Healing
the
Hurt
Child

Healing
the
Hurt
Child

*A Developmental-
Contextual Approach*

Denis M. Donovan, *M.D., M.Ed.*
&
Deborah McIntyre, *M.A., R.N.*

W. W. Norton & Company New York London

Permission was granted for brief excerpts from the following publications:

Anthony, E. J. (1986). Contrasting neurotic styles in the analysis of two preschool children. *J. Am. Acad. Child Psychiat.*, 25,1:46–57.

Donovan, D. M. (1989). The paraconscious. *Journal of the American Academy of Psychoanalysis*, 17(2):223–252.

Duke, P. & Turan, K. (1987). *Call Me Anna*. New York: Bantam Books.

Gardner, H. (1983). *Frames of Mind: The Theory of Multiple Intelligences*. New York: Basic Books, Inc.

Moskowitz, B. A. (1978). The Acquisition of Language, *Scientific American*, November.

Terr, L. C. (1983a). Chowchilla revisited: The effects of psychic trauma four years after a school bus kidnapping. *Am. J. Psychiat.*, 140:1543–1550.

Terr, L. C. (1985b). Children traumatized in small groups. In: *Post-Traumatic Stress Disorder in Children*, edited by S. Eth & R. S. Pynoos. Washington, D.C.: American Psychiatric Press, 47–70.

van der Kolk, B. A. (1987). *Psychological Trauma*. Washington, D.C.: American Psychiatric Press.

Printed in the United States of America

First Edition

Library of Congress Cataloging-in-Publication Data

Donovan, Denis M.
    Healing the hurt child : a developmental-contextual approach /
Denis M. Donovan, Deborah McIntyre.
        p.   cm.
    Includes bibliographical references.
    1. Child psychotherapy.   2. Abused children — Mental health.
I. McIntyre, Deborah.   II. Title.
RJ504.D65   1990   618.92'8914 — dc20   89-49420

0-393-70093-3

W. W. Norton & Company, Inc., 500 Fifth Avenue, New York, N.Y. 10110
W. W. Norton & Company, Ltd., 37 Great Russell Street, London WC1B 3NU

1 2 3 4 5 6 7 8 9 0

Foreword

As this decade begins, child psychiatry is in desperate trouble. The number of qualified applicants has declined to an all-time low and the rapidly dwindling number of training programs are unable to fill more than half of their vacant slots. Fewer than 100 child psychiatrists are involved in even part-time research and scores of fully-funded academic positions stand empty at major institutions. The medical/biological model that reclaimed adult psychiatry has little to offer child psychiatry and the only alternative available to most trainees, the psychoanalytic model, is seriously flawed and grossly inappropriate in these days of markedly diminished mental health insurance coverage. The committees and task-forces called to study these problems all conclude that the situation is critical, but their recommendations reflect a confusion of purposes and an implicit disbelief that child psychiatry has much to offer the burgeoning numbers of traumatized children in our society.

This pessimism, which pervades most training programs, is a message that is not lost on the medical students, adult psychiatry residents and other trainees rotating through child psychiatry settings. Nor do the child psychiatry residents escape this invidious process, which lowers their expectations of treatment outcome and their investment in the therapeutic process. Yet, the need for effective psychiatric treatment of children is greater than ever before. The incidence of all forms of child abuse has shown dramatic increases during the past decade. Sexual abuse, for example, increased by more than 300% between 1980 and 1988 as determined by the National Incidence Study conducted for the National Center for Child Abuse and

Neglect (NCCAN, 1988; Burgdorf, 1980). In addition, the drug epidemic has turned our inner cities into bloody battlegrounds with children witnessing and experiencing staggering levels of community violence.

Healing the Hurt Child offers a number of pivotal insights into the mental life of children that can serve as the foundation for a paradigmatic shift in our thinking about their behavior. In this extremely sensitive and optimistic book, Donovan and McIntyre elucidate a developmental/contextual approach to unexplained and disordered behavior. Starting with a reexamination of adult models of childhood cognition, we are offered a new way to see, to understand, and above all, to help children. This book is both deeply idealistic and realistically pragmatic, with specific guidelines for creating and protecting the therapeutic structure necessary to produce profound change.

In particular, *Healing the Hurt Child* introduces us to a number of conceptual cornerstones in our understanding of children's needs, problems and cognitive capacities. By demolishing the fiction of the Freudian/Piagetian child who must pass through a protracted period of imperviousness to psychotherapeutic interventions and revealing children to be, in fact, "obligatory slaves of logic," they remove the dogmatic blinders that have doomed so many children to sterile or destructive psychotherapies. The logical binds that children become entrapped in as they struggle to make sense of their lives and the therapeutic solutions to these binds are richly illustrated by detailed case histories. These vignettes, on first-reading often enigmatic, are worthy of careful study, as they provide priceless glimpses into the cognitive operations of children.

The developmental-contextual approach is outlined by principle and example and by pointedly contrasting it with conventional explanations of the same behavior. Child psychiatry is the last mainstream bastion of Freudian psychoanalytic thinking and Donovan and McIntyre's penetrating examination of the psychoanalytic model of the child readily demonstrates how much of that theoretical stance is driven by the therapist's needs and how little actually corresponds to the child's capacities and life circumstances. Behavior that is labeled as "psychotic" by such traditional approaches is shown to be profoundly "rational" when reexamined within the appropriate developmental and environmental context. That which has traditionally been labeled as Freudian "fantasy" is shown to be the child's operational hypotheses about the way in which the world works. And symptoms that by traditional standards would be considered immutable are shown to be readily modifiable once the therapist comes to understand that they are dictated by the logic of the child's hypotheses about reality.

Donovan and McIntyre are not afraid to claim miracles and approach even the most apparently hopelessly disturbed of children with the belief that profound changes can be accomplished in a short time, sometimes within a single session, and without requiring the child to consciously understand what has happened. We cannot all match their clinical acumen, sense of timing, and highly refined teamwork; the examples, however, provide a sufficient feel for the process to allow us to borrow their ears and eyes and adopt their perspective in our own work. While this is not a "scientific" book in the conventional sense, the reader is furnished with sufficient hypotheses and "experiments" to test their observations and approach in everyday practice.

The operationalized conceptualization of the "therapeutic space" is outstanding and should be incorporated into every child psychotherapy treatment setting. It is tragic that many child therapists are trained in settings where they are assigned a room on a session-by-session basis, producing a sense of discontinuity and insecurity for both child and therapist that thwarts therapeutic progress. The failure of training institutions to provide protected space for trainees, coupled with an "it's all grist for the mill" attitude, is indicative of their larger loss of sensitivity to the special needs of children.

Donovan and McIntyre are among the growing number of clinicians and researchers condemning the tyranny of our psychiatric and educational classifications systems. Prospective research shows that it is exceedingly difficult to assign valid classifications to a wide spectrum of child developmental processes or to make accurate predictive statements about outcomes as little as three years into the future. And yet children are by far the most classified and labeled group in our society. They suffer, without benefit of recourse in most instances, the institutional prescriptions of a system that seeks to pigeonhole them in "special" programs for the rest of their childhood. Less than 2% of students placed in special education programs, for example, ever return to regular education (Bartoli, 1989). The DSM psychiatric diagnostic system, likewise, creates its own self-fulfilling prophesies, frequently dooming children to life-long self-images as damaged, defective and untreatable.

These reductionistic, categorical classification systems carry the weight of federal law, the bureaucratic force of an enormous enmeshment of school and social service administrative agencies and the economic imperatives of third-party payment interests. Donovan and McIntyre illustrate over and over again how flawed and senseless these labels are and how they impede rather than contribute to the child's best interests. In large part the malaise of child psychiatry reflects the therapeutic nihilism inherent in the assignment of troubled young children to dead-end categories and programs. Yet the message of this book is that children are resilient and are capable of rapid improvement even in symptoms that are currently viewed as neuro-biologically determined.

Healing the Hurt Child is representative of the conceptual and clinical paradigmatic changes that must occur if we are to offer meaningful and cost-effective treatment to the coming generations of neglected, abused, and traumatized children. Donovan and McIntyre have carefully and lovingly integrated a wealth of recent information on linguistics, child cognition, behavioral states and dissociation into a realistic clinical approach that significantly advances our understanding of the cognitive-behavioral styles of children.

Frank W. Putnam, M.D.
Director, Dissociative Disorders Unit
National Institute of Mental Health

References

Bartoli, J. S. (1989). An ecological response to Cole's interactivity alternative. *Journal of Learning Disabilities, 22*:292–297.

Burgdorf, K. (1980). *Recognition and reporting of child maltreatment: Summary of findings from the National Study of the Incidence and Severity of Child Abuse and Neglect*. Washington, DC: National Center for Child Abuse and Neglect (NCCAN).

National Center for Child Abuse and Neglect (NCCAN) (1988). *Study of national incidence and Prevalence of child abuse and neglect: 1988*. Washington, DC: U.S. Department of Health and Human Services.

Contents

Preface

We live in an era which is witnessing the rapid remedicalization of psychiatry and in which "mere psychotherapy" is increasingly viewed with disdain as unscientific, unsophisticated and "just talking." Psychotherapy with children, especially very young children, appears even less scientific and sophisticated. For many it is "just playing."

We demonstrate in this book that, far from "just playing," competent psychotherapy with children is one of the most complex, subtle, sophisticated, and potentially powerful of therapeutic modalities. It requires of the practitioner a detailed understanding of how children think, interact, communicate, and change, an understanding rarely reflected in works on the subject. Unfortunately, the clinical field in psychiatry, psychology and social work tends to have its own literature, the result being that much of the excellent scientific research which should inform our clinical practice rarely, if ever, finds its way into works on clinical practice. In this book we integrate some of the fascinating research in cognitive studies, developmental psycholinguistics and traumatology with the sound and rational pragmatics of therapy.

Although there are exceptions, many of the most influential works on the psychological and psychiatric treatment of children and adolescents treat theory and practice as if they were parallel and not mutually informative. Of greater concern—perhaps because it helps explain why this is so—is the virtual absence of the person of the child from many of these influential texts. The 960 pages of the prestigious Rutter-Hersov (1985) child and adolescent psychiatry textbook, for example, contain not a single case history—not even in the chapters on therapy. We attempt to counter this trend both through the nature of our theoretical-clinical approach to the subject and also through the use of copious clinical examples throughout. Our hope is that the reader will come away from this book with an appreciation of the incredible complexity and plasticity of real children, the often horrible experiences that can befall them, and the genuinely useful methods that can help to make them better. Needless to say, we cannot possibly cover everything there is to know about child psychotherapy or even about therapy with the abused or traumatized child but we hope that the window we open on that complicated and rewarding practice will prompt the reader to pursue our leads.

While many technical issues are covered in this book, it is nonetheless a book born of clinical practice. Many hundreds of children and their families and thousands of clinical hours have forced us over the years to learn, adapt and change our views. While written at a desk, this book was not born at a desk.

WHO SHOULD READ THIS BOOK

Although this book is aimed, first, at students and practitioners of child psychotherapy, it should be of interest to anyone with responsibilities in the mental health professions. Child and adolescent psychiatrists, psychologists, and clinical social workers will recognize many of their own patients and challenges in these pages, as will educational psychologists, counselors and teachers, family physicians and pediatricians. It should be of special interest to those clinicians who work with abused and traumatized children. We hope that the book will be seen as more than a manual on child psychotherapy, however, and that practitioners and researchers committed to a "modern biological approach" to psychology and psychiatry will recognize in these pages the many challenges to cherished beliefs which experience forces us to confront.

Since quite a few parents we work with have read and understood many of the chapters in this book, we feel safe in assuming that it is also accessible to the average intelligent reader. Thus, we hope that it will be of interest to anyone with an interest in children—or in the human mind.

Finally, a word to the reader—especially if a student. Much of what is new in this book we learned because we were prepared to accept that what we were taught was not necessarily true. When the children we encountered displayed abilities that their extensive testing assured us they did not have, we questioned the testing—not the children. When we found meaning where other clinicians found only disorder and dysfunction, we questioned our colleagues—not the children. Critical thinking is rarely taught these days. In fact, the word "anecdote" has become anathema in our would-be scientific approaches—an extraordinary loss, for there are few greater teachers than the living anecdotes who walk through our office door. Do not lose interest in what you encounter every day. Do not cease to ask "Why?" There may well be parts of this book with which you disagree. Don't just disagree: determine why you disagree and then develop your ideas. There are no losers in a genuine argument. The late philosopher Walter Kaufmann was fond of quoting Thucydides and Nietzsche: "So averse to taking pains are most men in the search for truth, and so prone are they to turn to what lies readily at hand," and "Neither conviction nor sincerity is proof of truth." Don't confuse the trappings of science and authoritative assertions with simple good thinking.

We have taken pains in Chapter 1 to describe in detail what we think is wrong with contemporary psychiatry's view of the child because ours is a bizarre discipline in which the most mutually contradictory of theories and clinical practices can be entertained without the least discomfort. Were we not to draw attention specifically to what we feel are mistaken views of the child, any genuine contribution we might make to theory or clinical practice would be only another piece of conceptual baggage in an already overcrowded baggage car. All good thinking requires an ongoing conceptual housecleaning.

OVERVIEW OF THE CONTENTS

Chapter 1 begins with a critical look at the two principal obstacles to the development of good problem-solving child psychotherapy technique: the almost unquestioned acceptance of conscious awareness and self-observation that the field demands of the child patient, and the Piagetian view of the child as a self-contained series of progressive schemata which develop not in a context of dialectical mutuality with the world but through the solitary classification of objects and experiences. These attitudes and view result in a skewed adult-model view of the child that does not correspond to the fascinating complexities of real children. The psychoanalytically derived model of an "observing ego" slows the pace of cognitive and affective change and growth to that of a snail. The verbal approach of Piagetian psychology pathologizes development and cognitive styles which do not conform to its hierarchical stages while failing to recognize actual cognitive styles of children that suggest avenues for powerful therapeutic interventions.

This first chapter examines the unnecessarily pessimistic appraisal of the effect of traumatic experience on affect and cognition, as seen from the

Piagetian perspective. In contrast, it presents findings from developmental psycholinguistics which suggest a much greater richness and potential resilience on the part of even extremely young developing children. It further lays the groundwork for a post-Piagetian perspective to aid the clinician in developing assessment and treatment strategies which can turn "obstacles" into opportunities.

Chapter 2, in opposition to the prevailing view that children must pass through a protracted prelogical period of development, offers a view of children as obligatory slaves of logic and clarifies the confusion of logic and reasonableness of thought that pervades research and clinical practice. It examines the "logical binds" that can result from the early logic-driven misinterpretation of experience characterizing much of childhood (a phenomenon which, by the way, would keep the child therapist busy even if all proactive harm could be removed from human experience). This understanding allows us to see in the "fantasies" of the Freudian child something much more complicated and sophisticated: operational hypotheses about the structure of reality. The chapter closes with a look at the interactive styles of children which, when coupled with an understanding of the difference between language and speech, paves the way for the development in Chapter 7 of a semantics of play.

In Chapter 3 we present a developmental-contextual approach to child psychotherapy that makes it difficult to assign arbitrary, and often mistaken, meanings to "disordered" and "dysfunctional" behavior. We demonstrate through clinical examples how *DSM*-style nosologies can be logical, consistent, reliable, and "valid" — and still have no necessary truth-value. We then analyze the cognitive style characteristics of the abstract-categorical approach to evaluation and treatment currently prevalent in the clinical and theoretical literature and contrast it with our own developmental-contextual approach. This, in turn, allows us to distinguish between *diagnosis* and *understanding* and to develop an approach to child psychotherapy based on the latter. Borrowing from Carol Gilligan's work on the cognitive aspects of moral judgment in children, we contrast male-mode and female-mode thinking, an invaluable distinction in understanding the cognitive-behavioral styles of children. We outline the three dimensions of context which the clinician must recognize in order to understand the meaning of behavioral symptomatology and to devise therapeutic solutions. The chapter closes with a look at the narrative-contextual style of child patients and its implications for the therapeutic process.

In Chapter 4 we review some of the findings of the relatively new field of traumatology, which can significantly enrich the practice of psychotherapy with both children and adults. Beginning with behavioral states of consciousness, we review normal and pathological dissociation and the model of inescapable shock. We present a model of (even nonvolitional) trauma in the family as a form of inescapable shock, because there is no "real world" escape for the infant or child. The possible effects of inescapable shock are illustrated by the experience of an abused or traumatized child "trapped" between home and foster care or protective service. In a section on dissociation and dissociative techniques, we apply the findings of traumatology to child psychotherapy and provide case illustrations of dissociative techniques in child therapy. Behavioral memory and its use in therapy, as well as the intensely dissociogenic effects of family secret-keeping, are also reviewed.

Many books on child therapy provide, often in outline form, an approach to history-taking. In Chapter 5 we review history-taking in detail and walk the reader through the process, pausing at various points to illustrate with clinical examples the importance of both the interactive nature and the contents of the history. Stressing that the process of therapy begins with the very first (even telephone) encounter, we cover who to see and why, the initial interview setting, the various components of the history and the process of history-taking. We review and illustrate the benefits of a parallel therapeutic process with parents, especially with those who were themselves hurt as children—a process that begins intimately linked to the child's therapy. After outlining our approach to structuring the ongoing sessions with the child and parents, we close with a review of some of the techniques we have devised to help parents understand and utilize child logic, to reinstate benevolent parental authority, and to improve meaningful and productive communication between parents and child.

Chapter 6 presents our concept of the *therapeutic space,* which enables the clinician to structure and utilize the physical, temporal, and interpersonal space in which child and therapist meet. The chapter begins with a look at the child's experience of space, an experience of which the contemporary therapist, depending on age, may not even be aware. The child's sensitivity to space, its contents, and its interactive nature allows the therapist to define the therapeutic space through the elaboration of structure, rules, and boundaries. We offer a number of "operational rules" that further define the therapeutic space and illustrate their rationale with clinical examples. We examine potential threats to the therapeutic space that constitute the frequent challenges of children to the therapist's mastery of his or her own domain. The importance of the therapist's mastery of the interactive space becomes even more apparent when we examine the role of the therapeutic space in modifying the trauma response and the utilization of dissociative techniques in modifying the experience of inescapable shock.

In Chapter 7 we turn to techniques for the evaluation of therapeutic aptness, that is, the child's ability to utilize the therapeutic space in a creative manner: operationally to recognize in the therapeutic encounter a potential for communication and change. The understanding, gained in previous chapters, of the often unconscious and nonverbal, nondiscursive nature of child cognition and interactive styles allows us to develop in this chapter a semantics of play, to distinguish between semic and ludic play and to utilize the distinction both diagnostically and therapeutically. The distinction between the "just playing" of ludic play and the potentially powerful communicative content of semic play allows us to develop an operational assessment of therapeutic aptness. This permits the clinician to perceive meaning and structure in "disordered" or "psychotic" behavior and to move the child quickly — even in the first encounter — toward a resolution of logical binds or pathological confusions.

Chapters 8 and 9 present the hurt child in clinical practice, after reviewing the individual and societal blocks to the recognition of trauma and its effects. A categorical approach to psychotherapeutic techniques with the hurt child would make no sense from our developmental-contextual perspective. Consequently, the subheadings in these two chapters may seem contradictory — some are experiential (as in "abuse," "loss," or "being abandoned") and some reflect formal categorical labels applied to children (such as "learning disabilities," "attention deficit disorder," or "organicity"). Each, however, allows us the opportunity to illustrate clinical aspects of the developmental-contextual approach.

Chapter 10 is a critical look at a child psychotherapeutic style. A textual analysis of a traditional child psychoanalysis of a preschooler provides a dramatic illustration of how different abstract-categorical and developmental-contextual approaches can be. Much like a clinicopathological conference in medicine, this review allows for the opportunity to learn from what went unnoticed and — from the developmental-contextual perspective — what went wrong in a standard treatment.

Chapter 11 offers a contrast to the previous chapter and provides the reader with a detailed annotation of an initial psychotherapy encounter with a six-year-old child. Many of the theoretical and clinical issues discussed in the book appear during the course of this first encounter, which provides an illustration of the therapeutic potential of a developmental-contextual approach.

A WORD ABOUT OUR CLINICAL STYLE

We have spent nearly 30,000 patient-hours together, developing the approach and techniques outlined in this book. While there are many necessary variations on any successful therapeutic theme, we have found that a consistency of approach on our part greatly facilitates the therapeutic process. With very few exceptions, we work as a team, one (DM) of us working with the child and the other (DMD) with the adult(s). We meet together with child and parents or other responsible adults for the initial therapeutic evaluation, separate for the middle part so that child and parents can have their own space, and reunite at the end of the session. This pattern is repeated during the course of therapy—although the time spent together at the beginning and ending of the session is much shorter than during the evaluation session. We have found that this fosters a powerful parallel relationship between what are effectively the separate but intimately related therapies of both child and adult. It is rare in our 13-hour clinical days that both parents are able to be actively involved the therapy sessions because of employment constraints. When both parents are able to be involved, the parallel parent therapy often alternates between intense work with one parent at a time and with both. Occasionally we bring in other family members but we prefer to work through the child and parents. We have found that this approach gives us the best of family therapy techniques while maintaining the intimate privacy often required for the reparation of trauma, a style of great flexibility.

Healing
the
Hurt
Child

1

Complex Obstacles to a Simple Understanding of Children

The fact that so much of what is widely believed is wrong is great incentive for research.

Walter Kaufmann

PERSISTENCE OF AN ADULT MODEL OF CHILDHOOD COGNITION

Two major obstacles stand in the way of developing a conceptual foundation for good problem-solving psychotherapy techniques. The first, even for adult psychotherapy, is a misunderstanding of children which is based upon psychoanalytic dogma, dogma related to the structure of psychoanalysis — and not to the objective facts of child experience and cognition. This misunderstanding is due to the widespread persistence of an adult model of childhood cognition and behavior. The second major obstacle is the pervasive influence of the Piagetian perspective on the way in which psychology and psychiatry view cognitive development.

The Freudian Child: Pedestrian Self-Awareness

The notion of conscious awareness as a clinical *summum bonum* dates from Freud and can be summed up succinctly in his famous "*Wo Es war, soll Ich werden*" ("Where the Id was, the Ego shall be") (Freud, 1923). This idea of an "observing ego" is still very much alive in contemporary thinking about child psychotherapy (Shapiro, 1989; Sholevar et al, 1989), even among genuinely child-oriented authors such as Coppolillo (1987) who asserts that "the aim of treatment is self awareness" (p. 284):

1

For therapy to be successful the child must be an active participant in the process. This will involve the child not only as he reveals his inner world, but also as he helps to formulate the conclusions that the therapist reaches. The therapist should tell the child, by word, and later by attitude and deed that he will not reach conclusions about the child without the participation of the child, or at least the child's awareness. (p. 135)

This same view of the child can be seen in several examples from two encyclopedic child psychiatry texts originating in two different countries. The first examples are from *The Basic Handbook of Child Psychiatry* (Carek, 1979):

The ultimate aim [of therapy] is for the child to become freer within the experience, to gain a deeper awareness of himself and other, and to find a path to the reasonable expression of emotions. [. . .] Attainment of any of these goals [of therapy] may become an end in itself along the way, but ordinarily they constitute intermediate points in a process that culminates in greater awareness. [. . .] It is assumed that an expanded awareness of oneself and one's mode of relationship can be a powerful accompaniment of and, at times, the instigator of these psychological changes. (p. 36)

Carek notes that "What does happen in psychotherapy is in fact quite unspectacular." Given the spectacularly worrisome nature of much of the behavior which frequently occasions the entry of children into therapy, spectacular change would not seem an unreasonable goal.

The expectation that little such change will actually occur in psychotherapy is not uncommon in psychiatric texts: "Psychotherapy aims to help but not to cure and it is an open question how much change should be expected" (Wilson & Hersov, 1985, p. 835). Wilson and Hersov also see the "observing ego" as a prerequisite for psychotherapy, for they indicate that "children and adolescents should have all or some of the following capacities":

1. A sufficient degree of basic trust and ability to form and sustain a relationship with another person.
2. The capacity to distinguish sufficiently between fantasy and reality and to transfer feelings from one person to another.
3. The capacity to tolerate anxiety and intense emotions aroused in psychotherapy, without unmanageable loss of control.
4. The ability to recognize and verbalize thoughts and feelings.
5. The capacity for self-observation and reflection on the relationship between actions, thoughts and feelings. (p. 84)

Are these reasonable requirements, especially if our population is to include the very young? Not at all. These requirements are, in fact, much too restrictive. The fact is that the lack of those requisite capacities outlined in (1) above frequently constitute the very reason the child is brought for treatment. Of more concern, however, is the fact that these "capacities" do not correspond to how children think, interact, communicate or change. This is especially true of the very young child and, certainly, of the mentally handicapped child—and neither age nor mental handicap need necessarily be a categorical barrier to effective psychotherapy. Furthermore, while numbers (1), (2), and (3) above are reasonable *goals* of psychotherapy, they become unnecessarily exclusionary if viewed as prerequisites. Numbers (4) and (5) are not only unrealistic therapeutic preconditions but would also constitute ill-advised goals in most cases of child psychotherapy.

Children do not share many of the adult preconceptions and misconceptions regarding the process of psychotherapy. The average child brought for treatment does not arrive in the therapist's office thinking that therapy has to be expensive, prolonged or embarrassing, that it has to be work and cannot be enjoyable—or that radical behavioral or affective change is not possible on the very first encounter. Why destroy this marvelous potential plasticity with the imposition of an embarrassingly self-conscious adult pedestrianism?

The Piagetian Child: The Solitary Learner

It is generally agreed that a stage-related model of psychotherapy with children is not only appropriate but also generally more successful (McDermott & Char, 1984).

Traditionally, the Piagetian model of cognitive development in childhood has played a very influential role in how we view children, their abilities, and their dysfunction. A brief summary is helpful to see what has shaped our view of the child's capacities. Piaget's model of cognitive development is serial and hierarchial; it describes a sequence of phases through which the infant and child must pass by means of his/her action upon the world. For Piaget (1972), "There is intelligence before speech, but there is no thought before speech." Intelligence "is the solution of a new problem, the coordination of the means to reach a certain goal which is not accessible in an immediate manner" (p. 11). Thought is mediated by symbolic representations which Piaget views as a later development.

Following this initial period of sensory-mediated reflex responses, the infant arrives at a "sensorimotor" knowledge of the world through the construction of sensorimotor "schemata." This stage constitutes "a long period of pure action [which] is needed to construct the substructure of later speech" (p. 13). This "long period" of sensorimotor cognition lasts until about 18 months.

Not until about a year and a half to two years of age does the Piagetian child begin to acquire symbolic thought and expression, "the capacity to represent something with something else" (p. 16). At this point the child can"[represent] something by means of an object or of a gesture. Until then play was only a play of motor exercises" (p. 16). Piaget views this period as one of "preoperatory representation." (This concept is extremely important for our considerations, for, as we shall see, such a "preoperatory" view significantly limits the genuine communicative ability of children at this stage of development — or, rather, our ability to perceive and respond to that communicative ability.)

Following a long period of "concrete operations," the child is able — only at the age of 12 or 15 — to perform "logical" operations: "reasoning on propositional verbal statements," manipulating propositions in a hypothetico-deductive manner and comprehending probability (p. 20). (This received idea is also extremely important for children do not wait until the age of 12 to receive Piaget's permission to "manipulate propositions in a hypothetico-deductive manner." Thinking propositionally and being consciously aware that one is thinking propositionally are not the same. Nor does the former require the latter. The fact that hypothetico-deductive thinking does not arrive at a conclusion judged by adults to be veridical or reasonable does not negate the fact that the process was one of generating hypotheses and arriving at logical, if frequently mistaken, deductions.)

Finally, the cognitive growth of the Piagetian child depends upon two *functional* invariants of thinking: assimilation and accommodation. Assimilation consists of incorporating new experience into existing schemata and accommodation consists of readjusting schemata and structures to experience. Unfortunately, despite good evidence to the contrary, clinical technique is still based largely on profound misunderstandings of these supposedly stage-related abilities.

The Piagetian model fails to appreciate that the child's development takes place in a context of intense dialectical mutuality with the world.

Human newborns do not act like passive and neutral listeners. They prefer their own mothers' voices to those of other females, female voices to male voices, and intrauterine heartbeat sounds to male voices, but they do not prefer their fathers' voices to those of other males (Brazelton, 1978; DeCasper & Fifer, 1980; DeCasper & Prescott, 1984; Fifer, 1980; Panneton & DeCasper, 1984; Wolff, 1963). [DeCasper & Spence 1986, p. 133]

The phenomena referred to by DeCasper and Spence are not simple reflex behaviors. The use of rigorous experimental methods has led to some fascinating discoveries which indicate that [musician and conductor Boris] Brott's experience [of knowing "without ever hearing" pieces his mother, a cellist, had played while pregnant with him] is not just a curious anecdote. In fact, "a newborn infant younger than three days of age can not only discriminate its mother's voice but also will work to produce her voice in preference to the voice of another female." [. . .] "Apparently," they conclude, "the infant learned to gain access to the mother's voice" (DeCasper & Fifer 1980, p. 1175). Other investigators have also confirmed in the neonate a preference for the human voice (Butterfield & Siperstein, 1972). That this preference is due to prenatal experience is now confirmed for it has been shown "that neonates' early postnatal experience with a particular voice is not sufficient to alter their preference for that voice." Hence the hierarchical preference: the maternal voice is preferred over other female voices which are preferred over the paternal voice for which, in turn, there is no preference over other male voices. In utero recordings indicate that fetuses are exposed to frequencies between 125 and 1,000 Hz, frequencies which correspond to the range of mother's voice. (DeCasper & Prescott 1984). The most recent work yet indicates that newborns persist in a preference for the muffled voice over the non-muffled voice—which corresponds to their intrauterine experience of mother's voice (Spence & DeCasper, in press). DeCasper and colleagues conclude that their results "support the evidence suggesting that in-utero auditory experience affects postnatal behavior in humans" (DeCasper & Sigafoos, 1983), and that "newborns remember something about their prenatal auditory environment" (DeCasper & Prescott 1984). [Donovan, 1989a]

Thus, the mutuality missing from the Piagetian perspective begins even before birth, for the fascinating work of DeCasper and his colleagues highlights a capacity for mutuality that the neonate brings into the world. The capacity for mutuality present in early postnatal life has been amply documented by painstakingly rigorous research (Meltzoff, 1988a, Meltzoff & Moore, 1977; for an excellent discussion of the differential way in which infants perceive and act on persons and things, see Wolff, 1987). For Piaget, however, cognitive development—like a Swiss carpet—unrolls serially and systematically in an atmosphere of desolate affective and cognitive solitude.

CATEGORICAL DYSFUNCTION IN ABUSED, TRAUMATIZED, "LEARNING-DISABLED" AND PSYCHIATRICALLY DISTURBED CHILDREN

The Categorical Tradition

It will be easier to understand the hurt child and the lessons which his/her experience can teach us if we first shed the excess baggage of a mistaken perspective. But, in order to change perspectives, one must often look closely at what has previously been taken for granted: an unnecessarily pessimistic view of the categorical abilities of the child. What follows is a summary of a current review of the effect of abuse on children's thought as seen through the Piagetian lens (Fish-Murray, Koby, & van der Kolk, 1987). Although some of the children referred to in the articles summarized by Fish-Murray and her colleagues are "learning disabled" or psychotic, and not necessarily identified as abused, the same basic categorical assertions are made with regard to their cognitive state or ability. The following quotations are from the chapter on "The effects of abuse on children's thought" in van der Kolk (1987, all emphasis added). Note that these children are described in terms of their categorical "inabilities."

> Voyat and his group at City University, New York [Oram, 1978; Shackelford, 1977; Sloate & Voyat, 1983; Voyat, 1979], found that the cognitive organization of psychotic children was qualitatively different from that of normal children. They were *unable* to conserve and *could not* use the operation of reversibility at an appropriate age; thus they *could not* properly assess other people's intentions. They *could manipulate* materials but *could not explain* what they had done. The children *lacked playful imagination* and an *ability to interact* with the examiner. (p. 94)

> Working with Piaget and the Geneva group, Inhelder [1976] found that older psychotic children were *preoperational* and *could not understand* the concept of chance. They had more difficulty with *logical relations* than with *logical* classes. They had *poor linguistic skills* and *disturbed symbolic and semiotic functions* [. . .] (p. 94)

> Schmid-Kitsikis [1976], another Genevan, looked specifically at assimilation and accommodation in psychotic children [. . . These children] accepted the materials presented and *seemed to understand* the problem but *could not anticipate or come up with solutions.* [. . .] They *could verbalize* the instructions but *could not complete* the task largely because of interference from visual cues. (p. 94)

> Breslow and Cowan [1984] also found that [. . .] psychotic children were *unable to use anticipatory imagery.* [. . .] The authors concluded that *deficits in imagery* were central to the *disordered thinking* of the psychotic.

> The psychotic children studied by Caplan and Walker [1979] also had marked delays in acquiring *logical structures*. (p. 95)

> Dysphasic, dyspraxic, and dyslexic children have *specific deficiencies in symbolic abilities*. (p. 95)

> To summarize, children in the research studies reviewed above demonstrated developmental delays in several of Gardner's [1983] domains. The *ability to use mental imagery to solve problems* is particularly affected, indicating defects in the visual domain [. . .]. *Verbal abilities* and *social skills* are also notably affected.

The children coped with change by relying on sensorimotor action *instead of creating meaning through imagery or logical thought.* (p. 95)

Research [on cognitive impairment in abused children] confirms *developmental delays in verbal abilities* and in the ability to accomplish age-appropriate tasks of personality development. (p. 95)

The cognitive state of these children, as defined by the descriptions above, is such that they simply cannot accommodate (adapt) to the environment, new experience, etc. As summed up by Fish-Murray, Koby and van der Kolk (1987), "Thus far, our strongest finding in these abused children has been the inflexibility of organized schemata and structures in all domains" (p. 101). Hence their miserable performance on so many of the tasks presented them. Thus, the categorically negative descriptions of their abilities: they *could not*, they *lacked*, they were *unable*, had *deficits* and *disordered thinking*, specific *deficiencies* in symbolic abilities, etc.

Here we confront the need to balance the two often apparently contradictory attitudes toward the hurt child that will characterize our approach in this book: uncompromising realism and an equally uncompromising therapeutic optimism. Evidence is increasing that traumatic experience, as well as psychosis, can have powerful, long-lasting—and even permanent—effects on the developing organism (van der Kolk, 1987). But how can we determine when those effects constitute genuine structural and irremediable change—or, on the other hand, when they constitute a potentially remediable cognitive-behavioral style? This is not an academic question, since even some structural physiological changes induced by trauma may be reduced, or even reversed, by psychotherapy—changes more strikingly "organic" than the cognitive "inabilities" described in the previous section.

The meaning of the clinical presentations in the previous section can be radically changed by insights from recent developments in cognitive studies and particularly from developmental psycholinguistics. Unbeknownst to most workers, clinicians and researchers have managed to build a functional pessimism into our view of the child which is often unwarranted.

The Developmental-Contextual Perspective

In contrast to the categorical pessimism evident in the examples above, a developmental-contextual approach to apparent dysfunction provides a very different perspective, one that can move the clinician or educator beyond dead-end categorization to a pragmatic problem-solving. Whereas the categorical approach to cognition, affect, and behavior exemplified in the Freudian and Piagetian perspectives accepts the apparently phenomenologically obvious inabilities of disturbed and traumatized children, a developmental-contextual approach views the same behaviors as potentially communicative and as attempts by the individual to adapt—however maladaptive the "adaptation" may appear to the outside observer—to the experiential demands of his/her life.

To appreciate the substantial difference between categorical disorder or dysfunction, as seen from the traditional Piagetian perspective, and the potential communicative power of the same behavior seen in a developmental-contextual fashion, consider the example of an extremely bright two-year, nine-month-old girl who had been sexually abused by her father. To set the scene for an understanding of the communicative content of her behavior (and how her examiner failed to comprehend it) we note that she had been removed from her mother's home and placed temporarily in a shelter home. (Shelter homes are for emergency placements of relatively short duration, and are usually part of protective, rather than foster care, services.) She was ill at the time and did not get along well with the shelter home mother, who had many other children to look after. This is how this toddler's female examiner described the first encounter in her report to the court.

> Joy initially presented with no separation anxiety. She is a verbal, bright child, but rather flat in affect. She has an obvious articulation deficit. In an unstructured setting (play), she initiated no interaction with the examiner.

The expectation that this little girl should initiate interaction with a person she had never seen before illustrates the basic adult orientation with which the examiner began the encounter. To initiate interaction with another person is an explicit acknowledgment that one is consciously communicating. This, as we shall see repeatedly, is not standard fare for children, especially very young children who are just emerging from, or who may well still be in, a period of their life in which needs and wants are responded to by an understanding caregiver (often mother)—usually because the caretaker recognizes the need, not because the infant/toddler explicitly states it. As we shall see, because she required a conscious interpersonal sign on the part of her little patient, this little girl's examiner did not recognize that potential communication was occurring throughout the evaluation. (This expectation on the examiner's part may have also been due to the fact that, at less than two-years, nine-months, Joy scored an age-equivalent of 4.6 years on the Vineland Social Maturity Scale.) The examiner also views play as "an unstructured setting," which tells us that she is unlikely to recognize spontaneous activity within such a setting as structured in itself—unless, that is, it is explicitly directed as such to the examiner by the child.

Joy's examiner continues:

> Interpersonal relating was minimal, with Joy being rather detached. Upon direct examination and questioning, Joy was evasive and avoided especially any conversation with respect to her current placement, the problems between her parents, or genital stimulation. The only spontaneous conversation she offered was about a potential outing to the mall.

Not surprisingly, the only response to direct verbal questioning is noncommittal. However, the interests of Joy's examiner have now been explicitly expressed: Joy's current placement, the problems between her parents and genital stimulation. It is here that we will now be able to see how blinding an adult perspective can be when one is interacting and communicating with children.

Joy's examiner should expect that Joy's play will, in fact, be a *verbal-equivalent response* to the examiner's stated interests. This is just what happens, but Joy's examiner fails to recognize it.

> In contrast [to her lack of direct verbal response to her examiner, presumably], Joy was highly verbal and involved with the playhouse and the family. Her play, however, was disorganized, fragmented, and showed poor reality testing. Furniture was piled one on top of another, four or five pieces high, people were sleeping on the stove, in the tub, and on the sofa, rather than in beds.

True, the *scene* portrayed by Joy is "disorganized"; however, far from being "disorganized, fragmented and [showing] poor reality testing," Joy's *use of the objects found in the evaluation room* appears to constitute an eloquent description of the disorder she presently finds herself in, namely that of the shelter home situation, having been abruptly and inexplicably wrenched out of her parents' lives. Anyone familiar with the often overcrowded conditions of protective service shelter homes will not be at all surprised by Joy's play description, for beds may, in fact, often be found in the most bizarre of places, including halls and even dining areas, and are often many to a room. This was Joy's "reply" to her examiner's first "question." Her replies are serial, orderly and eloquently expressive—entirely consistent with her advanced linguistic capabilities. Her examiner doesn't recognize this, however, for she is looking for *verbal* communication.

Joy continues in her symbolically manipulative response to her examiner's questions:

> She identified the obvious boy (short pants, suspenders, short hair) in the family as "Joy" and maintained female gender for this child throughout, despite the presence and availability of a girl doll with a dress and long hair.

The cleverness and striking symbolic intelligence evident in this behavioral statement are not seen as such by Joy's examiner. Rather, Joy's behaviors are mistakenly labeled as pathological.

> Joy also shows confusion in gender identity which I feel is unusual for a child of her mental age. While one would not expect sexual identity to be completed at her intellectual and socio-economic levels especially, one might expect recognition of gender differences, even if not one of role differences.

Far from "showing confusion in gender identity," Joy is again making a statement. Following her examiner's serial order, this statement refers to "the problems between her parents, or genital stimulation." Joy's identification with the boy in the family is easily understood when one remembers that she has been abused by an adult male. The logic is simple and pristine: "If I am a boy, then Daddy will not want to play with me sexually." (Thus, it is not uncommon to find an abrupt change to tomboyism in a previously quite feminine prepubertal girl after sexual molestation by a male.)

That Joy is not at all confused about *gender identity*, as her examiner concluded, can be seen in the next sentence of the report.

> Joy insisted that a picture of my daughter (same age) was herself and saw no discrepancy or unusualness in my having a picture of her [Joy]. She maintained this despite being told otherwise.

Again, the logic of the situation is not difficult to understand: a little girl, torn from her parents, the latter in gross discord, and giving the indication of probable sexual abuse (certainly the fear of the consequences of belonging to one's own sex), encounters a woman (read "mother figure") who must like children because she works with them—and who must further like children because she has a picture of her own daughter on her office wall. Joy's verbal productions must be read here as part of the whole: "I wish I were *your* daughter. Then I wouldn't be in this horrible situation. You like children—I know because you work with them and have a picture of your daughter on the wall—and you would take good care of me if I were your child." (It is not at all unusual for children in extreme situations to ask their therapists or examiners to take them home with them or be their mommy or daddy.)

Thus, the eloquent commentaries of this child on the complex and scary aspects of her life were entirely missed by her examiner, as was what amounted to a request for help. Not only was the true evaluative potential of this first encounter lost, but so also was the powerful therapeutic potential—all because this little girl did not talk with her examiner like an adult.

LESSONS FROM DEVELOPMENTAL PSYCHOLINGUISTICS

It might be argued that too much is being "read into" Joy's behavior in the above encounter, that the meaningful connections between her activities are being provided by us rather than flowing logically from the behavior itself. Consequently, it could be argued, the very meaning of Joy's behavior might be just what her examiner said it was: disorganized and fragmented. Indeed, within our everyday adult perspective it may look that way.

"Horizontal" and "Vertical" Speech

There is, however, good developmental linguistics research which both indicates and illustrates that this is far from the case. The difficulty in recognizing Joy's communication as such lies in the fact that it was long mistakenly believed that at the one-word stage of language acquisition children were learning only word meanings (lexicon) and not syntax (how to put them together to generate meaning). Indeed, the adult expectation is that complex meaning will be expressed by linking words together "horizontally," as in sentences where subject, verb, and object express ideas and intentions. The obviously sparse and simple nature of early utterances hid a fascinating complexity which went, and continues to go, largely unnoticed.

Ronald Scollon of the University of Hawaii and Lois Bloom of Columbia University have pointed out independently that important patterns in word choice in the one-word stage can be found by examining larger segments of children's speech. Scollon observed that a 19-month-old named Brenda was able to use a vertical construction (a series of one-word sentences) to express what an adult might say with a horizontal construction (a multiword sentence). Brenda's pronunciation, which is represented phonetically below, was imperfect and Scollon did not understand her words at the time. Later, when he transcribed the tape of their conversation, he heard the sound of a passing car immediately preceding the conversation and was able to identify Brenda's words as follows:

Brenda:	"Car [pronounced 'ka']. Car. Car. Car.
Scollon:	"What?"
Brenda:	"Go. Go."
Scollon:	[Undecipherable.]
Brenda:	"Bus [pronounced 'baish']. Bus. Bus. Bus. Bus. Bus. Bus. Bus. Bus.
Scollon:	"What? Oh, bicycle? Is that what you said?"
Brenda:	"Not ['na']."
Scollon:	"No?"
Brenda:	"Not."
Scollon:	"No. I got it wrong."

Brenda was not yet able to combine two words syntactically to express "Hearing that car reminds me that we went on a bus yesterday. No, not on a bicycle." She could express that concept, however, by combining words sequentially. (Moskowitz, 1978, p. 96)

Behavioral Speech Acts

Rather than viewing each one-word utterance as if it constituted a sentence, it makes more sense to view such one-word utterances as *speech acts* (Searle, 1969) which, when taken together and experienced *in a context*, can be understood as *statements* (see Chapter 7). Much of the communicative content of infant and child behavior is lost upon the adult because no continuity is perceived. This, in turn, is further complicated by the received Piagetian notion that "until [18–24 months] play was only a play of motor exercises" (Piaget, 1972, p. 16). Why look for meaning, especially complex meaning, if the child is engaging only in "a play of motor exercises"?

The potential communicative content of much infant and child behavior can be revealed, however, if nonverbal behavior is looked at in the same way Scollon and Bloom looked at early verbal behavior. We can see clearly in Joy's play the behavioral equivalents of Scollon and Bloom's "vertical speech." Joy's behavior in the play clearly constituted what we refer to as *behavioral speech acts*. Behavioral speech acts are both potentially intelligible and potentially answerable. If this communicative quality is not recognized, the child's behavior may appear to constitute nothing more than "mere playing" or the "play of motor exercises"—as it did to Piaget. As with one-word or two-word utterances, behavioral speech acts must be viewed, not as discrete, but in serial fashion, or the meaning-content may be lost. Without the contextualization made possible by the therapist/observer's knowledge of the real-world circumstances of the individual's life, no communicative content may be recognized.

"Caretaker Speech" and Therapeutic Interaction

In the example above, Joy's examiner was misled by Joy's "verbal abilities" as revealed by standardized testing and appears to have thought that the test results indicated that Joy should be able to talk with her in a fairly sophisticated manner. But even though Joy was extremely bright and "highly verbal," she was still a toddler who had not yet reached her third birthday. Joy's examiner spoke with her in a manner characteristic of adult exchanges, a communication style very different from that usually employed by adults when talking with very young children.

Most adults tend to speak to infants and little children in a rather stylized manner, regardless of the language spoken. This so-called "caretaker speech" or "motherese" plays a very serious and sophisticated role in language acquisition.

> There is no question, however, that the language environments children inhabit are restructured, usually unintentionally, by the adults who take care of them. Recent studies show that there are several ways caretakers systematically modify the child's environment, making the task of language acquisition simpler. Caretaker speech is a distinct speech register that differs from others in its simplified vocabulary, the systematic phonological simplification of some words, higher pitch, exaggerated intonation, short, simple sentences and a high proportion of questions (among mothers) or imperatives (among fathers). (Moskowitz, 1978, p. 94)

Caretaker speech facilitates language acquisition because it intuitively utilizes patterns and sounds consistent with the child's developing linguistic abilities. Far from "talking down" to children, caretaker speech reflects a remarkable unconscious knowledge of the structure of language and the nature of the process of language acquisition. Thus, with some very simple techniques, linguistically naive adults manage to facilitate understanding, communication and the incredibly complex process of language acquisition without even being aware of doing so.

Several of the characteristics of caretaker speech are highly relevant to child psychotherapy technique and can be used to good advantage with younger children:

> For example, adults talk with other adults about complex ideas, but they talk with children about the here and now, minimizing discussion of feelings, displaced events and so on.

Adults accept children's syntactic and phonological "errors," which are a normal part of the acquisition process.

It is important to understand that when children make such errors, they are not producing flawed or incomplete replicas of adult sentences; they are producing sentences that are correct and grammatical with respect to their own current internalized grammar. (Moskowitz, 1978, p. 94)

Note some of the implications for child psychotherapy technique of this aspect of child language. "Adults talk with other adults about complex ideas": this is just what Joy's examiner expected of her; it constituted the interactional approach she adopted with a child who was, after all, only a toddler. She expected Joy "upon direct examination and questioning" to *talk* about the complexities of her life. As we shall see, children have a much more nonverbal, interactive and behavioral fashion of communicating. "Adults accept children's syntactic and phonological 'errors' which are a normal part of the acquisition process." At well under three years of age, this child is still intensely involved with "the acquisition process." Expecting Joy to talk like an adult, her examiner failed to recognize the *logic* of her verbal-equivalent responses, her behavioral speech acts. This was disorienting for Joy's examiner because she was aware of just how verbally agile this child could be (despite her "articulation deficit").

Thus, when Joy insisted on communicating as a child, her adult examiner failed to understand her—an unfortunate instance in which a child was misunderstood, and therefore misjudged. Various pathological labels were applied to this child when she had been not only normal, but eloquently so. At the very moment when she needed most desperately to be understood, the imposition of an adult matrix only worsened matters.

The Use and Abuse of the Cognitive Styles of Children

A final lesson from developmental psycholinguistics will illustrate why this book focuses on therapeutics—and not on forensics. Because clinicians are increasingly called upon to testify in court regarding alleged instances of child abuse and neglect (especially sexual abuse), they may frequently serve as (unwitting) extensions of the adversarial examination/cross-examination process. The testimony of a clinician involved in such a case is itself open to such examination/cross examination techniques, the practical goal of which is effectively to credit or discredit the testimony—not to search out the truth. This process is intensely rhetorical and often focuses on the narrow meanings of words and phrases in order to establish that a child can or cannot adequately and veridically testify to fact. Inconsistencies in a child's version of an event or a chain of events are often seized upon as a convenient, and often quite persuasive, means of discrediting a child's testimony. Attorneys utilize this ploy when momentary denials or reversals occur, even though such retractions and equivocations are now recognized as common in true allegations of abuse (Green, 1986). A closer look at the way in which children master linguistically concepts entailing opposites indicates that young children are not as genuinely confused as their language makes them appear to be.

One of the problems encountered in trying to understand the acquisition of semantics is that it is often difficult to determine the precise meaning a child has constructed for a word. Some interesting observations have been made, however, concerning the development of the meanings of the pairs of words that function as opposites in adult language. Margaret Donaldson and George Balfour of the University of Edinburgh asked children from three to five years old which one of two cardboard trees had "more" apples on it. They asked other children of the same age which tree had "less" apples. (Each child was interviewed individually.) Almost all the children in *both* groups responded by pointing to the tree with more apples on it. Moreover, the children who had been asked to point to the tree with "less" apples showed no hesitation in choosing the tree with more apples. They did not act as though they did not know the meaning of "less"; rather they acted as if they did know the meaning and "less" meant "more." (Moskowitz, 1978, p. 106)

The frequent tactic of dismissing a child's testimony (or past statements) on the grounds that the child literally doesn't know what he or she is talking about ("Your Honor, the child used the same word to mean both things") depends upon the premise that three- to five-year-olds use language in the same way as do the adversarial attorneys, the judge, and the jury—which is not the case. Eight-year-old Micah, whose fascinating exchange with his ten-year-old friend James is quoted at the beginning of Chapter 2, knows well the distinction between truth-value and the meaningfulness and logic of language, a distinction that adversarial attorneys would have us overlook altogether. Children are not as haphazard in their use of language as adults often think.

Subsequent studies have revealed similar systematic error making in the acquisition of other pairs of opposites such as "same" and "different," "big" and "little," "wide" and "narrow" and "tall" and "short." In every case the pattern of learning is the same: one word of the pair is learned first and its meaning is overextended to apply to the other word in the pair. The first word is always the unmarked word of the pair, that is, the word adults use when they do not want to indicate either one of the opposites. (For example, in the case of "wide" and "narrow, "wide" is the unmarked word: asking "How wide is the road?" does not suggest that the road is wide, but asking "How narrow is the road?" does suggest that the road is narrow.") (Moskowitz, 1978, p. 106)

The clinician who views the verbal productions of children from an adult perspective will erroneously conclude that many a child has no clear or unequivocal knowledge of historical events and/or that he is beyond the reach of psychotherapy. On the witness stand the child therapist who maintains that a three- or four-year-old's contradictory statements "really have the same meaning" can be made to look like an absolute fool. Yet the clinician who understands how children use such word-pairs can look like an absolute wizard when he or she facilitates the rapid reintegration of a "hopelessly disordered" child.

A POST-PIAGETIAN PERSPECTIVE

The mental health professions still tend to think of children as "concrete," immature and incapable of complex abstract thought prior to the age of 12 or so (Fish-Murray, Koby & van der Kolk, 1987; Tanguay, 1985). This view, an outgrowth of the Piagetian tradition outlined above (Piaget, 1972), places children in stages which do not actually correspond to their genuine cognitive abilities.

The Confusion of Language and Speech in Traditional Research and Practice

In fact, evidence is accumulating which indicates that our traditional view of the perceptual and cognitive abilities of children is a gross underestimate of their real abilities. Much of this confusion is due to the fact that traditional *verbal* interview techniques, used regularly since Piaget's original pioneering studies, fail to elicit the child's true cognitive capabilities, especially in the early stages (Borke, 1971, 1973, 1975, 1978; Brainerd, 1978a, 1978b; Gardner, 1982). This failure to recognize the child's actual abilities and stage-related cognitive style, due largely to a widespread confusion of *speech* and *communication* (Mounin, 1970), can cause us grossly to underestimate both the complexity and the power of the child's actual lived experience— and communicative potential. (The clinician, educator, attorney or judge who is prepared to judge a child's cognitive and intellectual abilities on the basis of tests such as the Stanford-Binet or the WISC-R should remember that Piaget himself worked for Binet on the early research and test development and that this verbal behavior approach has not changed appreciably in the interim.) When this distinction is made, Piaget's categorical view of the child's development and abilities crumbles.

Cognitive Style vs. Cognitive Capacity

Even some of the best work on psychological trauma (for example, van der Kolk, 1987) is hampered by an inadequate and mistaken view of childhood cognition. This view is curious because van der Kolk actually cites the very source (Gardner, 1983) that could have pointed him and his colleagues in a very different, and even more productive, direction. The following illustrates a view of childhood cognition which does not correspond to how children actually think, interact and communicate.

> Abused children are not as good at self-recognition, although they have acquired object permanency (i.e., they can remember objects but not themselves). Possibly they already have different levels of development among domains, normal for age-appropriate scientific logical inference but immature in understanding of self and others. The preoperational and operational abused children showed a cognitive delay in flexible use of operations. (Fish-Murray, Koby, & van der Kolk, 1987, p. 97)

While these authors point out that "the psychiatric literature has devoted little attention to the development of distinct cognitive competencies (cognitive domains)" (p. 89), they treat these different competencies as if they developed according to the traditional view. Piaget's serial and hierarchial developmental stages are invoked as an explanation for this finding. Yet the brief section on "Integration or Dissociation" in the same work (pp. 6–7) suggests a more realistic and cogent explanation: if abused children employ dissociative techniques so adeptly it is precisely because they *recognize* and *remember* themselves keenly. Such recognition of self and other is an absolute prerequisite to highly selective dissociation.

Abused children are not necessarily "preoperational"; rather, they refine and then often misapply complex cognitive techniques (*inter alia*, dissociative techniques), which the individual in the "average expectable environment" leaves largely behind. The child whose life or psychological self is repeatedly threatened may learn how to survive by refining the ability to modulate behavioral states of consciousness ("space out," depersonalize, develop amnesias, or even alter personalities) far more than his or her non-traumatized peers. Still, even the average adult does not leave his or her ability to dissociate behind entirely and when such phenomena (e.g., "driving amnesias") appear in adults, as they often do under varying conditions, we do not judge them to be "delayed." While hypnotic susceptibility in adults, for example, is recognized as an indicator of dissociative ability (Putnam, 1987, 1989), it is not viewed as a reflection of developmental fixation or delay. Rather, we call upon the adult's ability to modulate behavioral states of consciousness in order to resolve problems in the present.

We appear to treat the same phenomena in children in a more judgmental fashion because the adult is more verbally accessible and can call upon conscious awareness to initiate responses or change patterns of reactivity. This differential treatment reflects our pedestrian understanding of childhood cognitive styles. By means of nonverbal techniques, the adept therapist is often able to achieve the same results with an apparently "seriously delayed" child—and often more quickly than can be achieved with relatively normal adults whose painful self-awareness can present formidable blocks to therapeutic change. This apparently aberrant situation is due to the fact that children are normative dissociators—and abused and traumatized children are even more dissociatively apt. Thus, just as they can deny, "space out" or forget, so too can the child often change ("get well") rapidly without the painful self-awareness that plagues adults.

If, however, one takes a categorical approach based upon the received notions of Piagetian dicta, such change will be accidental, at best, and the observer/researcher/clinician will conclude that the child is "incapable" of age- and stage-appropriate cognitive tasks. Simply because children (or adults) behave *as if* they do not recognize self/other or other/other distinctions does not mean that they *cannot* recognize them. In fact, many clinicians who work with children with multiple personality disorder (MPD) (like Kluft or Putnam) remark about the ease with which change can occur when an abstract-categorical adult-verbal matrix is not imposed upon the child (see Chapter 2 and Donovan & McIntyre, in press).

Piaget's Verbal-Discursive Style

The key words, those which consistently lead to confusion, are *recognize* and *remember*. Both terms are verbs and are generally used in a transitive-active sense, as in "I remember" or "the child recognizes the photo of his father," the transitivity implied by the object of the verb (which represents the action of the subject). That conscious awareness is implied is easy to see. However, verbal techniques which purport to assess such recognition and remembering may—and often do—fail to elicit genuine memory and recognition. Gardner (1983) describes the problem with the Piagetian approach succinctly:

> . . . while Piaget has painted a redoubtable picture of development, it is still only one sort of development. Centered on the intellectual agenda addressed by the

young scientist, Piaget's model of development assumes relatively less importance in non-Western and pre-literate contexts and may, in fact, be applicable only to a minority of individuals, even in the West. The steps entailed in achieving other forms of competence—those of an artist, a lawyer, an athlete, or a political leader— are ignored in Piaget's monolithic emphasis upon a certain form of thinking.

Of course, Piaget's perspective might be limited, yet totally accurate within its own restricted domain. Alas, a generation of empirical researchers who have looked closely at Piaget's claims have found otherwise. While the broad outlines of development as sketched by Piaget remain of interest, many of the specific details are simply not correct. Individual stages are achieved in a far more contin-uous and gradual fashion than Piaget indicated; in fact, one finds little of the discontinuity that he claimed (and that made his theoretical claims particularly riveting). Thus, most tasks claimed to entail concrete operations can be solved by children in the pre-operational years, once various adjustments have been intro-duced into the experimental paradigm. For example, there is now evidence that children can conserve number, classify consistently, and abandon egocentrism as early as the age of three—findings in no way predicted (or even allowed) by Piaget's theory. [. . .]

Despite his skepticism about I.Q. items couched in language, Piaget's tasks themselves are usually conveyed verbally. And when they have been posed nonlin-guistically, the results are often different from those obtained in Genevan labora-tories. While Piaget's tasks are more molar and complex than those favored in intelligence tests, many still end up fairly remote from the kind of thinking in which most individuals engage during their normal daily lives. Piaget's tasks continue to be drawn from the benches and blackboards of a laboratory scientist. [. . .] Over and above its failure to convey the universal pattern of cognitive growth which all normal children are alleged to traverse, Piaget's scheme—re-stricted at its mature end to the classroom exercises of a high-school science class—emerges as even less relevant to that discovery of new phenomena or that positing of new problems which many consider central in the life of the mind. (Gardner, 1983, pp. 20–21, 21)

Referring only to their demonstration of the 12- to 21-day-old's imitative capacity, a capacity Piaget placed at 8 to 12 months of age, Meltzoff and Moore (1977) conclude "this result has implications for our conception of innate abilities and for theories of social and cognitive development" (p. 75). As we shall see below, recognition of the genuine cognitive capabilities and styles of children has profound implications for clinical practice as well.

TURNING TRADITIONAL OBSTACLES INTO THERAPEUTIC OPPORTUNITIES

We can now return to some of the findings cited by Fish-Murray and her colleagues to see if our new perspective offers any novel opportunities. We first ask: are all of the absolute negatives reflected in the examples of "cognitive dysfunction, as defined in the Piagetian developmental tradition," really so absolute? The answer is no. Put simplistically: you can't get five gallons out of a quart container. Anything more than a quart proves that the container was, in fact, larger than that size. Thus, when we begin to strip away the requirements that communication be consciously intentional and explicitly verbal, and when we realize that the nature of observational or investigational technique itself (as in interviewing or standardized testing) actually plays a role in determining the nature and contents of the response, we can see that some of the absolute negatives may be artifacts of the process. If we mistakenly equate language and speech, then it is easy to assume that the subject's response failure, or his/her inappropriate responses to verbally-posed discursive questions or commands, constitute proof of dysfunction or lack of ability.

Clinicians tend to take for granted that the questions traditionally asked (through formal interviewing or testing) will generate a reliable and valid assessment. For instance, consider the case of Donald:

Ten-year-old Donald had been served academically by the Educable Mentally Handicapped Program since he entered kindergarten. He was diagnosed by a large, university-based program for autistic and communications-disordered children as being "aphasic-like" and suffering from a "central language disorder." Despite his mother's protests to the contrary, Donald's EMH teacher continued to see him as "mentally retarded." "For example," she told Donald's mother, "when I last tested him one of the questions was 'If I put an ice cube in your hand, what will happen to it?' Donald's answer was, "I'll eat it!" Even when I told him, 'No, you're not allowed to eat it, so what will happen to an ice cube if I put it in your hand?' he still said, 'I'll eat it!' You see, he just doesn't understand the question."

As they entered the kitchen after returning home from school that afternoon, Donald's mother asked him nonchalantly, "Donny, if I put an ice cube here on the counter, what will happen to it." "It'll melt," he replied matter-of-factly.

Donald's teacher thought that she had "reframed" the question when she specified that he was not allowed to eat the ice cube. However, despite the fact that it had recently been discovered that Donald had been sexually abused by his father since infancy, Donald's teacher did not realize that the *context* in which she posed the simple question about the ice cube was that of *Donald's body* ("if I put an ice cube in your hand"). Donald did not have a "central processing disorder"; rather, he was terribly confused about boundaries, interpersonal and otherwise. He hardly knew where his own body started and stopped, let alone what constituted the structural boundaries of words, clauses, sentences, paragraphs or articles.

It was not that Donald *couldn't* process information properly (he could understand and follow instructions for extremely complex video games where *he* controlled the environment and the course of events); rather, he tended to turn into a joke or a game any such interaction — which is exactly how his buffoon of a father had treated him his entire life. Donald's genuine academic success did not begin until his real potential was recognized.

2

How Children Think, Communicate, Interact, and Change

James (age 10):	I just can't wait until we're able to travel in space because I want to know whether the universe is really infinite or whether it has an end, whether there's some wall out there.
Micah (age 8):	What would that tell you? You would still be stuck with the fact that the wall has another side.
James:	But there wouldn't be anything on the other side.
Micah:	You don't know that.
James:	Of course you do! There wouldn't be anything. There would be nothing. Nothing, stupid, is the opposite of something!
Micah:	Only in language.

LANGUAGE, LOGIC AND CHILD PSYCHOPATHOLOGY
The Obligatory Logic of Childhood Cognition

Growing out of the long Freudian-Piagetian tradition is an operative assumption that children pass through a protracted prelogical period of development. This assumption has significantly impeded our understanding of cognitive development and effectively cut us off from a wealth of psychotherapeutic techniques. Far from being "prelogical," children are, in fact, *obligatory slaves of logic*. We fail to understand this when we confuse reasonableness of thought and the "realism" of ideas and attitudes (i.e., whether they correspond to how things "actually are") with *logical thinking*. Logic is simply a relatively closed system of interrelating propositions—which may or may not be true. Thus the two-and-a-half-year-old who states confidently that "germs come from Germany" is well within the bounds of a certain linguistic logic. Because logic is a necessary characteristic of any developing language (natural or artificial, as in computer languages), logical structures must first be constructed in order for the thinker ultimately to escape the very logic that was necessary to guide the development of the facilitating cognitive structures. Thus, we must all begin our cognitive development as incipient obligatory slaves of logic if we are to acquire the cognitive skills (structures) necessary to become "mature" thinkers, i.e., to escape the orbit of logic itself.

When this early logic-driven state of development is understood, it becomes clear that it is not necessary to wait for a child to reach a given "stage" in order to make an effective psychotherapeutic intervention. In fact, understanding the "logical binds" in which children unavoidably find themselves allows the therapist to structure highly effective interventions at any stage of development. Consider the following example of one such "bind," and the strikingly simple intervention used to resolve it.

Christopher M. was a bright seven-year-old who was referred for evaluation by his school counselor because of escalating risk-taking behavior bordering on the suicidal, self-injurious acts such as banging his head on the outside of the school building, slamming his hand in a door or the school desk top on his head. Christopher's attention span had dwindled to practically nothing, his previously excellent grades had fallen, and he had become hard to handle and disruptive at school. He was also frequently putting his name under the "frowny face" on the blackboard.

What had happened to this previously well-adjusted academic achiever? Not long before the behavior change, Chris had looked both ways—and then rode his bicycle into the path of a car that had just sped around the corner. He was thrown some 25 feet and ended up in the hospital unconscious for hours with five broken ribs, a collapsed right lung, hard-to-control internal bleeding, and a broken leg. He was in the hospital for 12 days.

But why the change, and, specifically, why the development of *suicidal* behavior? Chris came from a family of Catholic converts. He, like the rest of his family, had undergone intensive instruction and continued to do so in his Catholic school. Chris was hit by the car on Holy Thursday. On Good Friday the chest tube was inserted to reinflate his collapsed lung. His mother and doctors were convinced that he was not going to survive. On Easter Sunday the chest tube was removed and Chris was pronounced "saved"—he would live.

During the initial therapeutic encounter Chris was asked where his name came from. "Chris comes from Christopher which comes from Christmas which comes from Christ," he replied. CHRISTopher = CHRISTmas = CHRIST. Chris' unconscious logic was pristine, clear and tight: "I died and rose again; I can die and rise again." There was also considerable guilt over wishing that his younger brother had never been born and named a junior (the "one true Son of the Father"), but this had more to do with the self-punitive aspects of Chris' behavior change than with the potentially fatal risk-taking. This guilt, moreover, would probably never have been actualized had it not been for the accident. But the core of what developed after the accident was his unconscious identification with the dead and risen Christ. In fact, Chris had gone to his mother one day with the family crucifix and said, "Look at this," pointing to the red wound on the figure of Christ, "Christ had a chest tube—just like me!"

Chris' response to therapy was striking and before long the worrisome behaviors and attitudes had changed. A few weeks before the first anniversary of the accident (Easter), however, Chris began to dart out from between parked cars in the school parking lot. It occurred to Chris' therapist that one logical link in the chain of meanings had been left untouched. So, when Chris' mother repeated her renewed concerns about Chris' behavior at the beginning of the next session, he turned to Chris and said, "You know, if you run out in front of a car now and get killed— you'll go straight to Hell." Chris looked absolutely stunned and had to sit back on the couch. "What?" he asked, shocked. "For Catholics, suicide is a sin, a mortal sin, Chris," his therapist told him, "and if you run out in front of a car and get killed, you'll go straight to Hell—with no waiting!" Chris looked puzzled. "But when I got hit by that car last year," he said imploringly, "I wouldn't have gone to Hell then—if I'd died—would I?" "No," Chris was told, "not last year. But then, you didn't *try* to get hit last year, did you?"

An even greater ease appeared in Chris' behavior and appearance after this session and he got through the Easter anniversary comfortably. He finished the school year with good grades in both conduct and academic subjects.

Children as Victims and Masters of Language and Logic

Children are both victims of language and logic and master manipulators of both.

Danny was an extremely bright four-year-old. At the time of his psychiatric evaluation for depression, oppositional behavior, rages, and repeated suicidal threats, Danny was terrified of "bad ducks." He thought they were lurking about the house, under his bed and even in the ceiling. There was, in fact, a pond not far from Danny's house and Danny's castration anxiety was obvious even to the lay observer. The meaning of Danny's fear of "bad ducks" who bite was at first taken for granted.

Some time later it was realized that a good family friend, who happened to specialize in air conditioning repair, had visited the home just prior to the inception of Danny's almost uncontrollable fears. He had come to give some advice to Danny's parents about the cooling problems they had been having. Danny was in his room playing when the family friend came through, accompanied by Danny's parents. "What's wrong?" Danny asked, aware that everyone seemed overly concerned. "Bad ducts," replied the family friend with a genuine air of great seriousness. "Where are they?" Danny asked. "All over," replied the family friend, "but mostly up there, over your bed." For months Danny slept with difficulty and talked constantly about getting away from the "bad ducks" he thought would come in his room. It was not until some time later that it was realized that the "bad ducks" were, in fact, "bad ducts."

Logical "Binds"

Let's take another example of a bright child caught in a logical bind.

An incredibly bright four-year-old girl was brought by her mother to a bridal shower. She had lots of fun being the only child amidst a group of somewhat silly women—until, that is, people started to get things together in preparation to leave. "You can't let them all leave yet!" she implored her mother, "please . . . !" She had a look of real disorganization and panic on her face. "Why not?" her mother asked. "Because Debbie hasn't taken her shower yet!"

Needless to say, everyone at the bridal shower thought the scene was hilarious. All the women thought the remark was precious. Still, it never occurred to the parents of this child that the night fears and difficulty sleeping which had brought her to therapy were due to something equally "logical" but untrue: that being "put to bed" or "put to sleep" meant "being killed and never waking up." But, after all, didn't this little girl's father work for the county dog control and didn't he "put dogs to sleep"?

There is a very thin line between humor and disaster in the logic of language. A class of nine- and ten-year-old fourth graders in a private school was asked to write one page entitled "Before I was born." They were asked specifically to write about where they were and what was going on before they were born. In response, a ten-year-old boy wrote:

> My mom got a prescription from the doctor. So she got the medicine. And took one and her stomach grew fat. When the pill grew, I came out. I saw all the blood and at dinner food fell on my head. And I had to take a blood bath. And the blood took me to the heart. And I saw a germ. I went back to the stomach. And then I went to the intestines and then I came out. Plop! plop! plop! plop! [spelling corrected]

This ten-year-old thinks that he was "pooped" into the world. This should not be surprising, given the way most adults talk about pregnancy. Although one hears the stilted use of "uterus" occasionally, most adults—and, consequently, children—refer to the unborn child being in the mother's "stomach." (There has even been a television commercial for an analgesic pain reliever in which the pregnant mother talks about the baby in her "stomach.") Thus, it is only logical that food should fall on the baby's head at mealtime; that is, after all, where food goes. Similarly, it is only logical that, if the baby is carried all that time in mother's stomach, it should be born anally.

In this class of 23 nine- and ten-year-olds, 19 placed themselves in their mother's "stomach." Only one child, who wrote with uncomfortable affected humor about the "Banana God," gave any indication of realistic knowledge of the process of conception, pregnancy and birth. (This boy's parents were surprised by the discrepancy between the apparently accurate knowledge of human reproduction in his verbal descriptions and his "real" beliefs as reflected in his written answer.) In the following chapters we will see that such logic frequently wreaks havoc in the lives of otherwise basically normal children.

Tina and Eve were both 13-year-old sixth graders in the first year of middle school. Tina was a poor-to-average student in a lower-middle-class family characterized by turmoil, discord and impermanence. Eve, on the other hand, was a straight-A honor student who was planning her high school career in a program for the academically talented. Her family life was pleasant and was characterized by affection, stability and predictability. Both Tina and Eve were seen in psychiatric evaluation because of severe gastrointestinal problems. Consultation was requested by Tina's pediatric gastroenterologist after extensive and costly investigations had revealed no physical cause for her multiple and persistent G.I. complaints. Eve was referred by her pediatrician after a period of constipation and over a week with no bowel movements. She had not responded to any medical treatment and was more terrified of the pain of passing her stool than she was of the clearly explained consequences of prolonged retention of feces.

Both Tina and Eve had had very similar experiences just prior to becoming symptomatic. Each had recently experienced her mother's bloody third trimester miscarriage at home. And neither Tina nor her bright, academically successful agemate had the slightest idea which "hole" babies came out of.

In Tina's case an awareness of the realities of how children think, as well as of what they know and often do not know, could have saved considerable grief and considerable expense, since Tina's family was uninsured and could not pay physicians' or hospital bills. In Eve's case, the resolution of the constipation was facilitated and accelerated by the decrease in anxiety and fear brought by a simple explanation of human anatomy and the process of birth. (Even with children as old as Tina and Eve we clarify anatomy by referring to the uterus as the "safe, special, clean place for babies which only females have.") Because of the inconsistency of parental care in Tina's case, resolution of her simple misunderstanding may have prevented the development of a pattern of abnormal illness behavior (Pilowsky, 1969), itself a form of abnormal care-eliciting behavior (Henderson, 1974), which seeks through factitious illness the consistent and basically unambivalent care which the medical community provides. In Eve's case our simple intervention reversed a process which could have become literally life-threatening.

FANTASY VS. BELIEF

The Traditional View of "Fantasy"

The cases of Tina and Eve offer the opportunity to make a distinction with regard to how children think which is long overdue in child psychology and psychiatry. Our understanding and use of the term *fantasy* have grown out of a long psychoanalytic tradition. Traditionally, fantasy has meant an imaginary scene in which the subject is a protagonist and which is related to wish fulfillment and intrapsychic conflict (Laplanche & Pontalis, 1973). Contemporary child psychiatry (Adams & Fras, 1988) and child psychotherapy (Coppolillo, 1987) texts continue to view "fantasy" in this fashion. Coppolillo suggests exploring children's "fantasies" during the evaluation.

After telling of night dreams, children can frequently tell of daydreams or fantasies. This often requires a bit of preparation and reassurance to the child that
daydreaming is not pathological and unique to him. A statement that often suffices may be, "most of us have daydreams, or make up stories inside our heads in
which we're heroes or the main characters. Tell me about the stories you make
up." (p. 137)

"Fantasy" for Coppolillo, as for most clinicians, is fanciful—like a daydream. It has a ludic quality about it and points to an elective, playful
relationship with ideas, hence its relationship to daydreaming.

It is worth recalling here the radical change in Freud's theory of the
etiology of hysteria when, during the fall of 1897, he abandoned the so-
called seduction theory of hysteria which viewed the condition as the result
of childhood sexual abuse. As Marie Bonaparte, who saved the Freud-Fliess
correspondence from oblivion, commented on the September 21, 1897,
letter, "Freud brought to light the 'lie' of hysterics. The consistent abuse by
the father is a 'fantasy.'" (Masson, 1984, p. 112, DMD's translation of the
French). The sexual abuse, however, was not a "fantasy"—and there is am-
ple evidence (Masson, 1984; Wolff, 1988) that Freud was well aware of this.
(Some therapists appear to need to conceive of "fantasy" in this way, for it
allows them to avoid seeing the painful, even terrifying, realities in the
child's life.)

A More Serious View of "Fantasies"

Tina's and Eve's "fantasies" about the birth process can hardly be described as "playful" or daydream-like. Rather they were extremely troubling,
even horrifying. In fact, they were not "fantasies" at all; rather, they constituted *operational hypotheses about the structure of reality*. In this sense,
their views were *beliefs*. The distinction is extremely important for the
understanding of children and for child psychotherapy technique. To have a
fantasy altered or interrupted can be disappointing or upsetting. To have a
belief changed or radically challenged, on the other hand, can be earth-
shaking in its impact. The impact can be positive or negative. In the cases of
Tina and Eve, the impact was extremely positive. Similarly, Danny, who
feared the "bad ducks" that would come and hurt him, was not engaging in
"fantasy." He believed that there really were such creatures which could hurt
him. Beliefs do not have to be conscious to constitute genuine hypotheses.
The thinking of children—even very young children—is much more complex
and sophisticated than is recognized by contemporary clinical psychology
and psychiatry.

"Fantasy" and Trauma

The child's reaction to trauma is often thought of as fantasy. A good example can be seen in the various reactions of the children in the 1976 Chowchilla school bus kidnapping, well documented by Terr (1979). The 25 children were transferred by their kidnappers from the school bus to vans in which they were driven around in total darkness for 11 hours without a break. From the vans they were again transferred to a buried truck trailer which the children referred to as a "hole" (since they were put into it through what appeared to be a hole in the ground). Terr summarizes some of the children's reactions to different experiences during the course of the complex kidnapping.

Seven children in both vans [. . .] believed they would be shot as they were moved one by one out of the bus or vans. They had seen or heard about movies in which soldiers were told to get out of trucks, only to be shot as they exited. Because of a discussion in the older children's van about being shot, some young-sters vied for position of exit. Debbie (10) recalled, "In the van, I thought they'd shoot the first 2, the middle 2, and the last 2, so I went third to get out." Jackie (9), who imagined being lined up and shot, remembered, "I had seen *Serpico*; there was a charter bus which pulled into a garage and they said they'd shoot them and then drove off. Well, maybe not *Serpico*." The children's fantasies of being shot have become the basis for repetitious traumatic dreams. (pp. 555–556)

Two episodes during the van ride were particularly frightening for the group: when the kidnappers filled the gas tanks with gasoline, and when they backed up the vans. Alison (10), who is asthmatic, believed that she was being asphyxiated during the refueling. "People cried, but I cried the most. I felt I couldn't breathe in there. When they put gasoline in, it made everybody cough and I felt I was suffocating. In the hole I couldn't get air. There was only one fan and everyone was gathered around it. I went back to the fan once in a while." One year after the kidnapping Alison's mother related, "The new car makes her go crazy. She says in the back of the car it doesn't get cool enough. She huffs and puffs and says she can't breathe." Carl (10) and Sheila (11) also reacted with fantasies to the refuel-ing of the van. Carl thought the gas was going to be used to "burn us up." Sheila thought the gas would "smother us." When the van was backed up, Alison, her cousin Sheila, and Bob (14) believed that the men had placed a rock on the gas pedal to back it off a cliff. The 3 of them awaited their free fall to death. (A TV or movie stunt may have inspired this fantasy.) (p. 557)

Although Terr refers to these children's thoughts as "fantasies," it is easy to see that these are not Freudian fantasies. Instead, these "fantasies" are clear-ly operational hypotheses about the nature of the events experienced by the children during the kidnapping, based upon the information directly available to them and on their past experience. Terr recognizes implicitly the real importance of the children's thoughts for her words reflect their real nature when she refers to them as *beliefs*.

Perhaps the fact that adults engage in so much fantasy (alternative views of the world *known to be false*) tends to make them interpret many of the beliefs of children as fantasies. It should be borne in mind as well that it is adults who create the fantasy productions (movies, television, written materials and toys) with which they, the adults, then fill the experiential world of children. While adults often wish that they could recapture the realness of children's "fantasies," it is the adult difficulty (to the point of inability) of experiencing as *reality* the (rationally recognized alternative) world of the child that contributes to a perspective in which beliefs are mistaken for fantasies. If adults really believed in "fantasy and reality" they wouldn't have to create so many literalistic fantasy substitutes: they could play like children — with whatever was at hand.

It is specifically the elective and playful quality of fantasy which is missing from so much of what has been called "fantasy" in the literature.

THE INTERACTIVE STYLE OF CHILDREN

Therapeutic Utilization of the Child's Interactive Style

Chris (see p. 27) was a very verbal seven-year-old. Consequently, words could be used to undo, as it were, the logical bind in which he found himself as a result of the series of catastrophic coincidences following the accident when he was hit by a car. An example from the very first encounter with this bright, verbal child, however, illustrates how interactive communication can be more effective than words as such.

> During his first session in the playtherapy room, after the focus of activity had changed from the initial drawings on the table to play on the floor, Chris mentioned, almost in passing, that everyone was born with a penis, that half the population seemed to lose theirs — and he was very, very scared of losing his. Chris' examiner simply picked up Mr. Kangaroo (a stuffed animal), looked him over carefully, and then opened the roof of the large open-sided dollhouse to reveal the attic. She then put Mr. Kangaroo inside, closed the roof, and, a moment later, took him out. "Hmmm. Still the same," she said. She then repeated the process with Mr. Platypus, another stuffed animal.

Chris — at seven years of age — still sucked his thumb and wet the bed regularly, although they had not been presenting problems because they paled in seriousness when compared to Chris' suicidally risk-taking behavior. Both of these behaviors ceased as of the day of the intervention described above. It would have been a grievous technical error had Chris' therapist then pointed out to him (so that he would "understand" what had just transpired) that "not all babies are born with penises. Only boy babies are. And babies born with penises do not lose them" (hence the "same inside as outside" maneuver). The need to "make the unconscious (or preconscious) conscious" often leads therapists to *undo* verbally what they have just accomplished symbolically and interactively. Such verbalizations are perceived by children as proof that the adult did not really believe in what he or she just did and, consequently, tend to kill the "magic" of the intervention. Why? Because if the adult really believed that what he/she just did was real and effective, what would be the purpose of explaining it all? "Making the unconscious conscious" at this point is very much like the magician and illusionist David Copperfield's explaining how he just completed a breath-taking illusion: interesting, the audience would think, but why come back and pay another $25 to see it again—since it's not real?

Because children are normative dissociators (Putnam 1987; Donovan & McIntyre, in press), mild dissociative phenomena being both ubiquitous and normal in childhood, it is only reasonable to capitalize on this "ability" whenever possible. Good child therapy, like hypnosis and good mothering, utilizes and modifies *behavioral states of consciousness* (Wolff, 1987). (See Chapter 4 for a full discussion of normative and pathological dissociation and the use of dissociative techniques in child psychotherapy.)

The more highly symbolic children are in their expressive behavior (often referred to as "acting-out"), the more receptive they are to symbolic interventions which *remain within the metaphor* and the more sensitive they are to anything which seems to indicate that the adult does not really believe in the efficacity of their interventions. Many otherwise superb child therapists negate the power and effectiveness of their therapeutic interventions by requiring their child patients to acknowledge a conscious awareness of the content and process of therapy. Only experience, however, can teach when to resolve verbally and when to resolve interactively. Generally, the younger the child, the more interactive and symbolic the interventions. With some children only experience can be calming.

On the advice of her exasperated pediatrician, an enraged mother phoned the office. She was beside herself and wanted to sue because a "foreign" doctor had inadvertently given her 20-month-old son a double dose of antihistamine at the local emergency room when the child presented with a mild allergic rash. The toddler had an acute idiosyncratic hallucinatory psychotic reaction to the medication. He was terrified of the butterflies on his sheets, pillowcases and curtains which were all chasing him. At the time of the call, three days after the emergency room visit, this boy was still terrified, hysterically screaming and thrashing around as the car approached his house. He had to be carried forcibly into the house and could not be induced to set foot in his bedroom, in spite of the fact that all of the butterfly material had been removed the first day.

The boy's mother was told to go to the local hardware store and buy a cheap plastic plant mister bottle. She was to fill it with several inches of water and add just enough perfume to give it a smell. She was then to put the sheets, pillowcases and curtains back up and to tell her son that she had "a magic potion which turns bad butterflies into good butterflies." She was instructed to spray the door frame to the bedroom very ceremoniously and then to spray each butterfly. She was to do this with great theatrical seriousness. The toddler slept in his bed that night and the "bad butterflies" never returned.

No actual contact between therapist and child had taken place and yet the results were stunning, real and lasting—as they often can be in good psychotherapy. The intervention was based on an understanding of the intensity and realness of the child's experience and the richness of the imagination of children, a richness which can bring both complications and resolutions to their lives.

This case illustrates well how scotomatous and restrictive is the view which requires of child patients advanced verbal abilities and an awareness of self and the process of therapy.

A friend and colleague told of a visit which the late British child analyst D. W. Winnicott had made to one of his colleagues in Denmark. After Winnicott and his wife left, the children told their father what a marvelous time they had had talking with the nice Englishman. "We talked and talked and he had the most marvelous stories," they said. This is a beautiful example of the potential intense power of communicative behavior for Winnicott could not have "talked" to his colleague's children, and certainly not for several hours, for he spoke no Danish and the children spoke no English. (Colette Chiland, 1980, personal communication)

Children need not talk to be evaluated and/or treated psychotherapeutically. Yet few children who experience the intense communicative potential of a genuinely *therapeutic space* (see Chapter 6) will remain silent for long.

3

A Developmental-Contextual Approach To Child Psychotherapy

The obvious is that which is never seen until someone expresses it simply.
Kahlil Gibran

In Chapter 1 we saw how the meaning of a toddler's behaviors and utterances changed radically when viewed in the context of her life—or, rather, how it became more difficult to assign to them *arbitrary meanings*—and easier to perceive the genuine communicative content, when her behavior was contextualized. Behavior which had been perceived as "disorganized, fragmented and showing poor reality testing," as well as indicating "confusion in gender identity," proved, on the contrary, to be eloquently expressive of this little girl's real plight in a very real world. Joy was telling her examiner what her world was like and how she could imagine escaping harm. The problem arose because Joy's examiner, a traditionally trained Ph.D. clinical psychologist, assumed that the behaviors she observed were categorically indicative, rather than expressively communicative: looking for categorical disorders, she found them.

THE DIFFERENCE BETWEEN CATEGORICAL AND DEVELOPMENTAL-CONTEXTUAL APPROACHES

Pattern-Recognition vs. the Understanding of Experience and Behavior

The picture of Joy which emerged from her examiner's evaluation assessment did not have genuine biographical relevance. In fact, the narrative outlining Joy's life in her evaluator's completed report was more of a pathography than a biography. It was essentially an enumeration of everything that was perceived as wrong or dysfunctional in the life of the child. As such, it could not inform a genuine therapeutic assessment because it failed to identify the problem. Most case histories are pathographies rather than biographies and most diagnostic assessments are categorical descriptions of perceived dysfunction. The key is to distinguish between pattern-recognition and problem-recognition, a key that is found in the categorical/developmental-contextual distinction.

To understand this distinction, let's consider the increasingly important cornerstone of contemporary psychodiagnostics, the "lens" through which today's clinicians view the patient. The "lens," of course, is the *Diagnostic and Statistical Manual of Mental Disorders* (American Psychiatric Association, 1980, 1987) (currently *DSM-III* and *DSM-III-R*). A formal collection of descriptive labels, the diagnostic categories found in *DSM-III* are taken to "describe comprehensively what the manifestations of the mental disorders are" (p. 7). The circularity of this situation becomes immediately obvious: if the diagnostic criteria of *DSM-III* are assumed to describe comprehensively the manifestations of mental disorders, then mental disorders will have those manifestations outlined in *DSM-III*. What we have here is a form of circular acontextual pattern-recognition which assumes not only that the patterns described mean the same thing to different observers at different times and in different places, but also that they consistently refer to the same phenomena always and everywhere: "The purpose of *DSM-III* is to provide clear descriptions of diagnostic categories in order to enable clinicians and investigators to diagnose, communicate about, study, and *treat* various mental disorders" (p. 12, emphasis added). The word "treat" is exceedingly important here, for if the consistency of pattern-match implied above is merely occasional, or if the perceived patterns have different meanings (correspond to different things) at different times or in different places, then the certainty of diagnosis-treatment match is reduced to problematic, at best.

Being "atheoretical with regard to etiology" (p. 7), *DSM-III* is an acontextual instrument par excellence and is based on the erroneous assumption that observable appearances have the same meaning always and everywhere. But *meaning* is itself meaningless unless it occurs within a context; without a context there is no nonarbitrary way in which intelligibility can be assigned or discovered. In human experience, the generation of meaning always occurs in a context. Unless one is aware of the contextual meaning of a phenomenon, one is likely to assign a different, entirely arbitrary, meaning to it. The difference between typical pattern-recognition and contextual approaches can be seen in the following example, an example not from the clinical literature but from popular biography.

Patty Duke is an American actress whose television, film and stage performances have made her well-known to several generations around the world. As the dustcover of her autobiography *Call Me Anna* (Duke & Turan, 1987) notes, Patty's life appeared full and productive.

> The youngest person to win an Academy Award—for her performance as Helen Keller in *The Miracle Worker*—and winner also of three Emmys for outstanding dramatic appearances on television, Patty Duke is one of the most honored stars in America, a woman so respected by her fellow actors, she has been elected president of the Screen Actors Guild. With such unanimous public and professional recognition of her talent, Patty Duke would appear to represent the ultimate American success story. [. . . She] spent most of her childhood and teenage years in the public eye, yet even her most devoted fans had no idea of the life she was living offstage. (dustcover)

Patty Duke introduces her autobiography with an embarrassing anecdote:

> About two years ago I went to a meeting in the office of Sid Sheinberg, president of MCA and one of the most powerful men in the entertainment industry. I was part of an ad hoc delegation of Screen Actors Guild members, a gracious, dignified lady. Sid looked at me hard and said, "Well, it's been a long time, hasn't it?" And I said, "Yes, it has." Neither one of us went into any details. I just turned to the folks I was with and said, "Sid and I have had a few meetings in here." What I didn't tell them was that the last time I was in Sid's office, I shouted a string of obscenities and threw his Mickey Mouse clock at him for good measure. When people said about me "She's trouble," they weren't kidding.
>
> That all happened in 1970 [. . .]. I was guest-starring on an episode of *Matt Lincoln, M.D.*, starring Vince Edwards. We were on location on the palisades near San Pedro [. . .]. There had been a lot of technical problems that morning, the crew was tired and hungry and they wanted to eat, but it was decided that the actors would take lunch first so the crew could continue to set up the [. . .] shot. It was none of my business—none—but I couldn't keep my nose out of it. I decided I wasn't going to lunch until the crew went to lunch. Very unionistic. An argument ensued and I stormed off to get into a car and leave. (p. 1)

The argument escalated and Patty ended up throwing a veritable tantrum. When she wasn't allowed to leave in a vehicle, Patty hitched a ride on an army garbage truck and would not permit the limousine sent for her to enter the army base to which the truck had returned. Once back at Universal Studios, Patty got into a huge row with Sheinberg, told him he could keep his two thousand dollars a week—and threw the Mickey Mouse clock at him. She was suspended from the series and didn't work for a "very long time."

Until very recently that story was extremely painful to me. Every once in a while I'd run into a crew member from that time who'd start to tell it and I'd be mortified, I'd die. I'd even have a physical response to the memory, a tightening of my stomach. But now I'm starting to find it funny, almost as funny as the people who tell it.

The difference is that I know now what I didn't know then, that I was a manic-depressive, crazy as a bedbug. (p. 3)

Patty Duke must be, in fact, one of the most famous manic-depressives the public has known. Indeed, her clinical picture is classic: severe mood swings which are "unpredictable"; suicide attempts; striking and prolonged manic episodes with exorbitance and a marked decrease in judgment; depressive episodes which are also severe and prolonged; and an intense affective ambivalence. To complete the picture there is a family history of depression, suicide attempts, and alcoholism. Her relief at being diagnosed as a manic-depressive was instantaneous.

From that moment [when her psychiatrist disclosed the diagnosis] on, I wasn't frightened at all. It was such a relief, almost a miracle, really, for someone to give what I'd gone through a name and a treatment [. . .] The odd thing is, *when I was a kid and had those panic attacks, usually related to dying,* I used to pray for a pill. I'd say to myself, "There must be a pill. There's a pill for everything. There must be a pill for this." It turns out that there was. (p. 275, emphasis added)

Patty Duke views her terribly embarrassing behaviors of the past, her intolerable depressions and suicidal despair, and her sense of loss of control as due to a categorical disease. "All Lithium does," she tells us, "is help correct an imbalance that's already present in your body's biological systems. Most people who have this condition," she adds, "are born with it."

Indeed, Patty Duke's words echo the prevailing view of "modern biological psychiatry" (Wender, Kety, et al., 1986). This categorical position is well represented by Andreason (1984):

When a patient complains of such symptoms as low energy, insomnia, or hearing voices, the psychiatrist *assumes that the patient has a specific illness* and proceeds through a detailed history and physical examination *in order to determine what type of illness the patient has.* (p. 29)

This shift in perception [to the biological] suggests that we need not look to theoretical constructs of the "mind" *or to influences from the external environment* in order to understand how people feel, why they behave as they do, or what becomes disturbed when people develop mental illness. Instead, we can look directly to the brain and try to understand both normal behavior and mental illness in terms of how the brain works and how the brain breaks down. (p. 138, emphasis added)

A brief look at Patty Duke's life, however, provides a context in which to see her symptoms in a very different light. Under the glamour was horror and dehumanization. Born Anna Marie Duke, she grew up in a family with an alcoholic father and an emotionally ill mother whose behavior could be unpredictable and, at times, terrifying. She lost her father at six when he accepted being kicked out of the home by Patty's mother. Not long after that she was essentially given to a couple by the name of Ross who looked after her acting career. They stripped her of her identity and her name, controlled every aspect of her life for years, and gave her no sense of personal worth—very much as if she were imprisoned. Whether John Ross actually sexually abused her as well is unclear from the book. But, for the purpose of understanding the "meaningless" and embarrassing behavior she describes in her Introduction, we need only listen to Patty's description of her mother.

> . . . my mother could be warm and wonderful and generous, both of spirit and with things like ice cream cones and dolls, but much of the time she was not. [. . .] She's had to be hospitalized three times, the first when I couldn't have been more than five or six years old. [. . .] We had a fireplace in our apartment, boarded up as many are in New York, and a big cedar chest in front of it. We kids thought this was a great piece of furniture, but at times it was the dreaded cedar chest because whenever anything went wrong—if my parents had a fight for instance—the three of us were awakened, taken out of our beds, and lined up by that chest. He would be gone, she would be sitting in the chair, and we'd have to sit up all night with her. [. . .] Usually these episodes happened after she threw him out, but there was one time when he said enough was enough and he left. That was it for her. She lined us up by the cedar chest, said, "We're all going together," and turned on the gas. Now, she also left the windows open, but I didn't know that, I thought this was it. And we sat there for hours. (pp. 14–15)

Little Anna Marie's mother tried to kill her—but that clearly wasn't the only time Patty thought she might die. Her early years were filled with violence and chaos.

> When I was little, it seemed that every holiday, every event that's supposed to be joyous and wonderful—Christmas, Easter, graduations, weddings, birthdays—turned into a nightmare for my family. [. . .] Almost every Christmas, my father would get angry about something and there would be an argument, and before anybody knew it the tree was gone, out the window and down into the street. [. . .] My brother and my sister had miserable fights. My sister has scars all over

her body to prove it. [. . .] I remember [my brother] Ray pushing Carol so hard he accidentally sent her out of our fourth-story window. [. . .] If my mother found out what Ray had done, he would get killed. Though I got threatened more than I got hit, my mother was very, very physical. The steam would build up in her, she'd go completely out of control, and all of a sudden we'd get a whack, a real unpremeditated backhand whack. She had a phrase that always terrified me: "Wait till I get you home." [. . .] (p. 9)

I said the Confiteor [at Catholic school] letter-perfect and [the priest had to give me the prize]: a huge, hideous Mary that glowed in the dark. I'll never forget it; it scared the life out of me for years. [. . .] I was really convinced that anything you did that didn't exactly follow what the Commandments said or what the nuns said or what your mother said was going to cause you, truly, to burn in hell. My imagination flourished in this state of absolute terror. (p. 17)

Patty Duke was an abused, terrorized child whose mother tried to kill her and who handed her over to a couple who continued to terrorize and dehumanize her for years—no matter how "perfectly" she behaved. Like many abused and traumatized children, she "was desperately emotionally attached to [her] mother"—a dependency cultivated by the Rosses, the couple who "killed" Anna Marie and replaced her with "Patty," who treated her "as if I didn't exist," and yet who made her entire show business career possible. This is a pattern seen in patients with striking dissociative features, especially multiple personality disorder (MPD) (Putnam, 1989, p. 172).

How does Patty Duke's introductory example of manic-depressive "crazy" behavior look if we now see it in the context of her life? We purposefully omitted several phrases—those italicized below—in the original quotation. Their relevance will be much more obvious now that the context has been established. Patty Duke unwitting describes the context of her "crazy" and "meaningless" behavior.

That all happened in 1970, *when I was pregnant* but no one knew it. I was guest-starring on an episode of *Matt Lincoln, M.D.*, starring Vince Edwards. We were on location on the palisades near San Pedro, and *I was hanging off a cliff, supposedly committing suicide.* There had been a lot of technical problems that morning, the crew was tired and hungry and they wanted to eat, but it was decided that the actors would take lunch first so the crew could continue to set up the *suicide* shot. It was none of my business—none—but I couldn't keep my nose out of it. I decided I wasn't going to lunch until the crew went to lunch. Very unionistic. An argument ensued and I stormed off to get into a car and leave. (p. 1, emphasis added)

Far from meaningless, crazy and simply the expression of a psychiatric "disease," Patty Duke's behavior was strategically, if unconsciously, brilliant. The scene which was going to be set up during the interrupted lunch break was a *suicide shot*—and she was pregnant at the time. If a pregnant mother commits suicide—even in imagination—how many die? Two: mother and baby. Clearly, the reenactment of a terrifying scene from her own childhood was emotionally intolerable for her, so intolerable that an actress (who actually needed the money at the time) would jeopardize her very career to avoid it. And that is exactly what Patty Duke's "meaningless" behavior accomplished. That the whole experience evoked *behavioral memories* (see Chapter 4) can be seen in her on-going reaction to the memory of the event. They are psychophysiological reactions to the original trauma which are triggered by recall.

> Until very recently that story was extremely painful to me. Every once in a while I'd run into a crew member from that time who'd start to tell it and *I'd be mortified, I'd die*. I'd even have *a physical response to the memory, a tightening of my stomach*. But now I'm starting to find it funny, almost as funny as the people who tell it.
>
> The difference is that I know now what I didn't know then, that I was a manic-depressive, crazy as a bedbug. (p. 3, emphasis added)

Patty Duke's autobiography is an extraordinary account of the experience and subsequent effects of chronic childhood abuse and trauma. It is replete with vivid descriptions of many of the experiences and clinical phenomena covered in this book: the multiple personality aspect of *The Patty Duke Show* (thought up by writer Sidney Sheldon who felt Patty was "schizoid" and therefore ideal for the part in which she played identical cousins); the night terrors of her son MacKenzie, who was terrified of his mother's "unpredictable" behavior changes; the psychobiology of the trauma response; and her "panic attacks, usually related to dying." The interested reader can spend many hours correlating Patty Duke's early experiences with her "meaningless, disordered" behavior, an excellent exercise for anyone genuinely interested in understanding the experiential antecedents of a whole panoply of post-traumatic pictures. Most post-traumatic sequelae are not beautifully chronicled by well-known performers. Most are to be seen in the cases of children who "fall through the cracks" of education, psychology and psychiatry because no one sees the meaning of their behavior. (See also Chapter 8.)

The Meaning of Experience

Steve was a 15-year-old adoptee with a serious reading disability. Every year for the nine years of his public school life since the first grade Steve had been tested and retested by psychologists, psychoeducational experts and psychiatrists. Consistently over the nine years Steve's diagnosis of dyslexia remained the basis on which he was assigned to Specific Learning Disability classes. Apart from the cursory mention of his adoption after being removed from dangerously poor living conditions, only the scantiest reference to Steve's life was to be found in the many reports which accompanied him to his evaluation.

Steve's history, as reflected in all the school reports and psychologicals which accompanied him, certainly made him look dyslexic—and he did have great difficulty when presented with graded readings. Steve seemed nervous when asked about reading and even more so when asked to read aloud. He smiled too much, fidgeted, and would maintain only the most fleeting eye contact. Yet the picture changed considerably when a more detailed history was taken.

Before his adoption Steve had lived in numerous farm camps, following his migrant farmworker parents from job to job. At six, just before entering the first grade, Steve accidentally overturned a kerosene stove, burning his upper torso and arms so badly that it would later require five separate plastic surgeries for him to be able to move his arms normally at the shoulder. His entire upper torso and arms were a confluent mass of scar tissue.

While Steve lay burning on the floor, his mother, seated less than five feet away, *continued to read* her book. Even as his father scooped him up and placed him in the bathtub to put out the flames and cool him down, his mother *never so much as looked up from her book*.

These were the circumstances under which this child entered first grade and faced the task of learning to read. Shortly after the accident, Steve and his two sisters were taken away from their parents and separated, Steve going into medical foster care and his sisters into regular foster care. As minority children, they were not easy to place adoptively. Steve was even harder to place because of his newly scarred appearance and the daily nursing care required. As a result, the children were placed separately and never reunited.

Seen in the context of this child's life-experience, the *meaning of reading itself* is radically changed: no longer a "simple" developmental skill to be acquired with a certain sense of accomplishment, reading took on an "emotional charge," effectively signifying to Steve his mother's wish that he should die in flames. Once this context was established, the meaning of Steve's behavior that had resulted in the referral became evident: he had been caught setting fire to a woman's garden after stealing some of her vegetables.

The Acontextual Nature of Categorical Diagnoses

Bryer, Nelson, Miller and Krol (1987), using objective measures, found that almost three-quarters of 66 females consecutively admitted to an adult inpatient psychiatric unit had been physically and/or sexually abused during their lives—a finding higher than the already significantly high findings of other investigators (Carmen, Rieker & Mills, 1984; Emslie & Rosenfeld, 1983; Hussain & Chapel, 1983). When one bothers to inquire carefully into the history of severely disturbed adults, abuse is a frequent finding. Bryer and his colleagues conclude that "both clinical experience and these data suggest that the most distressed patients in the hospital may have been abused as children," and state that "instituting psychological and pharmacological therapies without knowing about the original trauma would be like treating the varied and chaotic symptoms of the Vietnam veteran without knowing about Vietnam or what happened there." Abstracted from the life-context of the patient, the clinical presentation simply corresponds to categorical patterns which yield categorical diagnoses—which, in turn, frequently prompt categorical mistreatment.

The professional reader of this book is likely to have more than a passing acquaintance with *DSM-III*. Think back to how you acquired your knowledge of that diagnostic manual. There have been, and continue to be, classes, seminars and even full conferences on *DSM* diagnoses. Entire texts are designed to be consistent with it (Adams & Fras, 1988; Kaplan & Saddock, 1985) and *DSM* primers abound (Reid, 1989; Spitzer, 1989). You probably learned *DSM* categories in much the same way one learns a vocabulary. The comparison is revealing: if one looks closely at the way children actually acquire their extensive vocabulary (the average high school senior leaves school knowing some 80,000 words), and at the way in which the average child is taught (a small number of words each week)—the first obvious conclusion we are forced to draw is that the 80,000 words could not possibly have been learned in vocabulary lessons. Even 100 words a week×40 weeks×12 years gives us only 48,000 words—and most children have only 20–30 words a week, and then only in certain grades. Thus, most of the graduating senior's 80,000-word vocabulary must have been learned *contextually*, in the process of living. This observation is important because the average person manages to communicate fairly successfully.

What happens, however, when traditional dictionary-based methods are used? Children create fascinating sentences.

> They find the unfamiliar word and then look for a familiar word or phrase among the definitions. Next they compose a sentence using the familiar word or phrase and substitute the new word for it. One of our favorite examples came from a fifth-grader who looked up the unfamiliar word *erode*, found the familiar phrases *eat out* and *eat away* in the definition and thought of the sentence "Our family eats out a lot." She then substituted *erode* for *eats out*; the resulting sentence was "Our family erodes a lot." (Miller & Gildea, 1987)

Clinicians often use nosologies in much the same way fifth and sixth-graders use dictionaries: they identify phenomenological patterns in clinical presentations and then match them with those in their *DSM* "clinical dictionary." The resulting diagnoses are "correct" but, as traumatology is increasingly demonstrating, they are frequently neither accurate nor relevant to treatment.

What about all the clinical examples, it might be argued, which are to be found in texts on the use of *DSM* diagnoses? Don't these examples contextualize the categorical diagnoses? No. Miller and Gildea note that "mistakes resembling simple substitutions appeared even when model sentences were given instead of dictionary definitions." The clinical examples in *DSM* primers are like model sentences: they are illustrations of categories—not examples of the discovery of contextual meaning. "Put at the front of your mind," Miller and Gildea conclude, "that a teacher's best friend in [fostering the growth of vocabulary] is the student's motivation to discover meaning in linguistic messages." A categorical pattern-match approach to human behavior (such as establishing a *DSM* diagnosis) is not a search for meaning: keep in mind that when the five blind men examined the same part of the elephant there was perfect inter-rater reliability and validity—and yet they were all wrong. Such situations are not uncommon, as we shall see below.

PATHOLOGICAL IDENTIFICATION

Contextualizing a clinical appearance may make it possible to distinguish between the two very different, but related, phenomena—*identity* and *identification*—a distinction which can make the difference between treatment and mistreatment.

When nine-year-old Catherine was referred for psychiatric evaluation she was in a class for the educable mentally handicapped and appeared to have mild cerebral palsy characterized by weakness, incoordination and mildly spastic posturing. Her measured I.Q. was 60 ± 5. When her adoptive father, a handsome quadriplegic confined to a wheelchair, accompanied her to one of her sessions, Catherine was asked to *imitate* her father's movements. Her strange movements and "spastic" posturing stopped instantaneously.

Catherine had spent the first three years of her life in a special children's hospital where she had numerous operations on her legs. Unable to use her legs for crawling, Catherine had literally grown into a horizontally experienced world, rather than transitioning early to the vertical world that we upright walkers take for granted. During those three years she was never once visited by her birth mother. When parental rights were terminated and she was thus freed for adoption, Catherine, along with another child, was sent to a preadoptive placement, where she was seen as "retarded" and treated as such. Thinking her seriously retarded, her would-be adoptive family made no attempt to encourage Catherine to engage actively with her environment. Nine months into this preadoptive placement, the family said they didn't want her—but did adopt the other child. By the time she came to her permanent adoptive placement, Catherine had already been abandoned twice.

It had never occurred to Catherine's workers at the special needs adoption agency that her need to identify, if not completely crushed by now, would be extraordinarily intense. Nor had it occurred to them that it would only be natural for Catherine, whose legs were still not quite right, to identify with the parent *most* like herself. Under normal circumstances, this would have been the parent of the same sex, but Catherine's incredible problems with her legs made for an instantaneous identification with her quadriplegic father. Catherine's father's self-care was impeccable—to the point that he was almost always doing isometric exercises in which he would straighten out his flexed fingers against his arms, his cheek, or the arm supports of his wheelchair. This stretching was one of Catherine's most common unconsciously copied movements. It made her look very bizarre.

Catherine was neither retarded nor cerebral-palsied, yet she certainly appeared to be both. Only her adoptive mother had consistently maintained that Catherine was a child of normal intelligence and abilities. Her horizontal perceptual relationship to the physical world and the movements she had so faithfully copied unconsciously from her handicapped father created an *appearance* which was grossly misleading. She was helped through psychotherapy to move from the educable mentally handicapped program at school to a normal classroom, doing grade-level work with average or above average marks. As is all too frequently the case, Catherine's transition from a mentally handicapped to a regular classroom took much longer than it should have (two years)—not because she could not have progressed faster on her own, but because of the incredible resistance of the schools to change her diagnostic category. She had been "identified" as handicapped and learning-disabled.

DIAGNOSIS VS. UNDERSTANDING

Over the years both Steve and Catherine had received consistent diagnoses from professionals ranging from psychiatrists, neurologists, and developmental pediatricians to psychologists and psychoeducational experts. All agreed essentially on what they saw and these views remained consistent over time. This would appear to reflect true validity and reliability, and yet all were wrong. Steve was not dyslexic and Catherine was neither retarded nor cerebral-palsied. The picture presented by each of these children was quite consistent—hence the consistency of the diagnoses over time. It is just this "picture," however, which was misleading. Rarely does the imposition of the *DSM* matrix on the child lead to therapeutically useful understanding.

The difference between categorical perception and operational understanding is of paramount importance in the psychiatric evaluation and treatment of children. Much more than adults, children are the passive victims of the way they are categorically perceived by their environment: rarely do they understand the process and they usually can't talk back. Once Steve and Catherine were seen as real persons, living in a context, relating to others and events and existing over time, the meaning of their behavior (and appearances) changed, as did their "diagnoses."

Synchronic and Diachronic Views of Behavior

What Steve's and Catherine's examiners saw was very much like a "snapshot"—and such momentary *synchronic* snapshots can be misleading. What was needed was a *diachronic* view of the child, a view *across time* (*dia*= across, *chronos*=time) which would provide a basis upon which to understand the meaning of the picture presented. The synchronic view of behavior is much like an electroencephalograph (EEG) reading: if the patient has a seizure during the procedure it will be recorded; if the patient does not, the reading will be "normal." A negative EEG does not prove that the patient is seizure-free, although a positive EEG does prove that the patient has an abnormality. Neurologists recognize that the 20 or 60 minutes of EEG recording represent but a brief moment in the patient's life; as such, EEGs constitute a synchronic view. Most of the pattern-recognition which generates categorical diagnoses is synchronic in nature—even when categorical nosologies require symptom duration to satisfy diagnostic criteria. As we shall see later in the book, a noncontextualized view is necessarily synchronic.

The Three Dimensions of Context

Context always has three "dimensions": environmental/situational, relational, and temporal. In Catherine's case one can see these dimensions clearly. Without the environmental/situational dimension we would have known nothing about how and why her unusual postural relationship to the perceptual world (her horizontal visual orientation) developed. Without the relational dimension we would have misunderstood the meaning of her postural mimicry, itself a form of love and identification. Finally, had we abstracted Catherine's appearance from its temporal (and truly developmental) dimension, its developmental meaning would have been lost—as, indeed, it was for all of the previous highly skilled clinicians and physicians who saw her as categorically impaired.

Catherine's case illustrates the difficulty clinicians may have in recognizing the temporal dimension when the perspective required is a diachronic one: the temporal relationship was drawn out over relatively long (developmentally formative) years. The incremental changes were so subtle that none of the clinicians recognized the process. The following example from adult consultative psychiatry illustrates how clear the three dimensions of context can be when the situation is acute.

Years ago the senior author was called to the orthopedic surgery ward of a large hospital to see a 60-year-old commercial architect who had sustained a compound fracture of his right femur in an automobile accident. Following successful open reduction of the fracture, Mr. W. was confined to bed in a traction-cast which maintained a gentle pull on his slightly elevated leg. Mr. W.'s orthopedic surgeon, to whom we will give the fictitious name of Dr. Reichenthaler, was extremely angry with Mr. W. because he had managed to break his cast on four occasions. Several times he had limped down the hall and was prevented from getting on the elevator only because house staff who knew his case happened to see him in time. Mr. W. was rather paranoid, suspicious and testy with the medical and nursing staff and would cooperate with very few of the medically sound and conservative requests that were made of him. Dr. Reichenthaler, furious with this patient who was ruining his own care, threatened with his just detectable Bavarian accent, "So he likes breaking casts! Fine! Let him break one more and I will show him what a cast really is: I'll body-cast him! And then I won't have to worry about him anymore because you can have him all to yourself up on psychiatry!"

Mr. W. was, indeed, a very strange person, strange because there appeared, really, to be nothing wrong with him. He seemed very normal in most respects and yet had a subtle, but bizarre, feel about him. Being somewhat closed-mouthed, Mr. W. would speak to his psychiatric consultant only for short periods of time, although he did appear to be warming up a bit. On the third day, after a fairly neutral and innocuous 15 minutes of conversation, Mr. W. leaned over to the consultant, who was sitting on a chair right next to the bed, put his hand up to cover his mouth, and said in a whisper, "How's your German?" Realizing that Mr. W. was treating him as a kind of "accomplice," the consultant leaned closer and replied, "I can fake it enough to get by if I have to. Why?" After another furtive glance around the room, Mr. W. looked the consultant in the eye and said, "Because I've got another escape planned."

It quickly became apparent that Mr. W. believed himself to be a prisoner in the infirmary of a German prison camp and was trying to escape. Apart from the attempts to get away, which resulted in the repeatedly broken casts, the manifestation of his psychotic delusion was so subtle that no one had even recognized it. Mr. W. was simply viewed as a "stupid" noncompliant patient whose only interest was in frustrating the attempts of his physicians to care for him.

At this point Mr. W.'s consultant, realizing that his patient had a very complex and organized delusion, assumed that its origins had to be found somewhere in Mr. W.'s life, even though the first history-taking had not been revealing. He gently interrupted Mr. W.'s escape-planning to retake the history. This is what he learned: Mr. W.'s great childhood dream—to become an architect—looked as if it were about to be shattered just as he was about to enter college. With the bombing of Pearl Harbor and the entry of the United States into the war, his long-planned career seemed unlikely. Not one to give up, Mr. W. went to his draft board and worked a deal: he would give year-for-year service as an architectural engineer to the government if they would allow him to defer his military service in order to complete his university training. His offer was accepted. Just as Mr. W. was entering college, his brother and only sibling, one year his junior, was drafted into the Army. No sooner had Mr. W.'s brother completed his basic training than he was sent to the front lines in Europe where he was immediately captured and interned in a German prison camp. There he remained for the duration of the war.

Mr. W.'s brother returned from the war with no legs. Two failed marriages followed, as did a series of unsuccessful jobs and a life which deteriorated into tragic alcoholism. While his brother's life was disintegrating, Mr. W. was prospering. By the time his car jumped the median on the interstate highway, breaking his leg and putting him into the hospital, Mr. W.'s survivor guilt must have been immense. He had everything his brother had always wanted: a bright, healthy, happy family, grandchildren, community respect, and an extremely lucrative business which had grown out of the education he had received while his brother suffered in the German prison camp.

Mr. W. had been perfectly fine, happy, productive and well-adjusted—until his leg was broken in the automobile accident. Then, as if to pay a debt to his brother, he unconsciously placed himself in a German prison camp infirmary—where his brother had suffered out the duration of the war. Perhaps the psychotic reaction would never have occurred had Mr. W. broken his arm instead of his leg, or had his doctor not been a Teutonic taskmaster with a German name and accent. The acute nature of Mr. W.'s situation made it easy to see the three dimensions of context. The environmental/situational dimension is immediately apparent in the circumstances of the accident and his hospitalization on Dr. Reichenthaler's ward. The relational dimension is clearly seen in the meaning of his hurt leg and the guilt he felt at having prospered while his brother suffered. Seeing Mr. W.'s clinical appearance in the context of his life revealed the temporal dimension: the quick succession of events in which his broken leg made him a virtual "prisoner" of a German "ward commander" constituted a *semic series*, a series of experiences linked by idiosyncratic subjective meaning—a veritable *catastrophic coincidence*. Only by contextualizing Mr. W.'s behavior was it possible to see the meaning of his self-defeating attempts to "escape."

"MALE MODE" AND "FEMALE MODE" THINKING

Returning again to Joy's encounter with her psychologist, we see two radically different ways of approaching the content of the interaction. Joy was telling her examiner about her plight almost as if she were recounting a story; there is a striking *narrative* quality to Joy's verbal and behavioral productions. Failing to see the narrative quality of her behavior, Joy's examiner perceived only *categorical* dysfunction. Following our analogy, Joy's examiner perceived only disordered syntax — and missed the semantic content. Bound to the coherent logic of a descriptive matrix, Joy's examiner failed to see the toddler's behavior as communicative and propositional. She described her little patient in *abstract-categorical* terms and failed to see the *narrative-contextual* nature of Joy's interaction. In fact, because she viewed Joy's behavior in abstract-categorical terms, her examiner failed to realize that Joy was interacting with her from the very beginning of the encounter. ("In an unstructured setting [play], she initiated no interaction with the examiner.")

We have borrowed the expressions *abstract-categorical* and *narrative-contextual* from Carol Gilligan's (1982) work on the development of moral thinking in children. When Gilligan noticed that the major studies of moral development (Freud, Piaget and Kohlberg), as well as other widely accepted general theories of development (Erikson), tend to define maturity normatively in terms of male development, she set out to develop a research strategy that would clarify the differences in male and female thinking about moral problems. When Gilligan examined the responses of 11-year-old boys and girls to the same moral issues problem, she discovered a striking pattern. A picture emerged of a stereotypic male morality (of rights and rules, mediated impersonally through a system of logic and law, resulting in an abstract-categorical "logic of justice") and a stereotypic female morality (of needs, obligations and relationships, mediated through a narrative-contextual approach to human problems, resulting in what Gilligan calls an "ethic of care").

Gilligan is cautiously conservative when she states explicitly that she is making no claims as to which mode of thinking is "better" or "worse." We, however, see in the two approaches a clear choice. For the choice to be explicitly obvious, the two styles must be contrasted and their logical and practical implications explored.

It should be borne in mind that the cognitive styles which Gilligan finds typical of male and female thinking are not limited by gender to any particular class of individuals, although they may be characteristically typical of certain classes. Nor are the two modes, which we shall examine more closely below, limited to thinking which involves the solving of moral dilemmas. Although each mode may be more characteristic of one gender than another, the modes of thinking Gilligan has defined can be found in both males and females and in our various institutions and disciplines.

If we accept that there are two different styles and orientations, two different approaches to solving moral dilemmas, then the important question is whether both of these modes of thinking reflect reality and truth equally well. The answer, as we have already repeatedly seen, is that they do not. There is a clear and useful difference between them. A diagrammatic representation, as in Figure 1, is helpful.

MALE MODE THINKING	FEMALE MODE THINKING
Abstract-categorical	Narrative-contextual
↓	↓
Rights, rules	Needs, obligations
↓	↓
Abstract categories	Relationships
↓	↓
PRINCIPLES	PERSONS
↓	↓
Meaningfulness	Truth-value
(Logic)	(Correspondence to fact)

Figure 1

The striking difference between these two modes is that the "male mode," with its abstract-categorical approach to problems, *does not require real, living persons*; conceptual categories alone suffice. (Bertrand Russell's analytic philosophy is a typical male-mode system, as are Freudian psychology and the process of psychoanalysis or *DSM* psychiatry. As we mentioned in our Preface, it is this unwitting acontextual and categorical orientation that allows a child and adolescent psychiatry text of "world" stature to have no case histories and no references to real, individual children—and yet no one notices.) We see this difference clearly when Jake, the stereotypic eleven-year-old boy in Gilligan's study of moral thinking in children, solves a moral dilemma on the grounds of competing rights: the right to life vs. the right to property. One can decide such competing abstractions without any reference to real people, their lives, or the human issues involved.

On the other hand, one cannot speak of needs, obligations and relationships without reference to *persons*—real people who live in a real world, who have histories, and exist over time and in a context. It is impossible to remain abstract and categorical when such an approach is taken. The significance of this difference becomes alarmingly apparent when we realize that it is entirely possible to protect all of a child's rights while meeting none of his/her needs—*and have the child die in the process*. Variations on this theme are experienced often by people who work with our large agencies and who see decisions made by policy (rule) while human needs play little or no role.

Contrasting these two modes, we again see the difference between *meaningfulness* and *logic*, on the one hand, and *truth-value* and *correspondence to fact*, on the other. In terms of human commerce, descriptions must be contextualized if they are to be anything other than categorical. And if they are, in fact, categorical, we have no guarantee that they correspond to human reality—no matter how coherent or persuasive they may be. Only by returning human problems to a human context (a context characterized by temporality and relationships), can we begin to discern whether descriptions have truth-value and correspond to fact—or whether they are just persuasive appearances. These differences are readily apparent in the cases of Joy, Steve, Catherine—and even Patty Duke.

THE NARRATIVE-CONTEXTUAL STYLE OF CHILD PATIENTS

Recognizing the Child's Narrative-Contextual Style

While children may be victims of categorical understanding (caught, for example, in logical binds), they are not categorical beings. They are narrative-contextual beings par excellence. Although the gender differences in cognitive style described by Gilligan can be seen in children even younger than the 11-year-olds she studied, children as a group tend to be narrative-contextual thinkers. Seen as such, they can provide the clinician with a wealth of information. As we saw in Chapter 1 with two-year, nine-month-old Joy, the child's productions *are* his or her communication. If an abstract-categorical approach is taken, then much of a given child's behavior may either be incomprehensible or appear to be "empty" play (see Chapter 7), leaving the clinician adrift without any sense of which direction to take. The following example illustrates how such "empty" play can become powerfully communicative if a context is assumed to exist and the child's behavior is taken to be narrative in nature.

Charlie was a five-year-old brought by his parents for psychiatric evaluation because of constant oppositionalism, disrespectful behavior, and general unhappiness. His misbehavior in the neighborhood had resulted in extreme social isolation and he seemed to have few, if any, friends by the end of kindergarten. Our standard extensive social-developmental history was exceptional in that it revealed no immediate clues as to the origins or meaning of Charlie's behavior. As always, we had asked—in the child's presence—about possible losses ranging from relatives or even pets to any abortions, stillbirths or miscarriages the parents may have experienced.

At the end of some 20 minutes with the child in the playtherapy room, Charlie's therapist returned to ask three questions of Charlie's parents, who were still going over details of the history. Did Charlie have a sister somewhere whom he had never met? Did Dad beat Charlie—especially about the shoulders? And did the family take showers together?

As the first two questions were asked father looked mortified. Mother's jaw dropped with the third. Charlie's father looked at his wife with an air of painful complicity as he turned to his examiners. He stressed that he and his wife had "no secrets," and then asked imploringly if he really had to answer the questions, seeming to imply that talking about these things openly might be bad for Charlie. He was told that since all of this seemed to have emerged from the very few minutes Charlie's examiner had spent with him, it was probably safe to talk about it in Charlie's presence.

Charlie's father swallowed, and said that, yes, it was "technically" true that Charlie did have a sister he had never seen. She must be about 20 years old. It had all taken place in Georgia, he said, and had happened while he was in the service. "It was a shotgun wedding," father added, "and by that I mean that the daddy had a shotgun. It was a shotgun divorce, too, the same day the baby was born." He paused. "But, you know, I never saw that baby. And, as far as I can remember, my wife and I have *never, ever* talked about that in front of Charlie. How could he possibly know about that? And, as for beating him, no, I've never beat him. I don't even spank. I was an abused child and I grew up thinking that abused children turn into abusive parents. So I've never spanked my kids. I just talk to them." (Charlie's father showed how he held them by the shoulders as he "talked" to them.)

He then looked at his wife who, in turn, appeared equally shocked by the questions. "You mean, it's not good to take showers with your kids?" she asked. No, she was told, five and eight were a bit old for boys to be showering with their mother. "Funny you should bring this up," she said, apparently a bit relieved to be adding some "important information," "but I always thought it was a bit curious that Charlie, the one who was born by caesarian section, never once asked about the big scar on my belly, but Hank, who was born normally, often did."

Both parents wanted to know how Charlie's examiner could possibly have learned those three things—the first two of which they thought they had never talked about—in such a short period of time. "Especially," they said, "since Charlie doesn't talk much."

Charlie's powerful "statements" about his life came in what might have been taken to be a rather mundane bit of "playing." Charlie wanted to play *Star Wars*, something which might have been mistaken for everyday "thematic" play, for after all, weren't many children playing *Star Wars* at that time, the films being at the height of their popularity? Yet there was something a bit strange and discordant about Charlie's *Star Wars* play. He wanted the hero, Luke Skywalker, to take a shower with Princess Lea. That, clearly, was not in any of the *Star Wars* movies. Thus, it was taken to be idiosyncratically meaningful. The following simple question was asked: who, in the series of movies, did Luke and Lea turn out to be? The answer was that they were, unbeknownst to themselves or to one another, long lost *brother and sister*. Similarly, discordant thematic material about Luke Skywalker's shoulders and the fights with Darth Vader led Charlie's therapist to explore the "shoulders theme" in the interactive play. Whenever strikingly discordant material is noted within otherwise "stock" thematic play, it is reasonable to assume that the thematic variations introduced by the child are not simply gratuitous but have real personal meaning. (The reader is left to wonder what the relation between Darth Vader's light saber and that "big scar" on Charlie's mother's abdomen may have been.)

What came out in the course of a rather brief encounter (less than an hour and a half) brought about some very significant changes in this family's relationships. Although Charlie was not consciously aware of what he knew about his father, the unconscious knowledge that his father had "broken the rules" appeared, nonetheless, to be sufficient to discredit Charlie's father as an authority to be obeyed. Acknowledging openly that father had broken the rules "a long time ago," and that he had been wrong to do so, allowed Charlie to reintegrate the family's explicit value system, a value system which would not have condoned father's past behavior. At the same time it returned to Charlie's father the authority to discipline his son without fearing that he would harm him horribly, an authority which had been doubly blocked by father's fear that he would be "constitutionally" abusive and by his sense of guilt for his own past transgressions. This short intervention brought an almost instantaneous sense of control to the family and resulted in a striking behavior change in Charlie. When contacted eight months later, that sense of control was still there and there were no complaints about Charlie's behavior either at home or at school.

Utilizing the Narrative-Contextual Style of Children in Research and Therapy

Although eleven-year-old Jake in Gilligan's moral dilemma study presented us with the epitome of abstract-categorical male-mode thinking (his rights, rules, and categorical imperatives), it would be fascinating to see what would happen to him were the context of the encounter to be changed from that of the research interview to that of the child-oriented therapeutic encounter. Leaving the adult discursive mode of verbal exchanges can actually bring about a shift to narrative-contextual thinking in even the most stereotypic of abstract-categorical thinkers (male or female). It does this by creating a situation of obligatory personalization; it moves the individual from the emotionally distancing neutrality of verbal description, in which everything can be argued out categorically, to an unavoidable involvement with an event. Having a context described verbally or in print and *experiencing* one are two very different phenomena.

Even moral dilemma questions such as those used by Gilligan or Kohlberg can be asked in a nondiscursive way: the situation giving rise to the dilemma of whether Heinz should steal the medicine from the pharmacist to prevent his wife from dying can be presented interactionally in a representational play setting. In that context, where the child is forced to identify with the various characters involved in the scenario, responses quite different from Jake's verbal response can be elicited—even from stereotypic male eleven-year-olds. While this can be done with adults as well, the transition to narrative-contextual thinking is much more easily accomplished with children and adolescents. In fact, as we shall see in Chapter 7, sometimes not only is it the only way to move adolescents out of a "categorical corner," but it can also facilitate the shift without any loss of face because it is all done privately in a small world in which it is safe to be vulnerable and to care about others. Male-mode thinking can be a marvelous defense against such vulnerability: there is great (apparent) safety in the impersonal universe of categorical truth and imperatives.

We saw earlier (p. 31) how strikingly different one child's views of human reproduction could be, depending upon whether they were expressed verbally or in writing. It has been our repeated experience that children and adolescents who steadfastly, sometimes even disgustedly, deny categorically a parent's version of an event or events of the week will do an absolute about-face in the playtherapy room. When the very same sequence of events is played out with dolls or stuffed animals in the privacy of the playtherapy room, the child who had, only moments before, complained bitterly that his parent was "lying," will rarely object to the portrayal. Surprisingly enough, the child will often begin to direct the scenario, playing it out like a movie director, frequently correcting the course of events. This is fascinating because the material is often genuinely embarrassing to the child. If the issue, occurrence or disagreement is left within the medium of the play—i.e., is allowed to be worked out and resolved within the interactional medium— genuine solutions or resolutions can often be brought about. If, on the other hand, the therapist mistakenly treats the child's implicit acknowledgment of the veracity of the parent's version as if it were an explicit acknowledgment that the parent was right, a categorical denial can usually be expected. Knowing that it is safe to be honest and vulnerable (because to do so is to deal with needs, obligations and relationships), many children and even adolescents will develop a sense of security with a mode of thinking that may otherwise atrophy with the passage of time.

4

Normative, Pathological and Therapeutic Dissociation in Childhood

You better be damn sure you understand a culture before you try to change it.
Clyde Kluckhohn

The therapist who is unfamiliar with both normative and pathological dissociation is at a significant disadvantage in work with all patients, but especially with children. Dissociative phenomena are so pervasive in childhood as to be normative. As such, they are part and parcel of a world the therapist must understand and be able to manipulate. As we will see below, the line between normative and pathological dissociation in childhood (and even in many adults) can be very thin indeed.

BEHAVIORAL STATES OF CONSCIOUSNESS

Drawing on the work of infant consciousness researchers, Putnam (1989) identifies two normative substrates for the development of multiple personality disorder (MPD). These also provide a key to the development of good psychotherapeutic technique with children in general: behavioral states of consciousness and their vicissitudes, and a specific behavioral state, normative dissociation.

Modulation of Behavioral States and Developmental Vulnerability

The central developmental task of infancy and childhood is learning how to modulate behavioral states (Prechtl, 1974; Prechtl & O'Brien, 1982; Prechtl, Theorell, & Blair, 1973; Wolff, 1987). In infancy behavioral states appear discrete and the transitions between states are often saltatory and abrupt, lacking the smoothness and fluidity of later years. Thus, the infant can change from calm and serene to inconsolably enraged in the space of an instant. Under normal conditions the primary caregiver, usually mother, aids the infant in modulating these behavioral states, helping to negotiate a transition from one state to another by providing guidance, support or response which is beyond the means of the infant. Often this transition is mediated simply by meeting the infant's momentary needs—feeding, cleaning, burping—or by providing a buffer between the child's experience and noxious environmental stimuli. The latter can range from assuring a comfortable position to an infant lacking the necessary motor strength and coordination, loosening a too-tight diaper, or regulating environmental temperature, on the one hand, to removing the infant from an inhospitable human environment, on the other.

The potential for pathological development is easy to see. The infant whose needs are not met appropriately, in a timely fashion, and within the limits of assimilability is clearly at risk as autoregulation of behavioral states develops. Similarly, the infant whose mother misperceives, misinterprets, or does not recognize the nature of her infant's behavioral cues cannot learn to modulate state in the same fashion as does the child whose needs are appropriately met. Since the mother's responses to her infant's behavioral cues (discomfort, pain, hunger, etc.) serve to shape the developing meaning of such experiences for the infant, the possibility for misperception and misinterpretation, or even mislocalization, is clearly there.

The nature and meaning of emotions are "negotiated" between mother and infant. Infant discomfort due to hunger or pain, for example, can be misinterpreted, misidentified and mislabeled by mother in terms of emotions or attitudes such as anger, hatred, or rejection. We see here the potential for the attribution of intent, which can become extremely confusing for the developing infant and child and significantly confuse the notion of agency. The results of such chronic misattribution can be seen in, for example, the child who cannot identify or localize his feelings, emotions, or discomforts (which makes them difficult to shape or resolve) and the child who grows into an "imposed identity" as a replacement for a dead sibling (Cain & Cain, 1964).

Returning the Dimension of Interactive Mutuality to Piagetian Psychology

The process of learning how to modulate behavioral states is central because, without the consistency and continuity of experience assured by this ability, the myriad tasks of cognitive and affective development would be insurmountable. Certainly language acquisition, the "jewel in the crown of cognition [which] defines what it is to be an intelligent human being" (Pinker, cited in Kolata, 1987), would be impossible in a sensorily chaotic universe. And just as language develops in a context of intense mutuality, so, too, does the ability to transition from one behavioral state to the next. We all begin life in a mediated universe and whatever may go wrong occurs in a mediated universe.

To the observer infant behavioral states can appear strikingly discontinuous over even a very short period of time. Putnam's discussion of the normative substrates of multiple personality disorder (MPD) suggests why this observation is important for all therapeutic work with children—and with many adults.

> The transitions between infant behavioral states exhibit psychophysiological properties that are highly similar to those observed across switches of alter personalities in MPD.
>
> As the child grows, additional behavioral states are added and the transitions between states are smoothed out, so that it becomes increasingly difficult to identify discrete behavioral states in children older than a year (Emde et al., 1976). In adults, discrete behavioral states are most clearly manifested in certain psychiatric conditions, such as the affective states seen in mood disorders or the anxiety states seen in the anxiety and phobic neuroses. Again, the switches between affective states and the onset-offset of anxiety states exhibit many of the psychophysiological principles observed in infant behavioral state transitions and the switches of MPD alter personality states. (Putnam, 1989, p. 51)

Consider once again the categorical "deficiencies" and "inabilities" of abused, traumatized, "learning-disabled," and psychiatrically disturbed children reviewed in Chapter 1. Viewed categorically, those children "could not" perform various mundane tasks; they "lacked" various abilities; they were "unable" to perform or respond, and had "deficits" and "disordered thinking"—all of which were seen as representing "specific deficiencies in symbolic abilities," etc. We can see clearly how such apparently disordered cognition could develop under conditions of abuse or inadequate parenting over time. Even the cognitive operation of *reversibility* requires, first, a consistency and continuity of experience to form the experiential "ground" upon which the "figure" of the cognitive operation can be reversed and, second, the ability to effect such a reversal. Children who have not learned how to modulate behavioral states will have serious difficulty with this operation, as they may with any operation involving seriation or variants.

But more important for our concerns here, both the process of learning how to modulate state (necessary to fix attention upon a given task, for example) and the process by which such abilities are measured occur in a context of mutuality. And just as infant modulation of state can be impaired because of inadequate or disturbed environmental mediation, so too can all varieties of state-dependent performance be impaired because of absent, inadequate or disturbed environmental mediation. In other words, just as traditional Piagetian verbal interviewing and assessment techniques can fail to elicit the true cognitive-performance abilities of the child (and thereby result in a significantly suboptimal assessment of genuine ability), so too can an unmediated or improperly mediated assessment (e.g., a WISC-R) result in grossly suboptimal findings.

If such test results are allowed to stand, the effects of trauma on childhood cognition summarized by Fish-Murray, Koby and van der Kolk (1987) may well become fixed over time, until they constitute a veritable cognitive style characterized by relative deficiency or disorder. However, if assessment techniques are modified in light of (1) our knowledge of the communicative styles of children which are often nonverbal and interactive, and (2) the realization that behavioral competence is optimized by appropriate environmental mediation, we may find that the appearance of categorical dysfunction can be remediated or reversed. To judge any individual's affective or cognitive (behavioral) competence without optimal environmental mediation is, almost always, to misjudge it. (Noting that Piaget's mother was mentally ill [Piaget, 1968], it is not hard to understand why he chose to view the subject as developing in a process of action-upon-the-environment, rather than through an environmentally mediated process of mutuality: the latter must have been much too threatening. Ironically, one can view Piaget's developmental psychology, and the developmental epistemology which informs it, as an astounding example of institutionalized intellectual dissociation.)

NORMAL AND PATHOLOGICAL DISSOCIATION

As we have seen, the lesson of Putnam's first normal substrate is that our assessment and therapeutic techniques must be mediative if they are to optimize behavioral response, adaptation and change. The lesson of his second normal substrate is that we surrender some of our most powerful therapeutic tools if we are not aware of, and prepared to utilize, the normative dissociative abilities of children. Any observant adult has seen normative dissociation in children, such as alterations in consciousness (daydreaming, "tuning out") or sense of self: "No, I didn't eat those cookies," replies the adamant five-year-old whose face is still covered with crumbs. To appreciate the dissociative nature of the child's response, it must be understood that, at that very moment of the denial, he neither remembers that he ate the cookie nor tastes the cookie still in his mouth.

We see in this single instance an illustration of the components of Putnam's description of dissociative states: "Dissociative states are characterized by significant alterations in the integrative functions of memory for thoughts, feeling, or actions, and significant alterations in sense of self (Ludwig, 1983; Nemiah, 1981)." At the moment he is confronted our five-year-old does not remember the *action* of eating the chocolate chip cookie nor his *thoughts* about getting into the cookie jar that preceded the act nor the *feeling* of enjoyment he experienced as he ate the cookie; his *altered sense of self* is strikingly evident in the absolutely sincere denial that he and the cookie-eater are one in the same person. An equally innocuous, although occasionally disturbing or disorienting experience is that of "highway hypnosis"—finding that one has no recollection of having driven the last three miles. Many people have experiences such as this, occasionally mechanically completing various acts or tasks, only to discover the process completed after the fact—with no memory of the experience itself.

At the Dissociative Disorders Unit of the National Institute of Mental Health, Putnam and his colleagues have developed an instrument which measures the frequency with which certain dissociative or depersonaliztion experiences occur, the Dissociative Experiences Scale (*DES*; Bernstein & Putnam, 1986). The *DES* has been used to survey a variety of normal and psychiatric populations.

Adolescents, as a group, receive a "relatively high median total *DES* score" (Putnam, 1989, p. 10), higher than normals, obsessive-compulsives, phobics, and epileptics—and exceeded only by schizophrenics, those with PTSD, and finally, multiples. Putnam notes that his team's findings are in agreement with those of other questionnaire-based studies (Harper, 1969; Myers & Grant, 1970; Roberts, 1960; Sedman, 1966). "Adolescents," he writes, "tend to report frequent experiences of 'tuning out' to external or internal stimuli and to report contextual shifts in their sense of self-identity—a finding that should come as no surprise to the parents of teenagers" (Putnam, 1989, p. 10). Children, however, are missing from the DES samples and, in fact, from consideration altogether—with two exceptions: the normative substrates of dissociation outlined above and the childhood traumatic antecedents of pathological dissociation—child abuse and, more specifically, child sexual abuse. (As of this writing, Putnam and his colleagues have developed a Child Dissociative Checklist, although it has not been standardized like the *DES*.)

The Dissociogenic Force of Trauma

The normative dissociative styles of childhood actually obscure their very presence: dissociation as a style is so pervasive in childhood that it is rarely recognized as such. Children, also, do not complain about dissociative responses and are not consciously aware when they use them. It takes a certain affective and cognitive maturity to be able to experience depersonalization as unpleasant: the self of the child is not as painfully self-conscious as that of the adolescent or adult.

The reader who has children, or who treats or educates children, will see a constant stream of dissociative phenomena simply by observing the everyday behavior of normal children. Young children can "forget" instantly. They can forget entire episodes or periods. They can access memory or produce information at one time or in one setting, and not at another time or in another setting. Their memory may be strikingly context-dependent. Even their apparent fund of knowledge may, at times, be context-dependent. They can deny with absolute sincerity acts or intentions just witnessed by adults. Children regularly "hear only what they want to hear," which really means that they, too, "tune out," just as adolescents do. The only difference is that the child is not painfully aware of the process, as the adolescent may be, and cannot give a reliable self-report.

Children don't complain of *ennui* or "not feeling like myself." Instead, the child whose cognitive-behavioral style has become literally a *dissociative mode* looks very bizarre and is usually quickly diagnosed as psychotic, having a "central processing disorder," grossly "learning-disabled," or presenting a severe developmental disorder. These children are caricatures of normal children. Unfortunately, even the familiar, when carried to extremes, becomes unrecognizable.

Thus, the adaptive nature of the dissociative response is easily recognized when seen as a response to extreme situations (Bettelheim, 1979; Bliss, 1984; Braun & Sachs, 1985; Frankenthal, 1969; Frankl, 1962; Kluft, 1984; Spiegel, 1984). However, when no clearly identifiable extreme situations are perceived, the dissociative nature of clinical phenomena may be missed entirely. The astute clinician will always look for such trauma in the history, even when no mention is volunteered. What is more surprising, however, is that the obvious dissociative nature of some clinical presentations is not recognized even when trauma of sufficient dissociogenic force is clearly present in the history.

George was three-and-a-half when his twenty-three-year-old mother dropped dead of a stroke at home just nine days after giving birth two weeks prematurely to George's first and only sibling, Billy. George, who had been a grossly over-mothered, shy, and retiring child, simply withdrew. He was referred for psychiatric evaluation and treatment because the schools thought that he was either autistic or mentally handicapped with a "central processing disorder." At the time of the initial evaluation, George was six years old, in a preschool class for three-year-olds, noninteractive, blissfully uninvolved and largely echolalic.

Nowhere in any of the previous evaluations was mention made of the sudden, unexpected death at home of George's mother shortly after the birth of his brother—except to note that she was deceased. One of the repetitive themes of most of the evaluations was that George "did not seem to understand" or "remember" what he experienced. Long after it was clearly and convincingly established that George was a child of normal intelligence whose bizarre clinical appearance was trauma-induced, his teacher in the Educable Mentally Handicapped Program of the school system maintained with uncommon tenacity that he was "retarded" (see Chapter 9, "Parental Death" for details of this child's treatment).

Putnam (1989) notes "the widespread nature of feelings of depersonalization, which are present in 15–30% of all [adult] psychiatric patients irrespective of diagnosis." He adds that "depersonalization syndromes are frequently associated with a history of sustained traumas (e.g., concentration camp experiences)." Having been grossly traumatized, George was further disoriented by the categorical and noncomprehending treatment he received. Unlike Putnam's adult subjects, George didn't complain of feeling depersonalized (in fact, he didn't complain of anything); he just *was* depersonalized.

Although the self-report of children is not like that of the adolescent or the adult (and consequently, we do not see categorical depersonalization syndrome in children as we do in adolescent or adults), many of the experiences of severely disturbed children are similar to those which lead to depersonalization. Many would-be normal children live the equivalent of concentration camp experiences.

THE MODEL OF INESCAPABLE SHOCK
Lessons from Military Medicine and Animal Research

Van der Kolk and Greenberg (1987, p. 67) note that animal research shows that the experience of inescapable shock depletes the central nervous system of certain neurotransmitters such as norepinephrine and dopamine, while the experience of escapable shock may actually increase them. The key factor in the debilitating ("helplessness syndrome") response to inescapable shock does not appear to be the shock itself (because of the normally subtraumatic level of current), but rather the experience of lack of control (the animal cannot escape even mild shock). The same level of electric shock without inescapability does not elicit a profound traumatic stress reaction. Furthermore, animals previously exposed to escapable shock are more stress resistant when exposed to inescapable shock than those without such prior experience.

> There is a striking parallel between the animal response to inescapable shock and the human response to overwhelming trauma. Grinker and Spiegel [1945] described many autonomic and extrapyramidal symptoms of catecholamine depletion following acute combat stress in World War II soldiers. These included masked facies, reduced eye blink, cogwheel rigidity, postural flexion, and coarse tremor of the extremities. Behavioral sequelae of catecholamine depletion following inescapable shock in animals closely parallel the negative symptoms of PTSD in humans. Van der Kolk et al. [van der Kolk, Greenberg, Boyd et al., 1985] proposed that the diminished motivation, the decline in occupational functioning, and the global constriction seen in PTSD are correlates of [norepinephrine] depletion. The symptoms of hyper-reactivity (i.e., startle responses, explosive outbursts, nightmares, and intrusive recollections) in humans resemble those produced by chronic noradrenergic hypersensitivity following transient catecholamine depletion after acute trauma in animals. (pp. 67–68)

> Some animals exposed to inescapable shock can be trained to avoid subsequent shock if they are dragged across the grid into a non-electrified area. This "putting through" procedure can even reverse some of the neurochemical changes due to inescapable shock [Seligman, Maier, & Geer, 1968]. This finding may have applicability to humans: therapists may have to perform the psychotherapeutic equivalent of dragging the patient into a non-electrified area; that is, actively encourage the patient to take action in order to reexperience control. This can attenuate some of the chronic sense of helplessness and victimization so common in people with PTSD. (p. 74)

While the psychobiology of trauma is fascinating and has profound implications for research and clinical work, its immediate usefulness becomes more obvious if we view it simply. If we take an animal—for instance, a laboratory mouse—and place it in a cage in which all touchable surfaces are (even mildly) electrified, there is no escape for the mouse. As noted by van der Kolk and Greenberg, "Anisman and Sklar [1979] found that shocks with no measurable effect on naive animals produced [norepinephrine] depletion and escape deficits in mice previously exposed to inescapable shock." Thus, the stress response of the mouse previously exposed to inescapable shock is overwhelming when the mouse is placed in a cage where the electrified grid is small and escapable. The previous experience of inescapability radically constricts behavioral and physiological responses to even minute aversive stimulation.

The Inescapability of Even "Mild" Childhood Trauma

Children differ in two extremely important ways from laboratory mice: they are cognitively and behaviorally much more complex, and the nature of inescapability in their lives is different. By virtue of the fact that infants, toddlers and children are literally dependent upon the care and goodwill of their caregivers for their very survival, the family itself can constitute an inescapable temporophysical space. Consequently, even "mild" abuse within the family can constitute psychologically inescapable trauma because there is no genuine real-world escape for the child. The child cannot pick up and go, trade or change families, or divorce his parents. And even when there may be genuine physical escape (running to a neighbor, telling a teacher, calling an abuse hotline), such escape may not be imaginable without an equally imaginable return to the very same family. The therapist who concludes that a child victim of family trauma was not exposed to inescapable shock because he or she cannot identify specific instances of gross invasion of bodily space or confinement abuse has failed to understand the experiential world of the child.

Let's now treat the child as if it were a mouse. The cage with the electrified grid is the abusive family. Protective Service becomes involved and removes the child, placing her in foster care. Consistency and continuity of genuine adult care, along with the absence of victimization, begin to give the child a sense of reliability and predictability. Good child psychotherapy is provided and the child's experience of escapability begins to acquire a genuine psychophysiological reality. The (not necessarily conscious) knowledge of an alternative to unavoidable hurt allows for a reintegrative process to occur.

Then—because our society does not understand that "family" is an operational, not a categorical, term—Protective Service, wanting to "protect and promote the family," removes the child from the safe and secure foster care setting and returns her to those who hurt her. There she is abused or terrified again. Having been removed from the cage with the inescapable electrified grid, and having been "dragged through" to a safe non-electrified area in a new cage, our "mouse" is placed back in the first cage. Through all of this she is told, if she is at all verbal, that all these maneuvers are to "protect her" and "for her own good." So, again, Protective Service must remove her from her parents and place her into foster care.

But this time she is abused by the foster "caregivers" themselves or by another resident of the foster setting, for 35% of abused children are reabused in foster care (Coppolillo, 1987, p. 347). In other words, this time our little child-mouse is *told* that the new cage into which she is being put is just like the first one where she experienced relief from the inescapable shock of the abusive grid—but it is not. To the experience of inescapable shock is added the extraordinary cognitive confusion of calling up "down" and right "left." So, to "protect" her a third time, our little child-mouse is removed again (if she is lucky enough to have the foster care abuse discovered) and placed again with her "family" or into a third foster care setting: from cage to cage to cage to cage.

It is not difficult to see how easily one could literally drive a mouse crazy. So what must the effect be on the infinitely more complex child? Unlike the mouse, the child interprets experience cognitively and with intense, idiosyncratic subjectivity—and not just physiologically (with all due respect to the complexity of mice). The child who receives a standard psychiatric diagnosis after being treated this way is being radically short changed.

The child-mouse parallel is easy to draw because an abusive family is like an electrified cage: overwhelming hurt and no escape. But the parallel holds for George as well, where there was no parental abuse. The dependency of childhood and the child's place within the family itself constitute the inescapability—even when there is no intentional proactive harm. Thus, children who are traumatized by experience which is unintended but still inescapable can be as affected as those who are hurt by the most cruel of abusers.

DISSOCIATION AND DISSOCIATIVE TECHNIQUES

It is generally agreed by researchers and clinicians working with traumatized patients that dissociative responses are adaptive at the time of the trauma (Putnam, 1989; van der Kolk, 1987). The self may have to be split, fractionated, or even denied entirely in order to assure psychological and, in some cases, even physical survival.

One of the purposes of dissociative techniques in child psychotherapy is to help the child to determine what he or she can, or cannot, deal with consciously. This should be seen as a process based upon a recognition of the nature of the cognitive and interactive styles of children—not as a first step toward bringing all issues into conscious awareness. It must be remembered that dissociative phenomena are not pathological in and of themselves; they become pathological only when they prevent adaptive change.

Ten-year-old Matt was extremely uncomfortable with our regular procedure of beginning each session by going over the activities of the previous week. Even though each session always began positively with a review of progress, good behavior, and accomplishments at home, in school, and in the community, Matt was intensely embarrassed by his mother's review of the week's problem behaviors or interactions. Matt's reactions to her open description of any negative occurrences were also intense; he would become upset, deny his mother's version of the week's events and call her a liar. However, in spite of the tough-guy attitude Matt affected, once in the playtherapy room he regularly allowed his therapist to play out the very same events his mother had just described—with stuffed animals. Not only did Matt never deny the accuracy of her play portrayal, but he also usually added details, frequently unflattering to himself, much as a director might embellish a scene in a play by adding directorial refinements to his actors' roles. At no point in the therapy did he ever acknowledge a conscious awareness of the absolute parallelism between the play and his mother's versions.

It is generally wise not to take such "indirect acknowledgment" of the veracity of a particular incident or assertion as a sign that the child is inviting the therapist to deal with the material by bringing the issues into conscious awareness. In Matt's case that transition never came, and yet the issues that blocked him from consciously acknowledging responsibility were resolved—all within the play. His behavior changed radically over time and his mother soon found herself with fewer and fewer such incidents to report at the beginning of the session. Another child, with a different interactive style, might quickly or slowly acknowledge the parallelism of the content of the play and the descriptions of his behavior at the beginning of the session. One could then pursue the issues openly. It must be stressed, however, that a move toward open consideration is not always, or even frequently, better: it simply reflects a different cognitive and interactive style.

Dissociative Styles as a Failure of Developmental Integration

A distinction, however, must be made between dissociative phenomena as potentially adaptive responses to overwhelming (even if subtle) trauma and dissociative phenomena representing a failure or disorder of developmental integration. In reviewing the role of trauma in the development of MPD, Putnam covers the spectrum.

The severe, sustained, and repetitive trauma that occurs during the early to middle childhood of most victims is thought to promote the development of MPD through several interconnected mechanisms. The first is a disruption of the developmental tasks of consolidation of self across behavioral states and the acquisition of control over the modulation of states. The recurring trauma (generally child abuse) instead creates a situation in which it is adaptive for the child to heighten the separation between behavioral states, in order to compartmentalize overwhelming affects and memories generated by the trauma. In particular, children may use their enhanced dissociative capacity to escape from the trauma by specifically entering into dissociative states. Dissociative states of consciousness have long been recognized as adaptive responses to acute trauma, because they provide (1) escape from the constraints of reality; (2) containment of traumatic memories and affects outside of normal conscious awareness; (3) alteration or detachment of sense of self (so that trauma happens to someone else or to a depersonalized self); and (4) analgesia.

In most MPD cases, the abuse is inflicted on the child by a parent or other caretaking figure. One of the most important tasks of a caretaker, particularly in early childhood, is helping the infant or toddler to enter and sustain a behavioral state that is appropriate for the circumstances. One only has to watch good parents feeding a toddler in public to see how they help their child achieve and maintain an appropriate state and how they suppress inappropriate states or help the child recover from disruptions of state. It is easy to speculate that the bad parenting accompanying abuse fails to aid the child in learning to modulate behavioral states. (Putnam, 1989, p. 53)

Developmental "Stage" vs. Psychophysiologic "State"

Children traumatized very early in life or children whose caretakers did not or could not mediate the process of integrative development in their infant may simply not know how to organize experience. Such children, like George above, may appear organically impaired. Their clinical appearance does not reflect a once-adaptive psychophysiological style; it reflects a disordered psychophysiological style. Repetitive environmental manipulative structuring, exquisitely sensitive to every interaction, may be necessary to build a coherent sense of self over time. (See Chapter 6 for the description of such structured and structuring interaction.) However, children whose dissociative maneuvers, no matter how bizarre, developed as self-saving responses to overwhelming trauma can use dissociation in the present just as they used it in the past. Such behavior, no matter how bizarre it may appear to the observer, represents a modifiable *state* — and not an inescapable *stage*.

Eleven-year-old Todd was physically and sexually abused and terrorized by his biological parents and while in foster care. In the Educable Mentally Handicapped Program at school, Todd still had not learned to tell time or make change. He spent much of his time in fantasy and related to most individuals or events in terms of movies or television shows. His mood swings were precipitous and his responses to frustration could be violently explosive. His social and interpersonal judgment was exceedingly poor and he tended to invade the physical and emotional space of others. He was, however, blessed with an infinitely patient adoptive mother.

Todd tolerated any criticism, no matter how minor, with great difficulty. On this particular occasion his mother noted that Todd had spent the entire week "glued to the television set, watching the children's network" on cable. Once in the playtherapy room, Todd's therapist went to a corner of the room next to the shelf holding the stuffed animals and sat down indian-style. She reached up to the wall and turned an imaginary control knob. "What are you doing? You look silly," Todd said, amused. "Leave me alone," his therapist replied, "I'm watching the Disney channel." With great patience, and with only a few replies to Todd to leave her alone and let her watch the television, she sat staring at the wall for a solid 45 minutes. Five minutes before the end of the hour she reached up, turned off the imaginary television set, and asked Todd to put away the few things he had played with in a desultory fashion while she had "watched television." Back in the room with his mother and her co-therapist, not a word was said about what had just transpired. Todd never again "glued" himself to the television while completely ignoring his mother.

Todd was a child who could deny ten separate acts within the space of five minutes. He had extensive amnesias for much of his abusive childhood which never resolved completely in many years of therapy. He had been blamed constantly for everything that happened in his world for the first years of his life and had been beaten brutally for events over which he had had no personal control whatsoever. Bringing the content of the interactive experience in the playtherapy room into conscious awareness ("You see how your mother must feel when you glue yourself to the TV?") would have resulted in an explosive outburst of hateful accusations.

It was not until nearly a year after the above session that it was learned just how extensively Todd's foster parents had projected responsibility onto him. With the recovery of the memory of the brutal and sadistic punishments they had inflicted on him for things over which he had had no control came a surprising increase in his academic performance as well as in his ability to tell time and count money. When Todd quickly made the honor roll his once obvious and long accepted mental retardation was quickly brought into question. It is exceedingly difficult to move a child such as Todd from one hierarchical Piagetian stage to the next. It is much easier to modify psychophysiological styles through interpersonal and environmental interventions—a process which can result in the development of apparent "stage maturity" over time. (See Chapter 6 for a detailed discussion of this process.)

Implications for Psychotherapy Technique

Because of the pervasiveness of normative dissociative responses in childhood, it would be totally impractical to attempt to bring into conscious awareness every instance of even pathological dissociative responses or patterns. Therapy would be reduced to the impotent pedestrianism of a centipede consciously trying to move every single leg. But even the potentially crippling dissociative response of multiple personality development serves a momentary adaptive purpose. Like Putnam, van der Kolk (1987, Chapter 1) notes that, "MPD illustrates how dissociation, and its resulting loss of memory for the trauma, allows the original distress to be walled off, while leaving the patient with a tendency to react to subsequent stress as if it were a recurrence of the trauma. The patient experiences the emotional intensity of original trauma without conscious awareness of the historical reference" (p. 7). Consequently, the therapeutic approach with adults has tended to concentrate on the retrieval and integration of traumatic memories (Greenberg & van der Kolk, 1987; van der Kolk & Kadish, 1987). This is often a process of collaborative exploration and retrieval, in which the patient's awareness of the process plays a role.

With children the process of retrieval and reintegration may itself remain largely dissociated from immediate conscious awareness. This is not to say that children never follow the adult model; some do and the flexible, astute therapist will capitalize on this ability. But we must repeatedly remind ourselves not to impose an adult discursive style upon the child. For many children such an interactive style will be foreign and very anxiety-provoking. Furthermore, because of the child's dissociative abilities, he may follow the adult path largely to please his therapist — and then dissociate the entire experience, leaving therapy with an impressive, but empty, piece of psychological baggage.

It is often felt that "traumatized patients are frequently very difficult to engage in psychotherapy" (van der Kolk & Kadish, 1987). The key word here is *engage*. Joy's therapist in Chapter 1 also viewed her little patient as difficult to engage because her model of therapeutic engagement was an adult discursive model. The more intensely understood traumatized patients — adults as well as children — feel themselves to be, the more likely they are to respond quickly to therapeutic initiatives. Because much of what they would talk about if they could is dissociated from conscious awareness, traumatized patients can rarely respond to traditional psychiatric or psychological inquiry. They also tend to experience such inquiry as aversive — first, because the style is so foreign to them, and second, because it signals to them that their examiner or therapist does not understand them and is therefore unlikely to be of help.

The hurt child, still alive but not very well in the adult patient, simply won't risk the investment. This, we feel, accounts for much of the hostility of adult patients who were traumatized as children or adolescents. The therapist who is not put off by this initial interactive style and who can genuinely, comfortably, and respectfully speak to the child in the patient (regardless of age) will find that these patients can be immensely satisfying. It must be borne in mind that the very same dissociative ability which allows them to "turn off," "space out" or treat the therapist as if he or she simply weren't there can be mobilized to effect equally rapid integrative change. Dissociation is neither positive nor negative, it is simply a psychophysiological fact. It can be used adaptively or maladaptively by the patient, and it can be elicited therapeutically or countertherapeutically by the therapist.

There is one caveat. Because the intensity of the experiential content of trauma itself alone can promote or maintain the attachment process (in a veritable psychophysiological sense), the pattern of addiction to trauma may be difficult to break. Furthermore, as van der Kolk and Kadish (1987) note, the "tremendous plasticity of dissociative phenomena" can result in a wide range of behavioral responses such as conversion reactions, fugue states, amnestic periods, derealization, depersonalization, reenactments and psychosis—all in the same individual. Such a repertoire of behavioral response represents an extraordinary chameleon-like *ability*. Traumatized adults may hesitate to give up such behavioral mastery even in spite of the great personal pain it brings. Fortunately, children hold much less tightly to such patterns—especially when they experience that positive plasticity can bring relief, safety, and a new and different sense of mastery.

We must be careful that we do not view the resistance of many traumatized adults to therapeutic change, especially at this point in time when so few clinicians are aware of those techniques and interactive styles which are likely to elicit genuine change, as representing an unalterable physiological outcome of trauma. Some trauma-induced physiological changes may be irreversible, such as the possibly trauma-induced precocious puberty currently being investigated by Putnam and his colleagues at NIMH (Putnam, 1987). Trauma-induced precocious puberty, however, represents a prematurely induced physiological *stage* of normal growth—and not a disordered *state*. We would suggest, based upon our clinical experience, a growing number of single-case reports (such as the case of the survivor of the Coconut Grove fire reported by van der Kolk and Kadish [1987]), and the logic of the stage/state distinction, that many of the psychobiological sequelae of trauma can be attenuated or even reversed. These include attention disorders and hyperarousal (from categorical Attention Deficit Disorder to full-blown mania); intrusive reexperiencing, including flashbacks, nightmares and night terrors (Donovan, 1989); and addiction to trauma. An example is previously diagnosed Attention Deficit Disorder with Hyperactivity (ADHD) that turns out to be anxiety-driven hypervigilance.

> Four-year-old Brice had a long history of physical and emotional abuse at the hands of his parents and an extremely chaotic life with multiple unpredictable moves as his parents attempted to evade the law. At three he had been present when his father raped, beat, and then stabbed his mother to death with a screwdriver. Brice wet the bed, and sometimes his clothes, was disrespectful to adults and invasive of everyone's personal space, and would not remain in his bed at night for more than a few hours. In preschool Brice would "tune out" the teacher and her aide. At the initial evaluation meeting Brice was in constant motion, climbing all over his grandmother who was sitting in an armchair, totally oblivious to the obvious pain he was causing her with his leather-soled shoes. Attempts to get him to sit in his own chair were unsuccessful until Brice's grandmother answered our question about what she had told him about the fate of his mother. "I told him that his mother is asleep in Heaven and that he doesn't have to worry about her." At this point his therapist stood up and leaned over the chair where Brice was squirming around on his grandmother's lap. She took him gently, but firmly, by the forearm and looked him straight in the eye. "Brice," she said slowly, clearly and with great seriousness, "your mother is *not sleeping. She is dead.* She is not sleeping," she repeated, "she is dead. Dead and buried. Buried in the ground. And she won't ever, ever, ever come back. She can't wake up because she's dead." Brice's overactivity ceased instantly and he became sad, quiet and normally responsive.

Pynoos and Eth (1986) have found in their work with children who have witnessed violence (including homicide, suicide, rape, aggravated assault, accidental death, etc.) that only when children are secure in the belief of their parent's physical death are they able to grieve openly. A central feature of their therapeutic interview technique involves the concrete representation of the act of violence in a drawing done by the child. In this instance, even though Brice's traumatic experience had occurred a full year earlier, he would not have been able to produce a drawing of any kind before this first intervention significantly decreased his anxiety.

BEHAVIORAL MEMORIES

In Chapter 1 we saw that the content and complexity of children's thought and communication appear significantly greater if we avail ourselves of the insights of developmental psycholinguistics. With this switch inperspective alone, little Joy's "disordered" play became eloquently expressive and our view of the communicative content of behavior widened. That particular developmental perspective significantly enriched our approach and offered potential diagnostic and therapeutic tools. In Chapter 3 we added the contextual perspective to our approach (to understanding Joy's behavior), thereby significantly decreasing the possibility of imposing abstract categorical meanings upon human experience and behavior—putting the child, as it were, back into child psychiatry.

An important contribution to the understanding of the memory of trauma comes from the ongoing work of Lenore Terr (1979, 1981, 1983a, 1983b, 1985a, 1985b, 1986) at the University of California at San Francisco. Because she has been following a series of trauma victims over a number of years, she has been able to investigate clinically what happens to early memories of trauma. The following clinical example from Terr's work illustrates the distinction between behavioral and discursive memory.

Perhaps the most fascinating single finding from these small groups was the type of memory still evident in children who were traumatized prior to the establishment of any real verbal ability. The three youngest children [pornography victims and possibly sexually abused] at the Hillgards' Day Care Center—Gloria (0–6 months), Sarah (15–18 months), and Brent (3–24 months)—each could produce no recollections in my office in response to such questions as "Did you ever go to somebody's house for babysitting?" or "Do you remember the Hillgards?" or "Tell me about your babysitters." Yet they demonstrated for me a striking kind of perceptual memory of the trauma, through their play in the office or through their fears that they described. Two-year-old Gloria smothered my small dolls with much heavier dolls, with blankets, or with cars and trucks that she placed over them (like adults on top of children). She jabbed her finger into the "vagina" of a doll immediately upon undressing it. She poked this doll, as she looked about my room, seemingly trying to determine when I would be looking away.

Brent, at four, constructed a hotel in my office where, he said, "Movies are being made." He set up a line of truck drivers waiting to get into the hotel. "They take pictures with their clothes off," he explained as he played. "They like to. . . . The children fight and play around. The parents also have to take their clothes off. They sometimes take their picture, too, without clothes. . . . They are Gumdrop Grandma and Gumdrop Grandpa. . . . The children like taking the pictures. They get excited. Then their penis unties—looses off. It comes off their bodies. They like to lose their penis. Then they get it back. The people at the hotel run and run to get it [the lost penis]. . . . When the children stop playing, fussing, and taking pictures, their penis gets very softer. When do I get out of here? . . . The guy drivers are going to fight and fuss. They're going to play with *his* penis. The Grandma wouldn't, but the Grandpa *would*. The guy in the car carrier likes it. Grandpa Gumdrop plays with his penis. . . . The guy is real quiet on the truck now that he has played. He's stopped talking." (In actuality, Brent's speech, which had developed early, entirely ceased for several months when he turned two.)

In four psychiatric sessions with me and in one with another child psychiatrist, Brent Burns demonstrated absolutely no verbal memory of the ordeal, which he must have experienced between 3 and 24 months of age. He could not remember the Hillgards [who ran the day care facility] at all. He listed babysitters who watched him from age 3 on, in response to any questions about sitters or day care. Yet Brent's play almost exactly duplicated much of what had probably happened to him. (Terr, 1985, pp. 65–66)

When to Remain Within the Dissociative Style of Behavioral Memory

By the time Terr and her colleague interviewed Brent, two years had passed since the sexual abuse and pornographic filming had taken place, an interval which constituted literally half of the four-year-old's life. Brent's safety and security had presumably been assured over that period and yet only in a dissociated fashion could he access the memories of what had occurred. In contrast, two-year-nine-month-old Joy, whose meaningful "meaningless" behavior we have considered in the preceding chapters, was still in the midst of an abusive and intensely chaotic situation when she was first evaluated by a female psychologist. It is not surprising that, notwithstanding her advanced verbal abilities, she was not more forthcoming with an examiner who gave no indication whatsoever of understanding her plight or of viewing her behavior as anything other than "disordered." Had Joy's examiner been more understanding of the dissociative styles of children, especially traumatized children, she might have been witness to behavioral memories which preceded those of the shelter home placement, specifically of the sexual mistreatment itself.

Several months after the encounter with the psychologist, Joy, in a much more understanding clinical setting, responded to a verbal question about being touched inappropriately by turning to her male psychiatrist and away from her mother and the other female in the room. She unexpectedly pulled up her dress and held it up under her chin while she pulled down her panties, staring at the only male in the room all the while. She then spread her labia wide with her hands and smiled. She appeared oblivious to the presence of the two women. When Joy's mother, astounded by this behavior, saw that her daughter was making no move to bring the display to an end, she told her to pull her panties up and get back on the chair.

Startled, as if she hadn't realized that her mother was even present prior to being told to stop, Joy pulled up her panties and climbed back up on the large chair.

Although Terr does not tell us what the next step in therapy was, we assume that conscious retrieval of traumatic memories played a role in Brent's resolution of the past. Safe and out of harm's way, Brent could presumably learn how to integrate the memories of trauma in order to modify his cognitive style and lessen the likelihood of future reenactments, personal vulnerability, and the abused-to-abuser cycle. Little Joy could not. Abandonment of dissociative skills would have left her vulnerable to collapse of the self: she was, by no means, out of harm's way and was not to become so for several years following her first evaluation and subsequent psychotherapy. Joy's therapist had to accept the necessity of using dissociative techniques as a means of maintaining psychological integrity during a period when environmental safety could not be assured by Joy's mother, social agencies, or even the courts. Because Joy had no genuine reason to expect or believe that the environment could assure her safety (because father had visitation), she could not afford to abandon her dissociative style.

Rhetorical attempts to persuade vulnerable children that the environment will be able to protect them—if only they tell everything they know and have experienced—are bound to fall on deaf ears. Only the experience of environmental protection over a significant period of time can persuade a child at risk that it is safe to abandon dissociative techniques. The fear of retaliation from the abusive environment is enough to guarantee this.

Mitch and his sister were six and five respectively. Both had been abused and deprived by their father and stepmother. Mitch's sister, while thin and clearly undernourished, looked to be her age. Mitch, however, although a year older, was thought to be a very sick three-year-old by the office staff at the time of the court-ordered evaluation. He looked much more like a miniature concentration camp survivor than a six-year-old boy.

In the presence of his six-foot stepmother, Mitch answered the questions about his life: no, he was never locked in his room and, yes, he always had enough to eat. Once engaged in play in the playtherapy room, Mitch was unaware that the very same questions were being asked in the context of the play. His examiner put the little boy doll in bed in the large open-sided dollhouse and said with typical childlike inflection, "This little boy's so hungry at night! What should he do?" "He should go to the fridge and get some food," Mitch replied in his garbled speech. "Do you get food from the fridge when you're hungry at night?" his examiner asked him matter-of-factly. "Oh, no," Mitch replied. "Why not?" she continued. "Because my door's locked." "From the inside or the outside?" she asked, still looking at the boy doll in bed. "From the outside," Mitch replied.

Taken to the small clinic kitchen after the "formal" interview was completed, Mitch practically dived into the huge tin of cookies when offered a snack. He scooped up literally armfuls and carried them back to the playtherapy room. When his stepmother reentered the office where little Mitch was holding a plastic bag filled with cookies to take home, she immediately exclaimed, "Oh, are those for me," and grabbed the bag from Mitch's hand, apparently caring little what the two clinicians thought of her action. Mitch, who had brightened considerably during the course of the evaluation, seemed to sink into himself. His spontaneity and eye-contact disappeared and his interactions with his examiners ceased as of that moment.

The purpose of the evaluation was to aid a child protection team in determining the cause of Mitch's apparent "failure to thrive." Interestingly, several workers continued to maintain that "Mitch's body could not use food properly" and saw in his interview behavior no indication of abuse or deprivation. Not until he sustained a broken arm at home and subsequently regained his growth curve in medical foster care did the workers accept that his "condition" had been due to human cruelty.

FAMILY SECRETS

Family secrets can constitute an incredibly noxious, pathogenic, dissociogenic force. A look at the nature of secrets reveals why. To conscious problems, conflicts or impediments there can be conscious solutions, resolutions or accommodations. Even to unconscious problems, conflicts or impediments there can be (at times brilliant) unconscious solutions, resolutions, or accommodations. But to secrets there can be no such resolution: they are, by their very nature, inaccessible. They are, therefore, by their very nature, unresolvable. Because of this, even otherwise innocuous, mundane secrets can exert a malignant effect on cognition and behavior.

One of the simplest examples is the effect of secrets on academic performance. Reduced to its barest essentials, school is a place where children tell adults what they know—through oral and written work. A family secret represents knowledge of which the child cannot even be aware that he is aware. This bizarre situation engenders "cognitive blinders" which are difficult to isolate to the home situation. Consequently, the child ends up not allowing himself to know what he knows or to tell what he knows — and academic performance falls, sometimes dramatically. Frequently, however, family secrets are not minor. They are parental secrets of which the child or children are assumed to have no knowledge. It has been our consistent experience over the years, however, that children often know much more than adults assume — at an earlier age and with much greater complexity than would be thought possible. Such split-off knowledge often permeates the child's play or thematic preferences. Not consciously accessible to the child, it is often present in the form of behavioral memories. (See the case of Charlie, pp. 50–52, for a striking example of behavioral memory.)

5

History-Taking, Tools of Logic, and Parent Issues

We must know history in order not to be condemned to repeat it.
George Santayana

A unifying thread runs through these issues of history-taking, logic, and working with parents that informs the whole of therapy. One can hardly know the history of the child without knowing the parents (or guardians) and one can hardly enlist the parents as therapeutic allies without acquainting them with a basic knowledge of how children think, interact, communicate, and change. And because children rarely manifest the behavioral or cognitive difficulties which bring them to therapy in an ecological vacuum, parent issues must be addressed creatively and successfully throughout the therapeutic process if genuine change is to occur.

The therapist's first intense contact with the parents usually occurs during the history-taking process. Discussing the (historical) context in which the presenting problems developed is the best way to generate and mobilize the parents' understanding of child cognition, while the history-taking process itself offers the therapist/co-therapist the opportunity to address the child and the adult simultaneously. This chapter deals with what both therapist and parents need to know and do in order to maximize the therapeutic potential of a clinical encounter.

STRUCTURING A THERAPEUTIC EVALUATION

The Importance of the History

The history is the most important part of the evaluation, because without the context it defines and its priming effect on the clinical encounter with the child the risks of a blind clinical interview rise dramatically. Because the history represents a view of the child, the family, and the problems which, ostensibly, bring them to therapy, it is helpful to get as many different views as possible. We ask that any assessments or treatment discharge summaries from schools, agencies, institutions, hospitals, or other clinicians be forwarded to us prior to the first meeting. Since the purpose of such materials is to understand how the child and his family have been, or continue to be, perceived and treated by other institutions or individuals, it makes little sense to have the material brought to the first meeting or to receive it afterward.

Although we view all such information as tentative, prior assessments, previous testing, treatment summaries, or school incident reports permit the clinician to began to see some of the broad outlines of the child's life, as well as some of the identified problems. This information also tells us how the child has been perceived—or misperceived—by the authorities in his life. Such foreknowledge allows the clinician to begin the actual encounter with a series of operational hypotheses and questions. It also alerts the clinician to potentially meaningful (and therapeutically useful) inconsistencies or omissions in the history; these may signal anything from an uncaring or inadequate parent to powerful family secrets which exert significant effects on the child's emotional and cognitive growth or adaptation.

The First Contact

The clinical encounter itself, as well as the process of gathering the history, actually begins with the very first contact with the family. The clinician whose scheduling is done by a secretary and who sees the child and family "cold," thus having no idea why the child is there, is off to a slow start. For this reason we return all calls and make all appointments personally. Many parents are literally astounded when "the doctor" or "the therapist" actually returns telephone calls and sets up appointments. While many of our children's parents view such contacts as "concessions" on our part or an imposition on our time, we do not. This experience can in itself be useful since we often have to ask parents to make significant concessions and sacrifices with regard to transportation, lost wages, and occasionally fragile relationships with family members or employers. The fact that we ask the same of ourselves makes the process of beginning therapy easier for many parents. Furthermore, given the decreasing insurance coverage for mental health services, even if we substantially lower our fees the cost of treatment is a genuine burden for many parents. Thus, when parents receive a personal call from the therapist after hours (often very much after hours!), their sense of being alone in making sacrifices diminishes considerably.

The personal and financial sacrifices of some "parents" can be subjectively even greater precisely because they are not parents: many of the children
we see are brought by relatives who have "inherited" the obligation of caring
for a child after the "real" parents abandoned or were unable to care for the
child. This is something they might not have chosen to do had circumstances
been otherwise. Thus, such a small thing as the way in which the first
contact is made can take on disproportionate technical and therapeutic importance.

While many parents take the initiative of calling to ask for help, many
others do not; they call because they were told that they needed help and
that they should call. There can even be substantial pressure on the parents
to seek treatment as an alternative to judicial action by juvenile or criminal
courts, by attorneys, or by schools because the child is on the verge of
expulsion or placement in a program which the parents find threatening or
unacceptable. Unless handled properly, such pressure can result in therapy
being perceived as a form of coercion or even punishment. Although such
pressure may seem a handicap, it actually offers the clinician an opportunity
to create an atmosphere of problem-solving cooperation in which an imagined resolution of the problem turns the tables psychologically and makes an
ally of the clinician. The first telephone encounter with the clinician can
reduce considerably the sense of guilt or stigmatization which parents may
feel for needing, or being pressured to seek, psychotherapy for their child.

Often the parent's brief telephone description of the child's behavior and
history will provide a key to a simple understanding of the actual problem
which, in turn, can prompt a simple explanation. Thus, the first telephone
contact can also leave the parent, guardian, or caseworker with a powerful
expectation of help. The clinician may then find himself or herself in the
very different, and much more therapeutically effective, position of being
perceived as an ally by two "opposing" sides.

The first telephone contact can also alert the clinician to other problems
which might not come to light in the first interview. As child therapists know
well, the presenting problem is not necessarily the real problem. The first
contact may reveal family secrets such as parental alcoholism or a parent's
prior psychiatric history—of which the child is supposedly unaware. Often
the caller requests that certain issues not be brought up; or there may be just
enough hesitancy in the caller's voice to suggest that all is not being said
(even though the formal process has not yet begun). Mothers have occasionally told us that they had given another child up for adoption before they
were married to this child's father and that either father or the child or both
were not aware of this fact. Some have desperately wanted to seek help, but
have feared that the process of "dredging up the past" would make things

worse. Similarly, mothers may indicate that they had an abortion early in their child's life. They may say that they do not want this material brought up in front of the child or, in some cases, that they do not want it brought up at all. These are times when telephone contact can be extremely productive and save considerable time and grief, for we can usually demonstrate easily to the parent that the child's behavioral problems reflect an unconscious knowledge—often extremely detailed and accurate—of the supposed secret. The parent can then be shown how that unconscious knowledge plays a major role in maintaining the present disastrous situation.

The parent thus faces the first of the many difficult or painful decisions of therapy, as well as one of its potential "silver linings"—that the resolution of one problem almost always brings about the resolution of other problems, and that it is difficult for just one family member to change or "get well" when things go right. Because these parents have often suffered silently for years in horrendous fear that their secret will one day be discovered, they usually greet with relief the opportunity of solving their child's problem while at the same time putting behind them the otherwise eternal threat that the secret represents. We point out that, had they not wanted an opportunity to resolve the secret once and for all, they would not have mentioned it on the phone. A simple denial during the office history-taking would probably have sufficed to prevent discussion of the issue altogether. This statement constitutes a nonjudgmental acceptance of the parent as a person while assuring him/her that good clinical judgment and practice would never allow a defensive parent to dictate the course of treatment. The exchange has a powerful triage effect as well. In our experience those parents who work through the first phone contact and follow through with treatment usually do well and generally profit personally from their child's therapy. They quickly become allies of the therapeutic process.

On the other hand, those children whose parent(s) insist(s) upon the clinician's collusion in secret-keeping tend to do poorly regardless of therapeutic technique, often with considerable dramatic acting-out (which effectively punishes and humiliates the parents publicly), although the actual content of the acting-out behavior is intelligible only to those who know the secret. To accept such restrictions is almost always to accept therapeutic failure.

Apart from the pain of guilt, a major motivation for continued secret-keeping is the fear that disclosure will irreparably destroy all parental authority. We point out that one of the reasons for the call was their child's lack of respect for adults and their own inability to control their child's behavior. Thus, their fear is not so much of losing authority but of never being able to regain what has already been lost. If necessary, we share one or more brief anecdotes to illustrate that they are not alone in this kind of predicament, nor will they be the last to resolve it. In our experience, most such callers make and keep their appointments and come to the first session with a strongly motivating expectation of help.

Some child therapists relinquish much more of their adult authority at the beginning of treatment than they realize. This seems to be done out of respect for a strange notion of "democracy," which blurs the boundaries between adults and children and their very different abilities, rights, and prerogatives. Thus, we cannot agree with clinicians like Coppolillo (1987, pp. 125–126) who suggest that the child be allowed to participate in the setting of the initial appointment even to the point of having the child call or talk to the therapist. In our view, parents are "big people who tell little people what to do—for the right reasons and because they genuinely care." Since so much of our therapeutic work aims at reestablishing benevolent parental authority, we see no reason to sabotage it right from the beginning. The parent who suggests to his or her child that he or she make the first appointment has already set the stage for the child to expect the "right" to cancel the next one.

THE FIRST SESSION: DATA-GATHERING AND INTERVENTIONS

Who to See—and Why

We ask that both parents be present with the child for the first meeting, indicating that the presence of both parents not only will help us know the family better but also constitute a message of united parental commitment to the child. In our experience, children whose mother, at least, is not willing or "able" to accompany them to the first session do not do well in therapy. If the initial caller is a grandparent (usually the maternal grandmother), we communicate this concern immediately. Grandparent-initiated calls may signal significant transgenerational family problems, which usually involve the discrediting of the mother's parental ability and authority by the maternal grandmother. On the other hand, occasionally only the grandparent may have the courage to ask for help, in which case one may be able over time to "lure" the fearful parent into the therapeutic process by establishing a productive and even enjoyable working relationship with the child and grandparents.

In those cases where one parent refuses to be involved in therapy, we suggest to the other parent (usually the mother) that this does not necessarily pose a major problem. We suggest to the involved parent that few things are more intriguing than genuine change, especially when change has been thought impossible and when the child's behavior has been a major issue to the uninvolved parent. We suggest to the involved parent that she not worry but, rather, that she view the process of drawing the uninvolved into therapy as a challenge. We are not always successful but the approach does bring in a significant number of "refusniks." It is always fascinating when a matriarchal grandmother or great-grandmother (in a family with neither fathers nor grandfathers) requests an audience to "set us straight." Several of these "matriarchs" continue to return to see us every time they are in town—even though they have moved out of state. Occasionally the most resistant parent becomes the most poignant and rewarding patient.

Frequently, parents want to bring the entire family or ask if they should. While many of our colleagues prefer a full family approach, we find that we are more successful, and more quickly so, if only the designated patient and the parent(s) are present. In fact, because in our experience children change more quickly and more completely when the need for their own personal space and privacy is recognized and respected, we ask parents not to bring siblings (especially babies) whenever possible. All it takes to undo an otherwise productive session is for the child to discover his or her sibling misbehaving—even minimally—in the waiting room on the way out. Children delight in the proprietary privacy of the relationship with their therapist. We try to avoid blurring the home/therapy boundary by not recreating the family in the office.

If the child is involved with social services or the courts, or if the problems occur primarily at school, we ask that the caseworker or school personnel with the most complete knowledge of the reasons for referral be present. We do this to insure that the history will be as complete and accurate as possible and to minimize the adversarial relationship between home and institution. We are much more likely to provide a genuine therapeutic service to the child or adolescent if all adult parties involved feel that they are part of a common process. In those cases where parents are either uninterested or extremely defensive, the caseworker may play a vital role in maintaining the family in therapy or in extending the parent-therapy into the home setting.

The Initial Interview Setting

After the parent, guardian, or caseworker has filled out the registration form, we invite the child and accompanying adults into the office study. The study itself is not "child-proof." It has a large library filled with thousands of books and a computer, printer and typewriter all within a child's reach. We expect even the most disturbed children to respect this space and its contents, and it is only the very rare child who does not. Similarly, we expect the parents or caretakers to oversee the child's behavior in the office: how and/or whether they do so can be quite telling. As with every aspect of our approach, the fact that we see the child and parents initially in a setting which is not child-proof conveys implicitly our expectation that the child will be able to adapt to the constraints and requirements of the real world. Thus, without saying a word to the child or the parents, we begin the formal process with powerful therapeutic optimism. Child-proofing an office, on the other hand, constitutes an implicit invitation to disrespect conventional rules and boundaries. Many colleagues, on seeing our office, have remarked that we must not mind taking real chances with our property; however, in over six years not once have we had anything damaged or destroyed.

Taking the History: The Family Context

The parents and child are invited to sit down together on a couch facing the two seated co-therapists. Much can be learned just by seeing how and where on the couch the two or three people sit. Our couch has three fairly large cushions such that each family member can have his or her own space. Although we make no attempt to utilize the seating arrangement on the first encounter, at the second encounter we ask the child to sit properly on his or her own cushion, a simple thing which encourages safe individuation and the acceptance of interpersonal boundaries. (It also helps discourage the nonverbal communication implicit in touching, which can prevent a child or parent from saying what is really on his or her mind.)

We introduce the history-taking process by telling the child and parents that we have "a rather formal and structured way in which we like to get to know the people we work with" and to understand why they have come to see us. We outline that structure by telling them that we are going to spend about 15 to 20 minutes together discussing the family, the problems which have brought them to see us, and the details of the child's life. We explain that after the initial information-gathering we will separate; the child will spend some time with the co-therapist in another room and then "we will get back together to see if we can make some sense of all this—and talk about how to make it better."

With parents (as opposed to guardians or caseworkers), we begin the formal history-taking with a question calculated to ease tensions: "Now, for the hardest question we're going to ask today—how old is Mom?" Since the first set of questions frequently brings up difficult or painful subjects, this very first question (begun with great seriousness and completed with a smile) sets a counter-tone. Because a woman's age is treated in our culture (if only facetiously) as a "secret" and as an issue of potential vulnerability and embarrassment, this simple question is utilized—much like a hypnotic suggestion—to signal the fact that serious issues are going to be discussed but that ours is a safe place to do so.

After the father is asked his age, we ask the parents specifically when they were married, about "children from this marriage," and whether any children were lost: "Were there any abortions, stillbirths, miscarriages or child deaths?" This gives us the opportunity very early in the encounter to begin to understand the meaning of any perinatal loss. Many interview outlines include a variant of this question but treat it as a simple informational issue. The context of perinatal loss, however, can be much greater than that reflected by a simple tally of miscarriages, because of the effect of such losses on subsequent attachment and projected identities (identities projected onto the child). If the miscarriages or stillbirths were late in the pregnancy we ask whether there was any closure to the experience: was the baby buried, were there services, etc.? (Later, when the child is in the other room, we ask about mother's ideas of what happened to the baby: was it cut up, buried, thrown in a wastebasket, used for medical research, etc.?) If the answer to the question about lost children is a categorical "no," we are even more specific: e.g., "three pregnancies, three children?"

We ask matter-of-factly about previous marriages, which may bring an overt or covert sign from one or both parents that certain things are not to be mentioned. We respect such requests and continue on with our questions in as subtly reassuring a manner as possible. In such cases, we pursue the details after the child has left the room with the co-therapist. If one of the parents present is a stepparent or if the present parent is a single (although not necessarily divorced) parent, we ask specifically about the reasons for the separation or divorce, although we leave to the brief longitudinal review of the child's life the details of his experience of the parents' relationship and the circumstances of the family breakup. We also ask whether any other persons have lived with the family during the child's lifetime, as well as who is presently living in the home. Not infrequently there are other individuals in the home, a fact which would be left undisclosed if not asked about specifically (even though the intake form asks about "others in the home"). This includes pets, a question which occasionally reveals powerful traumatic losses.

If the parents carry pictures of family members, we ask to see them, explaining that it helps to make the people in their lives more real to us. Striking similarities or differences can be informative. We have even seen deceased family members in pictures who were not mentioned in spite of detailed questioning. In one case the husband was consistently absent from

the multitude of photos "because he always takes the pictures." This husband was also absent from the interview—and largely from the family as
well. It is extremely important to ask to see pictures of dead siblings, for they
often provide invaluable clues to the meaning of the presenting problems.
Although this part of the history can be detailed and often extremely informative, rarely does it take more than four or five minutes.

The History: Identifying the Problems

After this brief but necessary overview of who's who in the child's world,
we ask the parents to be very specific about why they "have come today." (We
make no references to "therapy" or "psychiatry" or "treatment."* We point
out that it is very important to be open and frank about their concerns and
to describe in detail the cause of their concern—even if this repeats what was
said during the initial telephone contact. Some parents ask to wait until the
child has left the room before going into details. Similarly, many therapists
like to meet first with the child's parents alone and then to meet separately
with the child. Whether initiated by the parents or the therapist, the results
of such an arrangement are the same: unless the child hears an unequivocal
statement of the problem—at least as perceived by the parents, guardian or
caseworker—therapy begins adrift and directionless. The clear statement of
the perceived problems *contextualizes* the process of therapy which began
with the first telephone contact.

We do not ask the child to "tell us what is wrong" or "why you are here."
It is hopelessly inefficient to wait for a child to state resolvable problems:
children often can not and adolescents often will not. It also places the
therapist in a potentially compromising position, caught between the problems as perceived by parents, school, or even the juvenile justice system and
the problems as perceived or presented by the child or adolescent. As we saw
in Chapters 1 and 3, without the contextualizing effect of the overt delinea-
tion of the problems, the child's behavior in the playtherapy room (or the
adolescent's interaction in the office) is potentially emptied of communicative meaning. And certainly in the case of adolescents, we have no guarantee
whatsoever that the patient will either admit that problems are as stated or
volunteer the information on his or her own. Even in those cases where the
identified problems are factitious, mistaken, or reflect difficulties with the

---

*If the child—or, more often, adolescent—remarks at this point that he doesn't need or like
"shrinks," we take advantage of this to lighten the atmosphere by pointing out that we are
"expanders"—not "shrinks" or "brain-suckers" or any of the other colorful terms our devotees
come up with.

parents themselves rather than with the child, they must nonetheless be stated explicitly to be resolvable. Once in the confines of his own space (the playtherapy room or another office), the child cannot react or respond to the stated problems if he or she has not heard them. Consequently, we are firm about getting the adult responsible for the child's or adolescent's treatment to state openly every concern which has prompted the evaluation.

The History: The Child's Personal History

Once the problems have been sufficiently outlined, we move to the child's personal history. Having developed a genogram (McGoldrick & Gerson, 1985) as we learned about the family (leaving sufficient room for corrections and emendations), we have a cursory "picture" of events prior to the child's birth. We then begin the longitudinal history by asking where the child was born and for details of the pregnancy, labor and delivery. Often in traditional history-taking biographical confirmation of categorical diagnoses is sought, e.g., perinatal distress in cases of "attention deficit" or "learning disabilities" or a family history of "major psychiatric disorder" in cases of suspected psychosis or affective disorders. Since the psychotherapist faces the same challenge—to solve the identified problems—regardless of categorical diagnosis, such pattern-matching is of no interest and of little usefulness.

This part of the history-taking frequently provides a useful glimpse of the parents' categorical view of their child, in this case an example of projected identity.

The father of a 10-year-old with a long history of "learning disabilities" and "central processing disorders" attached great significance to Phil's "full breech delivery" and the fact that the umbilical cord "appeared to be" wrapped around his neck. "I was really worried when I saw what was happening," he said, "I knew we were going to have difficulties." Despite the fact that his son was of normal birth weight, knew the alphabet at two, and could read with good comprehension at three, this father saw Phil's obvious oppositionalism in developmental tasks which required cooperation (such as toilet-training) as a sign of "brain damage." This was significant, not because the perinatal and developmental information was indicative of a categorical disorder, but because Phil's father, who was himself three months premature and weighed only slightly over 3 lbs. at birth, attached no significance to his own much more obvious—and much more potentially dangerous—perinatal circumstances. Concerns about his own safety, well-being, and developmental potential, which had been denied or minimized in this father's mind, were clearly projected onto his son.

Each of the developmental history questions can provide information which is not only informative but also potentially therapeutically useful during the initial interview with the child.

One mother, for example, said of her seven-year-old that he had been "born dead" but that "the doctors brought him back to life." This child, who had overwhelming fears of going to sleep at night and was seen by the referring physician as "crippled by anxiety," underwent a profound and positive change simply on learning "from a doctor" that his mother's version was not true: he had not been "born dead." He had had difficulty breathing on his own but his heart was beating and he was very much alive. Once his airway was secured he did fine.

Had this child not been present during the history-taking his examiners would not have been able to witness the striking increase in this child's baseline anxiety when his mother described him as having been "born dead."

Following the perinatal history we make a quick, but thorough, year-by-year survey of the child's life up to the present, including health, development, academic history, and family events. Although our note-taking is structured to assure that the standard categorical questions (health, development, academics, peers, previous treatment) are not neglected, we have found that a year-by-year, rather than categorical, survey creates a more vibrant picture of the child (or adult) as a person and tends to provide more therapeutically useful clues.

Apart from the raw data provided, this very process can be enlightening when the child is present. A dramatic example of such parent-child interaction during history-taking can be found in Chapter 9 (Steven). In some cases much of the actual work of therapy itself can be accomplished at this point in the interview.

An extremely overactive six-year-old was brought by his single mother, Mrs. T., who described her son as having "maximal brain damage" and "learning dispilities." Indeed, the six-year-old was in constant motion, blinked frequently, and nibbled on his fingernails which were already chewed down to the cuticle. After she described her son's extremely tortuous and precipitous premature delivery and the relatively few postnatal complications which ensued, Mrs. T. was told that her son must have had excellent doctors. "Not at all," she exclaimed, throwing up her hands and looking toward the ceiling, "it was the Good Lord that fixed him!"

As soon as the therapist had determined that, apart from his nervousness, Mrs. T.'s son was neurodevelopmentally precocious and quite able to attend, he asked her if she was a "born-again" Christian. "Absolutely," Mrs. T. replied. "And that means," her examiner continued, "that you believe in the Bible as the literal word of God." "Absolutely," she repeated. "And that God made the heaven and the earth and everything that walks upon the earth?" "Absolutely," she continued with an evident sense of righteousness. "And that God created man and woman in his own image—and that that includes *all* men?" "Absolutely." "So that means that God must have made doctors, too?" Mrs. T.'s face reddened, she hesitated, and then replied with significantly less enthusiasm, "Well, yes."

At this point her examiner looked her sternly in the eye. "Let me tell you something, Mrs. T. Either you think the Good Lord is a used car salesman—and a dishonest one, at that—or you've lost your faith. Now, you go to [a nearby discount department store] and buy your son a pair of boxing gloves. They cost six dollars. He wears them 24 hours a day, except for meals. Understand?" "Yes, sir," Mrs. T. replied. "And you come back and see me next week—same day, same time."

The following week when Mrs. T. and her son arrived for their appointment, the six-year-old walked in calmly, smiling, and holding his hands up so that the therapist could see the new fingernail growth. He then climbed up in the therapist's lap and held his hands out flat so that the therapist could see even better. "You didn't buy the boxing gloves, did you?" Mrs. T. was asked. "No . . . they were too expensive. I couldn't afford the $25." [The therapist had seen the gloves himself only the week before and they were, in fact, only $6.] "I thought of putting sox on his hands," she said sheepishly. "But you didn't do that either, did you?" the therapist asked. "No, sir, I didn't." "Well, then," he said matter-of-factly but gently, "I take it you must have refound your faith."

In this case a maneuver was used with a parent that we use daily with children: Mrs. T. was backed into a "logical corner" from which the only "step" was into health. Only the occasional first encounter will move so quickly but the therapist must be prepared for the eventuality and capitalize on it when it occurs.

The year-by-year review of the child's life includes all significant family events as well. The process gives both parents and child a sense of the significance of experience in the development of the problems which have brought them to therapy. We discuss the meaning of many of the events covered, but not all. Parents vary in their responsiveness to a collaborative attempt to understand the meaning of events in their lives. Most are captured by the process and become quick allies. Some, however, are extremely uncomfortable—especially after years of unsuccessful treatment elsewhere—with a process that seems to move too quickly. Only through experience can clinicians develop the judgment necessary to determine how quickly to move.

The advantage of a longitudinal look at the child's life can be seen in the school history. When school performance, behavior, or attendance is seen in parallel with life events, it is often easier to see why problems occurred. Frequently, a child's (or adolescent's) academic performance has been so bad for so long that school authorities lose sight of the fact that it was once good or even excellent. Even neurological trauma cannot account *categorically* for a decrement in academic performance, unless and until psychological causes are ruled out. Depression, a disastrous rearrangement of self and body-image, as well as confusion about agency and ability, can all affect a child after accident or illness such as to create the *appearance* of inability. By placing such disastrous events as accidents or catastrophic illness within the developmental context of the child's life we gain a perspective which may suggest psychological approaches to a rekindling of ability.

We take the same approach to a brief history of the parents' health. Accidents, illnesses, and even absences are reviewed, for they are all experiences for the child as well. Even when the child appears to understand the parents' description, it is useful to ask the child about the event. One six-year-old stated assuredly that she had been sent to stay with her divorced father "while my mommy was in the hospital for a hysterectomy." Asked what "hysterectomy" meant, she shrugged her shoulders.

The History: The Parents' Personal Histories

Once the child and co-therapist have left the office parents can be questioned about the details of their own lives. We take much the same longitudinal approach with parents as with their children, beginning with the place and circumstances of their birth, their parents, their siblings and their siblings' children. Often, as we review their lives, themes will emerge which are very much related to the child's problems.

The stepmother of a suicidal 18-year-old was being asked whether her own mother had lost any children when she happened to notice an article on sudden infant death syndrome on the desk. "You know, that's interesting," she said matter-of-factly. "My mother was 10 when her mother had the last baby at home. After the doctor left my grandmother called my mother over to the bed, held up the brand-new baby and smiled—and then broke its neck. She told my mother, '*You* did that.' And the death was put down as a 'crib death.'" It had never occurred to this woman that her mother, who was only 10 at the time, must have been horribly affected by what her mother did to her. Nor could she see how she was now unconsciously pushing her stepdaughter, whose own mother had died of cancer five years previously, into a suicidal depression.

In this case the first encounter with the "responsible parent" was predictive of the course of events in therapy, for this stepmother could not be induced to see the incredible cruelty in her grandmother's act or to admit that its effect on her mother had affected her own life at all—although the results were readily apparent even to casual observer. The psychological blinders this woman had developed as a child extended to her present relationship with her stepdaughter: "mothers" were never responsible for anything affecting their children—especially their death.

THE ONGOING THERAPY: A SYNERGISTIC PROCESS

Parents need to understand and establish structure, rules, and boundaries, as much as children need them. Linking the adult's therapy to the child's allows the parent's therapist to treat the parent's view of the child's treatment much as a clinical supervisor would. (In fact, for the process to work well the parent must become a genuine therapeutic ally at home.) The parent sees both therapists structure the therapeutic experience on an ongoing basis, a quasi-participatory experience that allows the parent to identify with both child and therapist simultaneously and to take from each process what serves best. The parent's active participation in the child's treatment allows any personal success for the child to serve as a kind of implicit "permission" for the parent to experience a parallel success. Much like guided imagery, parallel co-therapy with parent and child facilitates a working-through of the adult's childhood issues (which can range from witnessing the murder of a parent, rape, or other trauma to more mundane losses); at the same time it is face-saving in that the identification with the child allows the parent considerable opportunity for vicarious work.

Structuring the Ongoing Therapy Hour With the Parent and Child

With very few exceptions we have a standard structure for our work with children and their parents. It is already present and reflected in the structure of the first therapeutic evalution: we meet with the parents and the child (or adolescent) at the beginning of the session, separate so that parent(s) and child have their own space, time and therapist, and then meet together again at the end of the session.

At the beginning of each session we review the time that has passed since the last session. Unless there has been an absolutely calamitous disaster, we always begin with the positive. Most children, like most parents, teachers, and clinicians, have a tendency to notice primarily the negative. Consequently, we try to reverse this as quickly and as consistently as we can. After the positive events of the week have been reviewed, and progress noted, we turn to the negative. It is often difficult for parents—who feel like they are "ratting"—to say openly how their child has behaved, and it is not unusual for very important information not to come up until the child and co-therapist have left the room. We then explain, or reexplain, as often as we often must, the priming and contextualizing nature of the information at the beginning of the session.

At the end of the session co-therapist and child return (always knocking and waiting for an invitation to enter) to close the encounter or to discuss or resolve important issues prior to the end of the session. We find it very difficult to accomplish all that needs to be done in a 45- or 50-minute "hour"—a time segment established by tradition for the therapist's convenience, not for the patient's needs. Consequently, all of our sessions are roughly one hour long (except for first encounters, which are $1^1/_2$–2 hours in length and involve both clinicians).

Co-therapy of Parents Who Were Hurt as Children

Although we try to work with all parents concurrently, and much of this work develops into a genuine psychotherapy experience for the involved parent, some work with parents can be particularly intense. One of the advantages of a co-therapy approach is that the child's experience as therapy progresses presents the parents with a "mirror" in which to see both the hurt child in themselves and the child who can be helped to heal that hurt.* Many parents do not realize how constricted their own range of personal opportunities has been until they begin to see their son or daughter grow in

---

*"Co-therapy" here does not refer to the constant presence of two therapists with the same patient but, rather, to a parallel process of therapy with the parent that begins intimately involved with the child's personal therapy. Usually, the first and last five minutes of the session are shared: the session begins with both therapists, the child, and the parent present. The parent's therapy—which can be intensely personal or of the child-guidance variety, depending upon the needs of the individuals involved—proceeds in a parallel fashion. About a third of parents involved in such parallel therapy elect to continue on their own after their child's therapy has been terminated.

therapy and discover new potential. Often developments in the child's therapy serve to trigger memories in the parent—usually the mother—which in turn create therapeutic opportunities for the parent.

The first time we saw Donald and his mother Marcie he was nine. He sat on the hood of the family car in front of our office while his mother dutifully tied his shoelaces for him. Donald had been "identified" as "aphasic-like," "communication-disordered," and consequently, "retarded" by a well-known program for autistic children in another state. At the recommendation of the program, he began school in classes for the educable mentally handicapped. Although he had been "identified" as educable mentally handicapped in three states, some confusion over what was "really" wrong with Donald brought him to us for a psychiatric consult initiated by the school system. Donald's mother decided to bring him back for therapy following the evaluation.

Marcie quickly became as involved as her son. In response to the easily made discovery that Donald was not retarded, but rather an exceedingly confused bright and complicated child who was achieving well beneath his ability, Marcie suddenly recognized her own brightness, complexity, and underachievement. She had dropped out of college, married one of her instructors—a marriage which turned out to be a disaster—and given up job opportunity after job opportunity. The longer she remained married the less attention she paid to her appearance, her weight, and to the orderliness and cleanliness of her home.

Marcie's reaction to our discovery of "the real Donald" beneath his "retarded and crazy" appearance was to wonder what had ever happened to "the real Marcie." A short time into therapy she realized what had happened to "the real Marcie." Eight years old and in the third grade, she had been sexually abused by an older man who lived next door and who gave her quarters for "being good." Embarrassed and extremely confused by the fact that she had "accepted money for sex," the eight-year-old did not tell her mother. Instead, she waited for her mother to realize what was happening and that something was wrong.

This memory led to a double realization: first, that she had done for her children—and for Donald especially—what her mother had failed to do for her—read her mind. Hence, Marcie responded to her son's needs before he could even verbalize them—and much of Donald's "communication disorder" was due to this anticipatory activity. Second, she saw that the pattern of her underachievement and lack of self-respect reflected her own sense of badness and worthlessness following the abuse when she was eight.

At this point, she also began to wonder if Donald's father could be sexually abusing him, and if it could have anything to do with Donald's difficulties. In fact, it was discovered that Donald's father had abused all five children over a period of 20 years. With the resolution of her own sense of badness and worthlessness came an ability to use therapy much as a child uses the support of a caring parent. In less than two years, Marcie divorced her husband, moved her family twice in search of better schools and better living conditions, developed an ever-growing sense of personal pride, and received many thousands of dollars in raises as she advanced from the bottom of her company's ladder to a management position.

As the amnesias, selective memories, and denial faded, Marcie was able to puzzle out the reason she had not told her mother about the sexual abuse by the next-door neighbor. "I felt very, very dirty and very useless," she said. "Whatever made me go off with that man and collect quarters? Even then I sensed that this was wrong and that I was doing it for a reason." Subsequently Marcie found "the reason" in one of her most vivid memories as a child: when she was four her mother had threatened to send her away to an orphanage because she had wet the bed. Since, in her experience, her mother already viewed her as bad, she simply gave up expecting her mother to understand.

When Parents Do Not Change

The process of psychotherapy progresses best within a context of healthy mutuality, just as does the development of cognitive and affective structures. Thus, it matters little on which side of the wall (playtherapy room or office) the first genuine change takes place. The first change will tend to serve as a catalyst for the ensuing changes. However, when the adult fails to change even when the child changes, the therapeutic process with the child may be doomed to failure.

Morris was an 11-year-old black fifth grader who had failed three grades by the time he was placed in the Emotionally Handicapped Program at age 10. There he was seen as hyperactive, oppositional, disruptive, and aggressive. He threw chairs and desks and got into fights. Then, suddenly, Morris' teacher, thinking that he had been absent for two weeks, discovered that he had simply been behaving so well that she had not noticed his presence. Curious about this, she asked his mother if anything had happened and learned that Morris had been given an over-the-counter medication for "whiplash" he had sustained when he fell off his bicycle. Convinced that some ingredient in the medication had radically altered his behavior, Morris' teacher requested an evaluation.

The evaluation revealed that the only possibly active ingredient in the small dose of the medication he had been given by his mother was an antihistamine. There were no signs of any organic or neurodevelopmental impairment in Morris. Morris was therefore given a placebo, which we purposefully called CALMOGESIC, and told that it was so potent and so expensive that he could take it only on Mondays, Wednesdays, and Fridays. We informed his teacher that we had identified the "active ingredient" of the medication he was taking when his behavior improved and asked her to monitor his classroom behavior for an eight-day period, during which he would take the more potent substance. Morris' behavior remained excellent.

Morris' mother drove over four hours round-trip to keep his appointments. This was a hardship for her but she was willing to endure because of her commitment to her son's future. Morris' mother had been a cleaning lady most of her life. One day she saw an ad in the paper for nurse's aid training. She enrolled and changed her situation considerably. After a few years she realized that she was "basically a nurse's cleaning lady" and went back to school, this time becoming a practical nurse. After ten years of this work she came to the same conclusion again, and again returned to school.

When we met Morris' mother she was the nursing director for a highly specialized hospital medical service. "I'm the oldest of six, he's the youngest of six. My life's over but his is just beginning," she said. "I want him to have every opportunity." We told her we disagreed; her attitude "simply wouldn't work." At 45, she just wasn't old enough for her life to be "over." She could, for example, try to provide for Morris by giving him a $10 allowance every week—something she never had—but what if, when he went to get it out of the bank at 21, he discovered it was all counterfeit? She could also dress him in the finest of clothes, but what if the image he saw in the mirror never changed? *She,* we pointed out, was Morris' mirror. If she didn't change, why should he believe that he could? That was one of the "silver linings" of this kind of therapy: it was hard for just one person to change. But that meant that she would have to realize that, although her work life had changed immensely, her personal life had not. She still had an alcoholic husband who did nothing and whom she supported, as well as nieces and nephews whose parents preferred to surrender the responsibility to her. She had no life of her own.

For the several months during which Morris' mother considered these things during her hour, Morris' behavior was excellent and he showed progress in school. But she did not change: she continued to work nearly 20 hours a day at work and at home and to solve everyone else's problems while expecting, and getting, no support from family or friends. Morris' teacher also announced that, in spite of his excellent behavior and our recommendation that he be mainstreamed, he would have to remain in her Emotionally Handicapped class for the duration of the year "because I don't keep anyone for less than a year in my class." When his mother announced that she could help him change his life but not her own, Morris' newfound self-esteem fell precipitously and his behavior became disruptive and aggressive again and remained so over the years.

Because children are such ecological beings, without the necessary environmental support even the finest of psychotherapy techniques quickly reach the limit of their effectiveness.

CHILD LOGIC AND PARENTAL STRUCTURE

Parents: Victims or Manipulators of Child Logic?

Parents need to understand how children think, interact, communicate, and change as much as clinicians do. We rarely spend more than one of the 168 hours in a week with their child. They, on the other hand, must deal with the rest. Thus, we spend a great deal of time reviewing with parents many of the same issues covered in this book. The difference is that the parents we work with have an immediately accessible "laboratory" to test our views and theories. That "laboratory" tends to follow them right into our office, creating a marvelous learning opportunity. As we explain how children think and the often formative role of logical structures in their experience and cognitive development, interactions between the parents and their child provide us with the dramatic illustrations. Since most parents provide us with these beautiful clinical examples, we rarely have to generate our own.

Many of the children we see are caught in logical binds. Naturally, part of the therapeutic process involves describing to the parents how this occurred and how we intend to resolve it. This leads quite naturally to a discussion of the logical nature of early child language and cognition and of the traps which adults inadvertently set for themselves. Very quickly, often during the very first encounter, we help parents to understand how children interpret and use language. For example, we all tend to assume that expressions of social convention are received conventionally. Such is not the case with children and many adolescents. Thus, interrogatives unwittingly used as commands can remain interrogatives in the mind of the child. "How about doing you home work? — no matter how forcefully uttered — remains a *question*. It is therefore logically satisfied by an *answer*. The answer, of course, is almost always "NO, I WOULDN'T!" Similarly, interrogatives such as "will you . . . ," "would you . . . ," "how about . . . ," "would you like to . . . ," "why don't you . . . " are rarely recognized as such by adults. Thus, when father, already overly tired from a long day's work, says to Johnny, "Didn't I tell you I expected your homework to be done — BY THE TIME I GOT HOME?" he doesn't realize that he has again asked a question. Neither, of course, does Johnny — at least not consciously. Unconsciously, of course, he does — and his equally unconscious reply is, "Yes, you did. So what? I didn't particularly want to do it." Later Johnny's father says, "I told you to do your homework." "No, you didn't," comes the adamant reply — and, again, Johnny is right: his father only *asked* Johnny if he remembered what he had said the day before. Thus, even parents must understand the difference between surface and embedded meaning. *Surface meaning* is the apparent conventional meaning of an utterance and *embedded meaning* is the literal (logical) meaning. Children are exquisitely sensitive to embedded meaning. (For the therapeutic use of embedded meaning, see Chapter 11.)

A strikingly pathological example of such embedded meaning can be seen in two separate cases. In the first case the embedded meaning appeared to represent the actual covert intentions of the parent. In the second it represented an unwitting command by an otherwise well-meaning mother.

Ian was an 18-year-old who used to like to play with the 13- and 15-year-old brothers who lived next door to him when he was a child. When Ian was seven the younger neighbor boy had initiated sex play in which he played the husband lying on top of Ian, who was supposed to be the wife. He also initiated Ian into oral sex. Soon after this initiation Ian was used in this manner by the older brother and became aware that the two brothers engaged in such activities together. They had a detailed repertoire of adult sexual practices.

About three years into this activity the boys' mother unexpectedly found Ian and the younger brother engaged in sexual activities in the neighbor boy's bedroom. "Don't *ever* let me catch you doing that again," the boys' mother yelled, and sent Ian home. "And she never did," Ian added as he recounted the sad story.

Although he had never given it any thought before, Ian realized on recounting his experiences that his friends' mother had not told them not to engage in sex play again, for she had told them quite explicitly *not to let her catch them doing so.* The sexual exploitation of this young child by his older peers did not stop with the discovery; it only became more secret.

Marcie, all five of whose children were emotionally and sexually abused by her husband over a period of some 20 years, realized, as she began to look more clearly at her own past experiences, that she had inadvertently communicated the same thing to her children's father during the one occasion she had confronted him. She had walked into the bedroom of the two younger children and found them and their father "with guilty looks on their faces." "If I ever catch you messing with these kids," she screamed, "I'll kill you!" Like the mother of Ian's neighbors, she never did catch her husband in the many degrading, hurtful and abusive things he did to the children.

Marcie's clear memory of what she had said, and her instantaneous understanding of it effective meaning, occurred as she listened to her therapist recount the story of the first instance above. "You know," she said, "I never realized it, but I did exactly the same thing." Such realizations are commonplace if one takes a narrative approach to such problems, sharing with patients or parents parallel stories. They rarely occur spontaneously, however.

These same observations apply to therapists as well. Questions like "What happened last week?" invite responses such as "Nothing" or "I can't remember." It is much harder not to respond to commands such as "Tell me what happened last week". Even if the child does not respond overtly to such commands, the child will most likely think a response. Thus, if you want to keep an issue alive, do not ask questions — issue commands.

Parental Blurring of Interpersonal Boundaries

Parents also continually blurr interpersonal boundaries with language. Parents who are upset that their child will not take responsibility nonetheless ask when report cards come home "How are *our* grades this time?" Those who cannot stand the fact that their child's room is a trash heap still say "*We've* not been keeping *our* room clean this week." Parents need to understand that this pronominal confusion radically blurs personal boundaries and diffuses personal responsibility. Once the parent refers to the child's bad grades as "our report card," personal responsibility has been diluted (or even assumed by the parent) in the mind of the child or adolescent. It is absolutely futile to try to get a child or adolescent to accept responsibility (for almost anything) while such conditions persist. Thus, we have to help parents to understand the often extraordinarily self-defeating mistakes they make.

Parental Hypocrisy

For children and adolescents categorical imperatives are subject to the same *logical* interpretation as are the questions and commands we have just reviewed. Consequently, if adults would have children follow categorical rules, they themselves cannot afford to break them categorically. Perhaps the simplest form of this bind is reflected in the common parental injunction to "do as I say, not as I do." Parents who continue to "do as they do" can count on their children continuing to "do as they do."

Parental hypocrisy falls into this category. Children are exquisitely sensitive to anything that smacks of inconsistency or hypocrisy. Most parents are not aware that categorical injunctions are perceived categorically by their children. Because we all have a tendency to a certain cultural and social relativism with regard to categorical injunctions, we may fail to see when our actions contradict our injunctions.

Stormy, 16, had already had a miscarriage by the time she came for therapy. She was brought by her divorced father because she would not follow household rules and was failing in school in spite of superior intelligence—when she was not skipping school altogether. She was running away from home continually and was drinking. In a word, she was "not following rules."

Stormy's father, a big, bright but insensitive man, could not understand why his daughter did not do what she was supposed to do. He wore "designer" tennis outfits with a marijuana leaf logo and kept a more than adequate supply of marijuana in his dresser drawer. When told that he would have to give up smoking marijuana if he wanted his daughter to follow conventional rules, he was confused: he didn't understand how what he did had anything to do with his daughter's behavior. It was not just his pot-smoking, he was told, he would also have to get rid of his marijuana logo tennis gear—no matter what it had cost him. Even when it was explained to him that the parallel lay in the fact that his use of marijuana was illegal, just as his daughter's use of alcohol was illegal, he couldn't understand the connection, and his daughter didn't stop drinking or breaking the rules.

As another example, not infrequently we have to point out that the discrepancy between the date of the parents' marriage and the birth of their first child is striking, so striking that there is little likelihood that any of their children have failed to notice (see Chapter 8). Consequently, it is unrealistic for them to expect their children to obey their prohibition of sexual experimentation.

Logical Problem-Solving Through Environmental Manipulation

Sometimes the logic of behavior is more abstract and its meaning may not be recognized at first.

Ron was a nine-year-old fourth grader who already weighed 115 lbs. He had few friends and was constantly unhappy and demanding. He was oppositional, disruptive, argumentative, invasive, and doing poorly in school. He also would not leave his parents alone. No matter where be began the night, he would eventually end up in his parents' bed or in one of his sister's beds. He always managed to end up in someone else's.

Ron was the third child born to his parents. There was no difficulty with the birth of the first child, his older sister. But Ron's parents nearly lost their next child who had an Rh incompatibility. When Ron was born his mother was desperate to care for her baby. But, according to his parents, Ron was "allergic" to his mother's milk — a literal bodily rejection as experienced by his mother — and had bilateral inguinal hernias. He was also "a hyper and inconsolable baby." After various medications were tried, all of which made him even more "hyper," Ron's parents decided that their only recourse was to "rock" him every night. Thus, they began a ritual of carrying him every night as they walked around the house. This ritual was not just a family quirk: they *had* to carry Ron. They had to carry him because, if he raised his intra abdominal pressure too much, he could burst his hernias — at least, so Ron's parents had been told.

Ron was caught in the bind of needing to separate from his mother and feeling that his very survival depended upon her proximity: after all, he had been carried every day of his life for years. Finally, a solution was found: a water bed. Ron could "move" while not moving. His nights had been filled with constant movement since he was born. Only in constant movement could he find rest. The solution was pristinely simple: sleep plus constant motion. (Ron's other behavioral problems were harder to solve, for they required a change in many family members — something that was hard for the family.)

THREE USEFUL TECHNIQUES

The above concerns with the logical thinking of chilren have led us to develop several simple, but important, tools (or techniques) which can radically change the relationship between parents and children. The first is a very simple reporting device, which we call our "Smiley Face Chart."

"Smiley Face" Charts

For many of the children we see we use a chart, hand-drawn on half a piece of standard-size paper, which is divided into morning and afternoon sections. Although the recording can be more refined, we find that dividing the day into two parts is usually adequate. The parents or guardians are asked to rate the the child on his/her behavior, putting a "smiley" or a "sad face" for positive behavior and a "grr" or "growly" for negative behavior. The rating is based on several very general categories: being one's "terrific real good self," "following directions the first time," and a third category which is usually tailored to the individual child.

The chart allows us to illustrate another logical bind in which children are frequently caught. In most of the elementary school classrooms in our school district with some 90,000 students there is a "good" side of the blackboard and a "bad" side. The "good" side is indicated by the traditional "smiley face" and the "bad" side by the "frowny face." But a "frowny" is really a *sad* face. This means that those children who are genuinely sad because of real events in their real lives must be *bad* in order to get their names posted to the *sad* side of the board. Those early grade teachers who have followed our suggestion to do nothing more than replace the "sad" face with a mean "growly" have reported a "surprising" improvement in behavior in their classes. Children, we point out, will literally work at getting a "sad" face if they are sad—and if the "sad" face represents "bad" behavior, they are left little choice but to opt for bad behavior.

This chart also addresses the concern of many parents and teachers that the child is doing whatever she or she is doing "for attention." On our charts the happy and sad faces are both big and attractive, while the "growlies" are small. Furthermore, the happy and sad faces are drawn by the parent in pen while, the growlies are drawn very small and in pencil—because, we explain, the objectionable behavior is going to become less and less and, like a mark made by a pencil, can disappear because it is erasable. We point out that "all of the pencils in our office have erasers."

Many parents, in reporting their child's behavior for the week, use expressions like "he went completely out of control" or "he lost it." They fail to recognize that in using such expressions they are literally providing a reason and an excuse for their child's behavior: it was "out of control." This view of behavior must go if the child and parents are to change and maintain a healthy change. Thus, the chart's first behavioral injunction is stated in terms of agency: *"Choose* to be your terrific real good self." Parents are reminded not to use expressions that invalidate the child's freedom—freedom being the recognition of choice and the ability to choose (Wheelis,

1973). "Johnny lost control and trashed his room" becomes "Johnny *chose* to trash his room." There is little hope of any permanency in positive behavioral change if actions are operationally defined as beyond the child's control. While we do not require of the child a conscious awareness of the process of therapy, we do consistently require of the child a conscious awareness of his or her own agency.

Bradley was a six-year-old who weighed barely two pounds at birth and whose very survival was viewed as a miracle by his intensely religious family. Blind from birth, Bradley had been in special programs prior to school and was now in special classes for the blind. He was extremely oppositional and noncompliant, refusing to do even simple things for himself. This was extremely frustrating for his teachers, who thought he had great promise. They couldn't begin cane work, for example, until Bradley demonstrated the prerequisite use of his hands to feel his way around. This he simply refused to do.

We had begun the use of the Smiley Chart with Bradley, using pieces of self-adhesive weather stripping for smileys and round pieces of self-adhesive sandpaper for growlies. We quickly discovered that Bradley worked for the growlies because he loved the feel of the sandpaper! This was easily remedied, however, by omitting the sandpaper and leaving the growly space blank. And Bradley did love to feel the smooth soft weather stripping.

In therapy, however, it became obvious that Bradley was doing little more than nothing for himself because he was "waiting for God to give him sight." Consequently, Bradley *chose* to do nothing for himself. After all, if his very existence was a miracle, why couldn't God just work another and restore his sight? We had two responses. First, we pointed out to Bradley that God had equipped him with a very good brain and excellent hands to feel and do and that God was waiting for *him* to "get his act together." Second, we changed our first behavioral guideline, which had previously read "Be your terrific real good self," to "*Choose* to be your terrific real good self."

The next session showed that we were on the right track. Mother reported that Bradley's behavior had not been good. In fact, he had crawled up on his parents' bed the previous Sunday morning (which he often did), but this time he climbed right up on his father, raised up his buttocks—and farted loud and long right into his father's face. When he we asked him why he had done that, Bradley replied, "Because I *chose* to!"

Although the behavior was negative, it was nonetheless the first action acknowledged by Bradley as volitional. This opened the door to positive willed actions and to the exercise of those faculties "which God had so caringly provided you." The identification and mobilization of *agency* subsequently became a central feature of our therapeutic approach, as can be seen in detail in the annotated transcript in the last chapter.

Children, especially younger children, whose most recent behavior was better than the previous week, but still not satisfactory, are allowed to choose one color when the therapist makes up the chart. Better behavior yet allows the child to choose two colors. Even the color chosen by the child can signal a positive therapeutic development such as when a biracial child who enters therapy hating his dark skin finally begins to choose dark colors. Thus, we would never make "standard" Smiley Charts with a copy machine or a computer printer, for this would rob this little tool of some of its useful subtleties.

Far from being a "silly little chart" or a "behavior mod card" (such as are often used in schools), our Smiley Chart is an extremely powerful tool with many potential uses. It is a useful tool for shaping and improving self-image and for undoing negative identifications. We suggest to parents that they jot down a short note about the behavior—good or bad—to serve as a reminder during the beginning of the session when we go over the events of the week. This helps us (and them) see patterns. Extremely negative behavior that consistently appears on the chart is often reminiscent of that of the absent (divorced, abandoning) parent—usually father. When these patterns appear again and again, the identification becomes obvious to the child and parent as well, making the work of therapeutic undoing easier.

"Mad Pads"

Another technique for decreasing aggressive or destructive behavior in children is the use of what we call Mad Pads. We usually introduce the technique in the process of therapy with the child and then explain it to the parent(s) in the child's presence. We instruct the parents to obtain a newsprint pad, at least 12 by 12 inches in size, which is to be reserved *solely* for the purpose of getting rid of angry feelings. If the child is really angry at someone, he is to take the pad and draw whatever he is angry about, then scribble it out, tear up the sheet, and throw it away. It is extremely important to stress that the paper must be thrown away and not kept and that the Mad Pad is not to be used for anything playful or enjoyable: the boundaries must be kept clear. Similarly, the process is a private one: the child is not to share it with the person he is angry at. If a child does, it can become dramatically obvious just how powerful this little technique can be.

Seven-year-old Mick's father complained that our "Mad Pad idea didn't seem to work very well." His son had become extremely angry at a six-year-old neighbor who refused to let him join in a game. So, Mick went home, father explained, and got the Mad Pad and accosted his friend Timmy. "You see, Timmy, this is you," Mick told his friend as he drew a figure on the pad, "and this is what I'm going to do to you," he continued as he scribbled out the figure and tore up the sheet of paper. "Timmy completely freaked," Mick's father complained, "so I think your idea could be dangerous." We reexplained the private and symbolic nature of the Mad Pad and told Mick's father that we had never recommended its public use: "That's voodoo," we added.

The "Five Minutes"

Our third technique is designed to improve child-parent communication. Few children at the beginning of therapy share their true feelings, worries, concerns, criticisms, or fears with their parents. It is crucial to begin to establish, or reestablish, this process of communication as early in therapy as possible.

There are few experiences more powerful or more therapeutic than feeling genuinely understood. For many readers this will call to mind Rogers' (1955) concept of "unconditional regard," yet the approach outlined here is different in that it is exceptionally structured and time-limited and is designed to serve several specific purposes.

If, as we have seen repeatedly, much of children's maladaptive and disruptive behavior has communicative content, then it stands to reason that one possible means of decreasing such maladaptive or disruptive behavior is to provide an alternative channel for communication. This is easily done with what we have come to call the "Five Minutes." The purpose of the Five Minutes is to aid in replacing oppositional, passive-aggressive or self-defeating behavior, which has no clear, acknowledged *content* with potentially content-rich interactions. To give but a few examples, when a child fails in school, is disrespectful to parents or other authority figures or steals from them, or publicly embarrasses parents or family, a *behavioral statement* is being made. Rarely, however, are parents or authorities aware of the potential communicative meaning of such behavior. Without perceived communicative content there is no potential for resolution. A child who steals from a parent may be saying, in effect, that he feels he is unworthy of parental love, or even that he feels that the parent does not love him. A child who publicly embarrasses a parent may be making a graphic statement of his disapproval of past or present parental activity, e.g., a parent's infidelity. Or he may be acting out his anger about a past or present perceived hurt or failure of parental care. Such behavioral statements, however, are almost always doomed to self-defeating failure: they usually serve only to get the child further into trouble, worsen the diagnostic label or further convince parents, authorities and professionals of the child's intractability.

The Five Minutes, as simple-mindedly simple as it may seem, offers an alternative means of communication which can be intensely powerful. Again, however, we must stress that "feeling understood" is not necessarily a conscious experience for the child or adolescent. More often it is a *process*, the success of which is reflected implicitly in behavior change rather than explicitly in a conscious acknowledgment. For this reason, rhetorical attempts to convince a child verbally that he or she is understood are almost always bound to fail.

Many parents spend far too little time with their children, yet many parents contend that they have little or no time to spend. We begin, therefore, by acknowledging explicitly the difficulty most parents have finding blocks of time to spend with their children and by inviting parents not to set themselves up for failure by committing themselves to an impossible task. In a world of single parents, or one in which both parents work, it is not easy to find even 10 or 15 minutes a day on a regular basis. Therefore, we do not make big demands: we ask parents to set aside a special *Five Minutes* each day to spend with their child. This should be done on an individual basis, that is, one parent with one child. We explain to both child and parent that this special Five Minutes is set aside specifically for the child to share his/her thoughts, experiences, and feelings with the parent. We stress to the child and the parent that our Five Minutes is structured in a way that is both "unfair" and unbalanced: it is the child's time to know that he or she can share — in a respectful manner, of course — whatever is on his/her mind.

We have found that many families become quite attached to their Five Minutes and that there are frequently complaints — even from otherwise off-putting adolescents — when parents do not seem interested or fail to pursue the daily activity. To facilitate this process there are a series of "rules" or definitions that govern it:

1. *The time together is to be private and uninterrupted.* This means that mother or father will not answer the phone during this time or otherwise be interrupted. Part of the potential power of the Five Minutes is due the fact that it is very short: if the parent allows it to be constantly interrupted or abandons it, the child has every right to think, "So I'm not even worth five minutes!"

2. *The Five Minutes is not to compete with any other activity.* This

means that they cannot take place while traveling in a car or while engaged in any other activity such as sharing a chore with a parent. Often children will want to play games during the Five Minutes. It is explained from the very beginning that not only does game-playing defeat the purpose but also such activities are often chosen by the child as an unconscious means to avoid dealing with real issues. If the child avoids talking to the parent by engaging in such an activity, the parent is gently to remind the child that this is "our special time together and we can play a game any time." If the child persists, the parent is simply to sit out the allotted time patiently and without evidence of feeling of frustrated or rejected.

Children will often *think* thoughts that are for the moment unspeakable until they have become convinced *through experience* that, no matter what they think, the parent does not get upset and does not abandon the activity. In difficult cases, parents are cautioned not to lose faith in the process even if several months go by without any meaningful interaction.

One adoptive father, who thought that all our talk about "adoption psychology" was a "bunch of nonsense," was about to abandon the Five Minutes because his 10-year-old son simply "wasted time" and "always looked pissed-off." On this particular occasion, however, he came to the session with an unusual sense of enthusiasm. "I was about to give up on your stupid Five Minutes," he said with a conciliatory smile, "when Don turned to me last night and said, 'You remember, you told me that my biological mother was only 14, and that she didn't have any money, or any relatives, or anybody to take care of her, and that she just wanted me to have a good life with a real home and a family? Remember? That's what you told me. Well, that means that I have a perfectly good 24-year-old mother somewhere—and I probably have brothers and sisters, too.' I was astounded," Don's father continued. "I had never believed you when you said that he had to be thinking about these things." This brief Five Minutes marked a turning point in Don's therapy and the father-son relationship. Don's father realized that the previous two months of frustrated silence had not been "wasted." They established the experiential foundation necessary for Don to feel that his father's commitment to him was secure and could withstand his sharing thoughts about a "rival" family.

Parents and/or children may unconsciously try to lessen the intensity or seriousness of what may be brought up during the Five Minutes through physical contact or proximity. We first noticed this during ongoing therapy.

During a regular weekly therapy session, when the child returns from the playtherapy room, he may need to share with his parent something from the past or present which has hurt or saddened him in some way. We have noticed that at the very mention of the fact that "Johnny has something that he needs to tell you about," the child's parent will often pull the child closer on the couch or touch the child in some way. Even though the parent may say aloud that he or she (usually she) is listening and ready to hear whatever the child has to say, the nonverbal message is very different. The adult's need for physical proximity or contact signals to the child a vulnerability not conveyed by the words, making it difficult for the child to carry through with whatever he had decided in the playtherapy (or other) room he was ready to do. Such cues from a parent will often prompt a retreat from "confrontation" by the child. When this happens it needs to be brought gently to the parent's attention so that the "confrontation" can become the "communication" it was to have been.

Such unconscious nonverbals are easy to spot and to control in the therapeutic setting. This is not the case for the setting of the Five Minutes. Not uncommonly, we will discover that parents who appeared to have a sensitive understanding of the subtleties of the Five Minutes interaction are actually giving their children backrubs or rubbing their feet during this special time! Needless to say, a child whose back or feet are being pleasurably rubbed by a parent is not very likely to bring up difficult or painful issues. One has to ask specifically about the logistics of the Five Minutes, because even the most therapeutically committed parents can defensively defeat its purpose in the nicest of ways.

3. *Barring impossible situations, the Five Minutes should take place every day.* Not infrequently we hear that the Five Minutes had been abandoned or skipped because the parent and child had just had "the most marvelous discussion in years" earlier that day. We stress to parents that, even in such situations, it is important to continue the Five Minutes. We point out that if parents skip the Five Minutes because of spontaneous communication earlier in the day, they run the risk of a paradoxical "backslide" on the part of their child. The logic of the child's inner reaction runs: "You say the Five Minutes is important, and then I tell you one thing on my own, and what do you do? You give up. So the Five Minutes wasn't ever really that important to you anyway." The child may also feel that the committment was to a process, a "technique," and not to him. We help some parents who are regular church-goers to understand the potential power of the ritual and repetitive nature of the Five Minutes by asking them if they would give up going to church just because they felt a sense of satisfaction in prayer earlier during the week.

Building provides a useful analogy: one can build an extremely strong foundation with very small bricks, provided that they are placed consistently and regularly. And, just as in construction, one cannot make up for leaving out a number of bricks by inserting a cinder block. The purpose of the Five Minutes will be defeated if a parent who has missed a number of Five Minute sessions—for whatever reason—tries to make up by extending the length of the Five Minutes to a total of those times missed. As with any foundation-building, one must simply resume where one left off and put each real or experiential "brick" in place. Needless to say, if a particular Five Minutes happens to develop into an extended period of genuine discussion, that is fine. But, in this instance, "more" is "better" only if it develops naturally.

For some children, whose parents must be out of town on a regular basis, a short phone call—designated specifically as the Five Minutes—can maintain a continuity which would otherwise be broken.

4. *The relationship is, of necessity, an unbalanced one.* It is the child who needs to feel understood and accepted by the parent—not the parent by the child. This concept is difficult for certain parents to grasp and accept, especially if they feel that they have been putting up with an unbalanced situation long enough. At these times we hear reactions such as, "You mean, I just have to sit there and take it, no matter what he says? That's not fair." Indeed, the Five Minutes is not structured to be fair—that would mean an equal part for each participant. Or some parents may feel that having the Five Minutes on a daily basis even when the child misbehaves amounts to rewarding the child for misbehavior. It must be stressed that the fact that the parent will listen to the child without explaining, excusing, or offering alternative perspectives in no way "lets the child off the hook" with regard to parental structure or rules. In fact, in some families (or foster homes) the Five Minutes may be the only time an extremely off-putting child is unable to elicit a negative reaction. Such "islands of understanding" may be necessary just to foil a child's otherwise successful attempt to ruin all relationships.

To facilitate the therapeutic aspect of this process, we have developed three "rules" designed specifically for the parent: (1) *Do not explain*, (2) *Do not excuse*, (3) *Do not offer alternative perspectives*.

We often fail to realize that an explanation is really an implicit correction. As such, it says simply and powerfully to the other person that he or she is wrong. Consequently, even if the child *is* wrong about the facts of a particular incident or about the true intentions behind a particular act, it is extremely important not to offer an explanation. Similarly, explanations are often excuses which amount to "I didn't really mean what you thought I meant." Such a statment also tells the child that he or she is wrong. So does the offering of an alternative perspective. And the end result is a sense of frustration ("What an idiot! Not only was I wrong to feel this way, but I was also wrong about what happened") and a return to passive-aggressive, contentless behavioral reactions. A single example provides a good illustration.

Bert (Chapter 5) was a 14-year-old with post-traumatic cerebral palsy which significantly affected both motor coordination and speech. He had been hit by a car when he was four and was unconscious for months. It was thought at first that he would never get out of bed and, subsequently, that he would never move beyond a wheelchair. When we met him he was on arm-grip crutches. Bert lost his father through divorce shortly after the accident. Extremely "macho," Bert's father could not bear to deal with a son who could never follow in his footsteps.

Bert's abysmal self-esteem was reflected in his poor attention to personal hygiene and lack of care for his own things. His constant passive-aggressiveness reflected an all-pervasive anger which Bert smilingly denied. For years Bert had denied any anger over the accident. Fortunately, Bert's mother understood well the purpose of the Five Minutes and the reasons for the three rules. Thus, when Bert finally allowed himself to get angry at his mother and demanded angrily during one of their daily sessions, "Where were *you* when I got hit?" she did not become defensive. She could have explained truthfully that she was on the other side of town, buying groceries, and consequently, could not have been there. She could have further excused herself by clarifying Bert's perspective — again, truthfully — by saying that it was Bert's father who was supposed to be looking after him and that it was he who chose to lie down and take a nap, thereby allowing his four-year-old son to ride his Big Wheel down the driveway into the rush-hour traffic. But instead, she replied simply, "You must have felt terribly abandoned by me" — a statement as true as the others she could have made but one which simply acknowledged that she understood how her son felt. With no other interventions, and within days, Bert's personal hygiene improved and his constant passive-aggressiveness eased considerably.

Previously, Bert's mother had found it very difficult to face the anger implicit in Bert's behavior, as if to do so constituted a tacit admission of guilt on her part. She had, in effect, colluded with her son in an implicit avoidance of the issue for years.

Such "knee jerk" reactions are extremely common. We all have a tendency to defend ourselves against a sense of guilt and responsibility, even when we know intellectually that there was nothing that could have been done under the circumstances to prevent the tragedy in question. Such a defensive need is probably all the more intense when the genuinely responsible individual, like Bert's father, is no longer available to absorb the reactive anger. Allowing her son to express his anger and to feel understood—without defending herself as if she were actually responsible for his condition—did more to relieve Bert's mother's own painful sense of responsibility than all the therapy in the world. It also signaled to Bert that his mother was no longer tacitly accepting responsibility for something in the past over which she had, in fact, had no control. Her simple response to Bert's angry question served to break the vicious circle of her son's unconscious logic, which said, in effect, "You are behaving as if you are guilty, so you must be."

The Five Minutes can be a solution in itself. For instance, we may occasionally we will get a call from a parent or custodian who lives at great distance from the office and/or whose meager financial resources and insurance would make treatment even at reduced rates a burden. Or it may happen that a busy schedule simply does not allow time for an evaluation even on an emergency basis. If the caller is adamant about not wanting to go to another therapist for help, we explain the purpose and structure of the Five Minutes in detail over the phone and suggest that it be started that very day. Often the Five Minutes can serve to break a vicious cycle, as in the following example.

A woman called from a community several counties away, saying that she had learned of us from her neighbor who had attended one of our training sessions. She explained that she had become the legal guardian of Tim, her 10-year-old nephew, who had been mistreated and then abandoned by his mother, the woman's younger sister. She was desperately concerned about Tim because he was constantly both sad and angry; he was failing in school and had recently made several serious remarks about killing himself.

It quickly became apparent that this boy's aunt, with the very best of intentions, had made an unfortunate technical error by telling him that his mother was "ill," that she really did love him but could not show it, and that he was cruel and wrong to "hate" her. We told her that "it must be very hard and painful to see your own sister behave so horribly" and then pointed out that she had inadvertently defined "love" in terms of the severe abuse and abandonment her nephew had experienced. A quick explanation of the logic and egocentrism of children's thinking allowed her to realize that, if she described her nephew's mother as "good but not able to show it," then he must be "bad" to deserve to be treated so horribly. She also saw that by blocking his expression of (understandable and justified) anger at his mother, she was bound to push him further toward turning that very anger toward himself and others.

It was suggested that she not tell her nephew of her call to us and that she explain to him that she had been wrong to tell him that he shouldn't be angry at his mother for what she had and had not done. The Five Minutes would provide an ideal vehicle for this process, since it would help isolate the intense anger and sense of badness which was currently disrupting every aspect of his life. She agreed to try it for two weeks and then call back to report their progress or, if necessary, to make an appointment for the four-hour round-trip drive to our office. Almost three weeks later she called to say that there had been a "wondrous change" in her nephew's mood, behavior and attitude both at home and in school. A follow-up call a year later confirmed that the change had been lasting.

This example illustrates the potential power of simple interventions. Given both what this boy had lived through and the seriousness of his suicidal threats, many clinicians would feel that hospitalization would have been fully warranted. In this particular instance, a psychiatric hospitalization at this point in Tim's life would probably have done more to confirm him in his horrible self-image and sense of being bad than it would have helped. It would have affirmed his sense of dyscontrol and might well have sealed a potentially disastrous identification with a "sick" mother, powerless to do good. Instead, a "good mother," with little more than telephone guidance, facilitated a genuine resolution of Tim's situation, returning to him a sense of agency and human value. We all need to feel that we can "provoke" human—especially maternal—care, and that we are worthy of it. The Five Minutes is structured to facilitate this process.

Every once in a while we receive a call from a parent two to three months after the termination of a very successful therapy, announcing that their child has "slipped back into the old behaviors." The first thing we ask is: "Are you still doing the Five Minutes?" Usually the answer is, "Umm, well, no. I thought that was part of the therapy." "No," we answer. *It is part of the relationship.* Start the Five Minutes up again and call back in a few weeks. If you still need to come back then, we'll arrange it." Rarely does the child or adolescent actually need to return.

6

The Therapeutic Space

Le silence éternel de ces espaces infinis m'effraye.
Blaise Pascal

Some adult therapists may remember that *space* had a very different, special, privileged meaning to them as a child. This special meaning is harder to conceptualize today for our notion of space has been subtly, but drastically, changed in a way of which most of us are unaware. When the senior author was a child in the late '40s and early '50s, television did not occupy its current preeminent place at the center of nearly every child's universe: that relatively small two-dimensional screen (which, for all its color, brightness and action, is really a very dead space) simply was not there to provide all of experience on a platter. Space and its contents had to be created by the child— even in the case of radio and certainly in the case of books. Imagination had to "fill in the blanks," so to speak. The six- or seven-year-old listening to the old "Sky King" radio show had to imagine what Sky King, his niece Penny, their two-engine airplane and even their dog looked like. Such imagination is an act of creativity. There is no creativity involved when today's six-year-old watches Saturday morning cartoons or an action video movie.

The result of that need to imagine was a richness of experience, a panaesthetic sense of participation in the imagined which opened a multitude of vistas upon countless alternative worlds. It was nothing, for example, to turn the space behind the living room couch into a secret world in which one's primitive action figures could play out complicated scenarios. Blocks of wood or mundane household items were easily invested with intense meaning and brought hours of satisfaction largely unknown to today's child, who is soon bored with the television character figure that Daddy brought home from a multi-acre toy store. Never have children lived in such an

110

intensely fantasy-saturated world as they do today, and yet never have children been so fantasy-poor. The reader whose early childhood was spent largely without television will see in the repetitive, stereotyped play of children today a sad emptiness and a staggering lack of spontaneous creativity. And because our media-mediated life has become the unquestioned norm, we aren't even aware that we are quickly losing an entire dimension of human experience.

This is extremely important, for it may require a significant perspective shift for the younger therapist to realize how this change in our experience of space can radically affect the way in which we structure our therapy. When one of us was a child psychiatry fellow it was suggested that we watch the Saturday morning cartoons in order to know what children were seeing on a regular basis. This way, so the reasoning ran, we would better understand what we saw in the play of children we encountered in the clinic. The individual who made this suggestion, himself a board examiner in child psychiatry, even intimated that questions about the content of Saturday morning cartoons might show up in the oral part of the board exam. Ironically, this apparently sensible suggestion represented a complete misunderstanding of how children *can* think, interact and change—and an unwitting ideological commitment to the empty world of the television screen. Child psychiatrists who accepted the suggestion were not likely to learn how to structure the space in which they encountered children clinically. It was structured for them without their even being aware of it.

The *therapeutic space* is the physical, temporal and interpersonal space in which the child and the therapist interact. Because it is by nature a virtual and potential space, it is constantly being elaborated. Its definition is entirely operational: it exists only as it is experienced by the child and the therapist. Every physical object it contains contributes to the nature of its structure, as does the way in which time is managed. If this description is accepted, then the evaluation/treatment dichotomy immediately collapses: if the concept of therapeutic space is meaningful, it dictates that the child's very first clinical encounter be structured therapeutically. In fact, the assessment of the child's ability *to recognize and utilize* the therapeutic space will be seen later to be a central aspect of the initial evaluation of therapeutic aptness.

There are several very simple premises upon which the therapeutic structure must be built. For example:

1. Structures, rules and boundaries must be explicitly elaborated and implicitly maintained.
2. The therapeutic relationship and process should in no way collude

with that which may have hurt the child (intentionally or uninten-
tionally).

3. While the therapeutic process may facilitate the child's expression of
    mistaken or negative self-perceptions, it should never allow them to
    stand. This requires that harm to self, to others or to property not be
    permitted within the therapeutic setting.

STRUCTURE, RULES AND BOUNDARIES

The need for structure, rules and boundaries can be illustrated by a short
anecdote.

A number of years ago I (DMD) visited a small residential treatment
program for children. As we toured the facility the director, who was
aware that I had had the unusual experience of living for a year with
psychotic children in a unique 24-hour treatment setting, remarked that
none of the children in his program were as severely disturbed as those
with whom I had worked. "Except, perhaps," he added, "for Martin.
That's Martin over there," he said, pointing to a 12-year-old who was
staring blankly into the distance. "Martin is 12 years old and has never
learned to read. In fact, you can find him out here every evening just
staring at the street. If you ask him what he's doing, he says he's waiting
for the lights to come on. And if that isn't crazy," the director concluded,
"I don't know what is."

When I asked about Martin's background, however, I found that he
had had 25 foster care placements in the 12 years prior to coming to the
residential program. "How many children," I asked my host, "do you find
beating down the school doors at the end of the summer, trying to get
back into school? Few, if any. So children learn what they learn largely as
a favor to us. They learn first to please their parents and teachers—and
then, if all goes well, they continue to learn because learning has become
enjoyable in itself. Learning to read and write requires consistency and
continuity of perception—and these in turn depend upon consistency and
continuity of experience. And this is just what has been lacking from this
child's life. Convince Martin that he is going to be with you for the next
three years, and he will do you the favor of learning how to read. Now,
what makes me think that I'm right about this? The very thing that you
see as crazy in his life. What can one absolutely count on in the month of
November?—that the mercury vapor street lights will come on at 5:30
p.m., as will most of the car lights. For some reason, this is the one thing

that Martin has chosen to count on as absolutely reliable." Two months later Martin was reading and writing.

Two components were necessary to bring about the profound but simple change in Martin's behavior and academic success: an understanding of the dialectics of individual subjective experience and knowledge of how to structure Martin's experience in the new therapeutic setting. This chapter deals with the process of that structuring and its rationale in the outpatient setting.

Structuring the Therapeutic Space

Children, with very few exceptions, are intensely symbolic creatures. The apparent nonchalance and obliviousness of children mask the fact that they are, in fact, exquisitely perceptive of, and sensitive to, the space around them. Everything about the therapeutic space, therefore, is assumed to have intense personal meaning to the child. Once one becomes convinced that this is, in fact, the case and has lived it for a period of time, it no longer has to be thought about consciously each time a new patient is encountered. One must work to structure the space at first, however, and work to keep one's treatment of it consistent from day to day and from patient to patient. When consistency has at last become comfortable habit, all sorts of creative variations are possible. One should keep in mind, however, that just as the child needs the "ground" of the consistency of sessional continuity in order to express the "figure" of that which is unique in his or her life and therapy, so, too, does the therapist require a "ground" of consistent practice upon which to perceive the often incredible subtleties that constitute the "figure" of each child's self-presentation.*

Children must perceive from the very first contact that the very space they encounter "understands" them, that it is so firmly and consistently structured that (1) it is safe to be self-disclosing and (2) the space will make them feel secure. The following "rules" (or descriptions of the therapeutic space) have come to represent our minimum working definition of that space. Most of the "rules" listed here can be stated to the child as the need arises. Reciting them to the child as, literally, a collection of rules, however, is not helpful.

---

*While Milton Erickson, perhaps the most uniquely gifted psychotherapist ever to have lived, may have needed only himself and the patient, we have never met another Erickson and doubt that we ever shall. It is better to define carefully one's environment when one can, in fact, control it — and then wisely cultivate an ongoing refinement of one's technique.

Like nearly everything else in child therapy, their meaning is an operational meaning which is conveyed through the interactive process.

A reviewer of an early draft of this book could not fathom how therapy could be accomplished with the rigidity of so many "arbitrary" rules. Had she watched the therapeutic process through the one-way mirror, however, she would have been hard pressed to identify most of the following "rules" since they are, for the most part, elaborated implicitly in the interaction between therapist and child. Only certain "rules" are stated categorically to the child. The therapeutic space itself thereby becomes a kind of Bowlbyan "safe base" (Bowlby, 1973). As van der Kolk notes (1987, p. 16), "Like adults who identify with their terrorist kidnappers, abused children usually make a rapid accommodation to their environment by protecting and identifying with their abusers." The at times subtle but intense experience of the therapeutic space offers an alternative environment to the hurt child, one which promotes therapeutic change and resolution.

Operational "Rules" That Help Define the Therapeutic Space

1. No adults—with the exception of the co-therapist—are allowed in the playtherapy room. Parents are not allowed to enter the playtherapy room.

The playtherapy room must be the child's own personal space. Often children need to express feelings or talk about actual or imagined events, which they would never do if they thought that anyone, especially a parent, would ever know what they said. For many children the inviolability and privacy of their space represent the confidentiality of the therapeutic relationship itself. Maintaining this simple boundary is a much more effective means of establishing and maintaining trust than any number of verbal reassurances. Besides, it is impossible to know to what extent a given child's personal (physical or emotional) space may have been violated. (Remember that such violations need not necessarily have been humanly and purposefully abusive: even "natural" catastrophe can be experienced as an invasion of personal space.) Thus, it makes sense to protect the integrity of the child's space as he or she lives it. In the case of abused children, the playtherapy room may be the *only* space in the life of the child which is consistently safe, secure and inviolable.

Some clinicians and programs carry the exclusion of parents from the child's space to a degree that seems frankly punitive. The therapist and co-therapist represent the transitional link between the child's personal and private space and the parent. If a genuine therapeutic relationship is established between the therapist(s) and the parent(s), no sense of exclusion or rejection need develop in the parent(s).

2. What the child does and says in the playtherapy room is confidential—except for those instances when genuine care for the child dictates that something be shared with the parent or custodian.

Children need to know that not only are their parents or custodians not allowed to enter their privileged space, but they cannot even know what goes on there—unless the child elects to inform them. Consequently, we explicitly state to children that what goes on in the playtherapy room is between them and their therapist. *They* may tell their parents or custodian if they wish, but otherwise their confidence will be kept.

However, just as children cannot be allowed to rule the world, neither can they be allowed to dictate what should or should not ultimately be told to their parents by the therapist. Occasionally, the therapist may feel that certain information should be be shared with the parents even though the child protests that the "secret" must be kept. In such cases, after gently attempting to convince the child to assent, we simply cast the issue in terms of "another little boy (or girl)" who, of course, just happened to have a parallel, or nearly parallel, situation. Even the brightest and most critical of children tend to permit such a communication once the distance is placed between them and the imaginary "other child." Never have we experienced a breakdown in trust or in the therapy itself as a result of a necessary disclosure.

The above technique simply capitalizes on the normative dissociative ability of the child. Furthermore, any child therapist who does not assume that children want to be cared for and protected—regardless of how much the child may protest to the contrary—is taking a disastrous step. Ultimately, caring adults must decide what is best for the child. The pseudodemocratic imposition of adult values such as honesty and openness on the process of psychotherapy with developmentally dependent children (Coppolillo, 1987) is misguided and tends to blur intergenerational boundaries and confuse the child's sense of genuine agency.

3. Nothing is allowed to be taken into the playtherapy room and nothing can be taken out.

No matter how detailed, consistent and elaborate one's structure and rules may be, they will disintegrate into nothing if this rule is not consistently maintained—with very few exceptions (see Chapter 5 for our Smiley Face charts which are hand-made each week in the playtherapy room and then taken out.) The nothing in/nothing out rule helps operationally to define a boundary that will play a significant role in many children's therapy. The rule helps to engender a sense of respect for personal and interpersonal space—a space whose boundaries, especially in the case of abused or traumatized children, are often fluid or uncertain.

> Mae was an eight-year-old who had been sexually abused. When she became familiar and comfortable with the rules governing her hour, Mae tended automatically to remove those jewelry items which were not customary for an eight-year-old to wear. When it came time for her to leave her mother and follow her therapist to the playtherapy room, she simply removed those things which she knew did not belong there.

Children tend to be very understanding of these rules because they eventually contribute to a sense of groundedness and security.

> A bright gypsy-like four-year-old was told, just before going into the playtherapy room, that she would have to remove her lipstick. Her therapist told her, "if you were a real mommy, then you could wear your lipstick into the other room. You can put it on when you return." The child more than happily removed her lipstick.

This little girl had pierced ears and it was never suggested to her that she should remove her earrings. They were part of her normal attire, since she had worn them since six months of age.

Once children understand that this is the rule, many will try to break it. *How* they try to break it—and with what insistence—can be both diagnostic and prognostic. Most children will try to break this rule just to see if their therapist really means what he or she says—and if he or she cares. Thus, children hide objects in their pockets, put them in their armpits, cheek them, put them in their shoes or socks, etc.—any imaginable ruse to see if their therapist will really stick by the stated rule. If objects are found, they must be put outside the room, even if only just outside the door, otherwise the child will not trust the therapist (because he or she cannot control the space).*

Even little children are capable of thinking (alas, often rightly) that they

---

*This is not an absolutarian as it sounds. Children are not "inspected" to see what they have in their pockets. Children who are secreting items into the playtherapy room—as opposed to simply forgetting that they have them in their pockets—usually manage to communicate this to the therapist.

are smarter than their therapists. Such a conclusion on the part of a child is disastrous for the therapy—for it means that the therapy is seriously compromised at best or ultimately compromised, at worst. The child who thinks he or she is smarter than his/her therapist is most unlikely to trust the therapist enough to utilize the true potential of the therapy, or to be genuinely self-disclosing. This is especially true of abused children—and exquisitely true of sexually abused children. Here the invasion of space takes on very special meaning.

If the abused child succeeds in secreting an object into the playtherapy room without being discovered, then he (or she, but usually he) has effectively *raped* the therapist's space, which is tantamount to raping the therapist. One would think that abused children would wish the very opposite, yet the fact is that often they put their therapist to this very test. Failure to find the object and exclude it from the room can result in a failure of therapy. Abused children who manage to violate the therapeutic space without being discovered may present an illusory picture of therapeutic progress. This, however, usually amounts to nothing more than *theoretical compliance*. These children rarely change as a result of the therapy.

There are three very different reasons why a child would sneak something into the playtherapy room. The first, and most innocuous, is simply that the child needs to be reassured that the therapist is at least as smart as he or is—and to find out if the therapist will really stand the defined ground (and can therefore be trusted). Some children may not know why they try to sneak objects into the playtherapy room, only that they have a compulsion to do so. Such a need may represent a *behavioral memory* (Terr, 1988) and, as such, may be an indication that significant material is just beneath the surface. At such times, even though the child cannot state verbally what may have happened in the past, he or she will often act it out in the context of the interactive play. On the other hand, the child who *repeatedly* attempts to violate the therapeutic space for the perverse pleasure of doing so—and who is neither reassured nor dissuaded from doing so by a repeated discovery of his or her actions—presents a very poor prognosis, since this suggests a perverse psychopathy. The ability to *use* the therapeutic space signals a positive potential outcome for the child, whereas the repeated attempt to abuse and violate the therapeutic space signals a profound disturbance in those values which keep human beings from seriously harming others.

It is the child's experience of the therapeutic space that convinces him that he is cared for. The giving of gifts, recommended by some clinicians (e.g. Dodds, 1985) to convey this care to the child is unnecessary if the therapeutic space is genuinely elaborated. In fact, gift-giving may be counterproductive, for it conveys the therapist's uncertainty that the child will experience the process itself as therapeutic, hence the need for a "proof" of care.

   4. Everything in the playtherapy room has a place and that place never
       changes.

As of this writing, neither the contents nor the disposition of our playtherapy room have changed in the last six years. The power of the therapeutic space is increased dramatically to the extent to which order and sameness are maintained. Although adults may not pay much attention to such things, children are exquisitely sensitive to the structure and order of the environments they inhabit. The incredible degree to which they can pick up in therapy exactly where they left off the previous week should convince us of that. Again, one should also keep in mind that, for many children, the order and reliability represented by that space they visit for just one hour each week may represent *the only consistent reliability in their lives.* Consequently, one cannot overestimate its potential positive impact. Besides, if one is to view the process of therapy as anything other than a discontinuous, sporadic, more or less meaningful series of encounters, then sessional continuity must be maintained.

   Only the therapist who maintains such continuity is likely to learn from experience that children vary significantly in how they relate to the therapeutic space. Some children display an extraordinary sessional continuity, which is uninterrupted even by years of absence from therapy. On returning to therapy, they will "pick up" right where they left off, as if they had been there the day before. Others will have to be reinitiated into the therapeutic space through the consistent re-elaboration of the operational rules outlined here.

   How powerful can such a simple thing be? The answer can be seen in an interesting concurrence of events. A few years ago three potentially disruptive events occurred in the lives of our patients over a very short period of time: the authors of this book were married (and most of our little patients attended both wedding and reception); hurricane Elena hit and radically disrupted our relations with our patients and their families; and we moved our office into a new building with a playtherapy room which was strikingly different from that which had become comfortably familiar to our young patients. In fact, the playtherapy room changed from being perfectly square to being rather strangely shaped, from having a window to the outside to having a one-way mirror, from having all of the Lego objects well out of reach to easily within reach in a bookcase, to having a sink right in the room, and finally, to having one corner in which the carpet ran right up the wall (to create a delimited, safe throwing area). Fascinatingly, only two of some 60 child patients were at all disoriented by the move: a four-year-old who had witnessed the murder of his mother and a twelve-year-old extremely immature, retarded, physically and sexually abused child. The rest of the children simply picked up where they left off—as if absolutely nothing had happened in the physical world in which they encountered their therapist. This reflects the extent to which consistency and continuity of experience can ensure experiential stability. (A technical puzzle for the reader: why, when boundaries are stressed as so very important to the integrity of the therapeutic process, did the participation of so many disturbed children in the wedding of their therapists *not* adversely affect the treatment process? After all, we broke most of the "traditional" rules. The answer to this question, as well as why all the environmental chaos in the lives of our patients did not disrupt the therapy, will be found in the next sextion.)

This issue of structure and boundaries raises the very real question of whether intensive psychotherapy with children can be done successfully using a shared playtherapy room. Again, one could argue that it is the person of the therapist which counts the most. Still, children tend to perceive the environment in which they encounter their therapist as an extension of the therapist—and we know of no therapist so extraordinarily gifted that he or she can command the riveted attention of individual children hour after hour, day after day, when ambient chaos reigns. Clinicians working in a common setting, such as a mental health center, would be wise to establish some very tight ground rules governing the physical space of the playtherapy room, based on a genuine understanding of the importance of detail and consistency and continuity in the lives of children.

Eight-year-old Chuck had lived through very difficult times between his parents prior to their divorce. No sooner had they divorced than his mother was seriously injured in an automobile accident which nearly took her life. Just as Chuck was beginning to trust that she would be all right, a freak accident caused a department store window to fall on her, again resulting in serious injury and a prolonged hospital stay and rehabilitation.

Chuck became school phobic and developed an almost hysterical attachment to his mother. Chuck responded quickly to therapy and developed a number of techniques which allowed him to separate from his mother. One of these techniques simply involved playing checkers when the accidental occurrences of daily life made him feel that the safety and predictability of life were crumbling. He found the highly delimited form of the board and the dependability of the game's simple, unchanging rules tremendously reassuring.

At the time of Chuck's treatment our office was in the building of another medical specialist who saw as many as 150 patients every workday. The other physician and his staff did not really understand the seriousness of the distinction between a playtherapy room and a simple playroom and were not terribly concerned if their own children played there on weekends. One weekend they removed the checkers set.

When another totally unpredictable accident shook Chuck's family, Chuck immediately sought the comfort of his reliable checkers game when he entered the playtherapy room. Although the accident had occurred several days prior to his therapy appointment, Chuck had maintained the gains he had made in therapy—until he entered the playtherapy room and found that the checkers set was gone. It took several sessions to regain the lost ground.

The more subtle and complete one's control of the therapeutic space, the more intensely powerful one's therapeutic interaction can be. As the next few "rules" are considered, it should become more obvious why such tight control is necessary.

> 5. Everything in the playtherapy room should be put back in its place at the end of the session. Although the child is not required to do this personally, he or she should remain in the room until the original order is restored.

No child should be allowed to leave a therapeutic setting which is in a disordered state. Again, it is important to realize that the order provided by the intermittent therapeutic encounter may be the only consistent order in a child patient's life. Furthermore, it must be stressed that children cannot be expected to trust adults who cannot keep the world in order. The symbolic power of "putting things back where they belong" cannot be overstressed. Even if the child refuses to put things away, the therapist must not allow the child to leave the playtherapy room until order has been restored.

The therapist who is skeptical with regard to this particular rule has only to perform a simple experiment to discover its importance. If your practice has been simply to put things "away"—but not necessarily in the same place each time, establish an order in your own mind and begin putting each item in its own place at the end of each session. Even if your therapy room is shared, make an effort to see that those items your patient regularly uses are in their proper places when the session begins and that they are returned to the same places at the end—no matter how unorganized the other objects in the room may be. Carefully monitor your child patient's behavior both in and outside of the ensuing sessions. If you are consistent over time, you will see an improvement in the process of therapy as well as a burgeoning commitment to structure, rules, and boundaries on the part of your child patient.

We now have the answer to our technical puzzle in the previous section. Our patients experienced much disorder and disruption during the period of time when our practice was briefly closed for relocation. Hurricane Elena, the move itself, and the very different shape and fixtures of the playtherapy room doubtless contributed to a sense of disorder. One would expect that the participation of our patients and their families in our wedding and reception would, as well. Yet the temporal, interpersonal, and material structure of the therapeutic space remained intensely the same: although the shape of the playtherapy room changed, every object was in the same place (with respect to every other object) as before and was treated in exactly the same fashion. We had an expectation of absolute continuity of the therapeutic process. It was the power of the consistency, continuity, and predictability of the benevolent structure of the therapeutic space, we are convinced, that allowed for such a smooth transition.

6. All contents of the playtherapy room, with very few exceptions, should be *generic*. No recognizable "theme" toys should be found in the playtherapy room.

Needless to say, we want to know what is going on in the (real or imagined) life of the child—not what is happening on television. There needs to be, as well, a very real boundary between office and home. Consequently, in principle, the contents of the playtherapy room should not reflect what is likely to be found in the child's own world at home. There should be no "theme" toys—no Superman, He-man, Cabbage Patch dolls, etc.—nothing that will invite the reenactment of empty stories from the empty lives of television children. Contents should be *generic* whenever possible: black and white family dolls (or other ethnic family dolls, depending upon the therapist's geographic location), stuffed animals not likely to be found at home (such as the kangaroo, platypus and koala families in our playtherapy room).

No anatomically correct dolls are to be found in our playtherapy room or office. It is naïve to assume that children, especially immature, sexually abused children, simply accept such dolls as necessary hardware for the everyday clinician. In spite of their apparent understanding, many children will wonder why these adults have such strange dolls in their office. What do they do with them after hours? Where did they get them? The possibility of inadvertent sexual stimulation is clearly present, and no caring clinician would knowingly repeat any of the trauma the child has lived through. Such dolls are a forensic tool, the purpose of which is to allow children to convince adults that inappropriate sexual activity has taken place. They are, in no way, essential or even necessary for good child therapy (Donovan, 1988c).

The typical "anal stage preoccupation objects" of traditional child analysts, such as clay or finger paints, are not in the least necessary: children who continue to smear in therapy cannot be said to be making any kind of meaningful progress. Such things are usually diversions from the real, intense, and powerful issues that plague the lives of children. Even those children who are "anally preoccupied" need not act out those preoccupations; they need to be able to change, grow, and move on.

Similarly, most games are generally not necessary equipment; in fact, the presence or use of games often signals that the therapist does not know what to do with the child—hence the therapist and the child play games instead of utilizing the therapeutic space. (We have seen children whose "therapy" consisted of playing Nintendo video games with their therapist for upwards of three years.) Chess and checkers, however, may be of real use under certain, very specific circumstances. Some children need occasionally to return to activities in which the rules are simple, clear and cannot be broken. This has been the case in our experience for children who occasionally experience a real sense of dyscontrol. Such children, like Chuck, may occasionally have to play checkers, for example, because the delimited nature of the board and the simple unbreakable rules help hold their world together momentarily. We have seen children—especially children with seizures whose experience of the world as disordered and unpredictable required a repeated, stereotyped experience of order and predictability—for whom making sure the chessmen were set up properly was more important than any possible playing of the game. Another creative use of these two games (although checkers—because of its simplicity—is usually preferable) is to maneuver noncompliant, oppositional children into *demanding* that their therapist follow the rules. This can be extremely effective because it requires no conscious recognition on the child's part of what has occurred, and there is no confrontation.

Again, one should shy away from games with identifiable thematic content, such as board games like Monopoly or Clue. Nor do children who genuinely feel they are understood need manufactured "expressive" games in order to express themselves and communicate.

With only the rarest of exceptions, the therapist should never *allow* the child win a game of chess or checkers, to make up new rules or to break the traditional rules. The therapist who allows the child to win and yet thinks he or she is still in charge of the therapy is sadly mistaken (see the example of John's "northern therapist" in Chapter 11. For the potential therapeutic richness of simple board games, see Adele and John in Chapters 8 and 11).

> 7. In principle, nothing in the playtherapy room should be easily breakable.

If structure, security and integrity are to characterize the space in which the child and therapist meet, then it makes no sense that this universe should fall apart or be breakable. Adults should hold the world together, not let it fall apart. Because of the extremely self-referent nature of the child, and because children tend to confuse synchronicity of events with causality, children really do at times feel that their wishes or feelings actually caused events to occur. A colleague shared with us his experience as a young psychiatrist during the Battle of Britain. His psychiatric hospital had just sustained a direct hit from aerial bombing. The whole experience was so confusing and occurred so fast that our colleague didn't even realize that he had begun to run when the bomb hit until he stopped several blocks away and turned around. There, standing in front of him was one of his chronic psychotic patients, holding the remnants of a toilet chain. "God, Dr. Miller," his patient said, with a look of incredulous fascination on his face, "I knew I was powerful, but I didn't know I was *that* powerful!" Just at the moment the patient pulled the chain to flush the toilet, the whole building exploded, making Dr. Miller's patient just as much a victim of logic as are the children we work with.

Adults tend to refer to such occurrences in children as "magical thinking." Such thinking is not so much magical as it is logical. Because of the incompleteness of developing cognitive structures, limited and highly idiosyncratic perspective, and the rule of logic in child thinking, such synchronicity is experienced by children as causal. The fact that children can and do delight in the thought of extending such "power" into other realms of their world probably contributes to our view of the magical thinking of childhood. Viewing such thinking as "magical," however, tends to empty it of the at-times terrifying reality it represents to the child and makes it easier for us to dismiss the intensity of children's experience.

Realizing that one will encounter many such children over the years, and that one may not know until well into the therapy that such "catastrophic coincidences" have occurred, doesn't it make sense to safeguard against potential disaster? One of the goals of the therapy is to convince the child (something which cannot be done with words) that he or she simply is not that powerful. Thus, it is incumbent upon the clinician to structure the therapeutic space so that collusion with such beliefs is difficult, if not impossible.

There are two exceptions to this rule. The first is the box of crayons to be found in our playtherapy room. Our crayon box is an old jewelry box, rather dilapidated and certainly not very impressive. Its contents are many old crayons, none of which is new or intact.

Bert was a mildly retarded mid-adolescent whose cerebral palsy was caused by being hit by a car when he was four. Disrespectful, overly familiar, off-putting and invasive of personal space, Bert changed strikingly when he was asked to do two initial drawings and presented with the box of crayons. "This used to be a jewelry box," he was told as the box was placed in front of him on the child's table, "but it got broken. Still, it makes a perfectly good crayon box, don't you think? And do you mind if my crayons aren't perfect?" Like many genuinely handicapped children or children who feel themselves to be "damaged" or "broken" in some way, Bert smiled warmly on encountering the box of crayons.

Just as one cannot successfully reassure children *with words* if an object which is never supposed to break unexpectedly breaks in the playtherapy room, so, too, is it impossible to reassure children who feel damaged or broken that they "are really all right." They know they aren't, so attempts to tell them that they are amount to an insult. Presenting the box of broken crayons to such children symbolically expresses an understanding of their feelings and their sensitivity without forcing them to acknowledge either. Hence the power of something so very simple.

The second exception to this rule is an old wooden helicopter with a rotor that falls out if the helicopter is turned upside down, a toy far too drab and unsophisticated to be of much interest even to a six-year-old Nintendo owner.

Laurie was a 13-year-old whose severe club foot made her quite clumsy and self-conscious. She had never known her father and had been repeatedly sexually abused by a number of her mother's live-in male friends. Laurie's mother rarely called her while she was in foster care and missed most of the visits she was allowed to have. Her mother generally forgot her birthday and usually forgot Christmas as well. But every time the social services began to move toward termination of parental rights and permanent placement, Laurie's mother would appear on the scene with numerous formal complaints about the agency and loaded down with presents.

At this point in therapy a series of missed visits had made mother's lack of genuine concern painfully evident. Instead of recognizing this, however, Laurie complained to her social worker that her therapist was "trying to make me hate my mother." When Laurie's social worker brought this up at the beginning of the session, prior to Laurie and her therapist's leaving for the playtherapy room, Laurie's therapist made no attempt to deny the statement, even though she had never said any such thing. Instead, she asked Laurie what she would do if she were the mother and her daughter was in foster care. "I'd call every week," Laurie replied. "Well, what if the phone was busy?" her therapist continued. "I would try again." "But, what if it stayed busy for a long time—for more than an hour, say . . . ?" "I wouldn't give up," Laurie replied. "I would keep calling until I got through."

At this point Laurie's therapist took her into the playtherapy room where she became involved in a pile of papers kept under the sink, as if she were looking for one of Laurie's drawings from the previous week. "Here," she said, handing Laurie the old wooden helicopter, "do me a favor and see if you can fix the propeller." Laurie tried and tried but, since the hole for the shaft of the rotor was simply too big to hold the rotor in, she could not get it to stay. Finally, in exasperation, she handed it back, saying, "I give up. I can't fix that thing." Taking it back, Laurie's therapist asked, "Is it your fault that you can't fix it?" "No," Laurie said, as if nothing could be more obvious, "it's the helicopter's fault!" Then, and only then—and very, very gently—did Laurie's therapist say to her, "Is it your fault that your mother never calls?" Laurie broke into tears.

If the use of such objects (like the broken jewelry box full of imperfect crayons and the helicopter with its faulty rotor) is to work, it cannot be contrived. Although such interventions can be easily illustrated, only experience can tell the therapist when the time is ripe for their use.

8. The wherewithal to repair anything that could possibly be broken should be available, and the child should never be allowed to leave the playtherapy room until any item which accidentally breaks has been repaired. If such repair is impossible, the child should be made to replace the item—even if the parents must secretly be given the money to do so.

One can imagine the possible scenario if Laurie were to encounter breakable dolls in the playtherapy room: in anger she throws the baby boy doll (or the mother doll, for that matter) against the wall; it breaks—and she is confirmed in her mistaken belief that she does, indeed, have such extraordinary negative power. We cannot, on the one hand, state blithely that "children are concrete thinkers" and, on the other, remain blind to the practical consequences of such a realization. To allow a doll broken by a child to remain broken is to convey to that child that her worst fears really are true: she does have that much power. It also says to the child that adults allow bad things to happen and that they do not care enough to make them right. When an object which has been invested with intense symbolic and emotional meaning breaks, the results can be disastrous. (See also Chapter 10.)

> Tim was a very bright 10-year-old in trouble and failing in school because of passive-aggression and constant disrespect for his teachers. Adopted as an infant, he had spent five marvelous years before his big, strong, financially and socially successful father was struck with a literally disabling case of eczema—and changed overnight into someone much harder to be proud of. Tim denied strongly that he had ever been angry at his father for changing as he had, but persisted nonetheless in constant disrespectful interactions with him. Finally, during one session, Tim allowed himself to be angry at his father for changing and threw the daddy doll against the wall. The head broke off. Tim was not too disoriented by the event and successfully glued the head back on. However, on reentering the office where he and his mother had begun the session alone with the co-therapist, Tim saw his father, who had arrived late because he had gone to pick up some rose bushes for visiting relatives. No one had realized that Tim's father had lacerated his leg at the nursery (he was wearing summer shorts) and that blood had trickled all down his leg and dried. Any observer, however, could have read the look of astonished horror on Tim's face as he saw the blood: "I got mad and threw the daddy doll—and look what I did!"

This child had an absolutely horrible week after that session. His therapist, however, was able to use the series of events in the next week's session to demonstrate to Tim just how afraid he was of his own anger and how much he feared losing a parent for the second time if he expressed it directly. (Note that it is not just the conscious awareness of Tim's "fantasies" which brought about the therapeutic change; it required the experience of confronting his anger toward his father and living through the fact that nothing horrible came of it.)

9. No item in the playtherapy room should suggest or invite violent or hostile behavior or acting-out.

Children do not require toy guns, knives, or war toys in order to express angry or hostile feelings. This they can and will do symbolically when they feel that the "space" understands their symbolic expressions. Toys of harm and violence, however, are equivocal, to say the least: they can be intensely confusing to children because their presence must be explained. They are clearly viewed as an *invitation* to violent play and this constitutes a contamination of the child's space. Moreover, they can confuse the clinical picture presented. Since the vast majority of toys today appear to be related in some way to war or violence, inclusion of any of them in the playtherapy room only invites theme-specific play which may not reflect child-specific content. In a word: they are simply unneeded.

More importantly, such toys may be frankly antitherapeutic: anger and hostility may need to be expressed, but this should be done in a controlled fashion in order to bring about a resolution. It is a mistaken notion, based on 19th century Helmholtzian physics, that anger—like urine—is present in "quanta" which must somehow be expelled from the person. Fans "ventilate." People change symbolically. For this reason, do not invite a child to "beat up his pillow instead of people" and then expect that child to sleep well on the very place he has "put" all his anger. Such "techniques" do not resolve anger and hostility; they merely move from one expressive mode to another.

Nick was bright, confused and angry six-year-old whose oppositionalism and aggression toward peers and family had resulted in a school emotionally handicapped placement and a number of previous failed therapies. Each of the previous therapists had told Nick's mother that Nick "needed to get his anger out," and all had recommended various ways for him to displace it from real people. His last therapist had recommended that Nick beat up his pillow and not his family. During the initial evaluation in our playtherapy room, Nick's therapist asked him how he thought his pillow felt. "I think it would like to hit me back," Nick replied. Nick's aggression quickly abated when the reasons for his anger were discovered and resolved.

On several occasions during workshops we have presented in Europe, colleagues have suggested that perhaps our ban on toys of aggression and violence was due to the fact that violence is so common in the United States. Because their countries were less violent and more "liberal" and "tolerant" of individual expression, they suggested, guns, knives, soldiers, tanks, and cannons had a different meaning in their playtherapy rooms. Their comments invite two replies. First, it was interesting to find a disturbingly high incidence of sexual abuse—including violent or coercive abuse—among the cases of our European colleagues—suggesting that violence in the lives of children is pervasive. Second, the presence of items of aggression in the playtherapy room *suggests* and *gives permission for* violence no matter where in the world one might be. Because of their conventionality, toys of violence may actually serve the purpose of protecting the therapist from the full affective experience of the child's anger or rage. There is, in our view, no rational argument for the presence of toys of violence in any kind of therapy room.

    10. Harming self, other, or objects should never be allowed.

Children are exquisitely sensitive to the genuineness and effectiveness of the therapist's commitment to their safety and well-being. It is imperative to explain to the child at the beginning of therapy that one of the inflexible rules of the playtherapy room (and hour) is that hurting oneself or another person, as well as destruction of objects, is not allowed and that any such occurrence will *immediately* end the session. (An infrequent, but significant, exception to this rule will be illustrated on p. 00.) One must state explicitly that this includes the therapist and that he or she is not allowed to hurt or be destructive either.

    Children inevitably test this rule to see if the therapist really means what he or she says. The subtlety with which children can do this is astounding. Since nearly everything in the therapeutic setting is of a symbolic nature, the therapist must be finely attuned to these acts.

> Mike, 11, a bright, manipulative child whose constant testing of the therapeutic situation paralleled his constant lying at home, nonchalantly flicked a small Lego piece towards the therapist. "Okay, that's it," she said, "you know the rule: no throwing at people in this room. The session's over and you'll have to sit out in the waiting room until Denis finishes talking with your mom." Mike looked disgusted and incredulous. "You've got to be kidding!" he exclaimed, "You call *that* throwing! *You're* the one who needs a shrink. I barely touched that Lego!" Insisting that Mike knew the rules, his therapist ended the session but did not rejoin her cotherapist and Mike's mother in the other room. Nor did she indicate that the session had been ended prematurely. Both she and Mike simply reentered the other office at the end of the session—as if nothing had happened.

Mike's behavior improved significantly the week following the prematurely ended session and he was much more genuinely involved in the therapy the following week.

Children may actually lie to their parents, saying that a session which ended prematurely because they broke the "no hurting" rule was "fine"; they may even fabricate a complex content for the hour. This should not be viewed by the therapist as a negative occurrence but simply as the child's understandable need to protect the privacy and integrity of his therapeutic space. It is extremely important to explain to parents that the structural integrity of the therapy may be destroyed if the parents intervene because of anything the child does in the playtherapy room. They must be helped to understand that, without respect for those boundaries, the therapeutic space is lost. Equally lost may be the child's trust of the therapist if parents intervene by punishing or disciplining the child.

> Five-year-old Johnny punched his therapist in the mouth, unexpectedly and without any identifiable provocation, during his third session. Extremely scattered, "hyper," overly familiar, and disrespectful of the personal space of others, Johnny was devastated when his therapist abruptly stopped the session. A master of guilt-induced control over his mother, he simply couldn't believe that his therapist would actually stop *his* session. He began to wail and sob so loudly that it could be heard outside the building.
>
> When his mother and stepfather were told that he had punched his therapist in the mouth and that she had a bleeding lip, they wanted to punish him on the spot. It was explained to them not only that should they not do this but also that it was extremely important for them not even to talk about the event on the way home and to treat Johnny as if nothing had happened. If Johnny should start to talk about the incident, they were told, they should simply reply that whatever happened in that room was between him and his therapist and that they weren't going to talk about it. Johnny's parents accomplished this quite well and the following week saw a marked improvement in his activity level as well as in his respect for persons.

Unbeknownst to his mother or to us, this bright little five-year-old had been sexually abused under extremely tense conditions. The abuse had occurred during court-sanctioned visits with his schizophrenic father, from whom the mother was divorced. After the first instance of sexual abuse his father had taken Johnny outside and made him watch while he shot a pigeon. "That is what will happen to you," Johnny's father told him, "if you ever tell anyone what we did." This threat was repeated on a number of occasions.

The absolutely nonretaliatory, nonpunitive way in which Johnny's therapist maintained the structure, rules, and boundaries which constituted the therapeutic space eventually allowed Johnny a sense of security great enough to tell his therapist what had happened to him some two years previously. It was all the more important for his mother and stepfather to respect the rules of therapy for the long delay in the disclosure of the abuse was due, we discovered later, to Johnny's fear that he would be sent back to his father. As it happened, Johnny's mother would occasionally threaten to send him back to live with his father when he misbehaved. Needless to say, she was horrified to find out what her idle threats had represented to him.

To reiterate, the rule in our playtherapy room is that *any* proactive harm — real or symbolic — is treated equally: it ends the session and the child sits out the remainder in the waiting room. It is important to stress that the purpose of such a rule is to convince the child that the structures, rules, and boundaries of the therapeutic space are real and inviolable. It is neither to embarrass nor to humiliate the child. Consequently, at the end of the session, child and therapist reappear in the office in which the parent or parents are being seen concurrently — and not even the co-therapist knows that the child's session has been ended prematurely. The vast majority of children will not even let on that something has happened. Very few will tell their parents that their session has ended prematurely; in fact, those who do tend to take much longer in therapy. Clearly, the child's therapist must take an absolutely matter-of-fact approach to the enforcement of these rules. If the therapist indicates that he or she is put off by what happens, then the whole issue has been personalized and the power of the therapeutic space has been significantly diminished. Those who really want to work intensively with children should be forewarned that the occasional child like Johnny demands great patience and self-control on the part of the therapist.

11. Disrobing — even the taking off of shoes — is not allowed.

If one takes the symbolic world of children seriously, then the incredible complexity and subtlety of that world becomes apparent. Simple common-sense rules then govern how one behaves in the intense symbolically-loaded space in which the child patient and therapist encounter one another. It might seem normal and inconsequential for a tired mother to kick off her shoes and relax. But, to an abused child, taking off any piece of apparel can be much more meaningful than one might think. Consequently, it is easiest simply to establish the rule that, with the exception of normal outer garments, *all* disrobing is disallowed. Children who begin to understand what this means tend to protect the therapeutic space themselves.

> Joy (Chapter 1) returned at age four after a break in therapy. She had been sexually abused by her father prior to the age of three. In the office she tended to sit with her feet on the chair. When she was told gently to "put your feet down," she became extremely upset and began to scream, "I don't want to put my feet down!" Her mother, thinking that we simply did not want feet on our furniture, began to take off her daughter's shoes. "Don't do that," Joy's mother was told. "You don't seem to realize, but one should never disrobe an abused child under such conditions, not even by taking her shoes off." Once Joy realized that the rules were going to be maintained—even with her yelling and screaming—and that there was going to be no retribution whatsoever, she calmed.

While the operational rules in this chapter refer primarily to what happens in the playtherapy room, this particular rule applies to the entirety of the office in which we have contact with the child and parents. No one takes any article of clothing off in our office—with the normal exception of outer garments. This includes parents. We explain to mothers who decide to take their shoes off while their child is in the playtherapy room that the shoes must be on when the child re-enters the office at the end of the session. (In respect for normal boundaries, the child must knock before re-entering the office.)

> 12. In principle, home or school visits are not made by the therapist and/or co-therapist.

This may well be viewed as the most arbitrary, and therefore "rigid," of our rules. Yet our experience over the years has convinced us that we are wise to maintain it. Because of the intensity, however subtle, of our therapy with children we have found that anything which blurs the boundaries of the therapeutic space actually slows the therapeutic process, which, in turn, increases the cost and inconvenience of the treatment. The exception to this rule, for us, is when environmental harm is suspected and adequate assistance from social services is not forthcoming.

Often it is difficult to make a home or school visit without witnessing some inappropriate behavior on the part of the child. At that point it is almost impossible to avoid being asked what to do. If we comply, we are effectively discrediting the parent or teacher in the eyes of the child. If we do not comply, we have an uncomfortable situations on our hands. Consequently, in the case of behavior problems at school, we offer to meet with teachers, counselors, or psychologists in order to aid them in dealing with the child in question—but we refuse categorically to go to the child's home or classroom while the child is present. What parents and teachers want when they ask for such visits can be provided them without compromising the therapeutic space.

13. Any structure built by the child (e.g., of Legos) is to be disassembled by the child at the end of the last session, even if that session is the first encounter.

The child who looks during a first encounter and asks about the Lego objects on the shelves, and who is then told that they are things made by children who come to the office on a regular basis, may tell his examiner something about his potential prognosis. If he or she sadly starts to take his/ her Lego creation apart at the end of the session, one knows that one has, at best, a very difficult road ahead. If, on the other hand the child asks, "Can I put my Lego up there, too?" one knows that the child is invested—and, regardless of how negative the child may have been during the initial interview or the therapeutic evaluation, he or she will probably do well in therapy.

The child nearly always asks whom the Legos on the shelves belong to. If the therapist accedes to the child's wishes to add his or her Lego creation to those on the shelves, knowing full well that this child will never return, the therapist has rendered the child a real disservice. After explaining just what those Legos represent, the therapist must tell the child that, if he returns, he may then keep his Lego there as well. To do otherwise is a tease at best—and a horrible deceit at worst. As painful as it may be for the therapist to insist (without evincing a feeling of sorrow for the child) that the child's Lego creation must be taken apart, this is best for the child. Children can carry away much that is positive, perhaps even life-saving, from a single encounter. To allow a child who will not return to leave a Lego creation intact is a duplicitous tease which can kill the magic of that one encounter.

At the end of treatment, the child's Lego must be disassembled by the child. This is part of termination and closure. If the child has truly profited from the therapy, he or she will carry away far more than whatever the Lego may have represented.

The Diagnostic and Therapeutic Use of Time

Time, like space, is a dimension. As such it can be both an experience and a tool. Children use tools, as adults do—but not necessarily *like* adults do. An understanding of how children experience and use time can aid the therapist in clarifying diagnostic issues related to what the child is supposed to be able to do. For example, many children are said to be unable to attend, concentrate, and calm themselves motorically unless they have one-to-one attention. It is assumed that when these children lose the immediately preoccupying interaction of the other individual, their attention is then drawn off-task by peripheral stimuli and that they, therefore, find it difficult to concentrate and attend.

We structure time and create time boundaries by informing children that they will be told when only five minutes remain before they must pick up and put away and then rejoin their parent(s) and the co-therapist in the other room. Frequently, children who are said to be *unable* to attend, concentrate, or complete tasks will become disruptive and/or demanding when the five-minute limit is announced. At such times it becomes clear that the issue is not one of attention but one of control. These children have usually enjoyed the experience in the playtherapy room, may feel extremely comfortable and protected there, or may have disclosed fears or angers that they have not shared with parents or caretakers. If the parents or caretakers are confusing, chaotic, or provocative in their interactive styles, the child may become even more uncomfortable when the time limit is announced. At such times children may beg or plead with the therapist to extend the time in the playtherapy room or, failing that, threaten or become physically disruptive or aggressive as an attempt to extend the contact. Often it is not until children are able to let themselves be sad—not discuss it analytically—that they are able to transition from the self-contained comfort of the playtherapy room to other office.

Threats to the Therapeutic Space

One reason that so many child therapists play games and engage in other non-content types of activity may well be a keen unconscious realization of just how devastating the disarming remarks or behaviors of children can be. There are, in fact, many times when the therapeutic space is threatened with collapse, sometimes simply by happenstance. Occasionally a child who has been profoundly involved in an intense symbolic process will abruptly exit the symbolic. The therapist must take care not to lose his/her grip on the situation.

Neil was an exceedingly bright four-year-old who had been grossly sexually abused by his biological father about a year previously. At the very first encounter Neil gave the impression that he had engaged in intense symbolically manipulative therapy all his life: he seemed to sense the purpose of the structure and contents of the playtherapy room, and he set about putting his world back together almost immediately.

If Neil had a good week in which he behaved in neither an aggressive nor an inappropriate sexual manner, he was allowed to play with the little Lego policeman during his hour—his therapist, of course, modulating the contents of that play. On this occasion, Neil blurted out immediately upon entering the office, "Do I get to play with the policeman?" His therapist glanced at Neil's mother, who gently but quickly indicated that it had not been a good week and then elaborated. "No," his therapist replied, "not today. And you know what? The policeman has been very sad that you behaved the way you did this week. In fact, he's been crying." Totally out of normal character, Neil looked at his therapist as if she were crazy. "Are you kidding!" exclaimed this four-year-old with a knowing smirk on his face. "That policeman can't cry—he's plastic!" Unruffled, his therapist replied, "You're right, Neil. The policeman is plastic—but he's still sad and he's still crying."

Bright children, especially, will often try—particularly after real frustrations in their lives—to poke a hole in the structure elaborated by the therapist. Such attempts to embarrass and frustrate the therapist are usually so spontaneous that they occasionally surprise the child himself. Many adult therapists, especially those who have worked in emergency rooms or large state hospitals, will be familiar with this kind of challenge from a patient. It is a kind of put-down that brings the patient a momentary and illusory sense of power, agency and control, and probably serves to counter his/her sense of impotence and embarrassment. Whether the patient is a child or an adult, the response must be the same: we must assume that "deep down inside" the patient knows that it is all illusory—unless our response grants them the power they have just claimed. If one utilizes the very behavior itself, most children will quickly reenter the symbolic—just as Neil did.

Ricky was a 13-year-old who had been left cerebral-palsied by a boating accident when he was six. He neglected his hygiene, allowed himself to underachieve in school and was generally overfamiliar and insolent to one and all. He was a veritable master at getting other people to do things for him.

One day while I (DMD) was working on something else, I heard a pounding on my office door. Opening it, I found Ricky, who didn't know whether to laugh or be disgusted. "You get in here and tell your wife to stop being so stupid," he ordered. "You tell her that that's not a TV; that's a window. And tell her to stop pretending it is!" I stepped around the corner from my office and found my wife, Ricky's therapist, literally sprawled out on a large arm chair, moving in a spastic manner and saying repeatedly, "I'm handicapped. Change the channel. I'm handicapped." I looked at the floor-to-ceiling windows which actually made up the end of the room and said, "That is a TV, Ricky. That's one of those huge projection TVs, so just go ahead and change the channel—she's handicapped, you know."

I smiled and returned to my office, closed the door and resumed my work. Ricky stopped using his handicap as a manipulative tool after that session, became more respectful in his interactions with us, and began to talk about how he felt about his condition, something he had previously hidden under the disrespect of helplessness.

An Exception to the "No Harm" Rule

Occasionally one will encounter children whose aggressiveness or self-injuriousness requires a significant change in technique. These are children who simply will not accept structure or who are willfully destructive of it. One cannot group them by traditional categorical diagnoses, for each child's relationship with the therapist and the space within which they meet is different in some way. These children view themselves, and are viewed by adults, as uncontrollable.

We have often thought of these children as "omnipotent powerless" children. The contradiction lies in the fact that these children, whose sense of personal power may be absolutely immense, do not know how to elicit genuine care and personal respect. Hence they try to coerce it from their environment through the exercise of power. We assume, however, that, as much as children may crave power and as addictive as it may be, deep down they do not really want it: it is simply too scary to have that much power as a child.

Seven-year-old Adele (discussed in detail in Chapter 8), for example, would not accept structure, rules, and boundaries at first because her own experience of a seizure-dominated world was one of chaos and intrusiveness; she wanted to hurt others and invade their space as much as she was hurt and invaded by her seizures. There was no way in which our therapeutic structure could contain her without a significant modification because she accepted no conventional boundaries whatsoever. Other children who have lived through experiences of intense, uncontrollable invasiveness (e.g., accidents, multiple and repeated invasive medical/surgical procedures) may be intensely disrespectful and destructive of the structure of the therapeutic space. This can, of course, include children who have lived through traumatic abuse, in which their physical or emotional space has been repeatedly or intensely invaded.

We use the cautionary expressions "may" and "can be" because most children—even those who have been horribly traumatized—are exquisitely sensitive to the subtle features of the therapeutic space and are relatively quick to accept the structure, rules, and boundaries which constitute it and which it defines. The objective intensity of lived trauma does not necessarily correlate with the intensity of the child's lack of respect for personal and emotional space and for defining structures. This is why we formulate our rule about proactive harm in the therapeutic space so strongly: if the clinician abandons the rule too quickly, he or she may fail to elicit the therapeutic compliance of many (categorically seriously disturbed or disruptive) children and thereby fail to perceive their genuine therapeutic aptness.

Occasionally, however, children refuse to enter the playtherapy room, run out, or try to disrupt or harm its contents or the therapist. These children cannot be contained and controlled by symbolic structure at first. If the child leaves, we assure safety and supervision but do not attempt physically to bring the child back to the playtherapy room. If the child is genuinely harmful, self-harmful or destructive, we continue to address the powerful emotional issues already identified during the history-taking but restrain the child physically. This is done firmly but gently, with never more pressure than is necessary to immobilize the child. It is surprising how often the simple exercise of restraint, without any real application of strength, suffices to calm the child. Such children want very much to be controlled in a benevolent manner, but they are intensely sensitive to loss of face. It is crucial that the therapist inform the parents of the course of events in a manner which does not embarrass the child, i.e., privately.

The need to restrain a child physically in the playtherapy room, while arising much less frequently than the need to stop a session, must be handled in the same manner, always conveying a sense of respect for the person and privacy of the child. This stance of gentle respect may be difficult for the clinician to maintain, for children can be disgustingly disrespectful and cruelly hurtful at times. It can, upon occasion, result in bites or bruises (we have received both), but the outcome is almost always satisfying. We view such behavior as a test of the therapist's caring, power, and commitment to the child. The need for such restraint rarely lasts more than a few sessions—and it can obviate the need for hospitalization, a frequent response to such "uncontrollable" children.

Jill was a 10-year-old whose life had been chaos as her mother went in and out of psychiatric hospitals. All of Jill's life her mother had been extremely violent and unpredictable. Parental battles over custody contributed to the sense of chaos and uncertainty. At one point Jill's mother came to town and picked her up at the baby-sitter's without father's knowledge. It was several years before Jill's father was able to locate her in another part of the country. After a final court battle following one of Jill's mother's many suicide attempts, permanent custody was awarded to her father. Several months after Jill's permanent arrival in her father's home, her mother was accidentally struck and killed by a car as she crossed a busy street. Jill had little reaction to her mother's death but was upset that she was not allowed to visit her grandparents at the time of the funeral.

Jill was brought to therapy by her father and stepmother because of constant cruelty and tantrums when she did not get her own way, even over the smallest things. Her tantrums lasted an hour at a time, during which she broke and threw things, screamed that she didn't care if she lived, that she hated her father, stepmother, and half-sisters, and that she wanted to go back to her grandparents, with whom she stayed each time her mother was hospitalized. She was intolerant of her younger half-sisters and alternated in her behavior toward them just as her mother had toward her: one moment she was nice and supportive; the next she was mean and threatening. Jill also still wet the bed.

From the moment she arrived at the clinic Jill was "in a bad mood" and made it perfectly clear that she didn't want to be here. She was oppositional and insulting and slapped her therapist when told that she would have to complete a task. This began a series of sessions in which Jill made herself as unpleasant and mean as she could, attempting to bite, kick, pinch and hit or run out of the playtherapy room. When Jill failed to respond to the many symbolic interventions that usually serve us well with even the most resistant children, it quickly became apparent that an exception to most of our operational "rules" had to be made if Jill were to remain in therapy. The challenge to both parents and therapists implicit in her behavior was obvious: "I won't even begin to trust you unless you can contain me—no matter how mean and disrespectful I am." Since Jill had repeatedly experienced her mother being sent away to the hospital for her "uncontrollable behavior" and threats of harm or self-harm, we assumed that Jill's behavior in therapy and at home was effectively a test to see if we or her father and stepmother would send her away as well. Her cruelty increased at home, until her stepmother said, with tears in her eyes, that she would have to move out if the behavior didn't improve because the two younger ones were becoming scared and starting to copy Jill's behavior. With support from the co-therapist, she persevered and redoubled her efforts to provide structure without vindictiveness. Both father and stepmother were very understanding of the chaos and horrors Jill had lived through for so many years.

Jill's behavior in therapy, while clearly an attempt to test the caring and commitment of her therapists, quickly began to take on post-traumatic features. Jill's reaction to her therapist became more and more out of proportion until it became outright fear. While restraining her, Jill's therapist told her, over and over, that she was testing because she had never seen her mother change or get better in spite of years of psychiatric treatment and hospitalization. She was also reenacting the scenes in which her mother would leave, threaten to leave, or trash the house.

As her behavior got worse in the playtherapy room it began to get better at home. Finally, after weeks of physically and emotionally exhausting sessions, Jill allowed herself to cry tears of sadness for the first time. At the end of the session she told her stepmother that she was walking the four miles home. Her stepmother chose wisely to keep the boundaries between the intense physical struggles in the playtherapy room and the verbal control of home very clear—and allowed her to walk. Jill arrived home two hours later. She demanded the clinic number and called, telling her stepmother she would never return to therapy. When the answering service asked her for her message, Jill hung up without saying a word. Her behavior was excellent that week. The next week Jill acknowledged in therapy that her mother had tried to kill her on several occasions and that she had been genuinely in fear for her life.

Although Jill's behavior certainly appeared to warrant and justify it, hospitalizing this 10-year-old would only have served to confirm her in her disastrous identification with her chronically ill and suicidal mother. In Jill's experience psychiatric hospitals were not places that made people better. Jill had attempted with incredible persistence to get us to reject her and, effectively, to label her as untreatable. When, after weeks of efforts in this direction, she failed to elicit any negative reactions from her therapists, especially from her female therapist, Jill finally allowed herself to risk investing in the personal relationships she wanted so badly.

This case also illustrates why the categorical assessment of the efficacy of psychotherapy as a treatment modality is so unproductive. Had we given up out of exhaustion or therapeutic pessimism only a few weeks earlier, we would never have seen the behavioral changes that followed.

Some Remarks on "Transference"

If one takes seriously the way in which children think, interact, relate and change, and if the structure, rules and boundaries which constitute the experience of the therapeutic space are genuinely important, then we must ask whether there is any role whatsoever for the promotion and utilization of "transference relationships" in psychotherapy with young children. Is there *any* rationale for the application of this concept, drawn from adult psycho-analysis, to the treatment of children? We contend that not only is there no justification, but that it is literally a clinical impediment and represents an extremely self-referent need on the part of the adult therapist to impose a rigid view of how people think, relate, and communicate on children.

There is no need to wait for a "transference relationship" to develop with a child patient. In fact, promotion of a transference relationship blurs the interpersonal boundaries and shakes the structures upon which the child counts to manage the therapeutic restructuring of his disordered or danger-ous world. The very notion of transference implies an interpretive therapeu-tic style. Transference interpretations, in turn, require of the child a con-scious acknowledgment of the therapist's presence at a therapeutically opportune moment—and this can kill the magic of the symbolic nature of the event. A transference interpretation made to a four-year-old, for exam-ple, represents an intrusion—not an aid. It transforms the poetically rich potential of such an epiphanous moment into the self-referent pedestrian tease by an adult who, in reality, can neither rescue the child nor change his world in a material way. (See Chapter 10 for examples.)

Worse yet, when the interaction which occurs in the playtherapy room is seen in transference/countertransference terms, the locus of agency can be-come confused for both child and therapist (as strikingly illustrated in the case of Billy's analysis in Chapter 10). It is not surprising, therefore, to see children who come from previous treatments which took a traditional child analytic approach or a strongly analytically influenced approach, begin a new therapeutic relationship extremely confused about boundaries. As one such nine-year-old said to us, "Aren't you going to say, 'you seem to be treating me like your father'?" While it may be important for the therapist to understand who's who in the child's "inner cast of characters" in order to be able to intervene, it is simply destructive of the therapeutic process to do a running commentary on it.

THE ROLE OF THE THERAPEUTIC SPACE IN MODIFYING THE TRAUMA RESPONSE

The psychobiological changes induced by both acute and chronic trauma are experience-induced changes. Just as experience can be physiologically formative, so can it be physiologically reformative. The highly structured nature of the therapeutic space is designed to utilize normative dissociation, to accept and contain pathological dissociation, and finally, to make significant modifications in the latter. The extent to which this can be accomplished depends upon the nature, consistency, and continuity of environmental support and collaboration, the flexibility of the child's use of reparative dissociative techniques, and the intensity of the therapeutic space.

Putnam (1987) notes that many children who appear seriously fragmented with altered personalities "actually seem to come back together when you remove them from their abusive environments." Similarly, Richard Kluft (1987), who has worked extensively with children with multiple personality disorder, has found that some children give the appearance of literally waiting for someone to present the simple key to reintegration or to the rejection of the other, punitive or bad personality. In the face of the apparent seriousness of the disorder, this potential for rapid change should encourage the therapist to take a therapeutically optimistic stance—even when presented with very disturbed and previously "nonresponding" patients.

While "traumatized children often have a heightened sense of vulnerability" (van der Kolk, 1987, p. 15), if this is viewed simply as a phenomenon to be dealt with, it need not necessarily be an impediment to either evaluation or treatment. The highly structured yet benevolent nature of the therapeutic space can elicit a sense of comfort and relief in extremely vulnerable children; this is both therapeutic and of significant diagnostic importance.

Modifying the Experience of Inescapable Shock

Van der Kolk and Greenberg (1987) raise an interesting question when they note that the animal model of inescapable shock, "the only biological model for a major psychiatric disorder," has, surprisingly, "been applied principally to depression [learned helplessness] rather than traumatization." The effects of exposure to inescapable aversive events they cite include (1) deficits in learning to escape novel adverse situations, (2) decreased motivation for learning new contingencies, (3) chronic subjective distress, and even (4) increased tumor genesis and immunosuppression. As we noted earlier, van der Kolk and Greenberg draw our attention to a distinction which is of paramount importance to the treatment of traumatized children. "The helplessness syndrome that follows inescapable shock is due to the lack of control," they note, "rather than to the shock itself—in fact, the behavioral and biochemical sequelae of escapable shock are just the opposite of those of inescapable shock" (p. 67). The "striking parallel between the animal response to inescapable shock and the human response to overwhelming trauma" is important because "the symptoms of hyper-reactivity (i.e., startle responses, explosive outbursts, nightmares, and intrusive recollections) in humans resemble those produced by chronic noradrenergic hypersensitivity following transient catecholamine depletion after acute trauma in animals" (pp. 67–68). We have seen that the behavioral effects of inescapable shock can be reversed by a process of "dragging through" in which the animal is literally dragged across an electrified grid into a non electrified area. Because this process "can even reverse some of the neurochemical changes due to inescapable shock," they see an applicability to humans: "therapists may have to perform the psychotherapeutic equivalent of dragging the patient into a non-electrified area; that is, actively encourage the patient to take action in order to reexperience control."

While many therapists can attest to some experience of success with this kind of forced "abreaction," we offer a slightly more complex, and less potentially dangerous, approach. The adult therapeutic model calls for something resembling a literal reliving of the actual trauma. Even should such an approach prove necessary, there are many other ways in which a genuinely therapeutic space can have a profound impact on the traumatized individual. Everything about the therapeutic space which elicits a feeling of being understood, contained, and cared for constitutes a microresolution of the sense of inescapability. Every experience which enhances a sense of control and agency (i.e., being an agent, not an object) also promotes resolution. It is this ambient sense of structure, rules, boundaries and benevolent control that allows for a therapist-initiated expression of anger to occur without provoking in the child a sense of profound dyscontrol, a sense of dyscontrol which often characterizes "ventilation therapies" that are not carefully grounded in a secure context.

Every potentially failable task in the playtherapy room, no matter how subtle, offers the child an opportunity for integrative mastery. We have a "cascade" toy in our playtherapy room (a series of rectangular pieces of wood held together by straps such that when one piece of wood is turned down against another and released, it creates the illusion of literally tumbling down to take its place at the bottom) which is often presented to a hurt or traumatized child toward the end of the first session. The positive effect of "mastering" our "magic trick" on the comfort, attitude and openness to interaction of a previously closed, constricted, resistant or angrily uncooperative child seems all out of proportion to the simplicity of the act. Over the last six years, not a single child, regardless of intelligence or sophistication, has exclaimed with indignation that the trick was "too simple" or that "anyone can do it." This is telling for the "trick" is obviously something at which the child cannot possibly fail, given the nature of the toy.

This simple toy brings a much-needed sense of agency to the child and, often, a real sense of pride when he shows it to the adult who brought him. The power of this demonstration is further enhanced by the fact that the adult must watch from outside the playtherapy room, since adults are not allowed to cross the threshold. Thus, this innocuous bit of play embodies four powerful experiences for the hurt child: a sense of mastery and personal pride, an almost bodily sense of structure, the experience of being able to control and delimit the behavior of a familiar adult ("You can't come in, only kids can!"), and a sense of potential environmental safety since "the rules" do not permit adults to enter the room. The complexity of the child's experience and (largely unconscious) attention to minute detail create a situation in which every positive integrative experience can provide a sense of potential resolution, thereby countering the pervasive sense of inescapability. Because inescapability for the child is defined psychologically and not just physically (even though trauma may have entailed physical inescapability), multiple opportunities for symbolic resolution are potentially present for the child (although not for the mouse).

The subtlety of these interactions highlights just how mistaken it can be to assume that dramatic, and often threateningly disruptive or dangerous, symptom behaviors (e.g., multiple personality, amnesias, fugue states, panic attacks, explosive rages or reenactments, crippling fear or phobias) require equally dramatic therapeutic interventions for real and lasting change to occur. Since pathological dissociation is a self-preserving psychophysiological maneuver at a moment of extreme stress (subjectively perceived inescapable shock), every experience which is perceived (=lived) by the child as an escape-equivalent offers a potential opportunity for resolution.

Because dissociative techniques may have been utilized and experienced — sometimes for years — as self-preserving by the traumatized child, forcing the child to become consciously aware of the escape-equivalence of experience can empty it of its therapeutic force, produce therapeutic compliance (empty change), or even alienate the child. Children have no difficulty in believing (knowing) that change occurring in a dissociative state is real. Only adults require conscious acknowledgment to know that such change is real.

One of the exasperating consequences of the dissociative style of abused children is that they often remember the abuse in one context but not in another. As Putnam (1987) notes, "This, of course, drives the legal authorities up the wall because they'll tell one person but they won't tell another person. I think people don't realize how much these children dissociate, how much they can access that memory at one point and then not be able to access it at another." If children can access traumatic experience only in certain settings (such as the playtherapy room), it makes good clinical sense to allow the reparative work to remain in those settings.

We see again how very important the distinction between the two types of shock is. It is experience, not conscious awareness, which is psychophysiologically formative. Therapists who structure the therapeutic relationship in this manner are building an experiential "foundation" which can support a conscious retrieval and reexamination of past traumatic events if and when it is appropriate to do so. For adults and some children conscious awareness may be a means by which they can structure reintegrative experience on their own; but it is rarely curative in itself. Many therapists have the cart before the horse: even for adults, experience must often lay the foundation for any useful conscious understanding. Asking a child or an adult to understand intellectually a security contradicted by experience not only can be futile but can actually worsen the clinical situation.

7

The Evaluation of Therapeutic Aptness

So averse to taking pains are most men in the search for truth, and so prone are they to turn to what lies readily at hand.

Thucydides

Any use of a human being, in which less is demanded of him and less is attributed to him than his full status, is a degradation and a waste.

Norbert Wiener, The Human Use of Human Beings

Therapeutic aptness is the child's ability to utilize the therapeutic space in a creative manner: operationally to recognize potential in the therapeutic encounter for communication and change. The key word here is *operational*: the child's ability to "recognize" the multifarious potentials of the therapeutic space is expressed behaviorally—not discursively. How the child uses the therapeutic space reflects that ability or its lack. Consequently, the assessment is an operational one. With definition in mind, we see that it does not really make sense to divide one's clinical approach into traditional phases such as diagnosis, treatment planning and treatment—all the more so since many first encounters will be last encounters, especially when clinicians do many one-time evaluations for schools or agencies. Since many clinical encounters are one-time encounters and every encounter is a potential therapeutic encounter, it can be persuasively argued that one would be morally and ethically hard-pressed to maintain a diagnosis/treatment dichotomy. Given the unusually high incidence (85%) of unilateral terminations (Novick, Benson, & Rembar, 1981), the therapeutic efficacy of the initial encounter or first short phase of treatment may be crucial in the lives of many children.

PLAY AND "PLAYING"

Behavioral Speech Acts and the Meaning of Behavior

A deceptively simple distinction from the philosophy of language contains a wealth of practical significance for psychology and psychiatry. The

144

distinction is that between *sentences* and *statements*, a distinction noted by a number of developmental linguists and, in particular, by philosophers of language, for example Linsky (1967) and Danto (1969). Without this distinction, it may be impossible to know what is meant (intended) by an utterance. Linsky's (1967) summary of P. F. Strawson's (1950) criticism of Bertrand Russell's idiosyncratic use of logic clarifies this distinction.

> Sentences have meaning, but they cannot be true or false. Rather a sentence which is not meaningless can be used to make statements, some true and some false. Truth and falsity characterize statements, not sentences. And if the statement presupposed by a given sentence is not true, then nothing true or false has been stated, although a significant sentence has been uttered. (p. 98)

In other words, a sentence—no matter how meaningful—has *truth-value* only if it is a statement; and it is a statement only if it has a referent. Thus, the sentence "The King of France is bald" is eminently meaningful but has no truth value: it is not a statement for there is presently no King of France.

Realizing the importance of this distinction is not just an "ivory tower" intellectual exercise. When, in the middle of the night, the psychiatrist on call at the local state hospital interviews a 30-year-old female patient with a history of three previous hospitalizations for "paranoid schizophrenia" and asks her the traditional mental status question "What does 'People who live in glass houses shouldn't throw stones' mean to you?" and hears, in turn, "There's glass up my ass and I think you're crass," he concludes that his patient has a "thought disorder." What she said, after all, "made no sense." Is he right? When that same psychiatrist asks another patient what his problem is and is told, "I think I'm Jesus Christ," is he again correct to conclude that his patient is suffering from delusions?

The answer is simply that he cannot be sure until he knows what those two patients meant. Bearing in mind that "speech acts" are acts which express the utterer's meaning (Grice, 1967)—not the listener's conventional assessment of adult-mode grammatical appropriateness—we may not be too surprised to learn that the 30-year-old "schizophrenic" had been repeatedly sexually abused (including anal penetration with glass decanter tops) and that the patient suffering from "delusions" did not actually believe himself to be Jesus Christ; he only "felt crucified" by the overwhelming, but momentary, burdens of his life. Had the on-call psychiatrist contextualized the verbal productions of his patients, that is, understood them in thecontext of their life-experience, he might have avoided categorical mislabeling; thus, he could have been one step closer to resolving the human problems which brought these individuals to the hospital.

A Semantics of Play

The distinction between statements and sentences has profound clinical (and research) significance for understanding and assessing the behavior of children. Sentences, remember, are meaningful utterances which may, or may not, be related to anything real. They have truth-value if they are, in fact, *statements* — if, that is, they have referents. Thus, the following little paradigm suggests itself.

$$\text{statement} \longrightarrow \text{play}$$
$$\text{sentence} \longrightarrow \text{playing}$$

This makes it much clearer why "free play" has no place in psychotherapy with children: it is effectively empty of semantic content. Furthermore, even if the child being observed were so symbolically apt as to be constantly involved in symbolically expressive play, it would still remain an extremely inefficient way of obtaining information about the child, his thoughts, thinking, emotions and life. Sentences, remember, have no truth-value; only statements do. Consequently, it makes little sense to watch children playing cars, playing house, playing teatime, etc. For our purposes, these are *empty* activities: they have no *content* with striking relevancy to the child's life. It makes no sense to allow children to wander aimlessly about a playtherapy room, waiting for them to "say" something meaningful. The following paradigm, however, is useful:

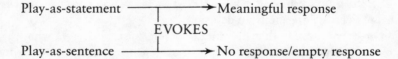

(Similarly, it makes no sense to allow adults in therapy to engage aimlessly in "free association," waiting for them to say something meaningful. Freud's followers have not yet realized that the free association method developed precisely because Freud did not know at first how to ask himself (or the patient) those questions which would be genuinely productive of veridical answers. Once he abandoned the so-called "seduction theory" which allowed him to realize the profound psychobiological effects of real trauma, free association as a technique was required in order *not* to come to the truth. Over time this "technique" has come to occupy the place that should have been filled by operational understanding.)

Semic Play and Ludic Play

We can now take our "semantics of play" a step further and refine our distinction a bit.

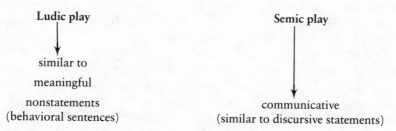

Ludic play

↓

similar to

meaningful

nonstatements
(behavioral sentences)

Semic play

↓

communicative
(similar to discursive statements)

Just as the psychiatrist must determine whether the patient's utterance is simply a meaningful sentence (with no real referents or truth-value) or a communicative statement in order to understand and respond in a helpful, problem-solving fashion, so, too, must the child therapist distinguish between *semic* and *ludic play*. Ludic play is much like a sentence: it is meaningful, logical, but it makes no statement. Ludic play is the empty play of playing house or playing cars.* Semic play, on the other had, is very much like discursive statements: it has referents and, therefore, potential truth-value.

The difference is easily seen. Consider, for example, a little girl "playing house." She takes the baby bottle, pretends to wash it and fill it with warm formula. She then feeds her baby doll. This is "just" playing, ludic play. It tells us nothing more than that she enjoys playing at the motherly activities she sees at home. On the other hand, if this same seven-year-old were to pretend to fill the baby bottle with scalding formula and to "accidentally" spill it on her baby doll, even the casual observer would recognize a "content" and would most likely be concerned with its implications.

To continue with our sentence-playing/statement-play distinction, what kind of response can one have to "The King of France is bald" when there is no King of France? The response will be word-play—whether it is recog-

---

*Because we tend to equate the ludicity of play (its particularly enjoyable nature) with play itself, we often fail to see that there are various kinds of play—ludic and semic play being the two most useful general categories. (Lest the reader think that we are disparaging the most traditional roles of play, let us indicate that this is not the case. Without ludic play there would be no human race as we know it: play serves numerous developmental, cognitive and social functions which are of utmost importance. The importance of ludic play cannot be underestimated. Still, this is not the object of our concern here. The reader interested in the multifarious aspects of play is referred to Fein and Rivkin (1986) and Rogers and Sawyers (1988).

nized as such or not. Similarly, the behavioral response to our seven-year-old's "playing house" will be the equivalent of word-play: meaningful and enjoyable, but of no therapeutic use. On the other hand, our behavioral response to the behavioral statement implicit in the scalding of the baby doll can be full of communicative possibilities. We can ask through play whether our seven-year-old has witnessed such "maternal" behavior or whether she has experienced it herself.

If we do not recognize and utilize the distinction between semic and ludic play—the distinction between behavioral sentences and behavioral statements—we lose the most powerful diagnostic and therapeutic tool in psychotherapy. And it must be remembered, as well, that communication, even complex detailed communication, does not require intent: the criminal who inadvertently leaves a multitude of clues does not necessarily intend to do so, nor is he aware of the process.

Communication and Speech

Most adults (even child therapists) still think that children must talk for their language abilities to be ascertained. But to oppose *language* and *communication* is to fail to realize that language must grow out of the dialectic of interactional mutuality (see Chapter 1). Thus, when we put child therapy squarely back into that context of interactional mutuality (which, obviously, cannot be the case when a child is allowed "free play" alone in a room), a wealth of therapeutic possibilities arises. Consequently, even before viewing the process in detail, we can safely begin to disagree with therapeutically pessimistic views, such as those that maintain that "psychotherapy with lower functioning children is difficult to justify" or that, for patients with diagnoses of psychosis or pervasive developmental disorders, psychotherapy "is a rational approach only in older patients (10 years or older) with communicative language, i.e., those with the best prognosis" (Adams & Fras, 1988, p. 364). As we shall see, therapeutic aptness must be determined individually with each child. One cannot categorically exclude a group, such as "autistic" children simply because they are "lowering functioning." In fact, not only is assessment of therapeutic aptness independent of *DSM* diagnoses, but a finding of genuine therapeutic aptness can significantly call into question a previously "firm" *DSM* diagnosis.

Communication Without Speech

The more intensely one is able to define one's therapeutic space, the greater the ability of therapy to facilitate the transition from *logic* to *elective*

assignment of meaning. Elective assignment refers to the (usually unconscious) assignment of meaning by the child to play which appears to be
caught in a rigid logical bind. Chris (see Chapter 2), whose intense identification with the dead and risen Christ locked him into a potentially fatal
logical bind, is a good example. The maneuver by which his therapist facilitated the reversal of his conviction that everyone was born with a penis and
that he was still in danger of losing his is another example of the facilitated
transition from the rigors of a meaningful logic without real-world truth-
value to an elective meaning with truth-value.

The therapist can offer, or even attempt to impose, a meaning upon
expressive, manipulative or even ruminative behavior, but such meaning
must be perceived and accepted by the child for there to be a genuine
assignment. It is *elective* in the sense that it allows for the development and
expression of a sense of agency on the part of the child and, as such, can be
immensely freeing. It constitutes, as it were, the cutting of the Gordian Knot
of the child's logical bind. This means that the therapeutic encounter has the
potential to free the child from the often paralyzing constraints of logic and
to effect a genuine cognitive restructuring. (It is not elective, however, in the
sense that the child must be consciously aware of the process.)

This, again, constitutes another reason to be wary of the evaluation/treat-
ment dichotomy. The following example not only illustrates the operational
facilitation of the transition from the bind of logic to the elective assignment
of meaning but also shows how a single brief intervention can shed light on
the child's ability to utilize the therapeutic encounter in an integrative manner.

George, who we first introduced in Chapter 4, was a severely disturbed
six-and-a-half-year-old still in a preschool class for three-year-olds. The
question asked by the referring Preschool License Board clinician was
whether George was "psychotic, brain-damaged, autistic or suffering
from a severe central processing disorder." In the course of taking the
history from George's father, we learned that nine days after his younger
brother was born two weeks prematurely, George's 23-year-old mother
had died suddenly and unexpectedly at home of a cerebral hemorrhage.
Three-year-old George had not been happy with the new baby his mother
had brought home from the hospital.

After considerable disorganized behavior which seemed to indicate
that he did not, in fact, understand the spoken commands and questions
of his examiner, George assembled a bizarre, distorted Lego object. It
appeared to be some sort of vehicle, although it had no clear front or
back and had six wheels going in various directions. When George took

his hand away from the strange-looking object his examiner reached over and quickly disassembled it, saying only, "It's dead." After a moment of apparent disorientation, George reassembled the pieces into two smaller vehicles with clearly defined fronts and backs and the wheels all properly oriented.

This single response, in the midst of otherwise grossly disorganized behavior, was seen as reflecting both this child's serious *psychological* disturbance — as opposed to the obligatorily disordered behavior indicative of brain dysfunction — and his capacity to respond in an integrative fashion to carefully formulated clinical interventions. The resulting therapeutic optimism was rewarded by significant positive change over the next two years, including a 30+point rise in measured I.Q. and a transition from the three-year-old preschool class to an Emotionally Handicapped public school placement followed by increasing mainstreaming into normal classes.

George had simply "shut down" in an autistoid fashion following his mother's death. Once he began talking coherently again he spent several weeks in therapy repeating obsessively, "I got mad at my mommy and she died," although there were no references to either her death or his sense of responsibility at home or at school. His examiner's one intervention, accompanied by the solemn statement "It's dead," permitted the beginning of a transition from the logical bind of having successfully wished his mother dead to a conviction that he and his brother (represented by the smaller coherent cars) would survive. The meaning of the object he had constructed was radically altered by his examiner's intervention, thereby providing a first therapeutic "out" while simultaneously permitting an assessment of this child's ability to utilize the therapeutic process. (See Chapter 9 for the completion of the case and the horrifying bind his younger brother found himself in when he was cognitively able to grasp the significance of his premature birth in relation to the time of his mother's death.)

OPERATIONAL ASSESSMENT OF THERAPEUTIC APTNESS

Dividing play into semic and ludic varieties and then making further operational subdivisions of these two major types facilitates a rational approach to the assessment of the child's ability to use the therapeutic space which can be illustrated diagrammatically. The operational concept is really an "if . . . , then . . . " approach to assessment, although the "if's" and "then's" are not expressed as such. Both clinicians and teachers may find this a useful way to express one important aspect of play.

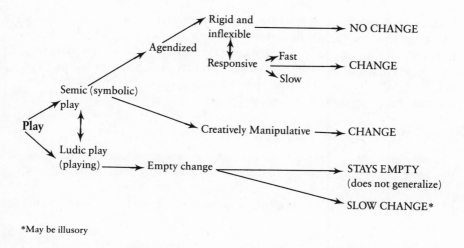

Figure 2. An operational assessment of "play"

Using the young child as our prototypical model, what questions must be answered operationally in order to permit a genuine assessment of therapeutic aptness? Among other things, we want to know if the child's symptom behavior is meaningful and, if so, is it potentially communicative? Does it represent an attempt to make sense of a confusing real-world situation or to solve a (perceived) problem—even if the resulting behavior is realistically maladaptive? Is the behavior responsive, amenable to change? Is it slow or fast to change? Is brilliant therapeutic aptness hidden beneath a veneer of apparent gross pathology, etc.?

Ideally, these questions can be both "asked" and "answered" during the first (evaluation) encounter, just as they were in the preceding example. Sometimes, however, they must be asked and re-asked a number of times before any rational assessment of therapeutic aptness and clinical prognosis can reasonably be entertained. Note that while it is perfectly reasonable quickly to entertain therapeutic optimism, it is not only unreasonable but possibly disastrous to jump quickly to therapeutic pessimism.

As we saw in Chapter 5, it should be kept in mind that the child who enters the playtherapy room has been primed by the initial encounter during which identities and problems have been operationally stated as the therapist has taken the history and listened to both the parents' and the child's concerns. Consequently, what occurs during the child's evaluation interview is at least potentially a response to what has preceded: a context has already been created in which to interpret (read "understand"—not "assign stock meanings to") the child's behavioral communications. In fact, the child's response during the initial history-taking may have already given strong indications of his or her openness to therapy. Although one may feel that the child's initial behavior has already given an answer, one must still begin with the most basic question: can this child play or "just play"?

Semic Play or Ludic Play?

Many children will recognize the intense symbolic potential of the play-therapy room immediately upon entering. This is easily seen in their almost reverent treatment of the space. Usually, however, one must ask whether the play the child engages in—even in a structured space—is ludic play or semic play.

> Mark, the seven-year-old son of divorced parents, whose father had been quite violent prior to abandoning the family, had been expelled from several private schools and was now being considered for the Emotionally Handicapped class in his new public school. Once the transition to the floor and the toys had been made, Mark was presented with the family dolls. After she made the father doll treat the rest of the family quite meanly, Mark's examiner had the boy doll leave for school. "How does he feel?" she asked Mark. "Let's play Legos," he replied as he moved to empty the box.
>
> Mark's initial drawing of "a house" and "the people who live in that house" had been equally devoid of human narrative content. "I like to play cars," he said as he drew what appeared to be a gas station. Mark drew cars parked in front of the house in which the people were supposed to live—but no sign of life was to be seen in the cars or in or around the house.

Much of this child's initial session continued to be devoid of content that related to events in his life. Granted, the emptiness of his spaces was symbolically expressive of the degree to which he felt himself to be isolated from persons—but nothing in his productions was indicative of therapeutic aptness. (It should be stressed that symbolic expression and the ability to effect—or accept—symbolic change are two very different things.) The bleak emptiness of Mark's first session had profound prognostic significance: years later, after failed attempts at a wide variety of interventions in a wide variety of therapeutic settings, Mark had not changed.

A striking contrast can be seen in the following first session with an adolescent.

Joe was a 16-year-old black high school student whose school-requested evaluation was somewhat of a mystery since he had already been permanently expelled for assaulting two teachers, a counselor and an administrator. Joe was an awesome sight. Big and muscled, he looked like an NFL lineman. During the initial history-taking with his mother present, however, Joe had taken out of his wallet a yellowed newspaper article about his best friend, who had died in a tragic car accident a year and a half previously. This he did spontaneously just after questions were asked about the family structure. In response to these questions it emerged that Joe's parents were not married. Not only did his father, who was relatively well-off and lived only a few blocks away, not contribute to his care but he also refused to acknowledge Joe as his son despite the fact that this was common knowledge in the neighborhood.

Once the drawings were done inside the playtherapy room, while Joe was still seated at the rather small child's table, his examiner took out the black family dolls, and put aside all but the father and baby doll. She then set the baby doll in the middle of an empty floor and threw the father doll behind the couch. "That dad won't even pay attention to the baby. How does that baby feel," she asked Joe. "Bad — and sad," he said, looking down at the floor and very dejected.

It was fascinating to note that school personnel were quite scared of this adolescent; after all, he had been expelled for assaulting adults. And yet not one reference to any hostility toward females could be found in the record. Joe had, in fact, done quite well in school sports — as long as the adult supervision was collegial and supportive. His problems occurred only when adult *male* supervision was dictatorial and patronizing.

The questions Joe's examiners asked him about family structure had elicited a touching display of affection for a friend who had died in an accident — when they could just as well have elicited an angry, off-putting, or otherwise negative response. This was taken to be a good first potential sign of treatability. It also served as the basis for his therapist's clinical judgment that it would be appropriate to "speak to the child" in Joe in the privacy of the playtherapy room portion of the evaluation. In fact, it was on seeing Joe's gentle sentimentality that his therapist decided to use the playtherapy room and bypass the office where she often saw adolescents. His subsequent response to the use of the black family dolls indicated not only an openness to symbolic play, but also a further willingness to share his emotional vulnerability, sense of shame ("bad") and sadness ("and sad"), and a lack of embarrassment over childlike feelings. This huge, powerful adolescent was very much at home sitting on the floor of our playtherapy room. Ironically, what was hard to assess here was not the therapeutic aptness of the patient but the therapeutic sensitivity of the adult environment and its willingness to change. Sadly, the environment continued to see Joe in terms of his categorical behavior ("he did assault school personnel, you know . . . ") rather than in terms of his impressive therapeutic responsiveness.

VARIETIES OF SEMIC PLAY

"Agendized" and Creative Play

Just as there was an absence of mutuality in Mark's "play," there was striking mutuality in the "play" between Joe and his examiner in the previous example. Not all semic (symbolic) play has this attribute of mutuality—or of mutability. Semic play can be intensely and creatively manipulative: some children give the impression that they have done nothing in life but wait for the opportunity to put together the symbolic "pieces" of their shattered lives.

Other children give the impression of being "stuck." These children present play that is "agendized." This play has symbolic content but is stereotyped and repetitive. It may be striking in its stereotypy or it may be quite subtle. In either case, it tends initially to be unresponsive to symbolic structuring.*

Sue was a five-year-old who was known to have been abused at home. In the playtherapy room she was in constant motion, setting down toys as soon as she picked them up. She did not respond in the first session to any structured use of the family dolls; rather, she kept repeating, "take the clothes off, take the clothes off" as she repeatedly attempted to do so. There was no cogent response on Sue's part to a multitude of very different interventions.

In this child's case the long-term physical and sexual abuse had taken a considerable toll—both cognitively and emotionally. While this first encoun-

---

*We realize that some readers may be uncomfortable with the term *agendized*. A number of other possibilities, such as *stereotyped, programmed, scripted*, suggest a volitional component which is not always, or even usually, present. *Traumatic play* (Terr, 1981) can be agendized. On the other hand, not all agendized play is, strictly speaking, [post] traumatic play. Wanting to avoid suggesting a particular origin for the psychological and behavioral content, we decided that the relative awkwardness of the present term presented less of a problem than the suggestiveness of the alternatives.

ter was useful in validating the seriousness of this child's disturbance (and thereby the need for the involvement of Social Services, Child Protection Team, Guardian ad Litem and law enforcement), it could not adequately assess her ability to use the therapeutic setting. It is important to note that this child's repetitive, nonresponsive behavior did *not* constitute obvious or obligatory grounds for inpatient treatment, for many children simply cannot attend and reorganize cognitively in an adaptive instrumental fashion while they are subject to (the gross or subtle) disorienting physical and/or sexual abuse. Hospitalization at this point would be a safety—rather than a clinical—tactic. While her behavior in the playtherapy room did not change significantly for weeks, it did change eventually, and when her safety and security were assured it underwent an astounding change.

Varieties of "Agendized" Play: Responsive

Although the child in the previous illustration was slow to change, she did change. She was able to use the therapeutic process in a most creative fashion when the chronic trauma was removed from her life. Intense, but patient, consistent, and nondiscursive therapy can effect powerful cognitive and affective changes in children like Sue. Such children must often proceed in serial stepwise fashion, building structure upon firm cognitive structure. Seen in this light, it is perhaps not surprising that the relative disorder and confusion of an inpatient environment containing many seriously disturbed children, while often thought of as more "intensive" treatment than "mere" outpatient therapy, can often slow the very process of assessing—or assuring—a child's ability to change. Multiple shifts per day and the unavoidable lack of staff consistency and continuity, as well as the unpredictability of other seriously disturbed children in the environment, may actually dilute both the diagnostic and therapeutic power of such a setting. Such an environment can unwittingly reinforce the addiction to trauma which is increasingly recognized as playing a major role in post-traumatic pathology (van der Kolk, 1987).

Just as Sue provided us with an example of responsive agendized play which was slow to change, Ellie provides an example of responsive agendized play which is quick to change.

Ellie was a six-year-old who behaved consistently like a dog when around family and friends and who clearly believed that her anger at her new little brother had resulted in the family's male dog's disappearance. (It ran away, only to be replaced by another male dog). When first seen in psychiatric evaluation, Ellie refused to talk and would only bark. She postured like a dog, licked her lips like a dog, panted, and even licked her father's hand. She entered the office from the waiting room on all fours and moved to the playtherapy room on all fours.

Ellie refused to do the drawings requested of her and evidenced only a dog's interest in the contents of the playtherapy room until her examiner offered her "a saucer of milk"—and then brought out the family dolls. "You say you love me," Ellie's examiner had the little girl doll say to her parents, "and yet what do you do? You go to the hospital and bring home a little boy! And you keep getting boy dogs and give away the girl dogs! You really like boys better—not girls!" Ellie barked ferociously *at* her examiner for the first time. She then said calmly, "I'm magic, you know. Watch . . . I can make things disappear." Ellie took a Kleenex and placed it over the baby boy doll she had previously ignored. Picking it up with the Kleenex covering it, she said, "I can make things disappear—forever."

Here we see the transition from the tyranny of *logic* to the potential freedom of *elective assignment of meaning*. Ellie's behavior changed abruptly in response to her examiner's simple statement of (one aspect of) the problem as she understood it: Ellie had wished not to have a little brother because she felt that her parents would prefer a boy. Her response to the intervention not only confirmed her examiner's play-statement but also constituted *an entry into semic play* when she barked at her examiner. (Again, we see that it is the behavior of the child which confirms or disconfirms the assignment of meaning—not a discursive acknowledgment or admission.)

Varieties of "Agendized" Play: Nonresponsive

Can a child's play ever be so rigid, repetitive, and stereotyped that it is categorically inaccessible to a transformational intervention? By this we do not mean "can stereotyped play be extinguished or suppressed?" We think such categorical inaccessibility is unlikely, for such a child would be extraordinarily bizarre—to the point of being effectively a nonperson (persons being essentially responsive beings). But there are, nonetheless, conditions under which play can become "agendized" to the point of being functionally nonresponsive—just as other behaviors can become functionally nonresponsive (as in the chronically hospitalized catatonic, for example). Here the determining factors appear to be time and the ability to effect real changes in the child's (or the adult's) environment. Consider first environment:

Art was a five-year-old who was hospitalized because of paralyzing terror which appeared to be induced, or accompanied, by hallucinations and because of very dangerous suicidal behavior. Art's response to therapy was extremely integrative and adaptive while he was in the hospital and his overt psychotic behavior disappeared within days. Themes of sexual abuse began to appear in Art's play and he eventually stated that he had been sexually abused by his father. During that period of time when it appeared that there was going to be a genuine resolution of the abuse, Art's behavior and play became more complex, more integrative and more adaptive. Then, suddenly, Art began to "just play" in therapy and all themes related to his life disappeared from the sessions. It was subsequently learned that Art's father feared a widening of the police investigation to include other crimes, such as child pornography and drug-trafficking, and had begun to put constant pressure on Art to say nothing.

This child's play remained symbolically empty and he was lost from treatment, as frequently happens when parents flee the law. It was strikingly obvious that he had become acutely aware that his therapist could "read" his play. This appears to have been a *conscious* realization in this very bright child. The guardedness which appeared in his demeanor was very different from the early lack of specific content. There is little doubt, however, that the content would have returned to Art's play had the greater environment been able to convince Art that his safety and security were assured.

Although initially it appears to reflect a genuine inability to respond, nonresponse can also be due to a need for consistent experience over time:

Dorothy was a patient confined to the "back wards" of a state mental hospital. Her chart had contained a diagnosis of "schizophrenia, catatonic type" for nearly 20 years. With the rare exception of an outburst of disordered agitation, Dorothy lay on her bed motionless day after day, her only responsive movements being to swallow the food she was spoon-fed at meals. When taken to the bathroom, Dorothy would sit for hours on the toilet if the staff did not return her to her bed. Struck by this pattern, a concerned and curious psychiatric resident had made a habit of spending an hour a day at Dorothy's bedside. During this time he often talked to her about the few biographical facts to be found in her chart or occasionally read, interrupting his reading every now and then to let her know that he was still very much by her side. The resident had just about given up expecting any response from Dorothy when, toward the end of the habitual hour one day, Dorothy almost imperceptibly edged her left hand over to his and softly touched his fingers. "I thought you had given up on me," she said quietly, still staring ahead, "until I realized that it was the weekend—and you never come on weekends."

A few more days with no response and this still enthusiastic and idealistic psychiatric resident might well have concluded that there would be no response from this "catatonic schizophrenic." Only when the experience of a caring presence had been experienced so consistently—and for what was obviously a long enough time—did this woman *risk* communicating directly with another human being. The story which subsequently emerged of the absolutely devastating rejection she had experienced as a child made that fear of risking such contact understandable.

THE USE OF PREVIOUS TREATMENT HISTORY IN THE ASSESSMENT OF THERAPEUTIC APTNESS

The Effect of Nontherapeutic Interventions on Semic Play

A first clinical encounter with a particular child for a given clinician may not be the first such encounter for the child. In fact, it is not at all uncommon to see children in evaluation who have had a number of prior treatments and possibly even many evaluations. It is important to have some idea of what occurred in previous evaluations or therapies, for the child's past experience may affect the way he or she enters upon the present encounter.

Not infrequently one will meet children whose previous therapists simply did not know what to do with them. (For example, many parents have told us about therapists who repeatedly did little more than play video games with their child.) In such cases the result may be that (potential) symbolic play meets an empty environment. Perhaps the most common instance of this situation can be seen in the multiply-tested school child—the child, for example, who is assessed repeatedly for "learning disabilities" when the problem is of a very different nature. What happens to such a child if his/her disorganization, underachievement, inattention, or poor conduct is the result of very real life events?

Many clinicians can look back on their past experience and remember such children whose behavior worsened over the years until they became frankly aggressive while the basic "response" of the environment was to test and re-test. Nonresponse can be enraging or disorienting; it may even precipitate a psychotic decompensation. Yet little was made of the child's life-context—perhaps a traumatic loss or a catastrophic experience occurring just prior to the initiation of the testing. This can be expressed diagrammatically:

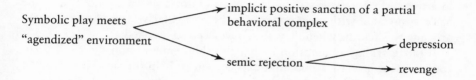

Symbolic play meets
an empty environment ——→ enraged depression ←——→ retaliatory behavior
                                                    → self-destructiveness
                                                    ↘ psychotic decompensation

Equally disastrous can be the encounter of semic play with an "agendized" environment. "Agendized" here has the same meaning as it does above in "agendized play." Some therapists have "stock" responses to categorically perceived problems. This, too, can be expressed diagrammatically:

Symbolic play meets   → implicit positive sanction of a partial
                                behavioral complex
"agendized" environment
                                                            → depression
                             → semic rejection ←——————
                                                            → revenge

One of the most common instances of this can be seen in stereotyped responses to, and advice about, the aggressive behaviors of children. An example can be seen in this "Coping with Kids" advice column from the *St. Petersburg Times*. The headline reads "When temper tantrum turns into scene it's time to teach child alternative behaviors." The "alternative behaviors" suggested by the columnist are typical of those we have seen used by child therapists.

> Dispel the anger physically by punching a pillow, wetting a washcloth and hitting it against the bathtub, stomping her feet outside or in the basement, throwing sponges against the side of the house, etc. Be creative together and devise other acceptable ways to express anger physically" (Alpert, 1987).

Far from helpful, this kind of advice constitutes both an implicit and explicit *positive sanction of a partial behavioral complex* which is now reinforced — not resolved. These children almost inevitably worsen in their behavior and frequently there is a generalization to other contexts, such as neighborhood or school. The logic is pristinely simple: this constitutes permission to be aggressive. As we indicated previously, it derives from what should now be the superannuated Helmholtzian notion that one needs to "dispel the anger physically."

There is a further complication in this kind of counter-therapeutic advice.

In the example cited the reasons for the temper tantrums of this mother's five-year-old daughter were never even questioned: they were simply acontextual. But the proposed means of resolution was highly contextual. The suggested substitute objects for this child's anger are all things which are loaded with meaning for a five-year-old: her pillow, her washcloth and tub, and her house. As one would expect when one keeps the logic of children's thinking in mind, the parent who follows such advice may next complain that the child resists bedtime and has trouble sleeping, won't attend to personal hygiene, and is disrespectful of family property. The parent, of course, does not realize that this is exactly what was set up by the "therapeutic advice" received from the previous therapist (or from columnists): paradoxically (but perfectly logically), things worsened instead of getting better. In a word: do not expect a child to sleep comfortably on a pillow he or she has just invested with great anger or to be particularly fond of taking baths or using washcloths when they, too, have been so invested.

If our working assumption is that the child enters upon the clinical encounter with at least a potential expectation of help (because that is what psychiatrists, psychologists and other "helping professionals" are for), then it is only reasonable to expect that a child whose symbolic communications go unheard is likely to be upset: angry or sad. The more often this occurs, the more potentially hostile and depressed the child (or adolescent, or adult, for that matter) can become. In the worst of circumstances, an "agendized" nonresponse to genuine communication and need can result in homicidal or suicidal behavior.

Perhaps the most grievous error in the psychotherapeutic treatment of children is the failure to recognize and mobilize health in the midst of what may otherwise appear to be gross pathology. While one cannot conclude, as we saw in the case of five-year-old Sue, that a lack of therapeutic aptness in the first encounter ensures (or even makes likely) a poor therapeutic prognosis, we can usually safely conclude that the ability of a child to utilize the first encounter in a creative fashion suggests a good prognosis—no matter how severely disturbed the child may have appeared prior to that time. An intensely positive therapeutic evaluation may not only demonstrate a previously unrecognized potential for adaptive behavior in some children but also obviate the need for hospitalization in certain cases.

8

The Hurt and "Broken" Child

Sticks and stones can break my bones, but words can kill.
A ten-year-old

A theme that will run through the rest of this book is that of the interpretation of experience and the contextual generation of meaning can have profound psychobiological consequences. We saw many of the cognitive, affective, and physiological consequences of trauma in Chapter 1 without identifying them as such. Those consequences were seen in terms of the categorical "inabilities" revealed by a Piagetian view of abused, traumatized, learning disabled, and psychiatrically disturbed children. However, to list the "effects of trauma" at this point would be most inconsistent with our developmental-contextual approach; rather, we prefer to discover them, as it were, in the process of trying to understand the development of disorders such as "learning disabilities," handicap or seizures, and the nature of the child's experience when categorical labels are peeled away. This, after all, is the task of the child therapist who would bring a genuine problem-solving approach to therapy. Although the major sections in this chapter deal with experiential and traditional diagnostic categories, the therapist's challenge is to see through the categories to the highly personal world of the individual child.

THE NATURE OF TRAUMA

Trauma is usually thought of as something strikingly out of the ordinary. When it is, it is easily recognized: brutal physical attacks, confinement abuses such as binding and gagging or imprisonment, or violent rape. These are experiences easily recognized as gross, terrifying, overwhelming, shattering, or unbearable. Sexual abuse, the most familiar form of trauma today, can be grossly traumatic — or it can appear to be "loving," "gentle," subtle. As such, it may not be recognized by the victim as something fearsome or even wrong, yet it can be extraordinarily traumatizing.

According to *Webster's New Collegiate Dictionary* (1961), trauma is "an injury, wound, shock, or the resulting condition," a definition echoed in 1970 by a standard psychiatric dictionary (Hinsie & Campbell, 1970): trauma is "an injury, something hurtful." Since we are not attempting to create a new category but rather to understand the effects of experience, we accept the simple and broad definition of trauma as *something hurtful*. Hence, many experiences can be traumatic, as we have already had occasion to see. Because trauma can be subtle as well as gross and terrifying, its effects can range from subtle cognitive skewing to gross psychobiologic change — or even death.

Regardless of form, all trauma is in some way unassimilable. For example, while most caseworkers and adoptive parents fear the anticipated "traumatic" effect of disclosure of adoptive status by a third party on the adopted child, and therefore attempt to "immunize" the child against the supposed "trauma" by forced early disclosure, few parents and professionals recognize the intensely subtle and potentially traumatizing effect of the "two mother dilemma" and the obligatory equation of love and abandonment (or even worse) on cognitive development brought about by early disclosure. Many experiences can be traumatic: abuse, neglect and mistreatment; divorce, alcoholism and parental illness or handicap; death of family members; the abandonment — often the repeated abandonment — of the adopted child, the child in foster care, or the "orphan." Some experiences that are rarely thought of as traumatic (or never even thought of at all), such as the miscarriage of a twin, can play traumatizing roles in the lives of children. Even apparently innocuous "family secrets" can be powerfully traumatic and deformative.

Blocks to the Recognition of Trauma

There are two blocks to the recognition of traumatic experience: the attitude of society in general toward children and the perception of the child by psychology and psychiatry. Although the former doubtless plays a significant role in the development of the latter, it is worthwhile considering them separately, for the child therapist will have to face each to be genuinely successful in the treatment of hurt children.

It is easy to look back and see the historical treatment of children as chattel and the objects of abuse. Contemporary literature on abuse often begins with just such a retrospective glance (Schetky & Green, 1988; Williams & Money, 1980) and the title of one introductory chapter by noted historian of childhood Lloyd deMause (1980) sums up how much society has supposedly changed: "Our forebears made childhood a nightmare." What is more difficult is to see, however, is society's continued negative view of children. For the clinician who would understand the real worlds of children, *The History of Childhood* (deMause, 1974) is required reading.

We live in a society steeped in contradictions: revulsion and moral outrage at child abuse, especially sexual abuse, and yet a monstrous hesitancy to recognize its prevalence. Ours is a society which both cherishes the child and collects Garbage Pail Kids trading cards. It is a society of contradictions in which "crib death" is a subject for neighborhood coffee get-togethers and television talk shows, and yet the medical literature takes several years before acknowledging research strongly suggesting that "crib death" may be far more than an idiopathic physiological disorder. During a presentation to the medical staff of a large metropolitan hospital, we pointed out that a multi-year study of sudden infant death syndrome (SIDS) in the District of Columbia (Luke, 1978), found that over 50% of the deaths occurred under conditions of bed-sharing, a finding which clearly called into question all the previous research on physiological causes. After our presentation a physician, who had served for eight years as a forensic pathologist for one of our largest cities, came up and said that she was astounded. "I had always thought crib deaths occurred in bed," she said, and went on to describe a case of identical twins who died of SIDS. At the very best, we replied, she had had one bona fide case of SIDS—and one infanticide. At worst, she had probably had a case of double infanticide. (What, after all, is the statistical likelihood of twins, even identical twins, dying during the same hour of exactly the same cause? Unless, of course, the cause was external?) As much as our society is fascinated by pain and talks of making it better, it is reluctant to see its own Garbage Pail view of children.

Such reluctance can be a powerful motivator when we choose our clinical approaches. It can be so insidious that we barely recognize it, so insidious that it makes it easy to accept the categorical myopia characterizing the field. Rather than learning from children how trauma hurts, we look for new categories of disorder. The following example, drawn from current child and adolescent sexual abuse research literature, illustrates well the need to look away from the problem by looking for categories of dysfunction.

Child psychiatry has been interested in the effects of sexual abuse and in establishing whether victims exhibit a unique symptom typology that can be characterized as a "Sexually Abused Child's Disorder" (Corwin, 1985). The idea grew with such magnitude that in 1985 a national summit conference on diagnosing child sexual abuse was held with the goal of developing the diagnosis and proposing it for inclusion in *DSM-III-R*. Although the concept was eventually rejected, empirical data was lacking to support or refute such a diagnosis.

To date, the psychiatric effects of child sexual abuse are only vaguely understood because of the myriad of complexities inherent to child sexual abuse research (Conte, 1985). [. . .] The majority of cases examined did not present symptomatology attributable to a psychiatric disorder. Victims who did have a *DSM-III* clinical syndrome were experiencing a variety of difficulties, including anxiety disorders and adjustment disorders. The range in levels of dysfunction suggests that a "Sexually Abused Child's Disorder" (Corwin, 1985) would in fact be inappropriate, as no common attributes or symptom clusters emerged for these children. The absence of a single psychiatric profile for victims of intrafamily child sexual abuse makes the evaluation of victims more difficult, as particular *DSM-III* criteria for identifying abuse and characteristics of victim's problems do not exist. (Sirles, Smith & Kusama, 1989)

The psychiatric effects of child sexual abuse are "only vaguely understood" not "because of the myriad of complexities inherent to child sexual abuse research," but, rather, because we mistakenly look to research and, consequently, fail to learn from that which is right before our very eyes. A search for categories—no matter how sophisticated the methods and the "data"—is not likely to find real children and their real-world experience, any more than a momentary "snapshot" view of an alleged abuser interacting with his child is likely to uncover a history of abusive behavior (Starr, 1987 cited in Froning, 1988). Thus, our failure to see as worrisome society's intense fascination with Garbage Pail Kids (reflecting our view of the child as a filthy monster) and with the "adoptable" Cabbage Patch Kids dolls (reflecting our tacit admission that the child is homeless within society) makes it easy to accept categorical approaches to diagnosis and treatment that are essentially devoid of contextually relevant human content.

A Not-So-Subtle Hostility Toward Children

We must now add a not-so-subtle hostility toward children on the part of the very professionals who should be assuring the child's safety and well-being. A striking example can be seen in the widespread tendency to disregard significant psychological and medical evidence of sexual abuse occurring during visitation with a biological parent. Sugarman and Kuehnle (1987, cited in Froning, 1988) found that 74% of the time allegations of sexual abuse were disbelieved by child protective service workers in spite of—not for lack of—the evidence. Yet research from the Association of Family and Conciliation Courts (Thoennes & Pearson, 1987) indicates that only 6% of allegations of sexual abuse made in the context of custody disputes is deliberately fabricated, a figure which is remarkably consistent.

> The five studies reviewed here [Faller, 1988; Jones & McGraw, 1987; Goodwin et al, 1979; Horowitz et al, unpublished 1984; Peters, 1979] and this study are consistent in suggesting a false allegation rate of between 2 and 8% among child and adolescent reports of sexual abuse. [. . .] the consistency of false allegation rates across studies is remarkable—especially given the diverse samples, the wide variation in evaluation procedures, and the differing professional backgrounds of the evaluators. [. . .] However, perhaps the most striking finding is evidence for what could be labeled an "eye of the beholder" phenomenon among a number of CPS workers. Specifically, these data suggest that a *subset* of CPS workers are predisposed against believing child or adolescent claims of having been sexually abused. As a result, these workers are likely to interpret ambiguous or inconsistent evidence as proof that the child's report is false, even though a more benign interpretation of the evidence in regard to the child's veracity may be equally compelling.
>
> The bias against believing the reports of children could be seen in the greater expectations of children lying and lower substantiation rates relative to peers among CPS workers in the False Reports subgroup. This bias was also apparent in the failure to question the validity of retractions of the child's allegation, despite obvious evidence of pressure or coercion to recant. It could also be seen in the incomplete or insensitive manner in which some investigations were conducted, the reliance on simplistic assessments of alleged perpetrators, and the confusion of the existence of a possible motive as proof of, rather than a possible explanation for, a false allegation. In its extreme, this bias could be seen in one CPS worker's adamant denial of the validity of a 9-year-old's allegation despite the perpetrator's admission of guilt and subsequent imprisonment. (Everson & Boat, 1989, pp. 234–235)

The failure of protecting agencies to protect, in spite of compelling evidence of harm to children and of their continuing vulnerability, constitutes a veritable societal attack on children (Rothenberg, 1980). The need not to see what we do to our children only serves to reinforce our commitment to depersonalized categorical approaches. Given this incredible blindness to the obvious, is it any wonder that we fail to see the full range of hurt in the lives of children? Only such blindness could allow for psychiatric research to categorize incest of four months' duration as "brief" (Krener, 1985) or fail to see the potential legal ramifications of such categorization (Donovan, 1989b; Donovan & McIntyre, 1985).

PHYSICAL AND SEXUAL ABUSE
Resolving the Sense of Guilt and Badness

Because of their self-referent and egocentric nature, children tend to treat experience as if everything happens to them, for them, by them, and because of them. This normal tendency is complicated by the abused child's forced physiological complicity in an experience that he or she would probably never have sought spontaneously. Unlike being robbed or beaten, being sexually abused elicits a mixture of emotional and physiological reactions, usually experienced as pleasurable, that can make the victim feel as if his or her body "wants" what is happening. The robbed and the beaten have no such experience unless the beating goes on interminably and begins to "feel like home." Even though abuse is initiated by the usually older and bigger person, the child or adolescent feels bad, dirty, and humiliated by what has happened, as if the responsibility were his. One of the first tasks of therapy is to facilitate the removal of this sense of guilt and badness. Usually, the clarification of responsibility and the cleansing of the self can begin in the very first encounter.

Twelve-year-old Jimmy was referred for psychiatric evaluation in view of possible placement in the Severely Emotionally Disturbed Program. Jimmy had always had an extremely chaotic family life: his father, hated by Jimmy's mother and her parents, had abandoned him early in his life. His mother, an ineffectual woman who saw nothing wrong with Jimmy's lifelong behavioral problems and academic failure, liked to check herself into the state mental hospital four or five times a year "for a rest." She had been married "three or four times" and had a number of children "here and there."

Although he had been in LD classes since the first grade, Jimmy's behavioral problems at school and at home quickly eclipsed his academic difficulties and he soon found himself in classes for the Emotionally Handicapped. Following a homosexual assault by three teenagers when he was eight, Jimmy's aggression toward peers and school personnel escalated to the point that he could not be served in a non-restrictive setting. Jimmy developed post-traumatic symptoms of fears of falling asleep, nightmare and night terrors and took to his mother's bed—where he was still sleeping over four years after the homosexual assault. Psychostimulants and antidepressants were prescribed by a child psychiatrist, who felt that "regular psychotherapy was not possible due to the family's instability and their inconsistency in keeping their appointments." The medications had only transient effect.

Jimmy was an attractive near thirteen-year-old who looked much more like a shy eight-year-old. He looked sad, fearful and apprehensive, and rarely looked up from his downward gaze. Jimmy sat on the edge of his chair during the initial history-taking, saying nothing. When it was brought up that "something bad had happened to Jimmy when he was eight," his mother interrupted, saying, "You see that he hasn't said a word yet. Talk about that and he won't say a word the entire time we're here." Jimmy's mother was told that it didn't matter whether or not he used words to communicate, but that it was important to be open about the bad things that had happened to him in his life.

Despite his apparent fearfulness, Jimmy separated easily and seemed more comfortable in the playtherapy room. He continued to hang his head and showed no interest in the contents of the room. When asked to draw our standard pictures, he drew them in brown. His "house" drawing had a large tree with a hole in it next to the house and "the people who live in that house" consisted of a mother, a father, and a baby in a carriage. The father had his fist planted in the mother's back and the mother was pushing the carriage away, a drawing which paralleled mother's constant attempts to flee abusive fathers while keeping Jimmy infantilized.

When Jimmy moved to the floor and the toys with his examiner, he immediately put the little boy doll in the bathtub. Knowing about the sexual abuse from the history, and seeing Jimmy's spontaneous move to place the boy doll in the bathtub, his examiner asked him about what had happened "up north." "I don't tell anyone about that," Jimmy replied. Asked how many boys there were, Jimmy replied, "Three." When asked gently what had happened, he said again that he didn't like to talk about it. His examiner then said that her understanding of "rape" meant that the boys must have taken their penis and forced it into his body and asked him if that was what happened. Jimmy looked at the floor and said, "Yes."

When she asked if the counselor at the time had helped Jimmy get rid of the feeling that he was "bad and dirty" for what had happened, he replied with a smirk, "No." His examiner then took a piece of paper and drew three outline figures on it. Reminding him that "we don't do this to real people in the world," she handed him the paper and a pair of scissors. He took them, cut the paper to pieces, and began to stuff the pieces into the dungeon of the toy castle. He was told to gather up the pieces of paper because there was something much more effective to do with "the pieces of those bad boys." Led to a trash compactor in another part of the office, Jimmy pushed the button and crushed the badness up.

His examiner then took some of our "Professional, Prescription Only" special red soap and told him that it would "wash away the badness and guilt" he felt for what had happened in the past. He scrubbed his hands with a surgical scrub brush, dried, and then started to throw the paper towel into the trash compactor. He was told that his towels did not belong in the same place as "those filthy boys" and was led to a clean wastebasket.

After returning to the playtherapy room and "cleaning up" the toys which had been left in disarray, Jimmy returned to the office where his mother was being interviewed. Crossing the few feet which separated the playtherapy room from the other office, Jimmy stopped talking; he said nothing more until he left. He sat down on a chair opposite his mother, who remained totally oblivious to him, reached into her purse, and took out an oversized set of playing cards. He carefully went through the cards, discarding all but four. These he spread out in his hand in vertical fashion. They were the four Aces with the Ace of Hearts on top. He looked at his examiner, pointed to the Ace of Hearts and then pointed to his own heart.

"Regular psychotherapy" may not have been possible with this child because of the chaotic nature of his family life—but good psychotherapy was. Jimmy Ace-of-Hearts, as we came to think of him, was a therapeutically apt child who would not have met the traditional criteria for individual psychotherapy but who began the therapeutic process himself when given the opportunity.

Despite his at first repeated insistence that he didn't want to talk about it, Jimmy nonetheless told his therapist about his life (through the drawings) and suggested that resolution of his sense of guilt and badness was possible (when he put the boy in the bathtub). What had appeared to be a major traditional obstacle to therapy in the other room—Jimmy's refusal to speak—was met with the clear suggestive statement that communication did not depend upon his use of words. When his therapist recognized his nonverbal communication and gently proceeded to provide the means to resolve the feeling of being "bad and dirty," Jimmy allowed himself to use words to communicate.

No attempt was made to render explicit Jimmy's exquisitely poignant and poetic expression of thanks to his therapist for "giving me my heart back." To have done so would have been to violate the private space this child's mother could not, or would not, protect, and would have killed the magic of the therapeutic moment. Although we saw Jimmy Ace-of-Hearts only once for no more than an hour and a half, he made it perfectly clear at the end of the encounter that he no longer viewed himself as a Garbage Pail Kid. Over the years we have received many letters and phone calls from children and, more often, parents who wanted to let us know that just that one visit had made a genuine difference in their lives.

Responding to the Idiosyncratic Needs of the Child

Most abused or traumatized children, like Jimmy Ace-of-Hearts, can resolve, or begin to resolve, the guilt or badness within the therapy itself. As we noted in Chapter 7, one of the purposes of the therapeutic evaluation is to assess and utilize this ability. Many children are so symbolically apt that they can "wash away" their sense of guilt and feelings of being bad and dirty with our special soap, or attenuate or even reverse the negative self-image engendered by the experience of abuse. Occasionally, however, a child may have to do so much more literally.

Larry was 14 when he came to therapy. It had been thought that his mild cerebral palsy, mild mental retardation, and severe "learning disabilities" were due to poor perinatal care and were congenital. Only in therapy did it begin to become evident that the brain damage was probably due to severe beatings and other physical abuse at the hands of his biological parents prior to Larry's entry into foster care, where he had been repeatedly sodomized by a male caretaker. Larry's poor personal hygiene and soiling were also felt to be related to his mild mental retardation and cerebral palsy. Normally, Larry was responsible for the initial cleaning of his soiled underpants. It was his job to rinse them in the toilet, as one would soiled diapers, and then place them in a bucket of bleached water to soak prior to machine washing.

When Larry's adoptive mother found him—and his soiled underpants— in the bathtub, the water a dirty brown, it became clear that Larry still viewed himself as literally filthy in spite of the therapeutic attempts to wash away those feelings symbolically and in spite of the fact that over six years had passed since his removal from foster care and subsequent adoption. Larry's therapist therefore bought two Fleet enemas and instructed Larry and his mother in their use. Only when Larry successfully gave himself the two enemas did his soiling stop and his personal hygiene improve.

It would have done no good whatsoever to try to persuade this fourteen-year-old that no ejaculate could possibly still be inside his body almost seven years after the abuse. Since the symbolic resolution had failed, we simply decided to accept Larry's literalism and help him "wash out the filth." Care was taken not to duplicate the abusive situation. Neither Larry's therapist nor his current caretaker, his adoptive mother, were directly involved in the actual administration of the enemas. Thus, Larry experienced them as purgative—not as invasive. The resolution of a symptom that had been consistently viewed as neurological by Larry's physicians in the past ("poor neuromuscular sphincter tone") prompted a reconsideration of both his retardation and his "organic learning disabilities."

This therapeutic maneuver illustrates one of the central features of good child psychotherapy technique: the generation of a potentially falsifiable hypothesis—which, if proved, results in therapeutic change—and an operational attempt to test it. Some therapists, like Coppolillo (1987, p. 253), seem to view the use of dramatic techniques which do not attempt to make the conscious unconscious or to resolve conflicts though conscious awareness as "gimmicky and tricky." Far from "gimmicky and tricky," the use of enemas by Ricky's therapist was a quick and reasoned application of good thinking to a clinical problem. (Since we tend to teach and learn traditional, rather than problem-solving, techniques in our training programs, anything out of the ordinary tends to get labeled in this manner—probably because the "mechanism of action" is not clear to traditional trainers.)

The Importance of Immediate Interventions

At the same time that the process of resolution and cleansing allows the child to begin to shed a horrible self-image, it also facilitates the rebuilding of basic trust, which can be so damaged by abuse and trauma. Trauma can destroy the "safe base" phenomenon, the certainty, conscious or unconscious, of the child that a particular individual or individuals constitute a safe haven in the midst of disruption or threat. Destruction of trust, fear of human closeness, and even fear of the mundane (Terr, 1979) can all be attenuated by the therapeutic process, as the sense of being understood, contained, and caringly "manipulated" by the environment grows in the child. Terr (1985b) points out that the sense of dyscontrol brought about by trauma can extend to the parents. "Embarrassed and frightened about their own vulnerability and loss of control in the past," she writes about the parents of the children in the Chowchilla kidnapping, "no one wished to be reminded of it."

One of the advantages of an immediate intervention, as we saw in the case of Jimmy Ace-of-Hearts, is the quickness with which the sense of dyscontrol and powerlessness can be dispelled. In the case of abused or traumatized children with at least one caring and supportive parent, the experience of that first encounter can be immensely relieving for child and parent alike. Since the parents' own sense of loss of control is further enhanced by not being able to make their child better, the actual experience of emotional relief during the first session can have a positive multiplying effect throughout a supportive family.

We have seen traumatic play, as described by Terr (1979)—a repetitive, unsatisfying, and driven reenactment which brings no resolution to the child—as well as repetitive dreams, fears, panic attacks, anxiety, claustra/ agoraphobia, and even hyperalertness and hyperarousal decrease dramatically after a single therapeutic encounter. The much increased self-injuriousness and self-destructiveness of traumatized children compared to controls (Green, 1980) can also often be attenuated by an intensely positive first therapeutic encounter. The incredible plasticity of children is one of the things that make therapeutic work with them so potentially rewarding.

For this reason, we feel that the therapeutic pessimism reflected in the view of some child therapists, e.g., Coppolillo (1987, p. 346), that "a period of three to six months in a stable, nonthreatening environment is helpful before beginning treatment" is unwarranted, although doubtless well motivated. Acute problems are best solved acutely. There is no need to wait until two-and-a-half to evaluate and treat a child who was abused or traumatized at the age of two. Any delay represents time lost. A six-month delay represents literally a fifth of the life of a three-year-old, during which the average clinician has no input to the environmental care of the child. And even good environmental care is often inadequate to the specialized task of reversing the effects of trauma.

The Meaning of Mundane Experience

Often children who have been abused or neglected react to everyday events in a manner that makes no sense to the casual observer. One of the most common causes of behavioral disturbance or otherwise inexplicable academic "regression" in a previously abused or traumatized child is the appearance in school work of a theme generically related to protection, harm or abandonment. When a parent or teacher reports that a child in treatment has suddenly taken an academic turn for the worse, the clinician should inquire specifically about the content of current course work.

Jeannie was a bright, loquacious, sexually abused eight-year-old with a penchant for the theatrical which could endear her to any talent scout. Despite her above-average intelligence and her more than obvious creativity, Jeannie was seen as "learning-disabled" and "unable" to do grade-level work in her Emotionally Handicapped class and was, thus, given little opportunity for challenge. Prior to beginning therapy, she had constantly been in fights with her female teachers.

Following a period of significant improvement in both academics and behavior, Jeannie dropped precipitously in her social studies grade and got into repeated trouble in class. She complained that other children were always getting her into trouble and that the teacher never disciplined them or protected her.

Jeannie had never completed an in-class open-book social studies test because the outburst which had started her "regression" had resulted in her being sent to the office. When the test question was found, it became clear why she had reacted so intensely. The test question was "What did the mother bear do to Davy because he tried to play with her cub instead of leaving it alone?"

When it was pointed out to Jeannie that the test question was about a mother (bear) protecting her child, and that during one of the times Jeannie had been sexually abused her mother was present in the same room, she immediately said that the guinea hens on her farm were more protective of their offspring than her own mother had been of her. She was quickly able to see that her feelings of being unprotected and vulnerable had been triggered by the test question—and that the other children were not really preferentially treated by her teacher.

When the primary environmental response to human cruelty is effectively to pretend that it simply does not exist, the issue is not "making the unconscious conscious" but, rather, simply removing affective blocks to normal perception. This girl's mother favored her brother in a most cruel fashion and had turned a blind eye to the abuse of her daughter, behavior that characterized her relationship with her children throughout their lives. Because most of the adults around her had not been willing to see this for what it was, this girl had compliantly narrowed her own interpersonal perceptual field to the point where, instead of being in the "gifted" classes her native intelligence and creativity merited, she was seen as having "learning disabilities" and behavior problems serious enough to warrant special education.

"LEARNING DISABILITIES" AND "ATTENTION DEFICIT DISORDER"

Prelude to Treatment: Abandoning Received Ideas Unsupported by Evidence

The child therapist who sees many children will repeatedly encounter those who have been diagnosed or labeled as having "learning disabilities."

The label will have been applied by psychiatrists, psychologists, pediatricians, clinical social workers, developmental pediatricians, child and general neurologists, school counselors, teachers, and parents. As Herbert Kohl (1988) notes in his review of Gerald Coles' (1987) book *The Learning Mystique: A Critical Look at "Learning Disabilities,"* there are a number of mental conditions, such as retardation and insanity, which are legally defined and which can lead to the legally sanctioned categorization of individuals. The category of "learning disabilities" has become so institutionalized that it is defined by statute.

"Learning disability" (LD) is the label applied to academic difficulties that are assumed to be due to neurological dysfunction in an otherwise globally intact individual. In fact, the categorization was initially applied to middle-class children who appeared to learn well in nonacademic settings but who did poorly in school in spite of obvious intelligence (as measured by individually administered intelligence tests like the WISC-R or Stanford-Binet). This simple definition persists today, as does the reductionist explanation for the "cause" of LD.

> Section 56026 of the California Education Code, for example, provides one of the strictest definitions of Learning Disability, and Title 5 of Section 3030J of the Administrative Code provides specific criteria and procedures for determining whether a student can be classified as "learning disabled." According to the law a "learning disability" consists of a disorder in one or more of the basic psychological processes involved in processing language or a discrepancy between intellectual ability and school achievement. (Kohl, 1988)

Coles (1987) summarizes the view of LD which has developed historically.

> Ever since Hinshelwood, a learning disability—by any name—has always been formally defined as a specific subset of low academic achievers whose serious academic failures could not be accounted for by their sensory functioning, intellectual ability (as measured by IQ tests), or emotions, which are generally normal. Nor can unfavorable circumstances or experiences explain the disabilities. These children by and large come from the middle class. Their homes usually seem to be materially comfortable and free of family or emotional problems; their schools seem to provide normal instruction which benefits most children. In learning-disabilities jargon, these sensory, intellectual, emotional, and environmental conditions are known as exclusionary factors, and excluding them as causes of the problem establishes or at least paves the way for a diagnosis of a genuine learning disability. Experts recognize that in some learning-disabled children the exclusionary factors might be evident, but in these instances they are judged to be a consequence, not a cause, of the disability. The disability might create emotional problems in the child, initiate conflict in an otherwise intact family, or lead to low

scores on intelligence tests because the child's learning has been hindered. Again, however, these conditions are not said to explain the disability itself, even though they may compound it. [. . .] Defining a learning disability does not stop with exclusionary factors. There is also an affirmative part of the definition: learning-disabled children are said to have a *neurological dysfunction*. (p. 11)

This view is echoed by the American Academy of Child and Adolescent Psychiatry in its *Facts For Families* hand-outs:

> A child with a learning disability is usually bright and initially tries very hard to follow instructions, concentrate and "be good" at home and in school. Yet he or she is not mastering school tasks and falls behind. Some learning disabled children also have trouble sitting still or paying attention. Learning disabilities affect as many as 15 per cent of otherwise able school children.
>
> It is believed that learning disabilities are caused by a difficulty with the nervous system that affects receiving, processing, or communicating information. Some learning disabled children are also hyperactive and/or distractible with a short attention span. (American Academy of Child and Adolescent Psychiatry, 1985b)

If, ultimately, learning disabilities (with reading difficulties among the most commonly encountered) are the result of innate, neurological "central processing disorders" (whether called strephosymbolia, word amblyopia, bradylexia, dyslexia, learning disabilities, hyperkinetic syndrome, minimal brain damage, minimal cerebral dysfunction, or Specific Developmental Disorders and Attention Deficit Disorder with or without Hyperactivity, as they are in *DSM-III*), the only approach offering any form of help would be a kind of educational physiatrics, augmented by medication affecting the central nervous system. This is, in fact, the position of the *Facts For Families* from the American Academy of Child and Adolescent Psychiatry (hereafter referred to as the Academy).

> The child psychiatrist will work with the school professionals and others to have the necessary educational testing done to clarify if a learning disability exists. After talking with the child and family, and evaluating their situation, the child psychiatrist will make recommendations on appropriate school placement, the need for special help such as special educational therapy or speech-language therapy and steps parents can take to assist their child in maximizing his or her learning potential. Sometimes medication will be prescribed for hyperactivity or distractibility. The child psychiatrist works to strengthen the child's self-confidence, so vital for healthy development, and also helps parents and other family members cope with the realities of living with learning disabilities. (1985b)

How does the clinician or educator know that a child "has" LD? First, since the underlying cause is said to be neurological, subtle signs of central nervous system immaturity or dysmaturity are taken to be indicative. Frequently, a history of perinatal distress or developmental lag is adduced to support this. Second, by definition, the LD child will do poorly in school. Finally, psychoeducational testing will demonstrate that he has LD. The "most frequent signals of learning disabilities" are listed on the Academy's *Facts For Families*. These are seen when a child:

- Has difficulty understanding and following directions.
- Has trouble remembering what someone just told him or her.
- Fails to master reading, writing, and/or math skills, and thus fails schoolwork.
- Has difficulty distinguishing right from left — for example, confusing 25 with 52, "b" with "d," or "on" with "no."
- Lacks coordination — in walking, sports, or small activities such as holding a pencil or tying a shoelace.
- Easily loses or misplaces homework, school books or other items.
- Cannot understand the concept of time; is confused by "yesterday," "today," "tomorrow."

Although remediation can help some of the reported 1.8 million children categorized as "learning disabled" in the U.S. in 1985 (according to the *Seventh Annual Report to Congress on the Implementation of the Education of the Handicapped Act* by the Office of Special Education and Rehabilitative Services (cited in Coles, 1987), the conclusion of the Academy's *Facts For Families* is a rather fatalistic one: apart from recommendations and medication, all the child psychiatrist can do is to help "parents and other family member cope with the realities of living with learning disabilities." If this statement of therapeutic pessimism does not reflect the true potential of child psychiatry/psychotherapy, it certainly reflects present realities of special education. James Lytle (1988, p. 118) of the Office of Research and Education of the School System of Philadelphia and the University of Pennsylvania Graduate School of Education notes that "chances are *less than 2 percent* that [an "identified" child] will ever again be a regular education student, and that the prospects of successfully completing high school will actually be diminished by accepting special education placement (speech and hearing placements excepted)." In fact, only 1.5 percent of special education students (speech and hearing excepted) ever return to the mainstream (James Lytle, personal communication, 1989).

The intellectually curious — and courageous — clinician would do well to read Gerald Coles' book, *The Learning Mystique: A Critical Look at*

"Learning Disabilities." The major (and minor) LD hypotheses, as well as the extensive research cited by LD proponents themselves to support the neurological etiology of learning disabilities, are examined by Coles in great detail. No theory of "central processing disorder"—from visual defects to acquired or hereditary neurological dysfunction—stands up to close scrutiny. In fact, what remains when all is said and done is ideological *belief* in the neurological causes of "learning disabilities" which can often be maintained only by clear-cut intellectual bad faith. As demoralizing as it may be, for it makes us face the bad thinking and even the bad faith that pervades much of the clinical and research literature, Coles' book should be mandatory reading for any clinician or educator working with children.

One of the keys to understanding the monolithic LD explanation/institution can be found in the few negative reviews of Coles' book. "Gerald Coles," writes Maya Pines (1988), in a book review cited in the newsletter of the National Institute of Dyslexia, "[. . .] would like to turn the clock back to the days when mothers were blamed for everything that went wrong with their children." He offers nothing in the place of a reductionistic explanation, Pines complains, a complaint echoed by Carl Kline (1988) who views Coles' conclusions as "dangerous because they perpetuate the self-protective myth of those educators who point an accusing finger at the parents rather than reexamining the educational system."

But what if the LD child with a history of perinatal distress, developmental delay, neurological "soft signs," and a confirmed "learning disabilities" diagnosis on psychoeducational testing can be helped to do better—or even very well—without specific educational intervention? Is he still "learning disabled?" The clinician who takes a problem-solving, developmental-contextual approach to "learning disabilities" will find himself in the same position as Coles and needs to be prepared for the potential slings and arrows from parents and teachers. Suggesting that there may be another explanation for a child's academic difficulties, other than an underlying neurological one, often elicits a very angry, defensive response, especially from parents. If the reductionistic "neurological" explanation is removed, what is left? The initial application of the LD category to middle-class children gives us the clue, as does Pines' and Kline's mistaken conclusion that Coles is "blaming the parents." How can often gross academic underachievement or even failure in an otherwise bright learner *with good parents* be explained except by a central disorder? The fear of being blamed for their child's problems which parents bring to therapy can be overwhelming. The clinician who would solve these problems faces two powerful obstacles: the institutionalization of LD in the American educational system and the fear of parental responsibility.

It is here that the value of a developmental-contextual approach becomes most clear: it offers the possibility of testing the worst-case hypothesis (that the child and family must learn to "cope with the realities of living with learning disabilities") while at the same time taking the first step toward change. If there is no unitary, reductionistic explanation for impaired learning, then each impaired learner must be assessed individually (whether the family is grossly dysfunctional or marvelous). As we saw in the cases of Steve and Catherine in Chapter 3, the traditional abstract-categorical approach to assessment can give results which are contextually wrong—and yet categorically "right."

One of the practical changes which Coles suggests to *prevent* and remediate impaired learning is to do away with "tracking," the stratification of the educational system through the grouping of children according to perceived ability in the earliest of grades. Such "tracking," done initially to facilitate learning (primarily reading), comes with time to be the justification for continued failure and underachievement: tracked according to "ability," children's ability comes to be reflected by the assigned track. The reader is reminded that, although "learning-disabled, hyperactive and cerebral-palsied," Catherine changed quickly when it was realized that those labels were incorrect; however, it took two years for her to escape the stratified classes which actually promoted her lack of progress.

Stratification and "tracking" have no place in psychotherapy: every child (or adult) is potentially treatable psychotherapeutically. Traditional approaches (Carek, 1979; Coppolillo, 1987; Wilson & Hersov, 1985) segregate patients (according to their ability to exercise conscious awareness and "relate" to the therapist) in the same manner that special education programs segregate students: both patients and students tend to remain in their respective categories in spite of therapy or teaching. No such "tracking" is necessary for the problem-solving psychotherapist.

Lessons from Traumatology

Some clinicians do not view trauma as having lasting effects on academic performance. Terr notes that in her experience traumatized children do not suffer academically.

> Children's work performance (school) rarely suffers for more than a few months after psychic trauma, as opposed to the long-term decline in work efforts experienced by many adults. This relative childhood immunity to work inhibition most likely directly relates to the lack of denial, intrusive flashbacks, and psychic numbing in youngsters. (Terr, 1985b, p. 52)

Terr comes to this conclusion based on her experience with children traumatized in groups, particularly the victims of the Chowchilla school bus kidnapping. We would suggest that her findings are not indicative of the nature of children's response to trauma, but rather of the therapeutic efficacy of her own research efforts with these children. A caring and competent clinician, Terr (1979) established a good relationship with the Chowchilla children and those parents who would participate, a relationship which has contributed important observations to the child psychiatric literature on trauma. Inadvertently, we suggest, she has illustrated one of our central points: even evaluations can be immensely therapeutic.

There are, in fact, many ways in which trauma can affect academic performance, and the effect need not necessarily be cognitive, though it often is. The cognitive effects of trauma in a child who is truant, for example, may never be observed because the child's "conduct disorder" successfully masks them, possibly even from the child himself. A number of items from the *Dissociative Behavior Checklist* developed by Putnam (1987) and his colleagues at the National Institute of Mental Health remind us that we must take into account the effect of experience—of which trauma is but one, easily recognized and intense variety—on cognition. These items, found in cases of severe trauma, seem as if they could have come from the Academy's *Facts For Families* sheet:

- amnesias: the child remembers in one context but not in another
- dazes and trances, eg., "spacing out"
- "attention deficit disorder," "learning disabilities"
- shifts in personality
- gets lost easily, loses possessions [or ideas]
- perplexing variations in skill and knowledge
- drawings reflect a real range in maturity level
- rapid regressions in behavior
- striking denial: "I did not just break that lamp!"

With these sequelae of trauma in mind, consider the case of an elementary school child with longstanding "learning-disabilities":

J. R. was a "learning-disabled" biracial 10-year-old whose black father had brutally raped his white mother when J. R. was younger. J. R. and his younger brother had both witnessed the "fight" and the bloody outcome. On this particular occasion, as the Christmas season approached, J. R. became increasingly edgy at school. Finally, on a day he had ostensibly looked forward to, J. R. "exploded" at his teacher, calling her obscene names and threatening to hurt her. The episode was initially seen by school personnel as an anniversary reaction to J. R.'s psychiatric hospitalization at the same time the previous year. However, upon closer inspection, the "anniversary" was found to be far more meaningful: J. R.'s hospitalization the previous year was itself part of an ongoing anniversary reaction. The year prior to the hospitalization J. R.'s father was released from prison and an attempt was made at reconciliation, which resulted once again in violence and another move as the family attempted to hide. Threats occurred *at school* where J. R.'s father would often wait for him outside the building or even follow him to his classroom.

The situation at school was complicated by the fact that the principal had been J. R.'s father's fourth grade teacher and apparently found it difficult to admit that "her" student had "gone bad"; consequently, she refused to cooperate by using J. R.'s initials instead of his father's name, James Robert (Jr.), or by keeping father away from the school. The year prior to the reconciliation J. R., his brother, and mother were living with the maternal grandmother during the much publicized sex abuse trial of J. R.'s maternal grandfather. Although the abuse was formally acknowledged by J. R.'s grandfather, he was acquitted on a technicality related to his daughter's recollection of her (young) age at the time of the abuse.

The event J. R. had been looking forward to was a major public celebration in which J. R. and his classmates were to participate. Three television stations were represented at the school, complete with reporters and equipment vans. The "explosion" occurred when J. R. saw the television crews. When the events were reviewed with J. R. in a calm manner he was able to identify the trigger for what had been a partial reenactment of the violent situations he had repeatedly lived through. J. R.'s experience of his grandfather's trial and the previous school principal's refusal to prevent J. R.'s father from entering the school grounds represented a failure of the "establishment" to protect him and his mother. The much awaited public celebration was terrifying to J. R. because he was certain that, with three television crews present, his father would certainly see him on television and thereby discover the location of his new school. Although J. R. was not consciously aware of his fear that his father would see him on television and be able to find him, he had reacted to the "public" appearance as if suddenly he were in a life-threatening situation.

As we have seen, experience need not be literally abusive or catastrophically traumatic to be powerfully formative. Given the relatively easy hypnotizability of children and the degree to which normative dissociation pervades their lives, it is not surprising to find a parallelism between the behaviors described on NIMH checklist and those listed by the Academy as "the most frequent signals of learning disabilities." In fact, when seen from the perspective of traumatology, "learning disabilities" and "attention deficit disorder" become symptoms and not diagnoses (along with distractibility, hyperarousal and hypervigilance, etc.). Given the subtle but powerful ability of psychotherapy to modulate behavioral states of consciousness (which we examined in detail in Chapter 6), the first step in a genuine psychoeducational approach to impaired learning involves resolving cognitive confusion and decreasing hyperarousal and dissociative distancing, resolving cognitive binds, and removing (the often simple) blocks to learning. Without such resolution even the finest of categorical remediation is doomed to less than optimal results, or even to failure.

Experiential Requisites for Learning

The process of learning depends upon consistency and continuity of perception, which, in turn, depend upon consistency and continuity of experience. Such experience is necessary for the development of spatial and temporal localization, seriation, immutability, object constancy and stable reference. The dissociogenic effects of trauma can lead to disordered seriation and localization, two important cognitive conditions necessary for the ordered development of cognitive structures and for nonpathological identity formation. Experience, as we saw earlier (Chapters 4 and 6), can be formative, deformative and/or reformative. The nature of experience is crucial for both cognitive and affective development. In the absence of consistency and continuity of experience, the appearance of categorical inability is frequently perceived by standard assessment techniques when, in fact, only *operational* inability is present.

> Jorge was a 12-year-old sixth grader in special classes for the severely learning-disabled who was referred for psychiatric evaluation because of inappropriate behaviors at school, such as profanity, physical aggression toward peers, work refusal, and making loud noises.
>
> Jorge was the second of two children born to his parents. About two years after his birth Jorge's parents divorced, only to be living together again before a month had passed. Having fought until the divorce, Jorge's parents lived comfortably together after the divorce for four years. During this time Jorge's father was extremely "irresponsible," making as much as a thousand dollars one week only to stay off work the next. Material goods—and big debts—accumulated until Jorge's mother could no longer stand his father's "inconsistency and irresponsibility."

In LD classes since the first grade, Jorge's "learning disabilities" had been identified in kindergarten, the year his parents separated again. Jorge did well in the first grade. The following year mother acquired a live-in boyfriend, Sam, who Jorge called his "stepfather." Unlike his father, Sam continued to maintain a positive contact with Jorge after he and Jorge's mother broke up—a confusing situation in which the meaning of togetherness, separation, marriage, and divorce became more blurred. Mother's sending Jorge to live with his father when she and Sam broke up further compounded the confusion. When he returned to his mother, another live-in boyfriend appeared. Unlike Sam, Freddy had a drinking problem and did not get along well with Jorge. At this point Jorge's "little fits" began at home and his angry outbursts escalated.

Jorge's academic history paralleled that of his home life. By the age of nine he had been retained twice and had attended eight different schools. As Jorge's behavioral problems began to overshadow his academic difficulties he was placed in the Seriously Emotionally Disturbed Program, but his mother removed him. At the time of the evaluation he was well below grade level for chronological age, with formal achievement testing scores ranging from 4.0 in math to 1.6 and 1.7 in reading recognition and spelling. Interestingly, his reading comprehension exceeded his reading recognition by more than half a grade level.

In school Jorge showed no effort, refused to follow rules, and was uncooperative and oppositional. He asked his teacher, "What will you do if I hit you?"—but never did. At 12 he presented himself as tough and "macho," smoked openly, made strange noises in class and used profanity, as if trying hard to put everyone off. While refusing written work and verbal class participation, Jorge did seem to like his teacher and responded to invitations from her to become involved in nonverbal class participation.

To add to Jorge's confusion, his relationship with his father was very different from his older brother's. Jorge's father was described as having been "a very good husband and father" during Jorge's brother's childhood, apparently providing him with a sound foundation that managed to survive subsequent developments. Jorge, however, was described by his mother as "short like his father" and "irresponsible like his dad"—two conditions which Jorge's mother was sure were due to "heredity."

When seen in the therapeutic evaluation, Jorge was an attractive near 13-year-old who presented with a mixture of ease and yet a macho "what am I here for?" feel about him. He sat calmly while his mother went over history and the reasons for the evaluation, after which he separated easily to be interviewed alone in the playtherapy room.

Although this youngster presented a street-wise front, it was decided to begin the therapeutic evaluation in the playtherapy room. Upon entering, Jorge was told "not to laugh" because his examiner had to be "ready to see kids this big" (indicating the size of three and four year olds). Far from being put off by a space clearly designed for little children, Jorge smiled upon entering and sat down comfortably in the small chair at the child's table. As paper and a box of crayons were presented to him, he was asked if it were okay with him that all the crayons weren't perfect. He indicated that he was comfortable with that.

After the completion of the requested drawings, Jorge's examiner brought out the stuffed platypus family and asked Jorge what it meant if the big platypus hit the little one and said "I love you" at the same time. At first Jorge laughed, a bit embarrassed. Then he said, "It's not love." Jorge's examiner then said, "But if you grow up thinking you're just like the big person [pointing at the big platypus], and you treat people the same way, is that love?" Jorge said, "I guess not." When asked whether his father loved him, Jorge replied, "I don't think so." Jorge was told that he was smart.

His examiner continued: "Now, if I tell you that this door is yellow and show you the door, what color are you going to say it is?" "Brown," Jorge replied, looking at the door on the Fisher-Price castle, which was, in fact, brown. "Now, just to stick to the idea of what 'love' is," Jorge's examiner continued, "what if I beat you [taking the big platypus and having it hit the small one] and shouted, 'WHAT COLOR IS THAT?' what color would you say it is? "It's still br . . . " Jorge started to reply. But as his examiner continued to have the big platypus pound the small one, Jorge added, "No, yellow, yellow, yellow! It's yellow!" "Right," Jorge was told, "you'd be smart to say 'yellow' and avoid the pain. Now, what happens when you go to school and are shown the same color? What answer are you going to give in school? "Yellow," Jorge replied, and smiled. "And what's going to happen to your grades," she asked. "Go down—because the color's brown, not yellow," Jorge said, his eyebrows going up. Again Jorge was told that he had a good mind.

"Look what's happened to you," Jorge's examiner said. "What's 'marriage'?" "When two people come together," he replied. "And what's 'divorce'?" "When they split," Jorge replied. "But what's the definition in your house? The opposite: they're married and they split up; they divorce and they live together." Jorge was then able to talk about how confusing his past life had been—his parents' relationship, the two live-in boyfriends, etc.

A Gray Oral Reader was produced and Jorge was asked to read. His immediate reaction was to try to give up. With consistent support, however, Jorge read—and read reasonably well, although below chronological grade level. When he came to the sentence "The boy began to cry," Jorge read, "The boy started to cry." It was pointed out to him that although the actual *word* was wrong, he had understood the *message*.

He then became rather sad and talked about his mother's car breaking down which had resulted in missing the first evaluation appointment. He added that he had missed his last visit with his previous therapist—and his first with us. Jorge understood immediately when his examiner explained to him that he often seemed to become angry when he was really sad.

The child was alive and well in this street-tough and off-putting early adolescent. Jorge's behavior problems at school had not developed in response to his supposedly inherent neurological "learning disability," but they were tactically very useful in avoiding any situation in which he would repeat failure upon embarrassing failure. When Jorge asked his teacher, "What will you do if I hit you?" he was expressing his uncertainty about the nature of emotional responses to negative events. In Jorge's experience, positive behavior or experiences could not be counted upon to produce positive results and causality was very confused. An initial encounter with an early adolescent who endeared himself to few adults gave the picture of a therapeutically apt youngster, still reachable, with genuine academic potential. That the schools had not recognized his real abilities was hardly Jorge's fault. It remained the school's challenge to change their categorical view of Jorge and to make it difficult for him to set himself up for apparent categorical failure, while taking advantage of the decreased hostility and defensiveness brought by therapy.

Language and the Described World

Stuart was a 10-year-old whose behavior and academic performance had been a source of great confusion to school personnel since kindergarten. His teacher noted that Stuart appeared to have few or no comprehension skills and that his verbal and written responses were for the most part nonsensical or inappropriate. He was noted to display some "typical aphasic characteristics" and to be self-stimulatory, often "shutting out" unwanted stimuli. Stuart was viewed as having a "central processing disorder," with the 40-point spread between verbal and performance IQ on the WISC-R seen as confirmatory. On the other hand, school personnel wondered if Stuart was psychotic, for his affect was generally inappropriate, his behavior was bizarre, and he was preoccupied by Japanese science fiction creatures such as Godzilla.

Stuart's mother was Japanese and his father American. They had met during one of father's Far East business trips and had married during father's return to Tokyo for a prolonged stay. When the couple moved to a fairly isolated city in otherwise rural North Dakota, Stuart's father insisted that only English be spoken to the new baby. Father was self-conscious enough as it was, and he was sure that two languages would only confuse the child.

During the history-taking, with both parents present, Stuart was asked if he spoke Japanese. He shook his head negatively and continued to smile. His examiner then asked him abruptly, *"Anata-wa hon-wo motte-imasu-ka?!"* ("Do you have a book?" in Japanese). Stuart looked disoriented but did not respond. When asked if he had understood his examiner's question, Stuart shook his head negatively and smiled even more. "Repeat what I just said," Stuart was told. "I can't," he replied. Stuart was told to "go ahead and try anyway," at which point he mumbled some nonsense syllables which ended with *"motte-imasu"* (the verb form *to have*, less the particle *-ka* which makes the sentence a question). Stuart clearly understood Japanese. In fact, Stuart's mother admitted when interviewed alone that she had secretly spoken Japanese to him since his birth. Only during a trip to Japan at age five to visit his mother's relatives had Stuart ever spoken Japanese openly.

Categorically, this child appeared to be either extremely cognitively impaired or psychotic. Contextually, he appeared confused, caught between two very different languages and two very different views of the world. He was further trapped by the necessity of keeping his entire Japanese language orientation a secret from the world: to have admitted that he understood what he heard would have left Stuart extremely vulnerable to the wrath of an unstable father. Furthermore, the genuine mutuality necessary for integrative cognitive development and language acquisition was present only when Stuart's mother related to her child in her Japanese "mode" — when she spoke Japanese with him. This experience created a cognitive skewing which significantly impaired Stuart's ability to function in a world mediated by the English language.

Without the developmental context in which to understand the clinical picture this child presented, Stuart would have continued to appear organically impaired (as the school believed he was) whereas there was, in fact, nothing *inherently* wrong with him. He was caught between two verbal descriptions of the world, one in Japanese and one in English. He could not let anyone know how or what he thought because that would be to betray the special world he shared with his mother—and father had laid down his dictum. English was, in fact, this child's second language—not his first. Only by contextualizing the "signs and symptoms of his disorder" did they become truly meaningful and take on genuine validity. Experiences can be extraordinarily deceiving.

While Stuart was burdened with keeping a powerful secret, much of the confusing clinical picture was related to the cognitive functions of language. The following example of simple secret-keeping illustrates how a consistent picture of "learning disability" can be created while genuine learning skills remain intact.

Secrets

As we indicated in Chapter 4, family secrets can constitute an incredibly noxious pathogenic, dissociogenic force. Although rarely can children keep family secrets without behavioral indicators of the contents of the secret or the child's attitude toward it becoming manifest, occasionally pathogenic family secrets will exert their force only in the academic setting. If we think of school in the very simplest of terms, it is easy to understand how this can happen: school is where children tell adults what they know—through written and oral work. It is very difficult to develop the cognitive blinders necessary for secret-keeping without having the process generalize to other areas, especially those specifically related to knowing and telling.

Gina was a bright, engaging and personable 10-year-old who had been "served" by the Specific Learning Disabilities Program since the first grade when it was discovered that she had a "selective math disability." By the time of her psychiatric evaluation she had been in special education classes all her life and had been treated with methylphenidate since the age of six for "attention deficit disorder." According to her parents, psychologists, and school system personnel, Gina had developed "emotional problems secondary to her learning disabilities." She had even spent several years at a school specializing in the education of "learning-disabled" children. Presumably, her difficulties in keeping up with her agemates and her frustration at not being able to achieve academically had resulted in the development of a contentious attitude, oppositionalism and a general disrespect for adults. Although formally designated as a "learning-disabled" child, Gina had come to be seen primarily as a behavior problem by her teachers and her parents.

Not even the taking of a history was required for Gina's problem to become evident. All it took was seeing the family. After the history was taken (which included our routine detailed questions outlined in Chapter 7), Gina accompanied her examiner to an evaluation room which, prior to the completion of our playtherapy room, was a normal office with a telephone and a corner reserved for our equipment. About 20 minutes later the phone rang in the office in which Gina's parents were still being interviewed: "Gina has a question she wants to ask her mother." When Gina and her examiner returned to the other office they found Gina's mother trying to smile and wiping away tears. Urged gently by her examiner to ask her question, Gina said to her mother, "Mommy, is Daddy my real daddy?" "Yes," her mother answered wisely. "He is your real daddy — but he's not your biological father."

A few minutes into the structured therapeutic interview, while drawing "a house" and "the people who live in that house," Gina had remarked nonchalantly, "My parents have the nicest wedding album, but, you know, I've never been able to figure out why the flowers in front of the church — which only bloom in the fall — were blooming in the spring." Gina's examiner handed her a paper and pencil and asked, "How long does it take to make a baby?" Within a few minutes Gina had figured out that she had to have been at least 15 months old when her parents were married.

Unfortunately, for reasons which could never be elucidated, Gina's father was deathly afraid of being an adoptive parent. Although he had adopted Gina shortly after he married her mother, Gina's father had demanded that the adoption be kept a secret. It was not that he was simply so comfortable treating Gina as his own daughter that adoption was not an issue. On the contrary, he was intensely uncomfortable with the idea. By the time the adoption went through Gina was nearly two years old. It was not until Gina began to learn arithmetic in school that her behavior became a problem. It had been assumed by one and all that the behavior change was secondary to the frustration brought on by her "selective math disability." Although her math "disability" disappeared with the revelation of her adoptive status, the improvement in her behavior was only momentary, for Gina's father continued to be extremely upset by the adoption issue, would not participate in therapy, and effectively sabotaged the process. The incredible power of the secret-keeping could be seen in the fact that this bright and observant 10-year-old had managed for her entire life not to know consciously what was obvious to the casual observer (that she and her father were as dissimilar as two members of the same race can be). The fact that no one had ever even broached the subject attests to the power that intense emotional need can exert to elicit collusion from an otherwise sensible environment. Even the environment can be collectively adept at dissociative maneuvers.

Secrets, Identification, and "Organicity"

Because the pervasive clinical orientation in psychology and psychiatry is categorical, clinicians often fail to realize when a clinical picture represents a developmental vicissitude rather than an inherent disorder. Perhaps one of the most frequently misunderstood of clinical appearances is that of the intense normative identification of a developing child with his or her primary caretakers. Because the process is pathological only when maladaptive, it is often difficult to recognize that an otherwise normal process may be producing a very disturbing clinical presentation. Catherine's identification with her quadriplegic adoptive father in Chapter 3 was so "natural" that it was mistaken for cerebral palsy even by experts is the field. One must recognize and remove (facilitate the removal of) blocks to healthy, adaptive identification if the way is to be opened for genuine psychotherapeutic or educational remediation. That is the challenge left to every clinician by Gerald Coles' conceptual house-cleaning.

Robert was a 10-year-old veteran of the Severe Learning Disabilities Program whose "organicity" had been apparent to school system personnel ever since kindergarten. Although Robert's "attention deficit disorder" and "hyperactivity" had been treated with Ritalin for years without appreciable effect, the suggestion that it might therefore be reasonable to discontinue the medication was met with great upset by the professionals involved.

Robert's "attention deficit disorder" and "hyperactivity" were fascinating in their origin and meaning. Because a bona fide hereditary neurological condition ran in Robert's family, Robert's maternal grandfather being the last family member affected, all of Robert's physical complaints were taken seriously. He had consistently had the best of medical evaluations. For example, when Robert once complained of "double vision" (an interesting term for a rather naive 10-year-old), he was taken to a highly specialized eye clinic where he was examined by renowned physicians. There appeared to be a "slight discrepancy" in binocular visual acuity *by Robert's report*, but the revealing thing about the ophthalmologist's report was the physician's curious marginal comment that "the patient does not appear to be malingering" when nothing of substance could be discovered in the examination. There had never been a question of malingering. What had the ophthalmologist reacted to without even being aware of it?

At the initial evaluation, after Robert returned to the office from the playtherapy room, he was asked if he knew what disease his grandfather had. "I don't know," he said, shrugging his shoulders. Robert was then asked how his grandfather was affected by the disease. Again he replied that he didn't know. Robert was asked if it affected his grandfather when he went to the bathroom. "No," he said with a smile. A series of equally absurd questions followed, all of which elicited smiles, until Robert blurted out impatiently, "No, it affects his *brain*." When asked how his grandfather's disease affected his brain, Robert replied, "It makes him nervous."

Clearly, Robert could be worried about a "nervous" disease running in his family. But there was a more bizarre complication which resulted in the strange subtlety of Robert's presentation which, in turn, had prompted the ophthalmologist to remark that he didn't think Robert was malingering. The ophthalmologist was absolutely right: malingering is a *conscious* behavior—and Robert was not aware of the meaning of his behavior.

When Robert and his mother arrived for the psychiatric evaluation, Robert's mother made a rather strange first impression: was she, we wondered, a chronic alcoholic, and slurring her speech for that reason, or was she a non-native speaker of English with a bizarrely idiosyncratic way of inflecting her speech? While Robert was in the other room his mother was asked if she had ever thought that she, too, might be affected by the hereditary disorder (spinal-cerebellar degeneration). (It was abundantly clear after taking the history and observing her for just a short period of time that she did, indeed, have the disorder.) Yes, she admitted with a sad smile of resignation, she was sure that she was affected for she became strikingly ataxic and her speech became slurred beyond comprehension with even the slightest amount of alcohol. She was not worried, however, for she knew that the disorder would result only in incoordination—not in intellectual decrement or gross motor impairment.

We now see the key to the ophthalmologist's strange remark. How does one categorize a person who *thinks* (unconsciously) that he has a hereditary disease of the "nervous" system and, consequently, *acts accordingly*? Such behavior is not malingering. The incredible cognitive confusion generated by seeing one's own mother progressively show the striking signs of a hereditary neurological disorder, while hearing her say repeatedly and categorically that the disorder is limited only to other relatives, must be overwhelming for a child. Hence, "Robert has been known to tell stories which he believes to be true" when clearly they were not. We see here an extraordinary complication of Robert's cognitive world. Learning and knowing, and telling others what one has learned and knows, are the stock in trade of school. Robert's mother was effectively keeping a secret, an unacknowledged secret which was obvious to anyone with a common-sense approach to the facts and a bit of family history. Yet none of the clinicians previously involved with this family had realized that Robert's mother was clearly showing signs of spinal-cerebellar degeneration. This scomotization of mother's illness illustrates the often extraordinary (and often extraordinarily subtle) cognitive collusion that can be elicited by the intense need to maintain a cognitive set (or perhaps more appropriately, an *affecto-cognitive* set). Robert's mother needed *not* to know that she knew that she was affected by the disorder.

What we see again is the often cognitively malignant nature of secrets (see p. 00). To repeat, secrets are by definition inaccessible and unresolvable. The effect of either tacit or implicit family secrets on the developing cognitive structures of infants and young children can be devastating. The effects of the cognitive skewing engendered by such differential knowing on academic performance can mimic genuine neurodevelopmental dysfunction or, if intense enough and longstanding, can lead to *functionally* impaired learning which may be difficult or, occasionally, even impossible to remediate.

In Robert's case the "attention deficit disorder" and "hyperactivity" ceased rapidly as order was restored to his internal universe. He was the victim of the mistaken (but linguistically logical) conviction that the effect of "nervous" disorders was to make one nervous. Relief was obvious when the whole issue was discussed openly with Robert and his mother. Bringing to light Robert's unconscious identity as a "neurologically nervous" person thereby opened the way to a much more genuinely valid assessment of his true neurodevelopmental status.

It is worth noting that previous evaluations had unwittingly reinforced Robert's unconscious view of himself as "damaged goods" by perceiving his problem generically and providing for it only a generic treatment, psychostimulants, which, of course, did not resolve his "nervousness."

Loss and Social Convention

Often the inception of impaired learning ("learning disability") is lost from view because it is too subtle and its meaning in the child's life is simply not recognized and, therefore, not understood. In Robert's case, only a contextualizing history and therapeutic evaluation could reveal the insidious process. In Gina's case, however, if the many clinicians who concluded that

Gina had a genuine "math disability" had been willing to entertain the notion that there was a life-relevant reason for an island of apparent inability in an otherwise good learner, four years of inappropriate medication treatment, repeated academic failure, and the development of "secondary" behavior problems might well have been avoided (not to mention the great financial cost to Gina's parents, insurance carriers and society at large). Similarly, Gina's father might well have been more open to a therapeutic resolution earlier in the process — before long years had passed which doubtless contributed to his feeling that it was "all his fault." The observant clinician will have many opportunities to see such nascent "disabilities" if he or she works with young children.

While still a baby, Jack and his two older sisters were abandoned by their mother, who left them at a baby-sitter's and never returned. Since their father was unable to care for them because of chronic illness, Jack and his sisters were raised by the paternal grandparents, in whose home they grew up healthy and reasonably well-adapted. Jack was a fourth-grader who generally got A's, B's, and C's in school. Apart from "laziness," there were few complaints about Jack's school work until his class began to study "The Family" in social studies. Jack was both upset and clearly disoriented when he failed a test in which he was supposed to mark the box which contained "a typical family." Jack had marked the box which contained grandparents and grandchildren — not the box with a mother, father, and children — and a big red check mark made it perfectly clear that he was wrong. Shortly thereafter Jack's grades in arithmetic dropped from B's and occasional C's to D's and F's. Although Jack didn't mention his new math difficulties to his grandparents, they discovered the change when the grading period ended and Jack reluctantly brought his report card home.

When the precipitous drop in Jack's math grade was mentioned by his grandparents at the beginning of the therapy hour, Jack was asked, "How many people are there in your family?" "Seven," he said without hesitation. When asked who the seven people were, Jack replied, "Grandpa, Grandma, [uncle] Henry, my sisters, me and my dad." Jack was then asked gently who got him up in the morning, made his breakfast, sent him off to school, made him clean up his room and brush his teeth. "Grandma and Grandpa," he replied. It was then pointed out to Jack that his uncle Henry was really more like a brother, and his father, whose chronic illness kept him away most of the time, was really more like an uncle — and that his grandparents, with whom he had lived nearly all his life, were really more like real mother and father. After a few more clarifying questions were asked, Jack was asked, "Now, how many people are there in your family?" "Six," he replied.

Although it was painful for Jack to realize that his father was not able to take care of him in a genuinely fatherly way, facing that sad fact brought Jack's grades back up. Things could now "add up" again in his life. We have seen many children undergo disastrous changes in the quality of their school work in reaction to very specific triggering events which had intense personal meaning in their lives. Rarely are the mistakes made at these times recognized as meaningful by the child's teacher, counselor or psychologist. If not recognized and resolved, such emotional interference in learning and academic performance can become a pattern whose historical roots are quickly lost from view.

The Psychotherapeutic Removal of Blocks to Learning

Because we are so used to categorical approaches, the invalidation of a convenient reductionistic theory can leave the clinician (or educator or parent) feeling that there is no approach to the problem. This is why categorists get so upset with the Gerald Coles of this world—it feels as if such ideological iconoclasts tear down the only structure we have to understand the world—and leave nothing in its place. The notion that power resides in the ability to name something is as old as man and permeates our myths and traditions and is at the heart of every nosology. Psychology, psychiatry and education are not immune to this intensely human need and tradition. Naming can be a form of mastery, but the mastery of naming and categorizing can also be illusory. As we mentioned previously, so many evaluations are really pathographies and consist of little or nothing more than the demonstration of pathology; what is missing is understanding. Children, especially hurt children, do not need to be mastered; they need to be understood. While understanding may involve naming, naming does not necessarily involve understanding.

What clinicians and educators alike tend not to realize is that understanding what something is *not* is the first and most significant step toward understanding what it is. If the facts supported the theories of a neurological etiology of the near epidemic of "learning disabilities" in American children, we, too, *might* begin to share some of the fatalism of the Academy's *Facts For Families*. But, even when genuine neurological impairment exists, only a developmental-contextual approach can provide a genuine operational assessment of ability and a basis for therapy—whether physical, psychological or psychophysiological. Abstract-categorical (nosology-driven) approaches cannot. Children and adults who believe themselves to be categorically unable become categorically unable. Only by mobilizing health and ability can one assess genuine potential. *That process is therapeutic in itself.*

As we indicated in Chapter 6, every potentially failable task presents an opportunity for integrative change. Even the most subtle and mundane of tasks offers this potential. But the ecology of child psychotherapy requires of the therapist a willingness to modify, whenever possible, the child's real world as well. In Stuart's case, the process of therapy could facilitate the removal of complex cognitive blocks to adaptive functioning. But to realize its full potential, it had to facilitate the resolution of severe family conflicts surrounding language and social stigmata. In Gina's case it succeeded only partially. While resolving the so-called "learning disabilities," therapy failed to change Gina's behavior because a very important part of the family was unreachable. In Catherine's case in Chapter 3, the transformational process of therapy was considerably slowed by the refusal of school personnel to accept the fact that she could have abilities incongruous with her outward appearance and her formal diagnoses.

The process of therapy works to reverse even the most minor of a child's convictions that he or she cannot do. This is one of the purposes of the "Smiley Charts" we use with so many children. Every session begins with the question "How was your week?" Often the answer is a vague "Okay." More often than not, however, when asked what was specifically good about the week, the child's the answer is "I don't [or can't] remember." Many clinicians ask similar questions, only to change the subject when the child gives a negative or non-answer. The "Smiley Chart" makes it difficult for the child not to remember because the parent is asked to note down, day by day, what actually happened. When the child is told to take a look at the chart and "refresh your memory," it becomes increasingly difficult for the child to remain in the "I don't know, I can't remember" mode. Similarly, acting out within the play specific happenings or formative themes (as when Jorge accepted a dictated perception) can have immensely powerful effects on the child's orientation toward knowledge and knowing. The revealing and resolving of family secrets can likewise have powerfully liberating effects upon cognition. Often the resolution of therapy issues unrelated to the specific learning difficulties can result in a significant improvement in class and standardized testing performance. We have seen formal IQ scores rise by 30–50 points as a result of therapy. Therapy did not increase the child's IQ, it only allowed for a more adaptive use and expression of the child's inherent abilities.

Although flexible responsiveness to the individual needs of the child is the keystone to successful therapy, a few guidelines may be helpful.

1. *Do not accept the appearance of categorical inability.* Even in cases of genuine handicap (see below), our working assumption should be that whatever abilities the child has are probably not being utilized to their fullest. The orientation that pervades contemporary psychology and psychiatry is a very pathocentric one: we take a pattern-recognition approach to the "identification" of categorical disorder, and then match categorical treatments. Consequently, the real potential of most children seen in therapy has probably not yet been recognized.

2. *Look for blocks to learning or performance that have their origins in the child's world.* Lack of environmental structure and consistency and continuity of experience, trauma—even subtle trauma—and family secrets can significantly affect cognitive development and performance. Often the discovery of a block to learning can be the first major step in its removal.

3. *Structure the therapeutic environment and the process of therapy such as to maximize competence.* Create opportunities for performance of those categorical tasks that are supposed to be impossible for the child. For example, in the case of a child with a "central processing disorder," work a series of complex commands (or situational demands for recall) into the play situation. In those cases where the child himself actually tells you that he or she "cannot do," you thereby demonstrate to the child that he or she can do. (Our one-way mirror is not for parents and school system personnel to view our assessment of "pathology"; it is so that adults can see children do those things they were convinced the children could not do.)

4. *Resolve and clarify cognitive confusions.* In Stuart's case above we saw that beneath the appearance of gross impairment was an extremely complex and bright child who actually knew two languages but who related to the world in two very different and confusing manners. The resolution of cognitive confusion paves the way for normal behavior, development, and, if necessary, remediation.

5. *Identify and undo pathological identifications.* Because imitation, most of which is unconscious, is such an elemental part of human development, the undoing of pathological identifications can free the child to resume or begin adaptive developmental patterns. This was strikingly illustrated by the cases of Robert and Catherine (Chapter 3).

Victims of Language

Over the years we have seen quite a few children who were thought by previous clinicians and educators to be mentally retarded. Often these children were in educational programs for the mentally handicapped and had formal IQ testing (WISCR, for example) which clearly "confirmed" the impression. Often they were said to have "central processing disorders" which prevented them from understanding what they heard. Still, the incredible complexity of these children's multi-leveled "fantasies" and the complex nature of the problems they created for themselves indicated that they could not be "simple" beings. In fact, for the clinician, possibly the most useful definition of intelligence is the following: intelligence is simply the ability to think complexly. The complexity of thinking does not assure that it will be "good" or adaptive: complex thinking can be problem-solving or problem-making. But it is not possible to think complexly and be dull—whatever "formal" testing may purport to "prove."

Ironically, not infrequently, children who are thought to have "central processing disorders" because of their apparent lack of understanding or confusion may, in fact, be so exquisitely sensitive to the semistic or symbolic meaning of ostensibly mundane behavior or utterances that they grossly overcomplicate the simple. Far from failing to process auditory or visual stimuli, as is often claimed by the evaluations which accompany these children, *they process too much*—and, often, too accurately. They understand too well what is really going on around them—while the environment works to make it appear that nothing is happening. (Not that bright children cannot misinterpret the meaning of experience; the fact that they often do so will assure that psychotherapy will never become obsolete.)

PSYCHOTHERAPY WITH THE PHYSICALLY HANDICAPPED CHILD

Rarely, if ever, does physical handicap constitute a block to psychotherapy with children or adolescents. All that is necessary is one channel of communication: the patient must be able to see or hear. (We are not "miracle workers": the blind-deaf are beyond our means.) We have, however, worked successfully with children who are deaf, blind, or unable to speak, as well as with those who are confined to wheel chairs or crutches. Not only is psychotherapy not contraindicated for patients with neurological disorders or mental handicap in which intellectual decrement, poor judgment, lack of an "observing ego," or impaired sensorium is traditionally seen as blocks, but it can often free otherwise unrecognized potential.

Anything which frees previously blocked communication can result in a functional increase in ability. Such was the experience when communications boards ("Blissboards") were introduced to nonverbal cerebral palsied-children previously thought to be retarded. When they were able to communicate by pointing to symbols and combinations of symbols on the boards, many children previously thought to be seriously subnormal were, in fact, found to be quite bright and teachable. In fact, it is fascinating to watch mothers from different countries, whose extremely poor English gives them the appearance of dullness, communicate rapidly and fluently via the communications boards—even though they cannot speak the same language. Because the primary concern in therapy is communication, and only secondarily speech, the fact that two mothers from different countries—or a therapist and a patient—do not *speak* the same language is of little importance to the process.

The Subjective Significance of the Handicapping Process

How an individual becomes handicapped is of paramount importance for the process of therapy for its meaning to the patient can vary considerably. Handicap is either congenital or acquired. If acquired, it can develop without obvious cause or its cause can be clearly recognized. Handicap which is caused can be accidental or volitional—although even volitional handicap (as when a child becomes palsied as a result of parental abuse) will often be treated by adults and children alike as if its cause were accidental. If handicap is acquired, it is important to understand the child's personal and family identity prior to the change brought about by being hurt purposefully, accidentally, or through illness. This identity involves not just the child's appearance and abilities prior to the change but also the expectations which parents and other family members may have had of the child. Photo albums can be helpful in this regard. It should be borne in mind that loss of function can be as psychologically palpable as loss of person. Whatever the handicapped individual can no longer do, or will never be able to do, represents a loss which can be as depressogenic as the loss of a loved one. Every handicapped individual must wonder "Why me?" and the handicapped child can develop extraordinarily complicated hypotheses ("fantasies") to account for the condition. The more than understandable anger at fate and the envy of the opportunities and abilities of others can seriously complicate the handicapped child's life.

Because pre- and perinatal care has greatly improved over the last decades, the number of children who survive previously fatal conditions or situations is persistently increasing. Consequently, handicapped children are likely to constitute an increasing proportion of the child therapist's caseload.

The process of understanding the meaning of acquired handicap presents an excellent opportunity to see the relevance of the three dimensions of context: environmental/situational, relational, and temporal. Consider how Ricky from Chapter 6 *became* a handicapped child.

While his father was inside napping, five-year-old Ricky rode his Big Wheel into city traffic and was hit by a car. At first Ricky was not expected to live. He was in a coma for months, confined to a hospital bed for many more months, and in a wheelchair for years. This was followed by years on crutches. When we met him at age 15 he was palsied, walked with sticks, and had palsied speech. Unable to square the condition of his son with his own "macho" attitude toward life, Ricky's father divorced shortly after the accident and left the family. During visits Ricky's father tended to be impatient and critical. Ricky's response was to become a master at passive-aggression.

The environmental/situational dimension can be seen in the meaning of how the accident occurred. The "accident" in which Ricky was nearly killed and which radically changed the course of his life was not a contingent experience of the unpredictable vagaries of the universe. He was not struck by lightning, hit by a falling boulder, or pricked by a poisonous plant. The immediate situational context of the accident was determined by his father's failure to provide expected benevolent parental care and supervision. The temporal dimension is reflected in the concurrence of harm and the failure of parental care. While both of these overlap the relational dimension, it was given its most intense meaning when Ricky's father left the family and his son because he could not stand his "broken" condition. The relational dimension might have been very different had Ricky's father accepted his responsibility for the accident and remained with the family to make the best of things.

Seizures as a Model of the "Damaged" Child

The child therapist who works closely with schools is much more likely to be asked if (or told that) particular behavioral problems are caused by neurological dysfunction than to receive a referral of an epileptic child for behavior which is felt to be independent of the disorder. In fact, in the large school system we work with, during the course of the year only one neurological condition was actually found in the forty-some children referred for formal neurological evaluation.

Seizures, like any handicap, are experienced. But the seizure experience is unusual in that it involves changes in consciousness which can range from the subtle absences of petit mal seizures to the experience of physical devastation in grand mal seizures. The pain of the seizures themselves, as well as injury that can occur during loss of consciousness or uncontrolled movement, can in some cases be made even more disorienting and confusing by pre-ictal auras which can be, as they were in the case of the great Russian writer Dostoyevsky, pleasant or even exquisitely sensuous (Alajouanine, 1963). Seizures can interrupt activities and relationships or even make them impossible. For some children the *dyscontrol* which characterizes disordered brain activity can become a part of the child's identity.

Seven-year-old Adele had had seizures since the age of 15 months. Ranging from grand mal seizures, which Adele said left her muscles aching as if she had been "beaten up by a gorilla," to profound clouding of consciousness preceded by stomachaches and followed by weakness and sleepiness which lasted for several house, Adele's seizures had resulted in any number of scrapes and falls and banged heads. Even though Adele's seizures were very hard to control (she had as many as 10–20 a day in spite of the best of neurological care), it was her behavior which brought her to therapy.

Adele was the only child either of us had ever met who had never played. She didn't play with toys of any kind, play with other children, or even watch television. Instead, she spent all of her waking hours invading other people's space. Intensely jealous of the ability of others to enjoy themselves and be without pain, Adele seemed driven to cause others to hurt as much as she did. If her experience of time, space, and relationship could not be free of unpredictable invasion and disruption, then, she reasoned, no one else's would either. Adele bit, kicked, pinched—and professed great affection and possessiveness. She recognized neither social nor personal boundaries and was therefore constantly "going home with" or "marrying" every newcomer. Or she was working to split people apart—such as couples.

Feeling that she could control nothing in her own world, least of all her own body and her own consciousness, Adele became a veritable master of controlling others. Constantly demanding things, attention, and involvement, Adele took things into her own hands if she didn't get what she wanted. If the family didn't listen to her demands, she threatened to run in front of cars or to jump out of windows or into swimming pools—and, of course, she couldn't swim. Adele was serious for if her demands were not met she would carry out her threats. Since her demands stopped only during her seizures, the danger was constant and real and life with Adele was extraordinarily exhausting.

Adele loved therapy at first because it was a new experience to possess and control. She wanted everything her way and simply containing her was an exhausting task. When her demands were not met at the office she threatened—and tried—to destroy whatever was dearest to her therapists. She was also the only child in years for whom our large bookcase holding the Lego structures built over time by children in therapy had to be removed every time she came for her session. The fear was not so much that Adele would overturn the large bookcase and injure herself; that was a risk which Adele's parents had simply come to take for granted over the years. Rather, the bookcase had to be removed because Adele would have destroyed all the other children's creations because they represented the ability of the other children to have fun. And if Adele did destroy anyone's property or hurt someone, it wasn't her fault: she *was* a seizure.

The first phase of Adele's therapy lasted nearly four months and was dedicated to undoing her identity as a "living seizure" and to taking every opportunity to delineate and preserve structure, rules, and boundaries while attempting to return even a minimal sense of control to her parents. Mr. Wolf, a hand puppet, became Mr. Seizure, who was bad and could be thrown against the throwing area of the wall. Simultaneously, and in contrast to bad Mr. Wolf, the goodness of Adele's body was reinforced exhaustingly. Because Adele picked her skin off until it bled, any small decrease in self-injurious behavior was greeted by her therapist with child-like celebration, until Adele began to care just a bit about how she looked.

This period was exhausting and painful for Adele's therapist who was bruised and bitten regularly. Yet Adele discovered that she could not anger her therapist no matter how much she hurt, or tried to hurt, her. So, realizing how much her therapist loved her playtherapy room, Adele, having run out of invasive and hurtful ways of taking control, said, "I know what I can do," pulled down her panties and urinated right in the middle of the floor.

After several months of futile attempts to control or destroy both the therapeutic space and her therapist's morale, Adele began to accept structure. The second phase of therapy lasted about three months and consisted almost exclusively of getting Adele to set up the chessboard. No attempt was made to play, not even checkers, which is much simpler than chess. Instead, repeatedly Adele put the chessmen in their proper places only to have her therapist sweep the board clean and start the process again. This is how the "game" was defined for Adele. Changes were subtle and the power struggles continued at home and in therapy, but bit by bit Adele began to accept structure and boundaries both in and out of therapy.

The process became less exhausting and more rewarding as Adele experienced personal, social and academic successes. She moved from the Physically Impaired Program where she had been viewed as uncontrollable and had to wear a football helmet for protection to a program for emotional and behavioral disturbance and even spent some time in a normal private school until the school's fear of her seizures brought her tenure there to an end. By the end of treatment she had friends she enjoyed, rode a bicycle and water skied behind the family boat, and was able to go on family vacations. Despite the remarkable change in her behavior Adele's seizures remained as intractable as ever.

Although we have encountered many such children, every therapist needs at least one Adele to learn from. The therapist who never actually experiences the profound and lasting changes such patients can undergo may never believe in their possibility. Such patients also tend to force the therapist to experience personally the inescapability of trauma and the maddening sense of personal powerlessness and dyscontrol that such initially "nonresponsive" patients can engender. At some point, the therapist who would really test the limits of treatability should take on an "untreatable" and "impossible" patient like Adele. Finding the patience to survive such an experience without becoming personally retributive or giving up can open the door to a recognition of the manifold subtle complexities inherent in "completely disordered" or "uncontrolled" behavior, thereby fortifying the therapeutic optimism that should characterize any caring clinician's approach to treatment.

9

Loss in the Lives of Children

There's nothing new under the sun but there are lots of old things we don't know.
Ambrose Bierce

Earlier we noted that what is often mistaken for ludic fantasy is, in fact, a complex, serious, and often scary form of imaginative hypothesizing on the part of the child, an anticipatory thinking-through of various possible explanations for why things are as they are. While anticipatory, such hypothesizing can be retrospective as well — an attempt to make sense of the past within the context of present knowledge and logical structures.

Children must make sense of the world as they live it. Their "interpretations" of the events in their lives quickly become part of their lives. Subsequent experiences are then understood in terms of preceding experiences. If events are overwhelming or profoundly confusing, the child's operative explanation may be very different from the consensual assessment of the same events. As bizarre as the child's understanding may be, however, it will always be found to be *logical*. The more these logical interpretations of events become additive, the more dysfunctional the child may become and the more bizarre his or her behavior may appear. In the practical world the functional rigidity of logical solutions to problems with variable contextual meaning can be disastrous. On the other hand, the effects of experience can be exquisitely subtle. One must simply accept the fact that experience affects some individuals with great and obvious intensity and others with great subtlety.

ADOPTION, FOSTER CARE AND "ORPHANS"

The adoptee who enters the mental health system is at a double disadvantage: the psychology of the adoptive situation itself complicates even mundane aspects of his life and its relevance to his problems goes largely unnoticed by caseworkers and clinicians alike.

The Overrepresentation of Adoptees in Psychiatric Populations

Child and adolescent therapists are likely to see many adoptees in their practice. Thirty years ago Schecter (1960) found that adoptees were grossly overrepresented in an outpatient survey, a finding subsequently confirmed in inpatient, outpatient, and mixed settings (Bohman & von Knorring, 1979; Goodman, Silberstein & Mandell, 1963; Humphrey & Ounsted, 1963; Kellman-Pringle, 1961; Menlove, 1965; Work & Anderson, 1971). Senior and Hamadi (1985) found a higher rate yet for adolescent inpatients: 21–24% of 12–18-year-olds admitted to an adolescent inpatient service consecutively over 18 months were adopted. Twenty-four and 18%, respectively, of their male and female adolescent admissions were adopted. Our experience with young women's residences (usually former homes for unwed mothers) shows an even higher rate than adolescent inpatient units, and we are told by case-coordinators at major insurance companies that adoptees constitute an inordinate percentage of child and, especially, adolescent psychiatric patients, although we have yet to quantify percentage.

Lest it be thought that the adoptee psychiatric population is an overrepresentation only because adoptive parents are more likely to seek out help, Jerome's (1986) long retrospective analysis of case records of children attending a children's mental health center from 1959 to 1973, which controlled for actual year-by-year incidence of adoptions in the population studied, found that "over a 15 year period the clinic adopted children were seen with *twice the expected annual incidence predicted from the community rates*" (emphasis added). Thus, he noted, because of referral pattern biases, there is "the possibility that the overrepresentation of adopted children seen at the clinic might be an *underestimate* of the number of emotionally disturbed adopted children that were being seen in the community as a whole" (emphasis added). This conclusion is supported by the large retrospective Scandinavian study reported by von Knorring, Bohman and Sigvardsson (1982), which found that "early negative experiences [. . .] *did not* explain the manifestation of psychiatric disorders in general. This is in line with our earlier studies where early life experience *did not* explain maladjustment or underachievement during school age" (emphasis added).

To the problems potentially inherent in the adoptive situation itself must be added the changing nature of adoption in the United States. From 1951 to 1971 unrelated adoptions constituted about 50% of adoptions (±4%). By 1982 unrelated adoptions constituted only 36% of total adoptions (National Committee for Adoption, 1985). To the unrelated adoptions which once constituted the majority of formal adoptions have been added an increasing number of foreign adoptions, including Korean infants and children and Vietnamese Amerasians. The placement of "special needs" (hard-to-place) children is not only increasing but has developed into a professional specialty with private organizations such as New York Spaulding for Children and other agencies supported by private and public funds. With the average foster child facing the loss of 2.3 foster placements prior to permanent placement (not to mention the loss of the original home) and some 300,000 children in foster care (Grabe, 1986), the child therapist is likely to see many such children. Furthermore, the number of already failed adoptions in foster care is considerable. And adoption disruption averages 13%, with the rate for older children as high as 25% (Grabe, 1986).

Common Behavioral Problems of Adopted Children

At no time over the past six years has the percentage of adoptees (children, adolescents and adults) in our 50–60 patient-hour work week dropped below 25%. It tends to hover at about 30% and has remained as high at 45% for months at a time when our caseload was at its peak of 13–14 clinical hours per day. Although over time we have become known as clinicians with a special interest in adoption and now receive referrals from schools, institutions, and out-of-state adoption agencies, that was not the case when the proportion of adoptees was at its highest. As a result of relatively long and consistent clinical experience with child and adolescent adoptees, and of an even longer consultative and training relationship with state and private agencies, we have seen the emergence of a remarkably consistent clinical picture. The following are common behavioral problems of adopted children as described by their parents:

- Stealing from parents and siblings. Taking money, usually available for the asking, from wallets, purses, or dressers.
- Sneaking, hiding and hoarding food. Parents often find caches, sometimes quite sizeable, of food in desks, dressers, and closets, or under beds. They are often puzzled, hurt, and disgusted when

they find old, rotting food hidden in their child's desk or dresser drawers.

- Worrying about seconds and thirds when food is readily available at meals and always in adequate supply in the home.
- Lying about *very* minor issues.
- Confabulating, making up fantastic stories — not infrequently about self and family.
- Treating minor acts as if they were great trespasses.
- Embarrassing family, especially mother, in public.
- Ruining birthdays, anniversaries and holidays. Mothers frequently complain that they are often treated disrespectfully by their child during the birthday party. Occasionally, refusal to celebrate and refusal of gifts.
- School underachievement or failure. Academic cheating when native ability would more than allow for average or even superior grades. Many of these children are formally or informally identified as having "learning disabilities."
- Stealing from teachers and peers, often from those who are most liked by the child.
- Going out of the way to get into trouble. Viewing oneself as a "jinx," as having "bad luck."
- Destroying parental, family property. Destroying one's own property or clothes. Often the destruction of the child's own things appears repetitiously "accidental."
- Sleep disturbances: difficulty falling asleep, nightmares, night terrors. Nighttime insecurity which has no objective cause.
- Failure to learn from experience.
- Indiscriminate attachment in bright, precocious younger children. Or failure to attach which the parents often think reflects an "inherent" inability to relate in the child.
- Steadfast denial of personal responsibility in the face of incontrovertible evidence.
- Aggression toward peers, insolence toward authority figures — especially in a self-defeating way. (Donovan, 1988a)

We find that, even when many of the problems and behaviors listed above are not mentioned specifically by adoptive parents during the first contact, a brief review of the list tends to elicit positive findings much more frequently than with children who are not adopted. Many of the adoptive parents we have worked with have commented that they found our questions about specific behaviors to be very reassuring. As one mother remarked, "If you've seen this so many times before, maybe it's not all our fault after all." One of the most frequent first responses to our questioning is "How do you know that?" Our clinical findings are similar to those of von Knorring, Bohman and Sigvardsson (1982). Whereas their finding was that "early negative experiences [. . .] did not explain the manifestation of psychiatric disorders" in adoptees, our finding has been the striking consistency of behavior problems among adoptees *whether the family is functional or dysfunctional.*

The Central Issues in the Psychology of the Adopted Child

The psychological blinders which have kept society and its erudite disciplines from understanding the real plight of the child are nowhere more in evidence than in adoption casework practice and the "expert" opinions which reflect or guide it. The adopted child has much to teach the child therapist, as we shall see below.

Needless to say, the adopted child may face the same problems that befall any child and his family—and many do. Even the mundane issues of life, however, can take on intense and idiosyncratic meanings for the adopted child. The reason for this is very simple: two extremely confusing issues may complicate the normal cognitive and emotional development of the adopted child—the *two-mother* dilemma and the *"she really loved you, but . . . "* dilemma. These issues are thrust upon the child—at the insistence of adoptions workers and "experts"—at a time when the child has developed neither the cognitive skills nor the sophistication necessary to deal with them without paying a significant price. The monolithic approach to adoption casework in this country dictates that the child be told about the adoption as early as possible. The position of most authorities is similar to the following response found in a respected medical journal to the question "When is the best age to tell children they are adopted?" To illustrate just how irrational "expert" advice can be, we have substituted "biological" for "adopted" in the following quotation.

> It is my belief that children should be informed from the very beginning that they [are] biological. This can be done in subtle and casual ways such as occasionally referring to the child as "my wonderful biological child" even in an infancy period. The comfortable and appropriate use of the word "biological" in reference to the child from an early age will permit the child to assimilate this fact without unnecessary and unexpected stress at any particular developmental stage of the child's growth process. (Kappelman, 1982)

If the need is for knowledge, then it follows that one should inform the nonadopted child of the fact that he is "biological." This basic attitude toward the implicit needs of the child is echoed by the *Fact Sheet* on "The Adopted Child" published by the American Academy of Child and Adolescent Psychiatry.

> Parents with an adopted child are concerned about whether, when and how to tell their child that he or she is adopted. They also want to know if there are special problems the adopted child typically faces.
>
> Child psychiatrists generally recommend that the child be told about adoption. This helps give the message that adoption is good and that the child can trust the parents. On the other hand, if the child learns about the adoption when older, he or she may feel anger and mistrust toward the parents, and may view the adoption as bad because it was kept a secret.
>
> The child should be given information according to what he or she can understand. In the early years, parents can say, "I am happy we adopted you," just as they would say, "What a beautiful baby you are." The baby does not comprehend the words in either case but understands the positive meaning. This helps set the stage for later discussion of adoption.
>
> As the child grows older, the birth parents' placement of the child in an adoptive home should be presented as an act of caring and concern. A possible explanation is, "At the time you were born your birth mother and father could not adequately take care of you. Because your birth parents wanted the very best for you, they made arrangements for you to live with a mother and father who were ready to love and care for you."
>
> Child psychiatrists have found that children have a variety of responses to the knowledge that they are adopted. The child may deny it or create fantasies about it. Frequently adopted children think they were given away for being bad or may believe that they were kidnapped. If the parents talk openly about the adoption and present it in a positive manner, these worries are less likely to develop. (American Academy of Child and Adolescent Psychiatry, 1985a)

We see here two extraordinary problems. The first is the totally irrational cognitive burden placed upon an immature and developing mind. The fact that the infant or toddler simply cannot understand what the experts tell the parent to say does not register on the experts. Babies have no need to "know" about adoption. They need love, care, nurturance, safety and challenge. Even the good psychological research on these issues agrees that young children do not understand these issues as adults would wish them to (Brodzinsky, Singer & Braff, 1984). So why persist?

The second problem forced upon the adopted child is the—unwitting, perhaps, but nevertheless real—equation of love and abandonment. The need to present these issues, and to present them in this manner, are adult needs and do not reflect the developmental needs of children.

The fact of the matter is that the unrelated infant adoptee must either have been given away by his or her mother or taken away from her. Children freed for adoption during the immediate postnatal period because of a maternal death are rare, as are puerperal deaths. (Even so, if that explanation is offered, the child must still face the fact that the "other" parent did not want him.) The experts tell adoptive parents to define this process as love and caring, failing to realize that this primes the child to equate literally *love* and *abandonment*. Hence the logical but perplexing behavior of many adopted children: the unnecessary stealing, the worry about and hoarding of food, the view of oneself as a "jinx," and the disorders of attachment — from indiscriminate attachment to failure to attach. According to the prevailing wisdom, attachment=abandonment and security=loss. Caught in a logical bind, adoptees cannot fault a mother who gave them up because, so they are repeatedly told, it was done for their own good. Blocked from feeling anger or resentment toward, or sadness about the loss of the relinquishing biological mother ("because she did it for you"), the adoptee often directs the anger toward his adoptive parents — and toward the adoptive mother in particular. Thus, genuinely caring adoptive parents are completely befuddled when their excellent parenting results in disrespectful, off-putting behavior in their child, and when they are repeatedly embarrassed in public.

Dawn had been neglected to the point where she failed to thrive and had been burned badly with cigarettes by her biological mother. Both the agency which placed her and her new adoptive parents told her (because the agency had insisted) that her biological mother had "loved her in her own way." Not until well into treatment, and just prior to the ultimate failure of the adoption, did Dawn tell her adoptive mother that she had never allowed herself to get close to her "because I thought you were going to hurt me."

The *two-mother dilemma* has profound potential cognitive effects as well. Unlike their nonadopted peers, adoptees who are told from infancy that they are adopted are forced into a bizarre position of *obligatory "fantasizing."* The average nonadopted child is not faced with the Sisyphean cognitive task of "filling in the blanks" of his parents' — especially his mother's — face because the "biological" parent is a known entity. Hence, the extraordinary imagination of many adopted children who come for therapy, the fantastic confabulations they concoct, and the compulsive, driven nature of their imagining. Children, remember, are obligatory slaves of logic for

many years. The results of early disclosure, totally inadvertent from a volitional standpoint, can be disastrous.

Will was a 10-year-old who was adopted from foster care at nine months
of age. His adoptive mother was an open, honest, and straightforward
person who tried to give real answers to real questions. Told to do so by
the state agency that had placed Will, she had told him about his adopted
status from the very first.

When Will inquired about the noises which he had heard coming from
the parental bedroom, his mother thought that it was time that he learned
the "facts of life" and therefore bought him the book *"Where Did I Come
From?"* which she thought well-written and informative. It did not occur
to her, however, that the question "Where did I come from?" is a loaded
one for an adopted child. She didn't realize, therefore, that she had inadvertently linked *sex* and *adoption* in her son's unconscious mind. Interestingly, the only question Will had about the book was, "What's the umbilical cord?"—that which links a baby to its mother.

Subsequently, Will asked about his birth parents, wanting to know
particularly how old they had been and whether they had been married.
He was told that his birth mother had been a teenager and that she had
not been married. As fate would have it, shortly thereafter Will received
his only introduction to explicit sex when he found a copy of *Hustler*
magazine next to a neighborhood garbage can. In it he saw scenes of
penetration and of a man with an enormous penis. Linking all the events
together unconsciously, Will later stated that he thought he was the product of a gross and pornographic teenage sexual orgy and that his birth
mother "must have been a whore."

Again, we must remember that these are not fantasies in the traditional sense
of the term; they are operational hypotheses about the structure of reality.
This generation of hypotheses about the structure of existence clearly constitutes a dissociogenic force that cannot help but have some effect on cognitive
development and academic performance. The incessant "day-dreaming" of
many adoptees comes to fill the time that should be devoted to enjoyable
learning.

Finally, if, as the Academy and nearly all traditional adoption casework
practice tells us to do, we tell the adopted child that the biological parents—
the biological mother especially—"really loved you, but . . . ," we inadvertently set the child up to conclude (logically, if mistakenly) that there must
really be something wrong with him or her. (Why, as many children have
asked us, would a good mother give up a good baby? The baby, they con-

clude, must have been "bad.") Hence the extraordinarily poor self-esteem of many adopted children in basically functional healthy families.

The irrational approach to adoption casework practice is not limited to that involving simple unrelated infant adoptions. Repeatedly, children who have been horribly abused and/or neglected are told that their parents "loved you in their own way"—even when the only tangible signs of parental attention are the cigarette burns all over the child's body.

Ten-year-old Jerry was born in a state mental hospital where his mother was incarcerated after she shot and killed Jerry's father. Five days after Jerry was born his mother hanged herself. After horribly neglectful care at the hands of relatives and nearly a year in foster care, Jerry was freed for adoption. Despite good care, Jerry lied, cheated, stole and was violently aggressive toward his mother. He constantly threatened suicide, so that knives and weapons had to be made scarce. He did poorly in school in spite of obvious above-average intelligence. (Asked by his mother why he hadn't answered the question about "the donkey" on the IQ test, Jerry replied, "Because a donkey is an ass and I didn't want to embarrass my teacher.")

One day Jerry stood up in our office and screamed, "If I had been a good baby my mother wouldn't have killed my father and then killed herself!" The following week his therapist arranged for a newborn baby to be brought to the office. Jerry was gently backed into a (literal) corner and given the baby to hold. "Now, you show me how that baby could be bad," she told him gently but firmly. "Show me," she repeated as she handed Jerry the bottle and had him feed the baby. "Go on," she said again, "show me how that baby could possibly be bad."

Only by seeing a real live baby—one that felt soft and good to hold and smelled sweet—was Jerry able to have any real sense that the individuality of a newborn baby is independent of its parents and their behavior. Only then could he turn his rage away from himself and his adoptive family to a more appropriate psychological target and be angry at his biological mother for not recognizing what a marvelous baby she had and for not caring enough about him to stay alive.

Another logical bind created by the "she really loved you, but" approach is the fear that the biological parents—especially mother—may return to steal the child. If, after all, only "unfortunate circumstances" prevented the biological mother from keeping her child in the first place, then what is to prevent her from wanting her child back now that she has the means to provide? This can be a horrible thought (conscious or unconscious) for the adopted child who does not want to lose his *real* adoptive parents.

> Jane was about three when her mother left her and her six-month-old brother at the baby-sitter's, never to return. By the time she entered therapy many years had passed and she was academically successful and well-behaved except for the oppositionalism which occasioned the therapy. As therapy progressed, her grandmother began to note other behaviors which she had always thought strange but not worrisome enough to do anything about. When Jane's grandmother remarked that Jane always slept with a huge pile of blankets and all of her many dolls tucked into bed with her, and that she would never allow the windows to be opened in her bedroom no matter how hot it got before the central air conditioning was turned on, it was suggested that grandmother simply ask Jane during their Five Minutes what she was afraid of. Jane answered: "I'm afraid Cissie [Jane's biological mother] will come back to get me and climb through the window."

This simple clarification allowed Jane's grandparents the occasion to assure her that she could not be "kidnapped back." Interestingly, Jane had treated the interval of several years since her mother left her at the baby-sitter's as if it were a very short time and her mother might, therefore, "come back" for her at any moment.

It is often very hard for parents (or professionals, for that matter) to understand that the child's need for security far outweighs any abstract "need" for categorical honesty. "Honesty" is not an absolute virtue. Thus, we wouldn't find it virtuous to accost an individual on the street with the "truth" that "you were the ugliest person I've seen all day." Similarly, the child's need for security far outweighs any abstract "need" of the relinquishing biological mother to have her image protected (or of the adoptive parents and caseworkers to protect that image). Many adoptees never voice the very conscious belief that they will be given up by their adoptive parents if the same fate that befell the biological mother—loss of family support, financial hardship, accident or illness—should befall them. Helping (even the healthiest and most financially secure of) parents to convey clearly to their adopted child that *nothing*—from illness to bankruptcy—could ever cause them to give up their child often brings about a much needed sense of security and removes the pressure of the constant worry about such eventualities.

We have followed the lead of one of our adopted little patients and no longer refer to biological parents as "parents." "Not my biological *mother*," the eight-year-old said in response to a question, "my biological *stranger*. If she had been a real mother she would have never given me away." Later, the parents can be told, when the child is older and genuinely secure in her sense of self and belonging, they can answer honestly (when appropriate and true) that the "biological stranger" really did do everything she could to ensure health, safety, and opportunity for the child she was giving up.

Adoption Psychology and Parental Pathology

The following case illustrates how many of the common behavioral symptoms of adopted children can be significantly complicated by real parental disturbance, as well as how useful history-taking in the presence of the child can be.

Ten-year-old Steven was brought for evaluation because he was felt by his school to have serious emotional difficulties. School personnel described Steven as distracted and fidgety and as having great difficulty concentrating on class work. His disruptive behavior had become truly worrisome when he began to make animal sounds in the classroom, to hit himself in the face, and to tear up papers and books. Steven was also noted to have bizarre thoughts about his body. He stuck a pencil in his navel, telling his mother that it "kept his arms and legs from flying off." Steven also engaged in bizarre activities which involved shutting animals, himself, or both into enclosed spaces—such as putting the cat in the washing machine.

Most striking, though, was his intense story-telling in which he would make up "strange, unusual, untrue but highly detailed stories" which adults around him would often believe at first, so convincingly were they told. Most of Steven's stories had to do with disastrous occurrences, such as when he told his parents that a school bus taking Steven and his classmates on an outing had had a terrible accident. He had described in great detail how the bus had run into a telephone pole and provided a more than graphic description of the horribly injured bodies of his classmates. Needless to say, there had been no such accident; in fact, there had been no outing at all. The entire story had been made up. Yet even his father, a polygraph specialist and an expert on insurance fraud, believed most of his stories at first.

Steven was adopted at the age of six months after Mrs. Smith had had 11 spontaneous abortions and had given birth to one living child, a girl, who was six when Steven was brought home. Shortly after bringing Steven home Mrs. Smith began to notice that he was "hyper" and soon had him on all sorts of diets, telling physicians that he was "allergic to everything." By the time he was five Mrs. Smith had taken Steven to most of the "fringe" professionals in the community, who had prescribed everything from herbs to tutoring for his supposed learning disabilities. (The fact that Steven had taught himself to read by kindergarten and was reading on a fourth grade level by the time he finished the first grade didn't seem to dissuade any of the experts from accepting mother's view of him as "damaged.") By the time he was seen for psychiatric evaluation Steven had taken large amounts of stimulant medication for over five years.

During the history-taking with Steven and Mrs. Smith present, Steven listened, transfixed, as his adoptive mother described in detail the 11 miscarriages. When she stated that she had carried one baby for six months, Steven exclaimed, "That was me!" Mrs. Smith continued, describing that pregnancy, oblivious to her son's interjection, saying, "but I never felt any signs of life." "That was mine," Steven again interrupted, referring to the pregnancy which had never shown "any signs of life." Although Mrs. Smith had voiced some concern over talking about such things in front of Steven at the beginning of the encounter, she appeared unconcerned when she described the rather rare disorder which presumably had caused the miscarriages and when she stated that an "autopsy" had been done on her womb "to see what it had done to all the babies."

When Mrs. Smith began to recount the adoption history and said that Steven had been brought home at six months of age, he interrupted again and said, "I did? I was?" With a look of total astonishment he said, "I thought you found me on the ground, laying on a blanket when I was six!" Mrs. Smith, unruffled by her son's exclamations, went on to say that Steven had "never really wanted to talk about it" ("But I do," Steven interjected), and that he had not been told much about his birth mother except that "she was a nice lady."

When asked from which adoption agency the Smiths had obtained Steven, Mrs. Smith started to reply "the American Cancer Society . . ." but blushed and corrected herself. "I mean the *Catholic* Society," she said. Although embarrassed by this slip of the tongue, Mrs. Smith could not be induced to see it as at all significant. Nor could she be brought to see the significance of the two fully-formed stillborn brothers who had proceeded and followed her own birth—not even when it was pointed out to her that she had described herself as "extremely hyper as a child" and that her descriptions of herself corresponded point-for-point to her descriptions of Steven as a baby.

What we see here is an incredible blurring of interpersonal boundaries. Mrs. Smith projected onto her adopted son extraordinary concerns about physical integrity and wellness. Thinking about all those miscarriages, the striking slip where she referred to the adoption agency as "the American Cancer Society," and the fact that her one successful pregnancy had produced a healthy girl (Mrs. Smith had four sisters), her examiner asked Mrs. Smith what she thought the sexes of her 11 miscarriages had been. "I never really thought about it before," she replied, "but I suppose they were male."

Identity being a key issue for adopted children, Steven never really stood a chance in this family. Imagine his bind: on the one hand, the identity projected onto him by his adoptive mother was that of a dead, fractionated, disintegrating baby. Hence the "It was me!" when his mother described the six-month (male) stillbirth. On the other hand, where would Steven's normal urge to be the natal child of his adoptive mother leave him? (After all, it is not at all uncommon for adopted children, especially those brought into a family with a biological child, to wish that they, too, had shared in the intimacy of being carried by, and born to, this *real* mother of theirs.) Such a fantasy could only be wrought with danger in Steven's case—for all the male babies died. Hence Steven's extraordinary preoccupation with sick, dysfunctional, disintegrating bodies—both his and those of others.

His symbolic aptness is evident in many of his stories, such as the one about the school bus. It takes but brief reflection to realize that there was a common theme to many of Steven's confabulations and bizarre activities. School busses carry children (like a mother's body carries children): in both cases, in Steven's mind, the results were disastrous. He was obsessed with such dangerous enclosures—as can be seen with his preoccupation with putting himself (and his pets) in places like the washing machine. That "special clean safe place for babies" which mothers have certainly was not safe in Steven's view. Caught between the need to identify with the imagined male biological child of his mother and the fear of the logical implications inherent in such an identity, Steven lived in a very confusing and dangerous universe. And since male babies died in his mother's universe, it was only logical that Steven should imagine all sorts of "magical" ways to prevent himself from suffering their fate. Hence his "bizarre" (and "crazy," meaningless to parents and school personnel) behaviors like sticking a pencil in his navel and then saying that it kept his arms and legs "from flying off."

And then there is the view of the adoptive surrender: Steven sees his life as beginning at age six years of age (although he had been told by his mother that he was adopted at six months), lying on a blanket, given over by "a nice lady"—certainly a convenient and safe way to skip a potentially dangerous part of his life. Over the years Steven's memories had been replaced by complex fantasies. These "fantasies," crippling though they were, were not a sign of "mental illness"; rather, they were logical, if bizarre, attempts on Steven's part to make sense of a very scary and confusing world.

The adoptive agency that placed Steven in the Smith household should have been concerned when (or if) they learned of Mrs. Smith's two stillborn male siblings and of her own 11 miscarriages. Unfortunately, in our experience, many, if not most, adoption agencies simply do not ask about such things. Or, if they do, they limit their questions to the couple's personal experience with conception. That childhood experience can significantly shape the meaning and impact of adult experience does not seem to occur to most workers. Frequently, facts such as these are not even to be found in the agency's social history. Yet it has been known for nearly 25 years that such losses can have a powerful impact on children (who—it should be no surprise to us—grow up to be adults and have, or adopt, children of their own) (Cain & Cain, 1964; Cain et al., 1964; Cain, Fast & Erickson, 1964).

The Adopted Child Grown Up

It is not only standard adoptions practice which can inadvertently create difficulties for the child. Even when one might think that the obvious would dictate the course of events, denial can wreak havoc.

Béatrice van Köln was a 35-year-old single woman whose "nordic" beauty was stunning. Following an automobile accident, in which her forehead had smashed the windshield when her car, traveling at high speed, hit a deer as it ran across an isolated country road, she developed headaches of such intensity that at the time of her referral she was taking upwards of twenty Percodan a day. Her general physician, concerned about what appeared to be an developing dependence upon synthetic narcotic analgesics, referred her for psychiatric evaluation.

When she was 12, and rummaging around her mother's closet, Béatrice came upon her birth certificate—and thereby "learned" that she was adopted. The fact that she was Catholic and attended Mass every Sunday, whereas her parents and siblings were Protestant and went to a different church, had never troubled her. Nor had the fact that her mother, father and siblings were short, swarthy, and had dark hair and brown eyes, whereas she was tall and had light hair and blue-green eyes. She had even managed not to notice that her siblings wore cotton underwear, whereas hers were always silk. Even the packages that she alone received from Germany, packages filled with all sorts of delicacies and fine clothes, failed to raise her curiosity. Finally, it had never occurred to her to wonder why she bore a name of German nobility while her family had a "plain old American name."

After she left home, Béatrice gave up her first child for adoption and gave the whole process not so much as a second thought. She was repeatedly unhappy in her relationships with men, often hurt, and finally found herself embroiled in the drug culture of Los Angeles, far from her home. After a series of abortions, she finally decided to have another baby—which was born dead—at home. Strung out on drugs at the time, she cleaned up as best she could and put the dead baby in the freezer where it remained for several days. An autopsy later revealed that the baby girl was anencephalic and had a huge "split" in the top of her head where the "soft spot" should have been. There were other congenital abnormalities but they paled in Béatrice's memory next to the image of the "split-open head."

It was not until she began therapy for her intractable headaches that Béatrice ever questioned her extraordinary life. It took but a moment to figure out why her headaches, supposedly due to the impact with the windshield when her car hit the deer, were impossible to treat. The dear had been a doe. And the doe was pregnant. Béatrice had killed a pregnant mother.

Like many female adoptees, Béatrice gave her firstborn up for adoption. Having repeated the rejection she herself had suffered when her mother arranged to give her away, she was thus psychologically free to keep the next baby and the series of abortions allowed her to "chose" her child. But it was born dead. Her sense of guilt was extraordinary and it was not until all of that was worked through that her "splitting" headaches went away and she could successfully decrease her medication. A series of *catastrophic coincidences* had locked in Béatrice's "agenda" (Chapter 7), and she was destined to pay an extraordinary price for what might have been—for another person under similar circumstances—nothing more than an unfortunate accident on a desolate country road. Again, only a contextualizing approach was able to make any sense of her condition and to provide a realistic resolution of the problem.

The Blindness of Psychology and Psychiatry to Human Suffering

Why the incredible blindness to such human suffering? Why do well-meaning agencies and professionals recommend that the adoptive parents tell their child "Your mother really loved you, but"? Why do so many parents follow this advice unquestioningly? Why does most of an entire literature on adoption ignore a child's cognitive ability to understand and place abstract notions of "right" and "honesty" above security?

One has only to look to Freud for the answer. Oedipus was the paradigmatic adopted child. Rejected and meant to be left to die in the present-day equivalent of a garbage dumpster, Oedipus passed through the "foster care" of the benevolent shepherd to the permanent adoptive placement with Laïus and Jocasta, the King and Queen of Thebes. His unresolved rage and identity-confusion led to extraordinary family disasters and, like many adopted children, he hurt the wrong parents. Ultimately, his life, his adoptive parents' life, and even the lives of his children were ruined. But Freud and his exegetes wear incredible blinders that keep them from seeing the obvious. Yet the obvious is accessible to anyone with the courage to see it. The key is to be found in Freud's "Oedipus complex," a notion so familiar that even lay persons who have never read Freud can recount it in outline form. In *The Interpretation of Dreams* Freud (1900) chose as the model for his oedipus complex Sophocles' drama *Oedipus Rex*.

> What I have in mind is the legend of King Oedipus and Sophocles' drama which bears his name.
> Oedipus, son of Laïus, King of Thebes, and of Jocasta, was exposed as an infant because an oracle had warned Laius that the still unborn child would be his father's murderer. (p. 261)

Bettelheim (1983) in *Freud and Man's Soul* seeks to clarify Freud's more humanistic side which he feels does not come across in the available English translations. Writing about the Oedipus complex, Bettelheim tells us that

> It is impossible to understand why Freud chose this particular term—this metaphor—if one is not familiar with the important details of Oedipus story. Unfortunately, most of the American graduate students whom I have tried to acquaint with psychoanalysis have had only the scantiest familiarity with either the myth of Oedipus or Sophocles's play *Oedipus Rex*. (p. 20)

Following Freud, Bettelheim outlines the source of Freud's ideas.

> The story of Oedipus begins with the incredibly severe psychological and physical traumatization of a child by those who should be his prime protectors: his parents. The infant Oedipus—born of Laïus and Jocasta, the King and Queen of Thebes, who have been warned by an oracle that their son is fated to murder his

own father—is maimed (a spike is thrust through his feet) and sent away to be killed. (pp. 20–21)

Again, following in a long, essentially uninterrupted, tradition, Bettelheim reduces the drama to its essence.

The Oedipus legend tells of a father's fear that his son will replace him; to avert this, the father tries to destroy his son. (p. 13)

Although Freud wrote to his friend Fliess about his understanding of the Oedipus complex in October of 1897, he waited until 1900, the beginning of a new millennium, to publish the theory in his *Interpretation of Dreams*. But is Freud right? What *really* happened in Sophocles' play? Oedipus, wanting to know his origins, has sent for the shepherd who found him and wants to know how he came to have the child he eventually gave to the King and Queen of Corinth. Who gave him the child, Oedipus asks the old shepherd (Sophocles, trans., Francklin, 1904).

Shepherd: He was called the son of Laïus; but ask the queen, for she
            can best inform thee.
Oedipus: Did she then give the child to thee?
Shepherd: She did.
Oedipus: For what?
Shepherd: To kill him.
Oedipus: Kill her child! Inhuman and barbarous mother!

Freud—and Bettelheim, who chides American graduate students for not knowing the play—are wrong. It was not Oedipus' father Laius who put him out to die as an infant. *It was his mother*. Freud has it backwards, and it is just this psychological blindness that has pervaded our view of the real and clinical worlds of children for ninety-plus years since the first publication of *The Interpretation of Dreams*, a fact that ought to astound and profoundly disturb. How such a monstrous reversal could have gone essentially unnoticed for nearly a century is amazing, given the tremendous number of people in countless professions who have read both Freud and Sophocles in the interim.

This reading makes it understandable that we should not see both the cruelty and absurdity of promoting the adopted child's potentially psychologically crippling view of the rejecting, relinquishing, or even abusive mother as "an act of caring and concern." Our often frenzied need to protect the image of the relinquishing mother is not based upon a rational appraisal of the genuine needs of the child but, rather, on our need not to see things as they are. This societal "scotoma" has clearly played a major role in determining what psychiatry has been prepared to see and deal with. That we are only beginning to become aware of its effect can be seen in the increasingly recognized failure of routine psychiatric assessment to detect histories of sexual abuse and physical assault in patients (Beck & van der Kolk, 1987; Jacobson, Koehler & Jones-Brown, 1987). We simply have not wanted to see the truth. Society and the helping professions have certainly been as blind as Freud—and Oedipus. The child therapist who would "do some good" must first "do no harm"—which requires that the therapist have his or her eyes far more open than Freud.

"Orphans"

Finally, a brief word about "orphans." Like Oedipus, most "orphans" have at least one living parents and, like Oedipus, most are sent away. The pain of their exile and of whatever mistreatment may have befallen them continues to shape their lives just as it did with Oedipus. In the orphanages with which the authors have been familiar, rarely did children without living parents constitute more than 2–3% of the institution population.

A woman in her fifties came to therapy because of an overwhelming sense of futility and powerlessness when her daughter insisted on marrying a previously married man with a child and a criminal record. It became quickly apparent, however, that her depression had long antedated her daughter's anticipated marriage. During a detailed review of her own childhood the woman stopped her narrative when she mentioned that at age five she and her older brother had been placed in an orphanage in spite of the fact that they had two living parents—and her mother had kept her younger brother at home. "I can't remember a thing from the time in the orphanage," she insisted. "Sure you can," her therapist replied, "tell me one." "I used to be locked in the closet—naked—when I wet the bed at night," she replied instantly. "I thought you couldn't remember anything from those years," her therapist said. "I didn't think I could," she replied, astounded. Despite the fact that the woman had lived in the community for some 30 years and knew the entire area well, for the next three weeks she was nearly 20 minutes late for her therapy appointment. The fourth week she told her therapist that she had realized on her way to the appointment why she had been late. "This is where those horrible painful memories are coming back," she said.

The challenges facing the therapist working with children from "orphan-ages" are very much the same as those to be faced in the adoptive situation: the recognition and resolution of rejection, abandonment, loss, and the human insensitivity and cruelty that are far more ubiquitous than we care to admit.

THE CHILD AS SURVIVOR

Recent years have seen an increase in interest in the psychology of the survivor. Niederland's (1961) work on the psychology of Holocaust survi-vors opened a new perspective on psychological trauma which has contin-ued to widen to include natural catastrophic trauma as well as man-made trauma (Eth & Pynoos, 1985; Figley, 1985; Figley, 1986; Horowitz, 1986; Krystal, 1968; van der Kolk, 1987). Some traumatic losses, however, may be so subtle that no one ever recognizes the powerful psychological role they can play. Yet children are frequently aware of them and can be seriously affected by them.

Sibling Death

The possible effect of the death of a sibling whose place and role in the family has already been established does not seem difficult to recognize or imagine, yet frequently the formative role of such loss is overlooked.

Marty was a four-year-old whose overactivity and immaturity were not hard to recognize. He occasionally wet his pants, regularly wet the bed, found it difficult to stay there and frequently crawled in with his parents at night. He was difficult to control, took direction poorly, and was disrespectful of adult authority in almost any setting. Aggressive toward peers, Marty was repeatedly being expelled from preschool. Marty was seen as "having ADHD."

During the course of Marty's treatment the authors got married. When Marty heard that this was in the offing he became quite upset and begged his mother, "Don't let them, Mom, please don't let them get married!" Marty's parents laughed when he told them why he was afraid for us to get married, thinking that they knew what he was "really" thinking about. "Because they'll sleep in the same bed!" Well, what's wrong with that, Marty's mother asked him. "But Debbie's *too big*," he replied with a look of upset and genuine worry. Beneath the apparently humorous con-cerns of this child about the size of his therapist lay some very scary thoughts. Marty's mother, like his therapist, was a nurse. She had not been able to prevent Marty's baby brother from dying a "crib death." Nor had the medical foster care she had provided to other children prevented them from dying as well. Marty was not thinking about sex, as his family had thought, but was afraid that his therapist's *male* partner would die in bed with the "big nurse," who would not be able to save him.

Although the contingent nature of the universe can be scary even for adults, a genuine accident is nonetheless more manageable and less terrifying than a sudden infant death due to failure to care. When Marty was able to understand that it was not his mother's fault if she could not "cure" the baby who had smothered in a sweater improperly put on by another child, his anxiety lessened.

Many children who lose a sibling feel responsible in some way for the death. If they were together at the time of the death this sense of responsibility may be even more intense. The sense of responsibility can be even greater if the child is literally left in charge of the sibling who dies or is killed.

Harland was a 10-year-old whose early development and behavior had been normal and adaptive in spite of an intensely chaotic home life. Following repeated episodes during which his mother would disappear for days or months at a time, Harland's parents divorced when he was one-and-a-half and Harland was kept by his father. When he was four Harland's first sibling was born, a baby half-sister with Down's syndrome to whom he became very attached. Because his mother, whose various homes he visited on a regular basis, did not take very good care of his new sister, Harland became even more protective. During one of his visits his mother left him in charge of the baby while she ran into a store "just for a minute." When she returned to the parking lot a half hour later Harland's baby sister was lying dead on his lap. An autopsy revealed a three-chamber heart and other serious abnormalities. None of this, however, was ever brought to the attention of school personnel or the public health physician who occasionally looked after the family.

Harland came to the attention of school personnel when his grades fell and he began to become preoccupied with girls and things feminine. In the third grade he chose to make a girl Pilgrim at Thanksgiving and told a teacher's aide that he wanted to be a girl so that he could wear pretty dresses. He talked of wearing make-up and tried to change all boy pictures to girl pictures when given coloring assignments at school. When he asked his mother for jewelry she bought it for him and he soon came to school with clear polished nails. He began to daydream much of his class time away and frequently "spaced out." His teacher became even more concern when Harland, for all the delight he seemed to take in pursuing feminine activities, began write her notes with drawings of a girl—and in big letters PLEASE HELP ME!

Harland's father remarried and life settled down at home. His new stepmother was very solicitous and took much time with Harland. When his stepmother gave birth to a new baby brother, a junior named after Harland's father, Harland took a turn for the worse. Upon hearing of the baby's birth he "accidentally" nearly hanged himself in the barn and began to have other "accidents" with increasing frequency. The desperate notes to his teacher accelerated until one suggested that, if he couldn't be a girl, he ought to be dead. Taken to the local mental health center, Harland was said to have a "gender identity disorder" and that a homosexual outcome was likely.

Harland did not have a true gender identity disorder (Stoller, 1985b). He had no doubts whatsoever about his gender. Nor was he on the way to becoming homosexual. He was, however, very close to committing suicide out of a sense of guilt and a dangerously intense sense of retributory justice. From a very early age Harland had realized that he was much more responsible than his mother. But the scope of his effective responsibility was limited by his physical size and maturity and by the fact that young children cannot become guardians of their little sisters in our society. That realization made Harland even more conscious of the desperate responsibility he felt for his sister's well-being. When her heart failed and she literally died in his arms in the back seat of the car, Harland felt that he had failed supremely. Because he had failed to keep his sister alive, he felt that he literally owed her his life. Since his sister could no longer be a living girl, he owed it to her to be one. In fact, he interpreted his insensitive mother's compliance with his requests to have his fingernails painted as her acquiescence to his requests—which meant to Harland that she agreed with his view of justice. He appeared immensely relieved when the logical bind was explained to him and his mother's lack of care was seen for what it was. Like Kluft's (1987) child multiples who seem to be "just waiting" for someone to give them permission to reintegrate, children like Harland who are caught in such logical binds are "just waiting" for an adult to give them permission to resolve them.

Harland's case highlights another important issue. It is not unusual for children who have developed normally in spite of adverse circumstances suddenly to take a turn for the worse. What is unusual, however, is for educational and mental health professionals to realize the significance of the preceding normal development: it is as if once a strikingly negative pattern is recognized, no notice is taken of antecedent health. If the professionals looking after Harland had taken his strikingly good early development into account, two realizations would have been inescapable: first, that he could not possibly have a core gender identity disorder and, second, that there must have been a precipitating factor. And there was: it was the birth of another half-sibling who was just as much at risk of maternal maltreatment and neglect as Harland's dead half-sister had been.

Roway was referred for therapy at age eight for lifelong and intractable nosebleeds that seriously handicapped his life. Occasionally requiring transfusions, Roway's nosebleeds occurred as often as three times a week, interrupting his mother's precarious work schedule so that she could take him home or to the hospital.

Because of the family history Roway's nosebleeds were particularly frightening to all involved. Roway's birth was induced several weeks early specifically so that his eight-year-old sister, who was dying of brain cancer, could name him. Two weeks after his birth, she died. Within days of her death Roway was found in his crib covered with blood. It was some time before the source of the bleeding could be determined and, when it was, it could not be stopped permanently by cauterization.

Roway lived in the very middle of the crack cocaine section of the city. Fights, muggings, and hold-ups were common in Roway's neighborhood. Shortly after Roway came for therapy his mother's purse, containing the money for the next two weeks' food, was snatched from her and a man was shot to death right in front of Roway's front door. Drug-dealing occurred regularly outside his bedroom window. Adding to all this confusion and danger was the fact that Roway's father, who was still married to his mother and who, in Roway's mind, should be home protecting his family, lived a mile or so away—with another family. He saw Roway only sporadically.

When Roway and his mother were seen in evaluation, he was asked what caused his nosebleeds. "When my tension's bad," he replied, explaining that high blood pressure ran in the family and that it caused the horrible headaches which presaged his massive nosebleeds. "When your tension goes up," Roway explained, "you have a stroke." When we asked what caused "tension" to go up, Roway replied, "When you get tense," inadvertently explaining why he sat so statue-still. Roway's mother also had high blood pressure. Hers was dangerously high but she was inconsistent in taking medication and in keeping doctors' appointments. She was also constantly threatened with the loss of her job—the family's sole source of income—because of the many absences necessitated by Roway's nosebleeds at school.

After clarifying the tension/hypertension confusion (shared by Roway's mother), we could see a real relaxation in Roway, who had believed for years that his mother could instantly die of a stroke if he did anything to increase her "tension."

Roway didn't have a nosebleed for 12 weeks after he began therapy — by many weeks the longest period he had ever gone without a bleed. In fact, he didn't bleed until the week of the murder in front of their house — and then he bled only when bumped on the nose while playing football.

This case was rich in possibilities and challenges — the first of which was to recognize therapeutic possibilities in the midst of what seemed like a disastrous environment characterized by danger, unpredictability, an unstable family, and a medically noncompliant mother.

While we assumed from the very beginning that we could teach Roway simple autoregulatory techniques that could control his bleeding, we felt that — even if successful at first — they would eventually fail or be abandoned as Roway's sense of dyscontrol reemerged after the support of therapy was withdrawn. Consequently, for the first 12 weeks Roway's therapist did not even address the issue of nosebleeds. Instead, she concentrated on those things in Roway's environment *over which he had no control*: his sister's death, the neighborhood drug-dealings, the robberies and murders, whether his mother took her antihypertensive medication — but, most of all, whether there was anything in the world that Roway could possibly do to *make* his father leave the other family and return home.

Even though Roway had to deal with the pain of paternal abandonment and neglect, he delighted in therapy, looked forward to it eagerly, and seemed to soak up everything it had to offer. His bodily defensiveness and fear of "tension" and strokes eased as his personal sense of responsibility took on normal proportions. Thus, when he had a bleed after being bumped in the nose, he was able to learn a simple guided imagery technique that "shut off the bleed like a faucet." The technique stood a much greater chance of long-term success because Roway's sense of personal responsibility and dyscontrol had decreased considerably — in spite of the fact that his environment remained as unpredictable, chaotic, and dangerous as before.

Parental Death

In order to understand children well enough to be effective, the child therapist cannot afford to take a categorical approach to "risk factors." The meaning of the death of a parent is highly subjective and must be understood individually with each child — even if statistically parental death does not appear to some to be a significant risk factor for the development of significant depression (Tennant, Bebbington, & Hurry, 1980). The relationship of the parent and child prior to the death, the circumstances of the death itself, environmental reaction to the death, and subsequent developments (such as remarriage, other accidents, illnesses, etc.) — all lend significant meanings to the experience.

George was three, and his newborn brother nine days of age, when their 23-year-old mother died of a stroke at home. Babied, over-protected, and yet intellectually stimulated by both parents, George was a complex and highly dependent toddler when his mother died. Father's response to the death of his wife and the loss of his children's mother was to become extremely depressed and ineffectual, only to be followed by a redoubling of the intense closeness to, and intellectual stimulation of, his children. Because of his own particular interests, George's father kept his little family in a world of fantasy in which movies, video games, and story-telling filled most of their time together. Apart from the relationship with his father, most of the "mutuality" George experienced in his life was with the family computer. By the time he was seen in psychiatric evaluation, George had been diagnosed autistic, schizophrenic, brain-damaged, and retarded. Placid, usually content with an empty smile on his face, George was manageable and presented no behavior problems for he interacted little with others. He was quite comfortable in a preschool class for three-year-olds when we met him at age six.

George's first truly intelligible words in therapy were "I got mad at my mom and she died." George had experienced no desire or need to have a sibling and had not wanted one. In fact, he was quite upset at his mother for bringing one home from the hospital. When she died at home only nine days after coming home with little brother Billy, George withdrew into an autistoid shell of silence (or minimal echolalia), little interaction with others, and the appearance of quiet contentment. His only real interest was in the constant fantasy world created nightly and on weekends by his father. Bit by bit he began to emerge from this shell in therapy, a therapy which painstakingly but gently reviewed every possible "accident" which occurred in the playtherapy room — and which involved several trips to the large cemetery across the street from the clinic. In the cemetery George's "I did, too, kill my mommy" was countered with repeated invitations to "see if you can bring a ghost out, if you're so powerful that your thoughts can kill." Eventually, George began to admit that his power was less than he had originally thought.

Because of George's intense cognitive confusion and his pervasive dissociative style he did poorly on standardized IQ testing with the result that he was "identified" as retarded when he entered school. It was difficult to get George's teacher to see him as an able—but extremely confused—child. When he announced in class, "I was black when I was three," his statement taken by his teacher to "prove" that his thinking was "completely disordered." Even when therapy brought an increase of more than 30 points in his WISC-R Full Scale IQ, George's teacher remained convinced that he was retarded.

As therapy worked to strip away the mistaken notions regarding everything George was *not*, his behavior normalized, interactions with others became more appropriate and socially productive, and he began to be "mainstreamed" into part-time normal classes. Just prior to Halloween and the anniversary of his mother's death, George's teacher decided to have a class Halloween party. She gave each child a small present such as a plastic Halloween pumpkin or ghost. Nearly eight months pregnant and only weeks away from "disappearing" on maternity leave, George's teacher gave him a small plastic glow-in-the-dark skeleton with its arm around the shoulders of a child skeleton. George became psychotic, stopped talking and "regressed." His teacher saw no connection between George's behavioral change and the "present" she had given him. George, who was seen weekly in therapy, required three sessions that week to regain his ground.

Intensely vulnerable because of the extreme dependency and blurring of interpersonal boundaries which his mother had cultivated, George reacted to her death with an overwhelming shut-down. Most of the therapy itself involved the clarification of interpersonal boundaries and an operational redefinition of agency in which George's overwhelming "power" was returned to its humbly human dimension. Every "accidental" occurrence in the playtherapy room allowed for an operational clarification of causality and responsibility. The proximity of the cemetery presented George's therapist with the opportunity to redefine his power dramatically while reinforcing the notion of the finality of death. The finality of death must be clarified for many children, who can easily view it as "just" a passage to "the other place" where their dead parent may be found. Such simple but dramatic clarifications can conceivably play a significant role in the attenuation of future suicidal potential.

As is often the case, the hardest part of George's therapy was the task of continually removing environmental blocks to health. It was not easy to get George's teacher to see him as being of normal intelligence or to recognize his intense sensitivity to the meaning of everyday events, such as her more-than-obvious pregnancy, her immanent "disappearance," and the adult-and-child skeleton toy she had given him. When he remarked in class, apparently for no reason, that "I was black when I was three," it took considerable explanation to make something very simple obvious. The only other child in George's class whose mother had died, and died recently, was black. Hence George's very understandable identification with a child who looked nothing like him.

It is relatively easy to understand the potential effect of a parental death on a child who is present and whose anger at the dying parent is obvious, but what of a child who is "too young to understand what is going on?" We hear this phrase frequently from parents, teachers and from colleagues. Thinking is an experience as much as witnessing. Ideas can be traumatic in themselves.

George's brother Billy was only nine days old when their mother died. But he had been born two weeks prematurely, was a very small-for-dates baby, and had not thrived initially. What, we wondered, would happen when Billy, who could read at three and used American Sign Language although he had been exposed to it only a few times at school, finally realized what his fate would have been had he been carried to term? He would have died in his mother's dead body. Not wanting to burden the imagination of a child already burdened by loss and a fantasy world encouraged by his father, we did not mention our concerns.

Several months later Billy suddenly began to become claustrophobic and to have panic attacks toward bedtime. He had night fears and night terrors, and found it difficult to breath lying down. These problems occasioned his entry into therapy. His anxiety was easily resolvable. Billy's therapist called her partner "the doctor" into the playtherapy room and said with great seriousness, "Now, Denis, you're a doctor, right? What happens if the mommy dies before the baby is born?" "The doctor takes a special clean knife," Billy was told, "and makes a big cut on the mommy's abdomen, all the way through to the special, safe clean place for babies which only mommys have, and takes the baby right out." "And does the baby get cut," Billy's therapist asked "the doctor." "No," he replied, "only the 'special, safe clean place for babies' is cut. The knife doesn't ever touch the baby." Billy's claustrophobia, his anxiety and panic attacks during which he found it difficult to breathe, his fears of going to bed at night, and the night terrors disappeared as suddenly as they had appeared.

A logical solution to a horrifying idea sufficed to resolve this four-year-old's fears. Fortunately, he did not object, "But, what if there's no doctor at home when the mommy dies?" Another imaginary resolution of the problem—probably having Billy's intelligent father stand in for the doctor—would have had to have been offered. It is interesting to note that one sees this sort of reaction to the retrospective past only in bright, complex children: dull children do not overcomplicate their own lives the way bright children do. It is also interesting to note that what we witnessed was the beginnings of a typical panic disorder. The average clinician—psychologist, psychiatrist, or child therapist—rarely sees the inception of such a disorder. Had Billy's panic attacks begun 15 years or so years later, when he was in his early twenties, the likelihood that the clinician responsible for his care would have recognized their origin in Billy's retrospective view of his own potential fate would be tantamount to nil. Thus, we have disorders "without causes."

The contemporary child's view of the finality of death is complicated by the nature of the constant portrayal of death in movies, on television, and in video games. In movies and on television, the same actors and actresses die over and over, only to reappear as different characters. In video games one's target may not "die" until the third or fourth time one "kills" it. As one child who had nearly perished in a dangerous accident told us, "You get to die three times—then it's over." Children's fears are further heightened by the nature of characters such as Freddy Kruger in the *Nightmare on Elm Street* movies. Not only can characters like Freddy Kruger not be killed—because they are already dead—but they attack you in your dreams. And for many children dreams are as real as waking life. Such "magical" power can put a child in the hospital.

A five-year-old, whose mother had died unexpectedly several months earlier, was coming for admission to a child psychiatry inpatient unit. During the intake evaluation she told her therapist, "You will die if you say 'Bloody Mary!' three times in a bathroom and then flush the toilet." The initially terrified little girl was then led to every restroom in the five-story building where she and her therapist flushed every toilet after yelling, "Bloody Mary! Bloody Mary! Bloody Mary!" When the rounds of all the toilets in the building had been made, the little girl's therapist said, "Well, I guess it doesn't really work, does it?" The five-year-old was seen a few times in outpatient therapy and dismissed without having to be admitted to the hospital.

Deaths do not have to be so overwhelming as that of a parent in order to affect a child strongly.

Trish was a five-year-old who was referred for hospitalization on a child psychiatry inpatient unit. She had become "violent and uncontrollable" at home. During the course of her intake interview Trish remarked off-handedly, "I killed a hamster with my foot." Trish's examiner, who had been seated opposite her, got down on her knees and looked intently at Trish's feet. "Which foot," she asked. "This one," Trish replied, sticking her right foot out tentatively. "This very foot," her examiner asked as she put her hands around the foot. "*This* very foot killed a hamster," her examiner continued dramatically as she gently removed Trish's right shoe. "This very foot *really* killed a hamster," she asked again as she slowly and deliberately slipped the sock off Trish's not-so-clean foot. "This," her examiner said gently and warmly as she cradled Trish's foot in both of her hands, "this is *the very foot* that killed a hamster?" Trish shook her head yes. "Looks like a very normal foot to me," her examiner replied, "and my hand isn't dead!"

Five-year-olds may or may not believe that death is real, scary, and final until they experience it. Trish had not believed her hamster would really die any more than she thought her dolls would. The experience of the agony and physical death of a real living being was intensely traumatic for Trish and locked her momentarily into a catastrophic identity. The gentle intervention above undid that pathological identity so quickly that Trish was able to be sent home safely without being hospitalized.

For a number of years we were fortunate enough to have a very large cemetery across the street from our office. That cemetery played a very important role in the therapy of many children we saw during that period. Children who were terrified that they would die were taken to see the graves of people who lived into their nineties or even their hundreds. Children who thought they could behave with impunity, take incredible personal risks, and that death was not real were taken to see the graves of children. Appropriate stories were generated to cover the circumstances of the dead children's death. Children who were genuinely afraid of ghosts, or who believed themselves to have unusual powers, were taken to the cemetery where, in spite of all their efforts and all their powers, no ghosts appeared. Suicidal children found in the cemetery a very palpable experience of their much less realistic fantasies. Many children needed a very concrete experience of the finality of death. Some children, who had lost siblings or parents, on the other hand, actually needed the concept of the soul in order to keep alive the idea of the loved person while allowing the physical self of the deceased to cease to be. When we moved our office to a space designed specifically for our therapy one 10-year-old asked his mother, "What will Denis and Debbie do without their cemetery?"

The Surviving Twin

Surviving twins are not as rare in clinical practice as might be thought. We have encountered so many over the years that the psychology of the surviving twin has taken on a special interest for us. Not every surviving twin we have seen was immediately recognizable as such, for not every death of a twin occurred late enough in life for the experience to be recalled as a loss. Thus, parents do not always mention the loss of the other twin even when it was a fully-formed stillborn child. And miscarriages of one twin must be asked about because they, too, may not be reported during history-taking. In fact, themes in the "fantasies," play, or acting-out of some of our patients (both children and adults) have occasionally been so striking that we were prompted to retake the history only to discover that there had been a perinatal—or even childhood or adult life—loss which was either wiped from memory or was simply felt to be irrelevant by the parents or the patient.

When we encountered our first case of a documented miscarriage relatively late into a twin pregnancy, we called an obstetrical colleague to ask about frequency of occurrence and how the event is handled when it does occur. Our call met with an unexpected reaction, which bordered on disgust, as the obstetrician suggested rather unpleasantly that we "would do better to pay attention to what happened to the kid *after* his birth and stop worrying about this nonsense."

In fact, many twin pregnancies result in the birth of a single infant, something of which our colleague was unaware. In at least 50% of twin pregnancies one fetus is lost—the so-called "vanishing twin syndrome." About twice as many twins are stillborn as singletons. Furthermore, as noted by Bryan (1986a, pp. 1044–45), "most twins survive the intrauterine death of their cotwin, physically at least, unharmed." Although most of these deaths occur during the first trimester, we have seen a number of adults and children whose twin miscarried late enough in the pregnancy for the experience to have constituted a genuine psychological shock for the mother. The perinatal effect of such loss is easily imaginable: disappointment, mourning, depression, or missed mourning can affectively color the crucial postnatal maternal-child relationship. The impact of such loss is usually grossly underestimated, if it is recognized at all (Bryan, 1986b). On the other hand, relief at the loss of an unwanted second child can bring its own psychological complications for mother and child. Such relief can be tinged with guilt for the mother—which may, in turn, be interpreted by the child as mother's happiness that her infanticidal wish came true. The physical process of birth itself can resemble a horror story with, for example, the presence of a macerated stillborn twin in a monochorionic pregnancy (Bryan, 1986a, p. 1045). As increasingly sophisticated technology allows for more and earlier interventions, such as the selective delivery of an acardiac, acephalic twin [a twin with neither heart nor head] at 22 weeks' gestation (Robie, Payne, & Morgan, 1989), we will still be faced with the psychological consequences of experience.

As children—who do manage to learn of these things far more often than adults would care to admit—acquire a veritable repertoire of visual images of imagined parallel events through television and movies, potentially horrifying "fantasies" can develop. The personal reality of such imaginings can make the video horrors appear pale in comparison.

Bobby was a 10-year-old fifth grader with a long history of "learning disabilities and hyperactivity" for which his pediatrician had been prescribing Ritalin regularly since the first grade. Bobby was viewed by his father, the school, and his pediatrician as "hyperactive, brain-damaged, and dyslexic," a categorization that Bobby himself was to repeat during the interview. He was referred for psychiatric evaluation and therapy, however, when he experienced a significant increase in his nightmares and fear of being left alone at night. Bobby dreamt nightly that he was trapped in a house which would not let him escape alive was also obsessed with *The Amityville Horror*, a horror movie the plot of which paralleled his dreams. His preoccupation with the dream-movie had taken on such proportions that prior to referral most of his free time was spent drawing complex escape routes and inventing powerful imaginary means of defeating the house.

Bobby himself was relatively calm and quiet with no medication. His neurodevelopmental exam was entirely normal and he exhibited none of the would-be stigmata of LD, such as letter or number reversals or word substitutions. In fact, not only did he read at grade level but a search of his clinic file revealed a copy of the results of recent standardized testing which indicated that, although in the fifth grade, Bobby's word-recognition and reading comprehension were on an eleventh grade level. Somehow this bizarre incongruity had escaped the notice of all the professionals involved in Bobby's care.

Bobby's history, however, suggested an explanation. Bobby's twin Robby had been stillborn. When Bobby was a toddler his mother had abandoned the family. And by the time he entered first grade, Bobby was a very preoccupied child. When this was ascertained, Bobby was asked to return the following week with a drawing of everyone in his family, including his live-in grandmother, his sister—and a drawing of what Robby would have looked like had he lived. Bobby returned with the requested drawings—and two identical school photos of himself stapled to separate pieces of paper on which he had written "Hi! I'm Bobby" and "Hi! I'm Robby." Since he had made marginal comments about his family members on the drawings (e.g., "prettier than I drew her" for his older sister), Bobby was asked what Robby would have been like had he lived. "Brain-damaged, dyslexic, hyperactive, and retarded," he replied.

There was nothing inherently wrong with Bobby. He was, in fact, a bright and imaginative child whose grades fell far below his documented academic achievement. So consistent was his "performance" with the "history of perinatal trauma" that the category match overrode the realities and none of his medical, psychological, or academic caretakers realized that there was nothing actually wrong with him.

The origins of Bobby's difficulties could be traced back to the day he was born. Bobby was caught in an intense logical bind brought about, in this case, by the good intentions of the family pediatrician. Hoping to soften the blow of the loss of one of the twins, Bobby's pediatrician told the parents that had Robby lived, he probably would have been "mentally retarded—but at least brain-damaged, hyperactive, and dyslexic."

Given the common family knowledge of Robby's would-have-been fate, Bobby faced a number of logical dilemmas which were extremely disorienting and scary. How can one be *identical* to someone who is dead? How could one brother get out alive—and not the other? How could Bobby's mother's body support one life—and not the other? Or did her body *allow* only one brother to get out alive? These terrifying questions about the "intentions" of mother's body were horrifyingly intensified when Bobby's mother actually abandoned her children. Bobby's self-image as the identical twin of a brother who would have been multiply handicapped left him functionally "multiply handicapped." He had to be "just like Robby" in order to be "identical." His fears, nightmares, and mounting obsessions with an inescapable murderous house reflected his "fantasy" about the "house" from which only he escaped alive when he and his brother were born. The clarification of Bobby's misbeliefs and the resolution of his fears through therapy allowed the gap between academic ability and performance to close and his sleeping problems to be resolved.

The Surviving Twin Grown Up

The problems of the surviving twin can persist into adulthood. Occasionally they may be resolved through life experience itself.

A man whose twin had miscarried at three months grew up intensely risk-taking. He played the most dangerous sports, took the biggest risks and, when he became of military age, volunteered not only for Vietnam but also for the most dangerous assignments. When his best buddy died in his arms his taste for risk-taking "vanished mysteriously," to be replaced by a gentle and quiet conservatism.

Such spontaneous resolutions, however, must be rare. More often one encounters fascinating "pathology" in adults who rarely suspect a connection between the loss and their present problems. Severe depression and self-defeating, self-injurious or even suicidal behavior are not uncommon.

Theo van Doorn was a Dutch musician and composer of some renown whose cyclic depressions, drinking and suicide attempts resulted in his hospitalization every few years. About two weeks prior to Theo's anticipated discharge date, the therapist who had worked with him since admission went on vacation. Theo greeted his new therapist with extreme rudeness when the new therapist, who also had an extensive knowledge of music, broached the subject. When his new therapist suddenly became ill and was absent for three days shortly after taking over his care, Theo signed himself out of the hospital against medical advice. Several days after his therapist's return to work Theo's wife called explaining that her husband had "really liked" his new therapist and that he was "confused, embarrassed and sorry" about his rudeness during the brief encounter. She said that her husband very much wanted to talk to the therapist but refused to come back to the hospital ward. A compromise was suggested and Theo's therapist agreed to meet and speak with him in the cafeteria. When the therapist, over three hours late because of an unavoidable emergency, finally showed up for the meeting in the cafeteria, Theo was still waiting—and immediately put out his hand in a warm greeting.

Theo and the therapist met informally three or four times over coffee and talked for hours at a time. At one point the therapist, upon learning of the one happy period of Theo's life, when he had had a series of homosexual relationships while living in Morocco, interrupted their conversation and said, "I'm going to tell you a story which I know will be important to you—but I don't yet know why. The story is about van

Gogh: Vincent Wilhelm van Gogh was born March 30, 1852—and died March 30, 1852. On March 30, 1853, one year to the very day later, his mother gave birth to another baby boy whom she again named Vincent Wilhelm and whose birth certificate number, like that of his dead brother, was also 29. This Vincent, of course, was the painter. Because his father was a Lutheran pastor, he grew up in a parsonage near the church cemetery in which the first Vincent was buried. For the first 18 years of his life, Vincent regularly saw the tombstone which bore his own name and the inscription from St. Luke 'Suffer the little children to come unto me.'

In childhood, Vincent developed a veritable twinship relationship with his younger brother Theo—a curious name similarity, don't you think!—and begin to fall apart when his brother became engaged, only to collapse completely when he married. When Theo 'disconnected' from Vincent, Vincent completely fell apart, attacked his closest friend Gauguin and shortly thereafter, on July 29th (the same number as the two birth certificates), died of a self-inflicted gunshot to the head." Theo van D. looked at the therapist in amazement. "How strange that you should tell me that story," he said, "because I was born with what the French call un casque de peau ["a flesh hat": the fetal remains of the undeveloped twin]. But your theory doesn't hold," he said with a triumphant grin on his face, "because my mother didn't tell me about it until I was 25—and I first tried to kill myself when I was 18!"

In retrospect, Theo's therapist realized that he had unconsciously inferred the formative role of such a loss in the development of his patient's suicidal depression from other aspects of Theo's history. Theo's artistic creativity and symbolic-mindedness made it easy for him to understand, with very little help from his therapist, the self-punitive nature of his repetitive suicidal depressions and the reason for his hitherto inexplicable happiness, productivity, and contentment during his long stay in Morocco, the only period of his life when he had been neither depressed nor suicidal. The culturally accepted male homosexuality there had allowed him to "reconnect" with his "other male half" without having to kill himself to do so. That realization brought about an immense sense of relief and the decision to move permanently to Morocco.

Miss L. was a 23-year-old exceptionally talented teacher-to-be. With Bachelor's degrees in education and music, she was at work on a third degree in art which would allow her to be an elementary art and music teacher. Extremely embarrassed, she announced that she had come for therapy because never in her 23 years had she been able to sleep with the light off. More embarrassing, she added, was the fact that she saw "creepy-crawly creatures" at night and was afraid that a hand would come up through the bed and pull her down to her death. She also had a horrendous compulsion to be first in everything she did, although there was no real competitiveness in this need. Miss L. just had to be first in everything: first in line, first in class, first in recitals, first in and out of elevators, always first.

Since I (DMD) had already treated Miss L.'s sister and was thereby forearmed with a detailed and extensive family history, I asked her how she, her sister, and brother were each "unique" within the L. family. After she gave me a number of examples I pointed out that her brother was the only boy; her sister was the only girl who was not a twin; and Miss L. was the only twin. She was astounded that I thought her dead identical twin had anything whatsoever to do with her need to have the lights on at night and with her "irrational fears." Our exchange continued.

D: Who was born first, you or Ellen?
L: I was.
D: So what would have happened to you if you had been born second?
L: I would have died! I never thought of that before.
D: That would seem to explain your horrible compulsion to be first, wouldn't it?
L: I would never have thought of that on my own, but it makes perfect sense.
D: What did Ellen die of?
L: Respiratory distress syndrome. We both had it, but she couldn't breathe much at all. She died two hours after we were born.
D: And what has your performance major in music been all these years?
L: Flute — winds, actually.
D: Right: *wind* instruments.
L: You know, that's incredible! Because I've always felt like I had only *half enough wind*.
D: So, this is all making sense so far. Now, think back, what do you think newborn nurseries were like here 23 years ago? What do you think you would have found there?
L: Well, babies and doctors and nurses.
D: What kind of babies would you have found in the equivalent of a neonatal intensive care unit — which is what you would have been in?

L: Really sick babies, babies who might die.

D: Do you think that there were times during the day when the doctors and nurses could afford *not* to worry about those babies?

L: No, I'm sure they had to watch them carefully all the time.

D: So, what does that have to say about the lighting back then?

L: That it must have been on all the time!

D: Right. It wasn't until later that it was discovered that maintaining day/night rhythms helped promote recovery—and that monitoring allowed safe light/dark alteration. Your very survival was linked *physically* through your experience with constant light. That's why you're scared to death to be without light at night.

L: That makes perfect sense, too, but what about my "creepy-crawly creatures"? I mean, I know there aren't "creepy-crawly creatures" around my bed at night.

D: Well, let's see if we can figure it out. What happened to you next? What was the next serious thing that happened to you?

L: I got croup at two-and-a-half and had to go into the hospital.

D: And what happened there? What did they do for you?

L: They put me in an oxygen tent.

D: All right. Think about that. What do you think things must have looked like to a bright, imaginative two-and-a-half-year-old as seen through the wavy plastic of an oxygen tent—what with all the hospital staff and visitors moving around out there?

L: Like "creepy-crawly creatures"! I can't believe how simple all this is! It all makes perfect sense. But "an arm coming up through the bed to pull me down"—how can that make any sense?

D: Did you see the Brian De Palma movie *Carrie*?

L: Yes.

D: Do you remember how it ended? It ended with Carrie's girlfriend sitting on her grave after Carrie's death in the school prom fire. Then, all of a sudden, Carrie's hand pushes up through the ground and starts to pull her friend down into the grave—only for her friend to wake up and discover that the horrible scene was only a nightmare.

L: So, that must be Ellen's hand coming after me—as if she were trying to pull me back *inside* so that she could get out first!

Miss L.'s second "brush with death," her hospitalization for croup when she was two-and-a-half, hit her where she was weakest: breathing— "weakest," however, not in a physical sense but in a *semic* sense (a sense in which the meaning of the experience was subjectively "charged"). She understood this immediately and the "creepy-crawly creatures" lost much of their scariness. In fact, this unusual opportune first encounter brought a great deal of resolution to Miss L.'s fears and compulsions. Those things which had been learned and then "forgotten" (her knowledge about the psychological significance of her birth order, her perinatal condition and that of her sister), or had been lived and then "forgotten" (her hospitalization, the fears it had reawakened and the form those fears had assumed), lost much of their pathogenic power with the insights of that first hour. An approach much more like that of child therapy was required to resolve her intense need for light. I explained to Miss L. that no matter how much talking, interpreting or working-through we might do, her conviction that she would not survive turning off the lights would not change—even though she understood perfectly well *why* she was so afraid of the dark. Consequently, our approach had to be one in which Miss L. would have to use her good intellect to push her through experiences which her "soul" told her she could not survive.

Miss L., who normally managed to get to sleep only between five and six in the morning, was asked when she would like to be able to go to sleep. She said that between midnight and 1 a.m. would be fine and explained that she was usually on the couch watching television at that time when she was living in her parents' home. Since she was a highly imaginative person, Miss L. was instructed to lie comfortably on the couch at her desired bedtime until she could *imagine* herself getting up. In her imagination Miss L. was to walk into her bedroom, turn the covers down, get into bed and settle in until she was lying comfortably on her back. Once this was accomplished, she was to retrace her imaginary path to the bedroom—this time in reality—stepping as closely as possible in the very footsteps she had taken in her imagination. On reaching her bedside, Miss L. was to look down until she could see clearly the image of herself tucked safely into bed. She was then to lean down and gently kiss "herself" on the forehead. At this point Miss L., whose genuine childlike love for the imaginary had lent a complicitous and even bubbly enthusiasm to the approach we were evolving, stopped me with a blush. "I couldn't possibly do that," she said. "Kiss myself on the forehead!" Not only would she have to kiss herself on the forehead, I continued, she was then to slip into bed, sliding right into her own image as if it were a sleeping bag which would contain her comfortably. She needed to do this every night and she had to stay in bed all night until her alarm went off the next morning—even if she were unable to sleep. If she was bothered by "creepy-crawly creatures," she was to cover her head with the pillow, but on no account was she to get out of bed.

It took about six weeks of courageous nightly footstep-following to move the hour at which she fell asleep from five or six in the morning (at which time she had formerly fallen asleep from exhaustion) to midnight or 1 a.m. Apart from the moral support Miss L.'s intellectual commitment to resolving her night fears *through action* required, our weekly therapy sessions were devoted to a fascinating inventory of the unconscious and fantasy world Miss L. had elaborated over the years. (Interestingly, I was not consciously aware of the fact that I was simultaneously addressing Miss L.'s need to "reintegrate her other half," as it were, through the guided imagery and guided "acting-out" whichI orchestrated for her until we had finished.) Five years later, Miss L. was still sleeping comfortably with the light out (Donovan, 1989a).

(For a detailed discussion of why traditional insight brought immediate relief of Miss L.'s compulsions and preoccupations, but not of her intense need for light, see "The Paraconscious" [Donovan, 1989].)

The Non-Twin

Just as the surviving twin is faced with the potentially horrifying asymmetry of his existence in the face of a non-existing "other half," so, too, must the child with twin siblings deal with the asymmetry of his position within the family. In our experience, the non-twin without singleton siblings is more frequently encountered in child therapy practice than the child who is at least partially "balanced" by one or more non-twins in the family. The non-twin is a veritable "odd man out," being the only family member not to form part of a "couple": the twins and the parents each form a pair. The asymmetry is to be seen in many other ways as well. In the case of samesex twins, the non-twin will often be the only family member to have his own bedroom. Unlike him, his siblings may dress alike—or even identically. His parents will have numerous activities together, as will his twin siblings, leaving his singleton activities to be experienced as solitary events.

The non-twin can develop a fascinating repertoire of alternative explanations for his solitary position within the family. The questions and logical binds in which the non-twin can become embroiled are similar to those one sees in surviving twins. Where is my twin? Is there still a baby inside my mother? Did the other baby die inside? Was it disposed of? Is my mother my twin? These questions can lead to bizarre preoccupations (such as one five-year-old we saw whose fascination with PCV pipes resulted in a collection of several thousand pieces and an compulsive need to hook things together).

Non-twins can also be exquisitely sensitive to any bodily "imperfections" that would tend to be overlooked by the average child.

The Ubiquity and Banality of Loss

Like trauma, loss is a lived event (even in retrospective memory) that has potentially highly charged meaning for the individual—even if the "loss" is not recognizable as such to the observer. Consequently, loss need not be experienced directly or be dramatic to be traumatic. As we saw in the case of George's younger brother, Billy, even ideas can be intensely, if subtly, traumatic. Children have no choice but to make sense of loss or other intensely meaningful experience in terms of their own logic and developmental perspective.

While it is understandable that few clinicians should bother to look for "traumatogenic ideas" when "modern biological psychiatry" is on the rise, the effective blindness to the real worlds of children to be seen in adoption casework practice is not so easily explained away. The clinician who wants to do genuinely intensive therapeutic work with children needs to adopt a more child-oriented and intellectually critical approach to practice. This means facing issues that are so troubling that several generations of clinicians, beginning with the founder of dynamic psychology and psychotherapy himself, have managed to avoid them altogether.

Obviously, one should attempt to change or to attenuate the effects of a deleterious environment as much as is humanly possible—as we did, for example, when we helped arrange for alternative housing in a safer neighborhood for Roway and his family. Failing this, the therapist has little alternative except to change the meaning of the child's experience of that very same environment—as we did when we helped Roway to change his sense of personal responsibility for murders, robberies, and a father who didn't really care—and the feeling of absolute futility and powerless that such a sense of responsibility evokes in a child. The resulting change in self-image and self-esteem is a central feature of successful therapy with hurt children, regardless of the cause of the hurt.

10

A Critical Look at a Child Psychotherapeutic Style

> Science is to see what everyone else has seen and to think what no one else has thought.
>
> *Albert Szent-Gyorgi*

Not only can a developmental-contextual approach provide a rational and problem-solving approach to the novel clinical situation, but it can also shed considerable light on any human situation—ongoing or past. Nowhere is this more evident than in in the comparison of traditional and developmental-contextual approaches to the same clinical situation.

THE CASE

An article by E. James Anthony (1986) in the twenty-fifth anniversary edition of the *Journal of the American Academy of Child Psychiatry* offers such an opportunity, for Anthony actually presents narratives of three child analytic sessions (10, 104 and 200) for each of two child patients. Anthony's stated purpose is to contrast the "neurotic styles" of these two preschoolers. This critique presents Anthony's clinical narrative in serial and verbatim form with running commentary, following a brief introduction.

The author's immediate introduction to the narratives and commentary is as follows.

To highlight the contrasts between the two cases during psychoanalysis, reports of sessions have been taken from the early, mid and late phases of the treatment with the analyst's commentary in terms of auto, micro, macro and transference spheres, media shifts, cycles of affect and the "analytic toilet."

The two cases Anthony chose to present were quite dissimilar, despite rough-ly equivalent levels of intelligence (IQs of 132 and 128) and age. Case I, Richard, came from a family whose "history was devoid of any striking pathology." Richard had extremely supportive parents and treated Anthony quite respectfully within the therapeutic context. He was clearly liked by his therapist and Anthony notes that "I was grateful for the chance to analyze this type of child." About Case 2, Billy, however, Anthony had "mixed feelings."

> I had known other Billys, but not analytically. Most of them had been encopretic and most of them had mothers with intense anal-sadistic drives. At first glance they looked doomed to pregenital existence, but I have seem them develop, in the milder cases, to a reasonable oedipal solution. Perspectives, during the anal phase, have a way of looking black and gloomy.

Of Billy's history we learn much more. Billy's father was discharged from the army as an "inadequate psychopath" and was to abandon the family during Billy's therapy. The maternal grandmother who lived with the family had been leucotomized for recurrent depression and one of her sons had commit-ted suicide. Billy's mother was preoccupied with his inner workings, present-ing at the diagnostic interview "clutching a specimen of Billy's stool which she wanted examined since she was sure that there was 'something bad' in it." This is Anthony's picture of Billy's beginnings:

> He began life with an unsatisfactory and short-lived experience at the breast. Over a period of months, during which he lost an appreciable amount of weight, his mother complained bitterly and inconsistently that he was a gluttonous sucker, that he never seemed to be hungry, that he hurt her nipples, that he sucked too hard, that he vomited her milk, and that, taken all in all, it was a horrible experience that she never wanted to repeat. (She later confided that the sucking gave her genital sensa-tions that made her feel guilty; she had similar reactions to intercourse.) The baby seemed unable to settle down to a regular existence and fought a running battle with mother over every mode and zone during the first two years. [. . .] Infantile colic, anorexia, recurrent vomiting, severe constipation, night terrors and temper tan-trums punctuated his miserable course of development.

At the beginning of treatment, Billy was four years, two months of age. Anthony indicates that he was seen five times weekly for a period of two years—for a total of 384 sessions. There was a break in treatment when Billy was admitted to the hospital for a few weeks but we are not told why. Because it was analytic treatment, there was an expectation that its length would be protracted. It was. By the time it was completed, *one-third* of this child's life had been spent in therapy—nearly one-half of his age at the beginning of treatment. This protracted approach to treatment appears to permeate all aspects of the therapeutic process for Anthony. Coppolillo (1987) notes in his book *Psychodynamic Psychotherapy of Children* that "E. J. Anthony (personal communication, 1964) maintains that in the psychoanalysis of children [a series of "interviews with the family in which their doubts and fears are expressed"] is sufficiently important to warrant seeing parents for as long as six months before beginning the child's treatment" (p. 199). In Billy's case, this pretreatment period would have taken an eighth of the child's life and would have incurred considerable expense.

Children, however, are incredibly plastic creatures, even those who have suffered greatly. For the most part, they do not share our adult preconceptions about how long, how hard, how costly or how *laboriously conscious* therapy should be. In fact, one of the very first assessments to be made in the initial therapeutic encounter (the "evaluation") is that of the child's *therapeutic aptness*, as we saw in Chapter 7. Therapeutic aptness is the child's ability to utilize the therapeutic setting and relationship in a creatively reparative and curative manner. The "therapy" does not await this assessment; on the contrary, it evolves, emerges within the assessment in a dialectical process. However, for the experience to be therapeutic in itself, there are certain structural and interactional parameters which must be elaborated and assured before (and as) the clinical encounter progresses. These we have outlined in detail in Chapters 6 and 7. This chapter will illustrate what happens to the therapeutic process when no structure organizes the space in which the child and the therapist interact and when preconceived notions about the child's "intrapsychic processes" replace an understanding of children. We will follow the process, as recounted by the child's analyst, in verbatim fashion.

THE TREATMENT

Billy—Session 10

Comes into his room and is silent as we unlock the cupboard to get his box [in which the items involved in his particular therapy are stored]. Looks apathetic and ill. Air of disinterest and detachment. Mutters to himself as he takes the box to the table and takes out the things. When he comes to a broken male figure—broken by himself in a previous session—he stops and stares at it, continuing to mutter. He returns to the box. (I say, "You don't want to play with a broken man.") He takes no notice and continues to empty the box, muttering the while. (I say to him, "You're talking in such a low voice that I cannot hear what you say.") He looks at me blankly and turns back to the box. (I say, "You want to say things but you do not want me to hear what you have to say.")

Billy clearly sees himself as "broken." We know from the history Anthony provides us of Billy's fear of a nonprotective, even sadistic ("poisonous") environment and of his tendency toward disintegrative disorganization. Supposing, then, that Billy's breaking of the male figure in a previous session was somehow unavoidable, the therapist must either help Billy to *repair* the figure or arrange for Billy to *replace* it (even if the therapist must secretly provide the child's mother with the money for its replacement). Failure to do so will significantly interfere with the child's conviction that he is understood and cared for by his therapist, at best, and thereby slow the process. At worst, it can not only destroy the therapeutic relationship, but also push an otherwise recoverable child into suicidal despair or psychosis. It certainly does not promote the development of a trusting relationship.

When Billy "stops and stares at it [the broken figure], continuing to mutter," what might he be muttering about? Perhaps about the fact that the figure is still there—and is still broken.

Allowing the male figure to be broken is the first major mistake illustrated here. Leaving it in Billy's box to be rediscovered by him is the next mistake. The symbolic meaning of both the destruction, and the therapist's allowing the broken male figure to remain as part of Billy's box (that which contains his identity within the therapeutic setting), is quite clear: "You break bodies; I permit you to do so—and I keep the figure here to remind you of your identity."

Anthony then states the obvious: "You don't want to play with a broken man." What is Billy's response? "He takes no notice and continues to empty the box, muttering the while." What Billy was probably muttering will quickly become apparent. Again Anthony "interprets" the obvious to Billy when he tells him that he is "talking in such a low voice that I cannot hear what you say." As we continue with Anthony's verbatim narrative, we see Billy's response.

He turns venomously and faces me, his eyes blazing with anger, "I hate you. You're a crazy man."

Even the most resistant child approaches the first encounter with a "helping professional"—especially a doctor—with some anticipation of help. All children, but especially those who have been hurt or perceive themselves to have been "broken" or "damaged" in some way, *test* their therapist quite early to see if he or she will allow them to remain trapped in their horrible world or miserable self-definition. If there is a self-punitive aspect to the child's behavior, he or she will test the therapist to see if the latter will, first, recognize it and, then, attempt to prevent or resolve it. If the therapist fails the child in this, the result may be depression, empty compliance, rebellion, or even worse. This is made even more disastrous when, in the course of colluding with the self-deprecating or self-punitive behavior of the child, the therapist also happens to be a likeable and/or sympathetic person. Empty stock "interpretations," such as those made here by Anthony, are then experienced by the child as a "tease" and cause the child to attempt further to integrate the therapist into his "inner scenario" in order to make some sense of the therapist's actions, the therapist thereby losing (at least part of) his privileged position vis-à-vis the child.

This interactive process, which so often passes for therapy, is strikingly illustrated in this first exchange between Billy and Anthony. Billy's response to Anthony's assertion that Billy does not want him to hear what he has to say is to say it quite clearly. Billy seems to be saying, "You're the doctor. Of course I don't want to play with a broken man! Deep down inside I don't want to have the power, even imaginary, to be able to break people, either. You should know this: you're the doctor. So why do you let me do it? And why do you keep this broken body around to remind of it? You don't *really* care about me. You're a crazy man."

But children in therapy are trapped, especially at four years, two months of age. If this big person isn't going to help them, who is? Thus, therapeutic compliance becomes the price of love and survival. How, then, except by acting out within the bounds of the only meaning-scheme that one knows, can the child react when—having been so angered by not having been helped to escape his universe of damaged and damaging bodies—he then encounters a kind and even sympathetic response from his therapeutic abandoner? The kind, but terribly confusing, response:

("Poor old Billy, you're pretty mad at me, because you're afraid I might do something to you.")

This is totally gratuitous, for nothing in Billy's behavior justified this statement. Billy will have to integrate it into his meaning-scheme, however, and this is what he seems to do.

His face goes blank. He stands silently for a while and then says, "What did you say? I didn't hear you." (I say, "Now it's your turn not to hear me.") But he does not smile back. Instead, he goes over to the window and, while looking out, rubs at his anus. He looks abstracted. (I say, "You don't want to stay near me while you rub yourself.") He immediately stops rubbing and shouts across the room, "Stop getting at me, you dirty old bitch." He sticks out his tongue and spits on the floor. [p. 51]

What we see here is a blurring of the very boundaries, both interpersonal and temporal, that should be protected by the therapeutic process. When the therapist does not protect and maintain those boundaries, he, of necessity, loses the experiential "ground" upon which to discern the meaningful "figure" of his patient's behavior and productions. Without control over the therapeutic space, the therapist is at a loss to understand the meaning of the interaction.

First we shall examine the structural components of this interaction, those which are inherent to the therapeutic relationship itself. Then we will return to the powerful meaning of Billy's responsive behavior.

The foregoing raises the fascinating issue we have examined earlier: whether there is any role for the promotion and utilization of "transference relationships" in psychotherapy with young children; whether, in fact, there is *any* rationale for the application of this concept drawn from adult psychoanalysis. Our contention is that not only is there no justification, but that it is a clinical impediment and represents an extremely self-referent need on the part of the adult therapist to impose a rigid view of how people think, relate and communicate on children—instead of understanding how they themselves function.

There is no need to wait for a "transference relationship" to develop with a four-year-old patient. In fact, promotion of a "transference relationship" blurs the interpersonal boundaries and shakes the very structures upon which the child counts to manage the therapeutic restructuring of his disordered or dangerous world. If we are right in thinking that what Billy needed, among other things, was both permission and the means to genuinely resolve his broken-self/broken-world bind, then the issue of the meaning of Billy's therapist allowing the broken male figure to stay in the box looms large. The breaking of the male figure offered Anthony what Henri Ellenberger (1973), drawing on Kielholz (1956) and Kelman (1960), calls a "kairotic [opportune] moment" par excellence. Billy's exit from his broken-self/broken-world vicious circle needed to begin somewhere: here was the perfect symbolically rich means to begin to effect it.

Instead, Anthony apparently did not realize that to require of a child a conscious acknowledgment of the therapist's presence at such a therapeutically opportune moment can kill the magic of the symbolic nature of the event. A transference interpretation made to a four-year-old at such a moment represents an intrusion, not an aid. It transforms the poetically rich potential of such an epiphanous moment into the self-referent pedestrian tease by an adult who, in reality, can neither rescue the child nor change his world in a material way. Sadly, the therapeutic potential of that moment was lost and Anthony was left no role except that of a "dirty old bitch" who was "getting at" Billy. (See below for the life-contextual meaning of Billy's behavior here.)

Because the interaction (or, rather, Billy's behavior) was seen in transference/countertransference terms, the *locus of agency* becomes confused for Anthony as well. We are told that Billy (a real person in a real world) broke the male figure in a previous session. Now the boundaries become even more blurred and confused when Billy's analyst accepts his little patient's attribution of agency to an imaginary "Mommy-lady."

> His hand goes back to his anus but he immediately withdraws it and comes back to the box. So far he has not played with any of the contents. Pulls out the female figure and then accidentally (?) the broken male figure. He tries to stand them up and the male figure falls down. He says, "She pushed him down and broke his leg. She did it." (I say, "The Mommy-lady hurt the Daddy-man, and now he's sick.") He says, "He's got to go to the hospital. [Anthony treats Billy at a hospital.] He's got to die."

By this point there is no possible positive outcome for the session. (Our expectation upon seeing the blurring of the hospital/home boundaries, incidentally, is that it will end with some sort of reference to a sadistic doctor— which, further reading will show, it does.) Billy had no choice but to remain within Anthony's metaphor: a constant repetition of the real-world problems from which Billy could not possibly escape. Anthony knew this fact about Billy's real life for in his discussion of Billy's therapy he tells us:

> Unfortunately, it was Billy's fate to return to an unbalanced, disturbing home from which the father had disappeared while mother and grandmother remained steeped in psychopathology.

The kairotic, therapeutically rich opportunities of the moment having been lost, Anthony further blurs the home/hospital boundaries with his interpretation. This is striking, for Billy had clearly broken the male figure himself and was therefore clearly personally responsible for its inability to stand. A reparative resolution would have radically altered the meaning of this experience for this child. Instead, Anthony left Billy no choice but to continue the blurring of boundaries and to put his anger where Anthony had clearly invited him to put it: toward his therapist in the context of a factitious transference. And, as we shall see below, this is just how the session ended.

Most children not only are content to remain within the "space" of a carefully structured therapeutic relationship, but tend, in fact, to become very protective of it. Rarely do children who are powerfully engaged in therapy violate the very boundaries they have come to depend upon for their sense of safety and security. (And often, in cases like Billy's where the home situation is chaotic and threatening, the consistency and continuity of that "safe space" may be the only experience that allows the child to survive an otherwise intolerable life.)

Consequently, when a child himself breaks those boundaries in the context of a therapy which is viewed by the therapist as dynamic and symbolic in nature, this is usually a sign that the therapeutic space has somehow "collapsed." And this is just what happens at this juncture. The reparative moment is (again) missed, the symbolic (of the child's agency) emptied of its power, and in its place Anthony imposes a symbolically impotent repetition of the inescapable. Billy's response is to exit therapy and to *talk* to his therapist: "If you won't help me in this (symbolic) world, then will you help me in the other (real) world?"

> Looks downcast and depressed. Turns abruptly from the toys and moves over to me, leaning against me. He fingers my tie, pens and handkerchief. "You've got a nice tie, I like spots. This is a nice pen. How many children have you got? (I say, "You're wondering whether I could be your Daddy because your Daddy's gone away.")

This simple verbal interpretation is, not surprisingly, taken by Billy to be an acknowledgment of his desire and an invitation to act on it. Billy then momentarily enters this world.

> He puts his head on my shoulder and nuzzles.

But the "real world" is that world where Billy's "symptom behavior" fails to bring relief or change. That world appears to have been invoked by Anthony.

> His hand goes to his anus. Then suddenly he pushes away.

Allowing Billy's head to be on Anthony's shoulder was a tease precisely because the world in which Billy can be Anthony's child *does not exist*.

Hence both the anger and the immediate return to the only world Anthony allows, the "transference."

"Hey, who you pushing around? Lay off, I tell you. Keep off. I'll tell my Mom."

While this does appear to be part of the transference "scenario," it is actually a very realistic response to the physical tease and to Anthony's blurring of boundaries. (Again, it is also something much more specific, as we shall see later.) Since Anthony keeps reminding Billy of his intractable parents, Billy has no choice but to couch his responses in those terms (while wishing for something else). Yet the potentially therapeutically rich part of this interaction lies in the aptness of Billy's responses to what Anthony actually does in the sessions. The tease of the physical contact, combined with what Billy clearly understood to be an invitation by Anthony to exit the symbolic, appears to have been horribly disorienting and frustrating. Billy's response is anger and then regressive self-soothing.

Goes to the end of the room and glares at me. "You dirty fucker, don't come near me." [A reversal of what Anthony had actually allowed.] After a while he squats down on the floor and starts to rock.

Billy's autistoid rocking is a powerful behavioral statement that his environment has become too stimulating and too overwhelming.

By this time Billy is in a horrible bind. He can't seem to do anything right. The symbolic is not open to him, and neither is the real. He has been momentarily forced into a quasi-psychotic withdrawal—so characteristic of children whose lives are made up of such constantly double-binding experiences. Anthony jolts him back to anger, however, with another tease.

(I say, "You're afraid to come near me and be close to me.")

This was clearly not the case for Billy had done just that. By forcing a conscious acknowledgment of Billy's impossible wish (to be his child), Anthony had emptied the act of its real-world comfort while, at the same time, calling attention to its very impossibility. Again Billy is told essentially that he cannot do anything right. His reaction:

He gets up furiously and charges down on me, pummelling me with his fists wildly.

The safety and security of the "therapeutic space" must be conveyed to the child operationally, through the very nature of its structure and the rules which govern its use. Thus far we have seen the disastrous results which occur when the simple premises for our operational "rules" outlined in Chapter 6 are not followed. Children are not discursive little adults. Not only do constant verbal reiterations of our good intentions fall on deaf ears, but they also demoralize.

> (I hold on to both his hands, and then his legs as he tries to kick and I say to him, "I know you're mad at me and want to beat me, but I cannot let you hurt me because that won't help you. It will help you if you talk to me about what makes you feel so bad.")

Since everything that Billy had done and said in the session up to this point had been an expression of how bad he *felt* (but had not been heard as such by his therapist), it must have appeared to Billy that Anthony was using the word "bad" in its other sense. This is confirmed by Billy's response.

> He relaxes against me and cries quietly saying, "Please don't hurt me. Don't send me to prison. Don't send me to the madhouse. That's where Mom says you'll send me."

(Note that this is a reiteration of Billy's acting-out a fear of being hurt, but Anthony does not hear it as such because of a preconceived notion of who's who in the oedipal cast of characters.) Billy's use of the word here clearly relates to a moral failing—not to "bad feelings"—for he begs not to be sent where "bad people" are sent: to prison and to the madhouse. Children, however, do not talk about "what makes you feel so bad" the way adults do—discursively. And it must have been very confusing for Billy to hear Anthony *say* that he won't allow the hurt, whereas Billy's *experience* of Anthony's "therapeutic space" is to the contrary. But even this confusion will be further heightened by the feeling of "sympathy" which is now to flow from Anthony.

> (I felt a wave of sympathy sweep over me and I say, "Poor old Billy, it's tough enough to feel mad at people and then frightened by what they'll do to you. I want to help you get over this.")

Which "people" is Anthony talking about? Billy's mother who threatens to send him to the madhouse? How can he possibly help Billy "get over this" without bringing about a change in Billy's real-world environment? The relief brought by feeling Anthony's "wave of sympathy" lasts but a moment.

He stays by my side for a while and then goes over to the table and comes back with a length of paper. "Where did I hurt you, let me see, I'm a doctor."

Anthony's marginal comment on Billy's utterances at this point is "Negative cycle separation." It is worth interrupting the narrative for a moment to discover what Anthony understands by "positive" and "negative" cycles in therapy with children. They seem to function independently with regard to the life situation of the child patient involved:

> A typical positive cycle may start with erotic feelings toward the analyst with a wish to make contact with him, and this may lead to fears of seduction, panic and feelings of outrage; a typical negative cycle may start with aggression toward the analyst followed by an attack on him, fears of retaliation, guilt reactions and evidence of remorse associated with attempts to make amends and placate the analyst. (p. 47)

We have interrupted the flow of Anthony's process notes to illustrate the extent to which the imposition of a rigid and inflexible conceptual scheme (in this case Anthony's "cycles" and "transference") can obscure our perception of what actually occurs in an interaction such as this. Billy's response to Anthony's expression of "sympathy" is, in fact, a bitingly accurate and cynical caricature of it. Anthony begins with the embarrassing tease of letting Billy know that he knows that Billy would like to have him as a father. When Billy begins to play out an incredibly rich symbolic statement of part of the difficult life he has had to live (see below), Anthony misses the symbolic communication and effectively "accuses" Billy of being afraid to come near him—in spite of the fact that Billy had done just that. Anthony does not wonder why a child who makes such a gentle approach for physical contact ("nuzzles") should immediately pull away as if assaulted. Following Billy's loss of control, Anthony describes what should have occurred (protection from harm). But Billy was "talking" about the real world, and Anthony is talking about the factitious world of the "transference" and of "cycles." Anthony ends these remarks with the words "you feel so bad," and Billy responds by begging him not to send him to prison or to the madhouse, thereby confusing "bad" (the feeling) and "bad" (the moral failing).

How, then, could Anthony's "Poor old Billy" expression of sympathy sound anything but patronizing when it terminates such a sequence of interactions? Billy's response to Anthony is an almost word-for-word parody of Anthony's previous intervention—right down to the "I'll help you get over this." How did the session end?

He puts the bandage in place, adding "If you get out of bed before you're ready to come home, I'll crack you on the jaw."

A sad and angry ending to a disastrous session which had begun full of therapeutic potential.

Although the repeated therapeutic openings were never perceived by Anthony and, consequently, never utilized, it would be an understatement to say of this child's productions that they were symbolically rich. Where we have found kairotic fullness, Anthony found only vacuous "circles." His comment on the session:

Comment
   Noticeable are the abundant aggression, the negative outcome to most cycles, the inability to play and the play disruption, his fantasy of a sadistic relationship between the parents with the mother dominant and the sympathy he evokes in the analyst.

It is fascinating to note what Anthony perceives as Billy's "inability to play and the play disruption": first, because not only was this child's play symbolically full, but it was also extremely caustic in its running commentary on Anthony's interventions; second, because this child's play was disrupted only by Anthony's attempts to impose a preconceived discursive adult matrix on a child who continued to ask—through his behavior and throughout the session—to remain a child. When Anthony persisted through to the end with his tit-for-tat and passive aggression, Billy simply turned the tables and told his therapist what he would do if he were in charge: If you get out of bed before you're ready to go home, I—the doctor—will crack you—the patient—one on the jaw.

One Hundred and Fourth Session

Anthony takes up the narrative 93 sessions later. It will be fascinating to see if anything has changed.

Billy gives me a big smile as I go to him. I hand over the key and he brings his box to the table. He asks: "Can I do my story (of previous session)?" (I say: "You do what you want to do.")

This child's need for structure was striking 93 sessions earlier. Billy's need to have adults structure the world in a safe, meaningful and constructive way is still very keen over a year later—in our view, a sign of optimistic resilience in this supposedly damaged child. This is true of all children, and it is a grievous technical mistake to think that non-direction is in any way curative. In Billy's case, it only paralleled the non-responsibility in his own world, thereby maintaining the blurred boundaries and preventing the therapeutically integrative play which should have begun to resolve many of these problems early on in therapy (indeed, during the very first encounter). Children crave power, but it is disastrous for them when they actually get it (symbolically or in reality). Thus, a response such as "Sure, you can do your story" can convey simply and pristinely a positive sense of agency to the child. "You do what you want to do," on the other hand, is ambiguous, open-ended, and potentially anarchical. Anthony's first response in this session is far more than nondirective, as we shall see.

> He picks out a small house, a car, a mother and father doll and a little boy (whom Billy has nicknamed "Silly"). Silly is a serial character and is featured most days in the analysis. Silly is an "id" personality who is not ashamed to do the most aggressive and ridiculous things, especially toward the parent dolls, who have suffered a great deal at his hands in the past.

Clearly, then, "You do what you want to do" is an open-ended invitation for Billy to become "Silly . . . an 'id' personality who is not ashamed to do the most aggressive and ridiculous things, especially toward the parent[s]."

The question with which Billy begins this session is brimming with therapeutic potential. Instead of functionally redefining Billy's question as a request "to do the most aggressive and ridiculous things," Anthony might have seen the potentially rich inner questions contained in an apparently mundane one: "Can *I* do my story, i.e., be in charge of it, be the agent of change?" and "*Can* my story change?" To use Anthony's terms, it is the therapist's choice: of whom is he ally, "id" or "ego," chaos or control? Anthony has already chosen chaos, and chaos is not curative. Has Billy become a theoretical convert?

> Billy provides a running commentary to the action. He kicks the Mom, she bashes him, then he kicks her again. He laughs. "Silly's a dumb guy."

Every day in our therapeutic world a child says something like this to us. He or she orchestrates a similar scenario, an acted-out repeat of their own dyscontrol, their own unresolvable chaos. What Anthony does not seem to understand here is that this acting-out within the play is a *test* of the therapist. "Are you going to let me persist in this useless repetition?" This is the question that is formulated behaviorally through play. Billy goes one step further, however. He makes an overt, explicit, literal discursive statement: "Silly's a dumb guy." "Yes, he is," Anthony could say at this point, and cleverly orchestrate a way out for "Silly" within the play. He could easily facilitate the transition of "Silly" to Billy. Instead, however, "id" continues. Anthony seems to forget that "unfortunately, it [is] Billy's fate to return to an unbalanced, disturbing home."

(I say, "Silly's not scared of his Mom anymore.")

What is Billy's choice, captive of the situation? He continues on for Anthony—but not without a price.

"No, he bashes her, and kicks her and knocks her down, he jumps on her." He begins to look anxious.

Billy has no choice within Anthony's "id" world. But he will have to pay with guilt.

"He's a bad guy. He should go to prison." He smacks Silly vigorously.

We are no further advanced after 103 sessions than we were after 9. Billy is still "bad." Silly, he tells us, should be sent to the feared prison of session 9. The boundaries are still blurred. There is no alternative but to be punished for his angry feelings toward his parents, about whom he can do nothing in reality.

But now Anthony is going to throw Billy yet another curve. Having invited Billy to "do whatever you want to do," and having pronounced that "Silly's not scared of his Mom anymore" after Billy beats her up in the play, Anthony now invites guilt for what he himself has just set up.

(I say: "Bill's sorry that Mom's hurt.")

This is a double disaster for Billy, for not only is he told to feel bad about what he just did (in the play), but Anthony switches from the metaphor of the play (Silly) to the reality of the little boy (Bill). Again, the boundaries are blurred and Bill, the five-year-old, is invited by his therapist to take responsibility for what Silly, the "id" personality, has done. Billy still cannot do anything right, not even in therapy. Thus the vicious circle of "I'm bad, so punish me. I'm bad, so punish me" must continue.

He throws Silly against the wall, "Serves him right." He holds the Mom doll up and very delicately smooths her down. "She's a fine Mom," he says. He strokes her again. He lifts up her dress and looks between her legs. "It's not nice. It's dirty. She's a bad Mom."

Knowing the theoretical orientation of this therapist, we will not be surprised to learn that Anthony sees in Billy's behavior signs of Billy's "castration anxiety." But what are we really seeing here? The answer is simply the not untypical behavior of a sexually abused child, or of a child who has been exposed to inappropriate sexual behavior.

By telling Billy that Billy himself (not Billy's play character, Silly) is "sorry that Mom's hurt," Anthony is telling this five-year-old that *he* has done something wrong. There are many, many ways in which a five-year-old can act out "being wrong," if that is what his therapist invites him to do. But why did this particular child choose this particular way? Why did he make this particular transition, linking his badness with mother's genitals? These questions are neither asked nor answered. Billy, who provides his therapist with opportunity upon missed opportunity, proceeds on to theoretical compliance, ending with an ultimate reassurance to his (male) therapist.

> (I say: "Billy's scared that Mom's got no widdler like Billy.") He shouts: "His Mom's got a widdler, too." (I say: "Billy's scared because his Mom's got no widdler.") He runs through the room shouting, "She has too"—over and over again, ending in a scream while he bangs on the wall—"has too, has too."

A very simple question—one which would have remained entirely within the context of the play and Billy's productions—would have been, "Why is she a bad Mom?" when Billy lifted up the mother doll's dress and looked between her legs. We could have been fairly sure that Billy's response to this simple question would have been apropos. Instead, however, an "interpretation" was imposed (violating, incidentally, the most cardinal of analytic rules: clarification before interpretation), and this "interpretation" directed Billy's response.

> (I get up to go to him, and he screams again, holding on to his penis. I say "Billy thinks doctor wants to take away his widdler.")

Our experience has been that boys between the ages of three and six will often bring up their confusion about the (existence of the) two sexes and their fears of losing what the other sex appears to have lost. This usually occurs within the first few sessions—if they feel safe enough to share such fears (see Chris in Chapter 2). But it is extremely unusual, however, for such fears to wait more than a hundred sessions before surfacing. Furthermore, it is also extremely rare for a child to go running about the room, clutching his genitals, especially after such a long period of time with the same therapist. Dyscontrol, however, is a characteristic of this therapeutic situation.

Now, if we return to the first session Anthony presented us, we have to wonder again about what motivated an apparently gratuitous comment on Anthony's part. Recall how Billy looked blankly at the box containing the broken male figure, "muttering the while."

(I say to him, "You're talking in such a low voice that I cannot hear what you say.") He looks at me blankly and turns back to the box. (I say, "You want to say things but you do not want me to hear what you have to say.") He turns venomously and faces me, his eyes blazing with anger, "I hate you. You're a crazy man."

Billy's response, we recall, was entirely consistent with that of a child who was allowed to maintain a broken self-image and an image of himself as "damaging" by someone who was supposed to help him. Yet Anthony goes on, in that tenth session:

(I say, "Poor old Billy, you're pretty mad at me, *because I might do something to you*" [emphasis added]

Billy's response was striking for Anthony's remark stopped him cold.

His face goes blank. He stands silently for a while and then says, "What did you say? I didn't hear you." (I smile at him, "Now it's your turn not to hear me.")

This tit-for-tat cost Anthony a possibly major insight into the life of this child. Billy asked a simple question: "What did you say?" Anthony retorts with a you-did-it-to-me-so-I'll-do-it-to-you, apparently not realizing that his last statement had been a very powerful one: " . . . you're pretty mad at me, because you're afraid that I might do something to you." "What," an alert therapist should think at this point, "does this child think I might do to him?" This is the point at which a simple discursive question is not only appropriate; it is mandatory. Anthony's response should have been: "Has anyone done anything to you?" That very open-ended question was much more appropriate to what Billy had actually said and to his personal reaction than was Anthony's next remark in the series:

(I say, "You don't want to stay near me while you rub yourself.")

If Billy were a sexually abused child, which is what is strongly suggested by his behavior within the therapeutic context, then his response to Anthony's intervention makes all the more sense.

> He immediately stops rubbing and shouts across the room, "Stop getting at me, you dirty old bitch."

So does Billy's response after Anthony interpreted the meaning of the broken male figure falling down as "The Mommy-lady hurt the Daddy-man, and now he's sick." After a short follow-up about how sick the man is, Billy became interested in some rather strikingly symbolic items: Anthony's tie, pens and handkerchief. When Anthony interprets Billy's interest in his long dangling appendages as a wish on Billy's part that Anthony be his father "because your Daddy's gone away," Billy at first "nuzzles," then "his hand goes to his anus." Reviewing this now a second time, we see the classical therapeutic acting-out of a sexually abused child, specifically, a young boy who has probably been abused by an adult (or bigger) male:

> He puts his head on my shoulder and nuzzles. His hand goes to his anus. Then he suddenly pushes away, "Hey, who you pushing around? Lay off, I tell you. Keep off. I'll tell my Mom." Goes to the end of the room and glares at me. "You dirty fucker, don't come near me." After a while he squats down on the floor and starts to rock.

Billy appears to have acted out a sexual approach (probably digital penetration), an attempt to fend off the abuser, and the threat to tell his mother. He called Anthony (who, by this time, had literally walked right into the scenario) "you dirty fucker" and told him straightforwardly "don't come near me." We can now wonder about the rocking as well. Is it autistoid self-soothing, or is it masturbation. Or are we witnessing the typical *behavioral memories* of abused and traumatized children (Terr, 1988, and Chapter 4)? Such rocking masturbation in children has even been mistaken for seizures.

Returning to session 104, we can only wonder what must have been going through Billy's mind at this time. Anthony had just got up "to go to him, and he screams again, holding his penis."

> (I say: "Billy thinks the doctor wants to take away his widdler.") He looks frightened and goes back to the dolls on the table. He lifts Mom's skirt and takes a longer look. He eventually pronounces his judgment. "She's got a big, big widdler. It's the biggest in the world."

By this time Billy is remaining more in control of his physical aggression toward Anthony. After 103 sessions, a bizarre sort of trust seems to have developed. Billy will remain "within the metaphor" through to the end of the session.

> He picks up the damaged father doll and pins up his trousers, and says quite solemnly—"Doctor's got no widdler."

Having been forced by Anthony's need to assign to the "phallic mother" the operative phallus (in the sense that French Lacanian analysts use this term), Billy takes away Anthony's "widdler" (a British slang expression for penis which figures prominently in Freud's "Little Hans" case, although it is not part of the vocabulary of the average, let alone disadvantaged, child in this country). Anthony continues:

> (I say: "Billy's taken Doctor's widdler away now. He's punishing doctor for scaring him.")

Anthony is absolutely right in this reading of Billy's behavior.

> He comes up to me, puts his arms around my neck and whispers in my ear: "You got one."
> *Comment*
> Billy's preoccupations with feces and smearing are well nigh over. He has moved into a phallic phase and his anal masturbation has given place to genital masturbation. He is sexually very anxious and is beginning to show manifest castration anxiety. Most of the other "psychotic" elements—the depression, mania and paranoid fears have disappeared.

One wonders what the outcome of this case might have been had Anthony thought that Billy's real-world life was relevant to what he did in therapy. Anal masturbation, use of expressions like "you dirty old bitch" and "you dirty fucker" are not things which typical fantasizing four-year-olds simply pull out of the blue—not even 4-year-olds whose mothers are preoccupied with their children's fecal productions. If Billy was, in fact, sexually abused, to what will he close his eyes as an adult as a result of this therapy?

Two Hundredth Session

Our concerns about what this child may have lived through (in his life) become all the more poignant as we look at his 200th session.

> Billy looks somewhat downcast as we walk into the room. He leaves his box on the table unopened. (I say: "You look sad today Billy.") He delays his reply and then replies—"Mom says I'm O.K. now." (I say: "She thinks you don't need to come anymore.") He nods, and then opens his box listlessly.

What happens next should never happen — even in an early session. Unless it is so horrible that it must be rejected, the future with which a child needs to identify should never be thrown away. Nor should it, for that matter, be allowed to be broken over and over.

> The old damaged father figure has been broken and mended several times, and done yeoman service. Billy throws him into the wastepaper box. He's no good any more.

Rather than recognizing and validating Billy's sad feelings for what they are, Anthony instead validates Billy's despair.

> (I say: "You feel like Mom's taking me away from you like she took Dad away.") He rummages in the box and takes out the Mom figure, also glued together. He throws her into the wastepaper box. She can go too.

This is a critical mistake, for one should never empty — or allow a child to empty — both the symbolic and the real worlds at the same time. (A brief thought about how voodoo works will explain why.) But this is what Anthony allows. Clearly, Billy's lot in life has not significantly improved. That means that what he gleans from the special hour with his therapist is of vital importance: an inner integration can often fend off outer chaos until the storm abates.

Even in a first therapeutic encounter (an evaluation), our second premise (pp. 111–12) stands: *While the therapeutic process may facilitate the child's expression of mistaken or negative self-perceptions, it should not allow them to stand.* Billy has just jettisoned mother and father. One would hope that, after 200 sessions, *Billy* would be a creative survivor. Sadly, however, it is not even a question of Billy — the real child living in a real world — for Anthony.

> (I say: "So Silly's going to be all alone now. What'll he do? He's only little.")

Almost a hundred sessions previously Billy had made it perfectly clear that he wished to be rid of Silly. "Silly's a dumb guy," Billy had told Anthony, apparently hoping that Anthony would agree with him and help him free himself from that horrible identity. Yet, Billy's therapist continues to identify Billy with Silly a hundred sessions later. Billy does seem to be a survivor, though.

> He says morosely: "He's Silly. I don't want Silly any-more." He throws him into the waste-paper box as well.

The symbolic is now absolutely empty. It is not hard to guess where Billy must turn at this point—again, after 200 hours of therapy.

(I say: "So only Billy and Doctor are left together.")

This is the same tease with which Anthony turned Billy's life upside down 190 sessions ago. Billy's response will surprise no one.

He looks at me and says: "Can I go home with you? I can clean my room."

This horrendously pathetic situation should never have been allowed to develop. Even leaving aside the issue of possible sexual abuse, no child patient should still harbor such very real wishes (not even "fantasies") of going home with his therapist after 200 hours of therapy. At the very least, this means that the therapist did not do what was necessary (through the means of social services, etc.) to remedy the living situation, or help the child weather the storm in the real world. There simply are no alternatives. Not for the child, at least. We are no further advanced than 190 sessions previously, for here is Anthony's reply.

(I say: "You sent off Mom and Dad and now you want to be my child and live with me.")

This is a repetition of what Billy had just said. Horror sets in. Something must be done to recover at least part of the symbolic, for the "real" is no different than it was 190 sessions earlier.

At this he looks even more anxious. He goes over to the wastepaper box and brings back the doll figures. He looks at them carefully. "It's alright. They're not hurt."

It is the therapist's job to protect the symbolic—not the child's. Children who are so symbolically apt that they can do so without aid rarely come to psychotherapy. This task should never have fallen to Billy, and certainly not after such a long time in therapy.

Adds, "They can come and live with us too. We can all stay together."

There are few things sadder for those who work with children than the experience of parents who do not care for their children, or of children who *know* that they are trapped in an impossible, uncaring situation. Billy knows this, and it is painfully evident. His English, usually excellent for a four-year-old (as the reader can judge), is going to suffer an interesting regression.

(I say: "Even your Dad?") He looks hard at me. "He's gone. Mom says he's sick and he's gone. He no wants me anymore." Tears are not far away.

Identification being a primitive form of love, Billy's "He no wants me anymore" is all the more striking. But the symbolic is not at issue in Anthony's world.

(I say: "That's how it is, Billy. No use pretending. It's just you and Mom and Nan now.")

Having nothing to carry with him, no organic transition that he is proud to make, Billy tries again.

He says: "When I'm big I can live with you."

The end result of this therapy appears to be that Billy must just face his lot in life, consciously acknowledge and accept that there is no exit, not even a symbolic resolution. Billy, however, remembers from early sessions that Anthony had told him that there was, in fact, a way to resolve these things. Maybe it will work now.

He closes his box and says: "Let's sit and talk."

Billy must have remembered that Anthony had said to him 190 sessions earlier, "It will help you if you talk to me about what makes you feel so bad."

(I say: "What shall we talk about?")

Aimless and adrift, the therapy does not know where to go. "Talking" is clearly of no use, so Billy returns again to the "real world" with a rather clever intellectual compromise of his and Anthony's positions.

He says: "Let's pretend I'm your little boy and you're going to the shop to buy me something nice."

Brilliant in its compromise use of pretending, this as a set-up, for Anthony cannot possibly fulfill any wish that may come now.

(I say: "O.K., I'm in the shop and I'm looking for something nice. What do I find?")

We know generally what Billy is going to say. And, again, this is tragic. His wish is unfulfillable, his need unmeetable. This is a disastrous ending to what had begun with such hope.

> He says: "You find a nice lady. You put me in her stomach. Then you help me out. Then we all live together."

Notice how his English has improved.

> (I say: "You're leaving someone very important out.") He says: "She can be the maid. She can clean up. That's what she likes."

Billy understands. What had his mother brought with her to the very first session? His feces.

> "She doesn't want to marry you. She just wants to clean up."

Again, what fascinating understanding on the part of this trapped child.

> "She can be the maid and if she's good she can sleep in my room."

So it ends. Anthony tells us that, "In spite of what he says, he has another six months to go in analysis." Still, Anthony assures us that this child—who still wants to go home with his therapist after 200 sessions, "sees his mother shrewdly in her fixated pregenital role and is conscious [sic!] of developing beyond her."

DISCUSSION

What makes psychotherapy with children so very different from most psychotherapy with adults? The answer to this question is dictated by the very real differences in how children and adults think, communicate, interact, and change. Our pedestrian insistence upon conscious awareness—something so foreign to the life and experience of the child, especially the very young child—leads many therapists into a discursive relationship in which both sides are left confused.

Essential to successful child psychotherapy is the notion of the *therapeutic space*, the physical and temporal space over which the therapist must have subtle, but powerful, control. Children are extremely sensitive to the consistency, continuity, and responsive nature of this space. It is a space in which words need not even be exchanged in order for very powerful communication or successful therapeutic intervention to occur. Some children who come for evaluation and treatment simply do not talk at first. Should this be an impediment to therapy? Should even complete deafness be an impediment to good child psychotherapy? Not at all. If one understands that the child's interaction with the contents and structure of the therapeutic space actually *constitute* the child's communication about his or her own life situation, and that the therapist's manipulation of that (physical, interpersonal and temporal) space actually constitutes his or her response to the child's communication, then the potential for therapeutic intervention is immense.

In the therapy sessions which we have reviewed, only one potential therapeutic vector was invoked: words. It is true that only three of 384 sessions were presented for our consideration. Still, the continuity evident in these three sessions is striking. Had they been sessions 1, 2 and 3, we would not have been surprised.

There was no indication that Billy's therapist realized that the very space in which they "encountered one another" was itself an almost limitless medium for communication and change. Instead, a rigid, repetitive, and stereotyped theoretical matrix was imposed upon the child. Some of the subtleties of a (rather disadvantaged) child's interactional communication were highlighted: his description, through the play and through his interaction with his therapist, of his life situation, his fears and his wishes; his attempts to resolve the impossible situation he found himself in, given this child's ability to imagine alternatives. Striking behavioral memories emerged that could have alerted his therapist to environmental maltreatment, had they been recognized as such.

When all this failed, Billy simply beseeched his therapist to take him home with him. His inventiveness in this regard went so far as to suggest to Anthony that he could "find a nice lady . . . [and] put me in her stomach. Then you help me out. Then we all live together." How this therapy might have proceeded had the child's life been more important than Freudian fantasies, we will never know.

An Initial Psychotherapy Encounter

A thing is not proved because no one has ever questioned it. Skepticism is the first step toward truth.

Denis Diderot, Pensées philosophiques (1746)

Don't oppose forces; use them.
R. Buckminster Fuller

Most of the clinical examples in the book have been fragments of sessions, chosen to illustrate particular technical issues. The previous chapter focused on the clinical consequences of not attending to those issues. What follows is a nearly complete (the tape ran out 9–10 minutes early) annotated transcript of a first clinical encounter with a bright, verbal six-year-old boy who was, at the time of his evaluation, in a psychiatric day-treatment program. His parents were concerned about a proposed change in his treatment plan which called for a transfer to an estimated 18-month residential treatment program and wanted to know if this were, in fact, their only option.

John and his mother flew to Florida from a Northern city, arriving on Friday and departing on Sunday. They were seen for two hour-and-a-half to two-hour sessions Saturday, with a break for lunch. There were two telephone contacts with mother and one with John the following day. John had fallen while exploring old Fort DeSoto in a nearby park and sustained a laceration of his forehead which required stitches in a local emergency room. Both the outing for lunch and the accident at Fort DeSoto allowed for an assessment of mother-child interaction, as well as John's immediate response to the therapeutic evaluation.

261

HISTORY AND PRESENTING PROBLEMS

John was the first child born to academic scientist parents, the product of a planned pregnancy with a very complicated perinatal course. Intensely set on experiencing fully and being in control of her delivery, John's mother was upset to learn several weeks prior to delivery that an unresolvable breech presentation would require a Caesarian section. John's mother agreed to the C-section with the understanding that general anesthesia would not be used so that she could participate fully in the delivery. Difficulties with the epidural anesthesia, however, resulted in seizures and loss of consciousness and an otherwise uncomplicated C-section under general anesthesia produced a healthy baby boy. Mother, on the other hand, experienced an overwhelming sense of dyscontrol with post-traumatic sequelae such as flashbacks if she did not get out of bed immediately each morning. She sought psychotherapy for her depression and sense of dyscontrol when John was a year of age.

John's infancy was stressful and his mother found it difficult, if not impossible, to console him. He would react to her insecurity and discomfort with crying and back-arching when held but was not happy when alone. John's development was extremely varied. He was precocious intellectually but had difficulty controlling body functions. Never completely toilet-trained, he developed all sorts of fears related to his body—such as that a mouse would bite off his penis if he wore training pants. Roughly the time John's brother was born his behavior problems began to be seen in day care. By age three he had had five different day care settings (due, however, to day care changes, not to John's behavior). In the final setting John began to hit and bite other children and refused to follow the rules or orders of adults. By the time he was referred by his elementary school kindergarten for psychiatric day care, John was sticking his finger in his anus and smearing feces on other children or on his clothes while laughing uncontrollably. He urinated in his clothing two or three times a day and picked his nose and ate the contents. He was generally "out of control," hitting and trying to butt his teacher in the abdomen, stabbing children with pencils and climbing all over the school furniture. He threw intense tantrums and had at times to be physically restrained while shouting "I'm the boss," "I'm in charge!" or "I have the power!" John was also noted to masturbate in the classroom or in therapy at moments of tension. At the time of this evaluation John's treatment team was recommending a prolonged residential treatment because of the severity of his "mixed personality disorder with borderline and narcissistic features."

INTRODUCTION TO THE THERAPEUTIC EVALUATION

In a transcript such as this, much of the interactional and environmental flavor of a child psychotherapy session is lost because behaviors are not seen. (Video recordings have a definite advantage over audio recordings in this regard.) The potential power of a first therapeutic interview is therefore only minimally evident. Still, this session illustrates the many therapeutic opportunities which are generally present in a first encounter, as well as the way in which a clinical impression based on history (which was abundantly present for this child), and on overt behaviors (which were consistent with history), can be significantly modified by the child's response to a highly structured therapeutic encounter. This is important because one of the central features of a first encounter should be an assessment of the child's *therapeutic aptness*—the child's ability to utilize the *therapeutic space*; that is, the child's ability to "recognize" in the therapeutic encounter the complex potentials for communication and change (see Chapters 6 and 7). This has profound implications for inpatient/outpatient treatment planning among other things.

Because children are exquisitely sensitive and responsive to both logical structure and the "diacritical marks" of discourse (tone, stress, temporal word-groupings, etc.), such modifiers are indicated in this transcript either by *italic* or by the contents of [brackets]. Nonverbals are also indicated by [brackets], as are the various interactions that are not evident from the verbatim transcript alone. Without *italic* or [brackets] the reader might not appreciate the very purposeful communicative structure of verbal interventions or might assume that conscious awareness of the content of those communications was expected of the child. While there is some obvious cognitive clarification (e.g., the anatomical specifics of parturition and the role of the baby, mother and doctor in that process or "what happens when you eat corn"), most of the understanding expected of the child does not require conscious awareness on the child's part; indeed, attempts to bring the child to conscious awareness generally kill the therapeutic moment and/ or result in nongeneralizable empty compliance. Instead, the child's grasp of the meaning and content of communications is judged operationally by his behavior.

A scientific approach to psychiatric assessment requires that one genuinely attempt to falsify one's worst-case hypothesis—in this instance that John is incapable of self-control (he is quoted by clinicians as screaming "you can't control me, I have the power"). The fortuitous converse of this is that falsification of the worst-case hypothesis strongly suggests the reality of a better-case hypothesis — or, simply put, that one can't get five gallons out of a quart container. We know from extensive records that the various clinicians involved in John's care saw him as extremely disturbed, requiring long-term residential treatment and *incapable* of significant modulation of objectionable behaviors in the present. Furthermore, we also know from records that John's primary therapist felt that John's "capacity for insight is limited by his extreme egocentricity and John's orientation to action." A significant goal of any truly diagnostic assessment, therefore, must be to attempt to falsify this thesis. The caveat regarding conscious awareness in children notwithstanding, we shall see that this child is capable of significant *usable* "insight."

In order to understand the rationale for some of the interventions in this interviews it is important to keep in mind that John had already had a long experience of psychotherapy; he was not therapeutically naive. Furthermore, one of the central issues in this family was mother's distrust of physicians, a distrust reinforced by very real terrifying experiences related to John's birth: John knew that his mother generally did not trust clinicians. It is important to bear in mind as well that, at the time of this encounter, John was being considered for long-term residential treatment, a consideration which clearly represented to this child and his family a failure of treatment to date.

Prior to the evaluation, records were obtained from the treating center and from the psychologist who had evaluated John at the request of the school prior to admission to the psychiatric day-treatment program. Telephone conversations with John's mother provided further information. Thus, prior to our first encounter, we had a good picture of John's development and behaviors as seen by his parents and by other clinicians. This made it easier to structure what was expected to be a one-time evaluation. John was told by his mother that they were going to Florida to meet with two people who might be able to make some helpful suggestions about his behavior. John's father, skeptical of all psychological treatment at the time, was not involved.

The evaluation began with an initial period during which we interviewed John and his mother together. During this time a relatively detailed history was taken and John's behavioral problems were enumerated. The purpose of the detailed history-taking was to prime the child for the therapeutic evaluation: the history-symptoms discussed prior to entering the playtherapy room form the *ground* upon which the *figure* of the child's productions can be understood as communicative and intelligible. Once John's problem behaviors were described by mother, he became extremely aggressive, trying to bite, hit, pinch or otherwise hurt all parties involved. John's aggression was also verbal—with repeated attempts to intimidate and scare. During this part of the evaluation John frequently had to be physically restrained. This was done in a matter-of-fact fashion with no evidence of anger, frustration, or lack of control on the part of John's examiner—although his mother's frustration was apparent. She was encouraged simply to keep talking and to treat the physical restraint of her son as an "ancillary" activity. John and his examiner then left the office where his mother was still being interviewed and entered the playtherapy room. Away from his mother, John required no further physical control of his behavior.

IN THE PLAYTHERAPY ROOM

J   Ah! Ha! [After entering the playtherapy room, John looks at the painted picture of a crocodile on the moat of the Fisher-Price toy castle.]

DM*   Crocodile, yeah. Crocodiles eat . . . eat people. And do they poop them out?

One of John's symptoms and objectional behaviors is that he sticks his finger in his anus, gets feces on it, and at times smears. It is assumed that this behavior is genuinely meaningful for him and that he does it for a reason. Knowing the complex history surrounding John's birth and the very typical ways in which young children (mis)understand pregnancy and the birth process, John's therapist begins immediately with an operational hypothesis and tests it out. (Many of John's behaviors and productions in previous therapy suggest this approach as well.) John's immediate response suggests that it is correct. His subsequent behavior in these two sessions will confirm that the hypothesis is correct. John is also extremely aggressive toward people and things. His immediate reaction to the crocodile suggests a projected identification. His therapist proceeds with this in mind.

J   (Giggles . . . shakes his head yes)

DM   They do, huh? Yes, they do . . . I see you shaking your head [yes]. Well, you know what the crocodile does all the time? He's always putting his finger in his bottom, back there, checking to see if a people's coming out.

J   (giggles)

DM   And then you know what that crocodile does sometimes? He picks

*The therapist is the second author.

his nose and then he eats it and then he looks to see if it's in there! Because one time when he ate corn, you know what happened?

J   What?

DM   What happens when you eat corn, John? (John points to his bottom.) It comes out, yes, right! So he wanted to see if the poop would come out, if the snot would come out. What else have you tried to see come out in your poop? What else have you been looking for? What else have you eaten that comes out in your poop?

J   Your brain . . .

As we have seen, children often think that mothers eat something—or even that they eat whole babies—which results in the baby getting inside their "stomachs." This is John's first suggestion that body parts are eaten.

DM   My brain? Well, I'll tell you.

J   Where's the people? [for the castle]

DM   Right up here. You can play with them if you want to. You're the boss *in this room*.

John's sense of omnipotence and his experience of adults as relatively powerless is evident from history and from his behavior at the beginning this encounter. We also know from records that John has been allowed repeatedly to act out aggressively (hitting, spitting, kicking, destroying property both in and out of the designated therapy room) and to experience bodily dyscontrol (masturbation). It is therefore exceedingly important to elaborate early in the encounter the *structure, rules, and boundaries* which help define the *therapeutic space*. His therapist accomplished this in a powerful, but subtle, manner in the two preceding sentences. "You can play with them . . ." defines John's play as occurring with the therapist's permission and simultaneously links his desire to do so ("if you want to") with her authority over the space. "You're the boss *in this room*" returns a sense of agency to the child while significantly limiting its purview. Repeatedly, as interactions permit, the child's behavior will be operationally defined in terms of a sense of controlled agency when he would otherwise have been threatening, bossy, or omnipotent. Note that John is not asked to acknowledge that his therapist is in control and that he is acting at her behest. Such an "interpretation" would only provoke violent resistance.

J   [Looking for Fisher-Price people] Where are the people that go in here?

DM   You have to use this kind [pointing to the shelf which holds the black and white family dolls, the puppets and the stuffed animals]. See this Mrs. Koala. She's got a baby in there. [DM takes

the large Koala puppet and places the small stuffed Koala inside her]
"Mrs. Koala, how did you get that baby in there? Did you have to eat
that baby first?" Mmmmmmm! Did she eat the brains? Did she eat
the brains?

J   Yep. (giggles)

DM   Well, I just saw at the grocery store that there were pigs' brains and
     cows' brains that were there. And another time I was at the grocery
     store, I saw that there were pigs' feet. But John, have you ever seen
     babies feet there? At the grocery store?

J   I saw their brains.

DM   Babies' brains?

J   Um hum.

DM   What did they look like?

J   Babies' brains. [matter-of-factly, as if to say "babies' brains look like
     babies' brains, stupid"]

DM   So did that mommy who ate the baby, did she eat the brains and
     then poop it out?

J   Yep!

DM   Well, that's what a lot of people think. But it's not true. . . . Be
     careful because they [the shelves] are a little wiggly and you don't
     want them to fall and hurt you.

Almost any incidental activity or occurrence during the session can have
great therapeutic and/or diagnostic potential. We know that one of John's
great fears is his own "uncontrollable" power. Here is the first opportunity to
underscore the fact that John lives in a contingent universe in which he is
perhaps less powerful than he thinks. "You don't want them to fall and hurt
you" ascribes to John a personal caring and concern which does not appear
to be recognized his psychiatric records, while letting him know that his
therapist cares about his well-being. It is also another opportunity to issue a
command (they have a cumulative effect on children) while only appearing
to be solicitous. John, in fact, complies with the command.

J   Hm um [agrees].

DM   So, you've been smearing your poop all over the place to see if there's
     people in there . . . as you shake your head . . . [John smiles widely
     while shaking his head no] Well, all these doctors up in [the North-
     ern city], they haven't figured that out, huh?

To say that John "tests his environment" would be an understatement. His
finger-sticking and feces smearing had been seen by his clinicians as evidence
of stage-related (anal fixation) preoccupations and poor impulse-control—

not as behavior reflecting a potential operational hypothesis for this child. This effectively left John's objectionable behaviors empty of content and thereby foreclosed any possibility of resolution. Being as bright as he is, John could obviously sense this—which further contributed to his false sense of power over adults (who John treated as though they were not very bright). It required acknowledgment and, then, resolution.

Note that the reference to "the doctors [up North]" was not made maliciously and the recording makes it clear that it was not meant to "undermine" John's current clinicians: the complicitous, child-like exchange between John and his therapist hardly resembled a calculated put-down of competing clinicians. Part of John's problem is that he thinks he is smarter than adults. Unfortunately, sometimes he is! In our clinical work, we always assume that a bright, articulate and creative child like John knows on some level that he has hoodwinked his previous therapists. Part of the "game" such children get into has to do with outdoing adults. They love it and get very excited by it. Unfortunately, winning such a game means losing for the child: children cannot hold the real world together. Consequently, the technique (executed spontaneously, not in a calculated manner) is to acknowledge the intelligence and skill of the child which resulted in the "win"—and then to take the child's (scary) power away while leaving him with the beginnings of a trust in the ability of adults to outwit him *for the right reasons*. In a word, that one statement (in the form of a question) respectfully acknowledged that John had won and simultaneously made it perfectly clear that he could not win with this particular adult. As is usually the case, part of the power of such an intervention lies in the fact that no conscious acknowledgment of the second part is required of the child: he keeps face while being reassured that some adults are smarter than he is.

    J   [shakes head yes]

DM And then you start biting people, wanting to eat them, right? But John, but have you . . . [John laughs] . . . pooped out brains and babies yet? [John laughs enjoyably again] But it happened to your Mom, didn't it? She had a baby . . . she had your brother Andrew, didn't she?

    J   Ah hah! Help. [makes an exploding noise and puts the mommy in the top of the dungeon].

DM She's in there.

    J   She isn't coming down.

DM Sometimes they get stuck. . . . There, she's coming down.

    J   Ha ha!

DM So you've been biting your mom and kicking the furniture 'cause you're mad at her for eating you, right? [John giggles with big

eyes] And eating your brother. My God! How on earth could a
mother eat somebody! Did she eat that baby, this mommy?

J   Yes.

DM   And then she's going to wait until she poops and then it's going to
come out, right? [John giggles] Well, then, what if, John, the baby
came out—and the mommy was knocked unconscious? Was this
baby so powerful that he hit the mommy and knocked her out?
[John laughs and shakes his head] You're shaking your head "yes"?
[nods affirmatively] "You bet! I'm so powerful, you better do what I
say, otherwise I'll throw this stuffed animal all over the room!
[throws the stuffed animal into the corner in which the carpeting
runs up the wall to form a boundaried, safe throwing area—with a
big bang] That's what I'll do! Otherwise I'll break things!" Now, I
needed not to do that, right? [inadvertently hit herself] Time-out for
Debbie. [gives herself a time-out] Time-out's over! And that's what
happens, John, if you throw things and break things. But . . .
did this baby knock that mommy unconscious? [John shakes his
head yes] How?

Further defining the therapeutic space, John's therapist elaborates and en-
forces one of the "rules" which govern it: no hitting or hurting. She gives
herself a "time-out" and then tells John "that's what happens, John, if you
throw things and break things." She does not even wait for a response,
however, because there is no expectation that he will throw or break things.
This interaction has now conveyed to John that the kind of dyscontrol he has
experienced in the past in therapy settings is not possible in the present one.
By finishing the exchange with the question "Did this baby knock that
mommy unconscious?" (a reference to his mother's seizure at the time of his
birth by C-section), she implicitly links dyscontrol, tantrums, fantasies of
hurting his mother, *and* the structure, rules, and boundaries of the therapeutic space, thereby emphasizing the integrative, reparative aspect of the encounter.

J   He did, that's how.

DM   How did you do it to your mother?

J   Rghhhhhh! Like that! [punches the mommy doll in the face]

DM   By punching her in the face? [he nods yes] But you were only this big.
[indicates the size of a small baby]

J   I still did it!

DM   Nope, you didn't do it. Babies just aren't that powerful. But . . .

No clarification of John's "fantasies" (read *operational hypotheses regarding
the structure of the world*) is undertaken without an attempt at resolution—

one of the characteristics of a genuinely therapeutic evaluation. John, however, is not ready at this point in the encounter to abandon his power—adults
have not yet been adequately demonstrated to be safely in control of the
world—and so he changes the subject back to the dyscontrol of falling.

> J   Everyone's falling down here. . . . [John pushes the dolls down the
>   dungeon of the Fisher-Price castle]
> DM Yes, they are. Now, when you eat a peanut butter and jelly sand-
>   wich, does that come out in your poop?

John's therapist regains control by using his play to establish a continuity with
the previous attempts at clarification. This is a double sense of control for it
interrupts John's acting-out of dyscontrol while taking a firm control of the
meaning of the play. We see here the usefulness of Saussure's (1959) notion of
the arbitrariness of the linguistic sign, as well as that of polyvocity: there are
several potential meanings which can be assigned to John's behavior (since we
can never know for sure what really motivated it). One possibility is the
dyscontrol of falling. Another possibility—and the one which his therapist
chose to pursue—has to do with objects going in one end of a tube (the
dungeon in the castle tower) and coming out the other. Here, again, what we
see is a felicitous choice of thematic continuity on the part of John's therapist.

Regardless of the "correct" meaning of John's behavior at this point, his
therapist will either assign a meaning or will ignore the behavior. It is in this
choice of meaning-assignment that the therapeutic potential of the interaction is to be found. *Intentionality* can be modulated by the interacting adult
(Greenfield, 1980). Good psychotherapy is constantly operationally redefining and modulating the intentionality of the patient. John's therapist did not
"change the subject" at this point but, rather, remained within the context of
his "what goes in must come out" hypothesis.

> J   Yes [John replies, peanut butter and jelly sandwiches do come out in
>   your poop].
> DM How?
> J   It does, that's how!
> DM Well, when you're checking around down there, have you seen pea-
>   nut butter? [John giggles and shakes his head yes] Nooo . . .
> J   Yesss. . . .
> DM No, you've checked enough times. How about grape jelly?

Rather than defining John's objectionable behavior as unacceptable, John's
therapist reassures him that it was eminently meaningful (but, again, not
requiring conscious awareness or acknowledgment)—and that it has adequately served its purpose—and can, therefore, be abandoned. If necessary,

this process will be repeated indefinitely. While this may require great patience of a child therapist, the results can be striking (as they were with George in Chapter 9).

> J   Yes! I found that.
> DM   You did not. But you keep checking, don't you? What else have you found? [John makes farting noises] Have you found babies' brains yet?
> J   Umhum, yep.
> DM   You did?
> J   Yep.
> DM   What did you name the baby?
> J   "Bugger."

John here links feces and "buggers": both are elimination products of the body; both come out of "holes"; and both are viewed as socially, aesthetically repugnant.

> DM   "Bugger"!? [both laugh] and where do buggers come from? That's right. Right there in your nose. Do you name the baby "Bugger"?
> J   Umhum.
> DM   Was it a boy-baby or a girl-baby?
> J   Boy! Did you see him when he went wrong-wrong-wrong and it's into flying into the hole? [picks up the mouse family (father, mother, brother, sister), choosing the set with the long tails]
> DM   Umhum. But John . . . [he pushes the mother mouse down the castle tower hole to the dungeon] You're real mad at that mommy mouse.
> J   Get down there and stay down!
> DM   And when we were in the other room you were trying to eat your mother, like I wouldn't believe! Gobble, gobble, gobble, gobble, gobble.

John's therapist makes an explicit link between the play and the real-world behavior in the other room. Although John's biting has an unequivocal aggressive and hostile quality to it, she operationally redefines it as "eating," thereby creating an opening for a symbolic resolution according to the consistent logic of John's constructions. This approach, maintained consistently over time, significantly increases the likelihood that such behaviors will be abandoned in favor of the experience of integrative resolution.

J And now you! [screeches . . . as he pushes the daddy mouse down the dungeon hole]
DM The daddy mouse, too, huh?
J Umhum.
DM The daddy-bear is mad at the daddy-mouse. [John pounds the daddy-mouse with the daddy-bear] How come? What did he do that was so bad. What did he *choose* to do that was so bad. [he continues to pound] Yoo-hoo, earth to John! What did he do that was so bad? [continues to pound . . .]

So much of John's behavior defines him as out-of-control and he has been seen consistently by adults as not having the capacity for genuine self-control. This intervention begins what will be a long series of interventions which define behavior *in terms of CHOICE,* thereby constantly stressing a more refined aspect of agency. The *italic* here represents the same sort of phonological stress which characterizes the manipulative interventions of Milton Erickson (Haley, 1973) in which commands are embedded within surface statements or interrogatives.

J Wait a second! Do you have something long and skinny?
DM Long and skinny like what?
J A straw.
DM How about a spoon.

It would be easy at this point to enter into a discussion of male and female anatomy, since it appears clear that this is what John is asking his female therapist: does she have a penis? In keeping with the much more effective technique of allowing most of the communicative exchange to remain within the metaphor, however, she chooses to resolve the issue implicitly, substituting a concave holding object for a long, narrow penile one ("pea shooter"= "pee shooter"). Even if this is not John's unconscious meaning, it serves the purpose of clarification while not exiting the language of play. Correct communications on this level are much more effective both in reassuring the child that he or she is understood and in effecting generalizable change.

J Yes.
DM Long and skinny objects are very useful.

John's therapist unequivocally affirms the goodness of his maleness while at the same time keeping the functional anatomy separate (in normal parturition, penises do not push the babies out).

DM   [John keeps on trying to push the dolls—which were stuck—down into the dungeon with the spoon. DM continues talking for the action.] Do you need to get them [. . .] out, 'cause you just pull them out from the bottom, that's what you do. "Oh, no, I don't want to put my poop in the toilet. [John's therapist has the boy-mouse go over to the toilet in the large open-sided doll house] I'm afraid I'll have a baby and I'll kill it!" . . . "No, no! I'll never go poop in the toilet! I'm afraid a baby will come out and then it will be my fault and then I'll kill the baby and it'll go into the toilet and I'll flush it away! [John laughs] I don't want to kill anybody!"

J   I do!

DM   You do? You want to kill somebody? Who do you want to kill?

John switches from the play to a statement about himself: "I do [want to kill somebody]!" At this point his therapist asks him a simple discursive question: "Who do you want to kill?" When John's response to this discursive intervention is to return to the play, rather than to answer it discursively, it is assumed that John is beginning to accept the boundaries between play and the world, and the discursive question is not pursued. To do so at this point would have risked blurring the therapeutic boundaries and thereby confusing the child. We also note the beginning of a series of manipulations in which murderous anger is attributed to fathers.

J   All right now! [screams] Go on! Go on! [growls]

DM   Boy, that daddy-bear's angry! Is he going to kill somebody?

J   [makes growling noises for the daddy-bear]

DM   You know what I think you're doing now?

This is the first time that John is asked to identify with his therapist and to speculate about the meaning of his own behavior within the session. It is done simply and matter-of-factly without breaking the cadence of the session.

J   What?

DM   Did you get "locked up" inside your mom's *special safe clean place for babies* and you couldn't get out? And were you afraid that if she went to the bathroom that she would poop you into the toilet and flush you away and kill you? [John laughs and shakes his head] Yes? Oh, John! And now you've been treating yourself as if you're supposed to be gotten rid of. You silly goose! You need to stop that! Sometimes if they go in head-first, it's easier. [DM puts the dolls into the dungeon hole in the castle tower. . . .] "I can do it!

I can do it! I can do it myself!" Is that what you want to do, push
people around like that? Who's called you "a little bugger"?

The "special safe clean place for babies" is anatomically different from
where urine and feces come from. This is a distinction we make every week
with children. John is an overly verbal bright child for whom technical
knowledge often represents a "parallel universe of words." His words, however exact and technical, do not necessarily correspond to his actual understanding of the concepts which we take for granted when we hear the same
words. This is abundantly confirmed by his behavior (checking on his
"poop", etc.). The anatomical differentiation is stressed—but not discussed.

    J   My mom. [not historically accurate]
    DM   She has?
    J   Umhum.
    DM   How about anybody else? So you just go around picking your bug-
          gers to prove to everybody that you are a "bugger" [. . .] and then
          they say that "you are what you eat," so are you eating? [John inter-
          rupts . . .]
    J   Buggers!
    DM   And then your name is "John Bugger"? [he laughs] Or just "Bugger"?
    J   My name's "John Bugger."
    DM   The other thing I don't quite understand is why do you *choose* to be
          so mean?

Without being made consciously aware of it, John has been asked to reflect
upon the complexity of his confused view of pregnancy, birth and the role of
babies in the process. Because his therapist knows well how much John's
parents—his mother especially—talk like adults about all these issues, no
attempt is made to engage John in a "discussion." Instead, once again the
stress is on *choice*: choosing to hurt, choosing not to hurt.

    J   Ah ha! [John pulls out the Wolf puppet]
    DM   Are you the Big Bad Wolf?
    J   Ah ha! [John "births out" the Baby Koala from the Koala puppet]
    DM   You did it! [meaning: successfully managed a safe birth] Did this
          baby almost kill that mother?
    J   Umhum.
    DM   "You bet! [John's therapist speaks for the Baby Koala John has just
          delivered] And if I want to beat somebody up, I'm going to—because
          I'm the biggest, baddest baby in the whole world, that's what I am!

> And I'll beat your brains in [. . .] and you better do what I say otherwise I'll kill you, too."
>
> J No you won't!

At this point the tables have been turned: John has been induced to identify with, and take the side of, the *mother* Koala. (Notice that John does this without any required conscious awareness.) Again, this allows him to begin to develop empathy—but without having to admit doing so, something which would surely result in a denial and a return to his "bad self."

> DM "I did it to my mother and I can do it to you!" [continuing to speak for the baby Koala]
>
> J Oh, yeah?! Hey, you! [makes an explosive sound]
>
> DM You can throw against that wall over there. [John's therapist exits the play for a moment to make a parenthetical remark.] Use that one. Boy! That's a big bear! [John makes loud "yeeaaahhh!" sounds] Now, who's this guy?

Again, the structure, rules and boundaries which help constitute the therapeutic space are explicitly elaborated. By making a statement outlining the rules ("You can throw against that wall over there"), John's therapist controls his behavior while giving him a sense of agency. The straightforward command "Use that one" facilitates a factitious choice which keeps freedom (the recognition of choice and the ability to choose [Wheelis, 1973]) within the bounds of acceptable behavior as defined by responsible adults. This is registered—but not noticed—by the child. Although the therapist has designated which stuffed animal or puppet may be thrown, she asks John to define what the object represents.

> J The mother.
>
> DM And who's this one?
>
> J The mother?
>
> DM Two mothers? [John laughs]
>
> J It's the daddy.
>
> DM Yes, you see, he doesn't have a hole. He doesn't have a place for babies.

John had chosen a puppet for the first "mother" and a stuffed animal for the second "mother." This allowed his therapist to reinforce the anatomical difference between the sexes, thereby reinforcing interpersonal boundaries as well. The large stuffed Koala is now defined as "daddy Koala." John can answer consciously that he knows well that men can't have babies. But "uterus" is too abstract and technical to be meaningful: that's why he is constantly checking his "poop." A "special safe clean place for babies," however, is a much more assimilable concept for a six-year-old. There won't be any "poop" in a *clean* place.

> J   I know . . .

By this point—barely half-way into a first clinical encounter—this child has already become an ally in the therapeutic process. He demonstrates that he is able to go back and forth between participatory and observing roles, one of the signs of a therapeutically apt child.

> DM   He can't poop them out because he can't get them in there! "Poop" is a *whole* different place!
> J   Ha, ha, ha, ha!

John is even able to laugh at a pun. He is clearly developing a genuine ludic quality to his interaction. Note that this is ludic playing within symbolic play—not "just playing."

> DM   And I ask you, John, have you seen any babies come out of your poop?
> J   Yes.
> DM   Bull! [another pun for a bright child] You haven't even seen jelly! You've seen corn, maybe. But I know when you eat your buggers, you haven't seen a bugger come out either, have you?

What follows is viewed as a confirmation of the *poop/bugger=baby* hypothesis. It is John's next utterance and behavioral statement in response to his therapist's question about "buggers."

> J   The little one went back into his mother. [John puts the little Koala back inside the larger puppet Koala]
> DM   He did?
> J   Yeah, because he was scared! Rghhhhhhh! [John makes the daddy-Koala roar]
> DM   He's a pretty scary guy. What's his name?

Rather than pursuing the question of what the "little one" is scared of, John's therapist chooses instead to make the link between the defense of being scary to others and the fear of being scared, thereby letting John know even more how much she understands what underlies his outward behaviors. This represents a purposeful therapeutic blurring of boundaries (John and father) within the context of the play and sets the stage for a later facilitation of positive identification with father's nonscary positive characteristics.

> J   He locked himself in [the house].
> DM   Just like the baby tried to lock himself back inside there? [DM. points to the little Koala inside the mother]
> J   Yeah. . . . Make him do some real mean things again.

Again, a fascinating about-face: John has just empowered his therapist to choose for him and asks her to "make him do some real mean things again," doubtless "knowing" full well that she will not. This represents a very significant step and is both diagnostically and prognostically extremely positive.

> DM   You want me to do that?
> J   Yeah.

John's therapist clarifies (and reinforces) that he, indeed, wants her—and not a play character—to make real choices for him. Unlike the purposeful blurring of boundaries within the play, this clarification highlights the difference between imagined actions and those of real people.

> DM   Well, I think I've changed my mind. I don't think I want *to choose* for him to be mean . . .

This is a purposeful affirmation of the ubiquity of choice: *all* of us have this ability to choose.

> J   Yeah!
> DM   I think you want him to be sad.

Again, an embedded command—"you *want* him to be sad"—the purpose of which is to facilitate an identification while making it possible for John to leave the anger and gain access to his underlying sadness. The sadness is resolvable; the anger is not.

> [DM. continues:] What's the matter, Koala? It wasn't your fault that your mommy almost looked like she was going to die. Oh, I know it's not your fault. You weren't a bad baby.
> J   She's *dead*. [with a sinister voice]

DM   She's just had a seizure. She didn't die.

The real-world circumstances of John's birth are again reiterated. It makes no sense to allow him to perseverate in his horrible self-image as a destructive baby.

J   She's dead.
DM   But you've been scared that she might die.
J   She's dead. She *is* dead. [makes a horrible threatening sound] The daddy's real mean.
DM   Yeah, he sounds it. How about your dad, is he real mean?
J   Umhum.
DM   He is? What does he do?
J   [Roaring sound] All right, big creature! I'll take care of this thing. [screeching sound—throws the daddy-Koala against the carpeted wall]

John chooses not to respond to a discursive question but, instead, continues with the play. Since the question had been asked about a real person in the real world, John's therapist makes a real-world comment, approving of his "choice" to remember and obey the rules:

DM   John, I really like the way you're following directions and only using the wall you can throw on. You're doing super.

One of the major concerns of John's treatment team was that he could not distinguish reality under stress. The operational distinction John makes by following the rules suggests real ability in this area.

J   Ha! Ha! [as he continues to beat up the daddy-Koala]
DM   Now, what if you look like that big Koala? [DM points out two boxes of Legos. The boxes are quite different in appearance but contain the same pieces] . . . Those are Legos . . . those are Legos, too. . . . Even though they look exactly alike, they come from two different places. They're not exactly alike . . . [points to the father and baby Koalas] Is this little Koala exactly like that big gruff daddy?
J   Yeah.
DM   No-o-o-o! No-o-o-o! [John continues to be mean, then changes and takes out the chess board]

What follows is another fascinating illustration of the therapeutic aptness of this bright child. He had been asked a discursive question by his therapist while he was beating up the stuffed animal that represented the (his) father. When his therapist does not interrupt the process and stop the beating, he seems to sense that she has not done her job (not letting him persist in a fruitless and scary exercise of pseudo-power) and changes the subject himself. It appears that he has realized that she is usually one step ahead of him, so he offers her the opportunity to regain her superior position in the real world with an invitation to play a game — a game an adult is likely to win.

J   I'm good at chess. Want me to challenge you?
DM If you want to . . .
J   I can beat anyone!
DM Okay, which one: chess or checkers?
J   Chess.
DM Here's the rules . . .
J   I know them.

This is taken to be another significant therapeutic move on John's part. He has chosen a game with complex structure and clear inviolable rules. Again, he is not asked to acknowledge consciously that he has chosen to side with — rather than against — rules.

DM Okay, what color do you want to be? Black or white?
J   [pauses . . .] Death . . . black! [almost whispers]
DM "Death black," okeydoke.

Because John seems to have chosen to test out whether his therapist can stop the process of his identification with deathly destruction within the sphere of the symbolic, she does not respond discursively to his "death black" comment. Rather, she allows the identification in anticipation of the opportunity for a corrective reparative response within the metaphor. Instead of saying to John, "No, you can't be Death Black," thereby attempting to block the identification, his therapist chooses to allow John to experience the fact that, even as "Death Black," he is just not very powerful.

J   The pawns all go up front [John repeats this over and over as he arranges the men]
DM Who taught you how to play chess?
J   Eddy, he's the only one who used to know.
DM Who's Eddy?

J   Oh, someone at school [a boy several months older than John and his best friend at school].

DM   How old is he?

Eddy is clearly not very important to John at this point in the session, so the question is not pursued.

J   Queen always goes on her own color.

DM   Right. Good memory.

J   Bishops can only slant. Knights have to move in an L-shape . . .

DM   . . . backwards or forwards, left or right . . .

J   Right. Rooks can go forward, sideward or backward. They can go either way.

DM   Right.

J   And they can go backwards and frontwards.

DM   Right. I keep the . . . [John interrupts loudly . . .]

J   Now the queen can go any way [practically shouting], any way — as far as she wants!

DM   As long as there's no one in her . . . ?

J   . . . way . . . [practically whispers]

DM   What about the king, though? Who's the most important one in the whole game?

J   Well, if you get the . . . if you *kill* the king and get . . .

DM   Not *kill* him . . . *catch* him . . .

Keeping the real world and John's fantasies quite separate.

J   Yes, you win the game.

DM   Right. No killing here, just capturing. Who goes first, you or me?

J   Well, the white always goes first. You can only move . . . [John illustrates moves] And knights can jump, too. They can jump over men. The queen can't jump . . .

DM   No, I have a clear path for her. [moves]

J   Pawns can only capture by slanting.

DM   You've got a good memory about rules — and you can choose to follow them. And you're doing good choices, John, choosing to be your "real, terrific good self," the way you . . . [brief pause] Are all babies born good or . . . [John makes a move] Oh, you can't do that . . . 'cause I can win the game, you can't move yourself into "check." It's against the rules to put yourself in danger. I would have won: game over. Bad choice, John.

While one should never *allow* a child to win a game in therapy (because it will destroy the child's trust in the adult as a competent, reliable person), there are times when one should allow the child to lose—and even lose repeatedly. This is not one of those times. This child is exquisitely sensitive to adult inconsistency and lives in a contingent and unpredictable universe in which his omnipotence is required to ward off disaster. This need for omnipotent control, of course, is also overly complicated by his confused sense of guilt for having "hurt" his mother. Structure, rules and boundaries are absolutely necessary for him—as is the protective structure of adult care. It would be a major technical error to allow John to "hurt" himself through an early bad move. Instead, it becomes an opportune moment to reinforce the notion of *choice* coupled with adult protection. John's verbal response to the intervention reflects an acceptance of that protective stance.

> J   Okay, well, how about . . . this. Let's see if I can free my queen in a safe way.
>
> DM   Oh, I like the way you're choosing safety. [John moves a piece, thereby freeing his queen but inadvertently allowing his therapist a 1-move checkmate] Okay, that's the same thing you did. [She demonstrates the obligatory checkmate which would result if John allowed his choice to stand.] I won. Do you want to play again? You can't put yourself in danger. It's against the rules to put yourself in "check." Where's the rules here? [John's therapist looks at the rules while a new game starts and John begins to get himself in the same trouble] That's why I keep these right here. Yes, it says, "The king may capture but it may not move into check, a situation where it would be captured." So, you can't move that. Otherwise I win the game. You can't do that on purpose.

It may appear here that John's therapist is just helping him to refine his chess-playing techniques. Actually, she is repeatedly not allowing him to hurt or endanger himself symbolically. She simultaneously displays that she is stronger and smarter (she can easily win), yet her primary concern is for John's safety and well-being—just like a parent.

> DM   [The game continues. John moves, freeing his queen] Boy, you are one super duper terrific *follower of rules* here!
>
> J   Why aren't you looking? I freed my queen! [nearly shouts, apparently feeling neglected while his therapist replaces the box top on which the rules are printed]
>
> DM   Umhum, sure did.

J   When you get a pawn to the end of the board, it turns into a queen. And it can move around like a queen.

DM   It doesn't turn into it. You have to trade it in, and if I haven't captured your queen, then I can't give it back to you. It doesn't magically turn into anything. [pause] But you're right, when it gets to the other end it can be turned in for one of the other pieces the other person has captured. Your turn. I moved here.

Even this board game allows for an ongoing clarification of John's confusion over the difference between sexes. His urge to identify with his mother—the super headstrong parent who will take on all the authorities in the world—is countered by a panic related to the real-world consequences of such an identification. Without addressing this explicitly, John's therapist deals with it implicitly through the metaphor of the game. Thus John's castration anxiety, so evident in his ongoing enuresis and in his past fear of having his penis bit off by a mouse, is addressed entirely within the play. Interestingly, this will free up his bishop. John leaves his preoccupation with the queen to turn to a more realistically useful piece.

J   Okay. [very softly] Ha! Ha! [long pause] I didn't realize my bishop could move. [long pause] Your move. [theatrically and almost inaudibly] Make him live! [imitates someone unknown] Now, [still almost inaudibly] I command you!

DM   Who are you imitating? [John ignores the question]

J   Okay, your move.

DM   Okay. Check.

J   Hmmm! Kings can move like this . . . but . . . double-check . . .

DM   Right.

J   I have to move like this, letting myself out.

DM   I like the way you're keeping yourself safe. *Good choice!*—following the rules and keeping yourself safe.

J   Can't do it!

DM   You *can* do it.

J   You can't capture my king when I'm safe, is what I mean.

John has just engaged in concentrated deliberation and has organized highly adaptive responses—all within the rules of the game—to serial frustrations. He also transitioned from a nonproductive, self-defeating preoccupation with a female figure (the queen) to a male figure with realistic—if less impressive—options (the bishop). This, too, is of significant prognostic import. His ordered, reasoned approach to this problem seems to suggest a prime time to return to the very opposite of such behavior: John's "disordered," "out of control" aggression. John's last clarification seems to indicate that he will correct a misunderstanding rather than acquiesce, implying that his acquiescence earlier in the session to some potentially controversial suggestions was, in fact, agreement.

> DM Now, what is this baloney, John, about you going around *pretending* you're a monster?
> J Nothing.

"Nothing" could be taken as a negative response to the question. Instead, it is treated as a confirmation of the embedded implication (*pretending*), and his therapist continues.

> DM That's good—because you are not a monster. You were not born a monster. All babies are born good—no matter which way they come out. And even the ones where the mommies have to have a cut in their abdomen up here [indicates the place], you know . . .
> J Yeah [very quietly] . . .
> DM Is that the baby's fault that they have to have a cut? [pauses when John does not reply] No.
> J I better get one of my rooks out here! If I'm going to capture this guy here.
> DM Good luck.
> J What?

John is momentarily confused by this encouragement. It is clear that his therapist will not *let* him win, and yet she wishes him good luck.

> DM Good luck. Wait. It's my turn [she moves] . . . now it's your turn. [pause] Check. You can't move yourself into check.
> J Now let's see what I *can* do. [with a determined, mean sound]

Therapists have the same choices that patients do. In this case, one can choose to respond to either of two potentially different aspects of John's response: his sense of agency ("I *can* do") or the striking meanness of his voice. His therapist chooses the former, totally ignoring the latter.

DM   I really like the way you are looking at what you *can* and *cannot do* — and following rules. What good *choices*, John. *Choosing* to be your terrific real good self. . . . Check . . . oh, no, I don't really want to do that . . .

J   Why?

DM   I didn't take my fingers off [the piece] because your bishop . . . [John interrupts]

J   Ah, ha! ha! ha!

DM   . . . so I'm not going to put my queen in danger.

J   Yeah!

DM   That would be a dumb *choice,* wouldn't it? [laughs] And grownups sometimes make dumb *choices,* but if you do it all the time, then they wonder about you. Even about kids that might make dumb choices. Do you know that you haven't picked your nose once since you've been here! . . . I haven't seen you "eat a baby." But you know, mommies have their stomachs up here, John, and then down here is the "special place for babies" and inside there is where the baby grows. And it takes nine months. It never is in the stomach. Lots of people say that, but they're wrong.

J   I know.

This "I know" has an entirely different feel to it. It is not the off-putting, cynical and sarcastic "I know" of early on in the encounter. John's voice is calm and affirming.

DM   I knew this one kid who kept wanting to eat all sorts of things, thinking that he was going to get a baby inside his stomach. Never worked! Plus, you're a guy. Guys don't even have a special place for babies! You just have a stomach, like ladies have a stomach, but you don't have that special place for babies inside there. *But,* can mommies have a baby by themselves?

Until now, John's only portrayal of father-type figures in the play has been negative. This offers him the opportunity to reverse that.

J   No, they need the man.

DM   That's right. The man is the most . . . is very, very important.

J   Yeah, because he has the part that they need to put together to build the baby.

DM   So your daddy . . . [John interrupts what was to have been her emphasis of how important daddies and their "parts" are]

J   He has the pieces.

DM Which pieces? You mean "little pieces of brains" and stuff that he gives to the mother?

J   [laughs] No, no. He has certain pieces . . .

DM He has the little tadpole-like thing called the "sperm" . . .

J   [interrupts] Yes!

DM Right. And inside there it's like a computer program. And the computer program gets with the mommy's part and then they make the baby.

J   Right!

DM Through his what? [*long* delay] . . . penis, right? Have you ever tried to get rid of your penis?

J   Um-um [no] . . .

DM Good, because they're very important, penises are. I knew this one boy who thought that . . . By the way, do mothers have penises? [John shakes his head no] Were they born with them and then they got cut off somehow?

J   No. [laughs gently]

DM That's right, cause ladies never . . . [John interrupts]

J   Why they talking about . . . like this? [John points to a rule on the inside of the top of the chess box]

DM Oh, that's "castling." If you've never moved your king and you've never moved your rook, but have moved the guys in between, one time in the game you can move your king two spaces over and your castle one over. Of, if it's on this side, how does it say, "the king two spaces and the castle three." See, you need to not destroy grownups because you need them sometimes to help you figure out what is going on. You're just six years old. You don't know everything!

J   What are they talking about here? [pointing to another section in the chess rules—as if to say "Prove it!"]

John seems to be saying that he will accept adult authority—but not on faith.

DM That's just showing where the king can move, and then I wrote some things in there which don't really go with the directions.

J   Why? [still as if to say "Prove you know what you're talking about!"]

DM I was going to continue a game with somebody once, but our time had run out. And so I wrote down where we had the pieces, so that when we saw each other again we could set it up the way it had been. That way we could continue. The game didn't have to end until the

game ended—not just because we ran out of time. [pause] Isn't it
your turn?

J   Of course, it's my turn! [very snotty] You didn't even learn how to
play!

DM   Want to put it up?

J   Locky locky locky . . . locky locky locky . . . [sings while pouring
the chessmen back into the box]

Again, John's therapist is presented with a choice: respond to the insolence
and negativity which has just appeared or emphasize the positive when
John's cooperative behavior is inconsistent with his verbal negativity. She
chooses to reinforce the positive.

DM   I really like the way you put those away nicely. Right underneath the
jewelry box there, where the crayons are. [indicating where to put
the chess set] Super! Now, you know what you just did?

J   What? [less snotty]

By concentrating on what John was *doing,* not on what he was *saying,* John's
therapist facilitates a return to a friendlier, more respectful tone of voice.

DM   You ended the game as if you . . . and we hadn't run out of time or
anything like that . . . and the game wasn't over . . . But does that
mean that either you or I died?

J   No. [back to his pleasant voice, takes the toy castle out and flicks the
flag back and forth]

DM   Have you ever made anybody die?

J   Nnnno. [gets rougher with the toy flag, knocking it back and forth
and making explosive gun sounds]

This is clearly a highly charged topic filled with uncertainty.

DM   Have you ever wished that your baby brother would disappear? I
knew this one guy who hated the fact that his mother always used to
be able to take the baby brother to work with her! Because the
brother was in here, you know . . . [points to her lower abdomen]

J   Yeah . . .

DM   And it was like . . . [John picks his nose and eats it] Do you need a
Kleenex? [he stops]

J   No. [sadly]

John had not picked his nose during the entire session until this discussion of the little brother being inside the mommy and hostile wishes toward a sibling.

> DM   The brother was in there [pointing to her abdomen] and it was like, "I'm so jealous . . . " [John starts to hit himself] . . . Don't hit people, John, not even yourself. [he stops]

John's response to a simple, gently offered reminder of one of the rules results in a quick cessation of the hitting—and allows the process to continue without disruption.

> [DM continues] He says, "I'm so jealous," he says, "I want to go to work with my mommy! I want to go to bed with my mommy! How come my baby brother does it? I'm older than him . . . and he gets to go with her!" Because you saw, when your mom was pregnant with Andrew, didn't you . . . ? [John smacks the flag on the castle even harder] And so one time he says, "Oh, I wish that baby brother would just *disappear!*" Did the baby brother disappear?
> J   No.
> DM   Try it on me. Tell me you wish I would disappear.
> J   I wish you would disappear! [sinister voice]
> DM   Didn't work! You're just not that powerful! [John continues to whack the flag pole of the Fisher-Price castle, perhaps suggesting to some readers who the imaginary "mouse" who would bite off John's penis was shortly after the birth of his brother] I like the way you're protecting your body, and not getting hit by the flag, and just letting it hit the spoon instead of your body. That's okay. *Good choice,* John! *Choosing* to be your "terrific real good self!"

Again, John's therapist chooses to respond only to the positive aspect of what John is doing—even though it would be easy to see his behavior as entirely negative. The result, again, is a cessation of the negative behavior. These positive responses to such interventions are powerful indicators of future therapeutic workability. This non-confrontational approach allows John to stop the negative behavior and change what he is doing without losing face.

> J   Where are those little tiny animals? [he asks with a demanding, growling voice] Hey! Who is this, a girl or a boy [he picks up the kangaroo] and where's the mother?!

DM   You decide.

J   Well, she doesn't have a pouch!

DM   No, she sure doesn't.

J   She should!

DM   She doesn't so she's . . . it's gotta be a dad. Right? Just a fat daddy,
      right?

J   [laughs] Wondering why he's having a baby! [laughs]

This ability to laugh at himself and the obvious silliness of some of his
worries stands in striking contrast to the belligerence of the first part of the
session. Sex, reproduction, babies, death wishes, castration anxiety and
gender confusion are all dealt with within the play itself.

DM   When I was your age I thought this one big man that I saw who was
      real fat, I thought *he* was going to have a baby! But, can men have
      babies?

J   No. [matter-of-factly]

DM   But they sure can get fat, can't they?

J   Yeah. [makes shooting sounds] You bring these guys back!

DM   Why do you always talk so mean, like that?

J   Cause I want you to do things.

Again, a striking change from the first part of the hour—and from his
behavior in the other office. Asked a simple discursive question about his
behavior, John answers simply and cogently. It has become safer for him to
admit that he needs to be threatening to get what he wants. Although this is
clearly one of his maneuvers when faced with anxiety-provoking material,
his therapist does not pursue this discursively. John is not asked to exercise
his "observing ego." Rather, he is simply told how to get what he wants in a
positive manner.

DM   Well, just ask me. "Debbie, will you please bring them over," and
      there they'd be!

J   Hmmm . . .

When his therapist acts out his bullying reaction to anxiety, John can laugh
at it.

DM   Makes me feel like I'm bad when you go, "Rgh! rgh! rgh! You better
      bring that over here right now!" [very loud . . . John laughs and
      laughs] But I didn't do anything wrong. But if you ask me nicely, you

know, [John still laughing], I put it right there. So, you're putting that baby right back into the "special place for babies" in that mommy, huh?

J   Way up in her head! [John pushes the little stuffed koala way up into the koala puppet]

DM   That's just a puppet. In a real, live person . . . [John laughs and snickers] Yes, you did put it way up there in her head. Can babies do that, though? Can they go back inside?

J   Yep.

DM   Nope.

J   Yep.

DM   Nope.

J   Yep. The mother got up. Look at the mother koala bear.

John has begun to imitate his therapist's way of talking. He ends with "the last word," but concedes through the tone of his voice. No intervention is required.

DM   Climbing. She has those special hands so that she can do that. Sometimes the platypuses feel sad. They say, "Gosh, you can climb so well. We wish we could climb as well." And it's because they're . . . They can swim in the water real well, but they can't climb as well as the koalas. Everybody has different things that they're good at. [John interrupts with a sinister laugh]

John is still not secure in his sense of being different.

J   Ha! Ha! Ha! The koala bear's [here the tape ran out]

John plays around with the daddy koala and ends up having him scratch the platypus with its paws. Again, John's therapist faces a choice with profound therapeutic implications: should she respond to the aggression? Instead, she sees this hurt as creating the possibility for a reparative intervention and John is invited to become "Dr. John" who can treat the animals. John responds to this intervention by having more of the animals be hurt animals, thereby giving himself the opportunity to extend the reparative moment. His therapist introduces a "mom with a baby who had to get out" and tells him, "You're going to have to get the baby out." Dr. John then uses his finger as a knife and takes the baby out, delivering the baby stuffed koala from the larger koala puppet. Dr. John then repairs the cut. By this time there are six or seven stuffed animals lying side by side, carefully and gently arranged by John, all recovering from their surgeries. This process takes a good ten minutes. John then ties up the daddy koala and sticks him in the dungeon [jail]. He then picks up the room without even being asked, putting everything back in its proper place. John makes the transition out of the playtherapy room properly but, once back in the other office, resumes his "snotty brat" aggressive behavior and tries to take over the situation, ordering his mother around and trying to hit or bite her.

DISCUSSION

At the time of this writing more than a year has passed since the interview above took place. Even though the results of our encounter with John were shared with his treatment team, John's therapist continued to maintain that John could not tell when he allowed John to win at chess, continued to view him as extremely dysfunctional and drive-driven and concluded that John "cannot use psychotherapy." John remained in day-treatment while parents and program personnel debated the wisdom of residential treatment. Our suggestion all along was to abandon the treatment setting in which John could not escape his identity as a dysfunctional child, incapable of using therapy, and risk enrollment in the public school program. Ultimately, John was transferred to an Emotionally Handicapped classroom in the public schools—where he was immediately recognized by his new teacher as a "gifted" student. John's behavior improved significantly with the transfer out of day-treatment.

Almost nine months after the first encounter, when John's parents felt that they could not mobilize any genuine therapeutic optimism in the staff looking after him, we began weekly 20- to 30-minute telephone sessions with John. The telephone sessions were conducted much they way we conduct regular therapy (a brief update and coordination time with the parent at the beginning and the end of the call)—except that the sole medium was voice and all action had to be imagined. Eleven months after the initial encounter, John's parents happened to be in the area vacationing and called requesting an appointment. This time father was present and lent his support to the process. John, much better behaved than at our first encounter, picked up where he left off and immediately asked to play a game of chess. In striking contrast to the first encounter, John quickly abandoned both chess and his mildly obnoxious behavior on being soundly beaten by his therapist in but a few moves. He talked openly about his life and his concerns during the remaining time.

John was quite capable of "using psychotherapy." Therapy, however, has to be capable of being used.

References

Adams, P. & Fras, I. (1988). *Beginning Child Psychiatry*. New York: Brunner/Mazel.

Alajouanine, T. (1963). Dostoiewski's eplilepsy. *Brain*, 86(2):209–218.

Alpert, L. (1987). When temper tantrum turns into scene it's time to teach child alternative behavior, *St. Petersburg Times*, Sunday, March 1.

American Academy of Child and Adolescent Psychiatry (1985a). Facts for families from the American Academy of Child Psychiatry: The adopted child., 11(4). Washington, D.C.: American Academy of Child and Adolescent Psychiatry.

American Academy of Child and Adolescent Psychiatry (1985b). Facts for Families from the American Academy of Child and Adolescent Psychiatry: Learning disabilities., 11(5). Washington, D.C.

American Psychiatric Association (1980). *Diagnostic and Statistical Manual, Third Edition*. Author.

American Psychiatric Association (1987). *Diagnostic and Statistical Manual of Mental Disorders, Third Edition — Revised*.

Andreason, N. C. (1984). *The Broken Brain: The Biological Revolution in Psychiatry*. New York: Harper & Row.

Anisman, H. L. & Sklar, L. S. (1979). Catecholamine depletion in mice upon exposure to stress: medication of the escape deficits reduced by inescapable shock. *J. Comp. Physiol. Psychol.*, 93:610–625.

Anthony, E. J. (1986). Contrasting neurotic styles in the analysis of two preschool children. *J. Am. Acad. Child Psychiat.*, 25,1:46–57.

Beck, J. C. & van der Kolk, B. (1987). Reports of childhood incest and current behavior of chronically hospitalized psychotic women. *Am. J. Psychiat.*, 144,11:1474–1476.

Bernstein, E. & Putnam, F. W. (1986). Development, reliability and validity of a dissociation scale. *Journal of Nervous and Mental Diseases*, 174:727–735.

Bettelheim, B. (1979). *Surviving and Other Essays*. New York: Harcourt Brace Jovanovich.

291

Bettelheim, B. (1983). *Freud and Man's Soul*. New York: Alfred A. Knopf.

Bliss, E. L. (1984). Spontaneous self-hypnosis in multiple personality disorder. *Psychiatric Clinics of North America*, 7:135–148.

Bohman, M. & von Knorring, A.-L. (1979). Psychiatric illness among adults adopted as infants. *Acta Psychiat. Scand.*, 60:106–112.

Borke, H. (1971). Interpersonal perception of young children: ego-centrism or empathy? *Develpm. Psychol.*, 5:263–269.

_____ (1973). The development of empathy in Chinese and American children between three and six years of age: a cross-cultural study. *Develpm. Psychol.*, 9: 102–108.

_____ (1975). Piaget's mountains revisited: changes in the egocentric landscape. *Develpm. Psychol.*, 11:240–143.

_____ (1978). Piaget's view of social interaction and the theoretical construct of empathy. In: Siegel, L. S. & Brainerd, C. J. (eds.), *Alternatives to Piaget*. New York: Academic Press, 29–42.

Bowlby, J. (1973). *Attachment and Loss, Volume II: Separation*. New York: Basic Books.

Brainerd, C.J. (1978a). *Piaget's Theory of Intelligence*. Englewood Cliffs (N.J.): Prentice-Hall.

Brainerd, C.J. (1978b). The stage question in cognitive-developmental theory. *Behav. Brain Sci.*, 1:173–213.

Braun, B. G. & Sachs, R. G. (1985). The development of multiple personality disorder: Predisposing, precipitating, and perpetuating factors. In: Kluft, R. P. (Ed.), *The Childhood Antecedents of Multiple Personality*. Washington, D.C.: American Psychiatric Press.

Brazelton, T. B. (1978). The remarkable talents of the newborn. *Birth & Family Journal.*, 5:4–10.

Breslow, L. & Cowan, P. A. (1984). Structural and functional perspectives on classification and seriation in psychotic and naormal children. *Child Dev.*, 55:226–235.

Brodzinsky, D. M., Singer, L. M., & Braff, A. M. (1984). Children's understanding of adoption. *Child Development*, 55:869–878.

Bryan, E. M. (1986a). The intrauterine hazards of twins, *Arch. Dis. Childhood*, 61: 1044–1045.

Bryan, E. M. (1986b). The death of a newborn twin: How can support for parents be improved? *Acta Genet. Med. Gemellol.*, 35:115–118.

Bryer JB, Nelson BA, Miller JB & Krol PA (1987). Childhood sexual and physical abuse as factors in adult psychiatric illness. *American Journal of Psychiatry*, 144(11):1426–1430.

Butterfield, E. C. & Siperstein, G. N. (1972). Influences of contingent auditory stimulation upon nonnutritional sucking. In: Bosma, J. (Ed.), *Oral Sensation and Perception: The Mouth of the Infant*. Springfield, Ill.: Charles C. Thomas.

Cain A. C. & Cain, B. S. (1964). On replacing a child. *J. Am. Acad. Child Psychiat.*, 3:443–456.

Cain, A. C, Erickson, M. E., et al (1964). Children's Disturbed reactions to their mother's miscarriage. *Psychosomatic Med.*, 26(1):58–66.

Cain A. C., Fast, I. & Erickson, M. E. (1964). Children's disturbed reactions to the death of a sibling. *J. Am. Orthopsychiat. Assn.*, 34:741–752.

Caplan, J. & Walker, H. A. (1979). Transformational deficits in cognition of schizophrenic children. *J. Autism Dev. Disord.*, 9:161–177.

Carek, D. J. (1979). Individual psychodynamically oriented therapy. In. Harrison, S. I. (ed.), *Basic Handbook of Child Psychiatry*. New York: Basic Books, Vol. 3:35–57.

Carmen, E., Reiker, P., & Mills, T (1984). Victims of violence and psychiatric illness. *American Journal of Psychiatry*, 141:378–383.

Coles, G. (1987). *The Learning Mystique: A Critical Look at "Learning Disabilities."* New York: Pantheon.

Conte, J. R. (1985). The effects of sexual abuse on children. *Victimology*, 10: 110–130.

Coppolillo, H. P. (1987). *Psychodynamic Psychotherapy of Children*. New York: International Universities Press.

Corwin, D. L. (1985). Sexually abused child's disorder. Paper presented at the National Summit Conference on Diagnosing Child Sexual Abuse, Los Angeles, California.

Danto, A. (1969). Semantic vehicles, understanding, and innate ideas. In: Hook, S. (Ed.), *Language and Philosophy*. New York: New York University Press.

DeCasper, A. J. & Fifer, W. P. (1980). Of human bonding: Newborns prefer their mothers' voices. *Science*, 208:1174–1176.

DeCasper, A. J. & Prescott, P. A. (1984). Human newborns' perception of male voices: Preference, discrimination and reinforcing value. *Developmental Psychobiology*, 17:481–491.

DeCasper, A. J. & Sigafoos, A. D. (1983). The intrauterine heartbeat: A potent reinforcer for newborns. *Infant Behavior and Development*, 6:19–25.

DeCasper, A. J. & Spence, M. J. (1986). Prenatal maternal speech influences newborns' perception of speech sounds. *Infant Behavior and Development*, 9:133–150.

deMause, L. (1974). *The History of Childhood: The Untold Story of Child Abuse*. New York: Peter Bedrick Books.

deMause, L. (1980). Our forebears made childhood a nightmare. In: Williams, G. J. & Money, J. (Eds.), *Traumatic Abuse and Neglect of Children at Home*. Baltimore: Johns Hopkins University Press, pp. 14–20.

Donovan, D. M. (1988a). Psychiatric implications of the disclosure of adoptive status. Paper read at the Annual Meeting of the National Council for Adoption, Washington, D.C., April, 1988.

Donovan, D. M. (1988b). Adoptee studies of psychiatric disorders. *Arch. Gen. Psychiat.*, 45:875.

Donovan, D. M. (1988c). Anatomically correct dolls: research vs. clinical practice (Letter). *Journal of the American Academy of Child & Adolescent Psychiatry*, 27(5):662.

Donovan, D. M. (1989). The paraconscious. *Journal of the American Academy of Psychoanalysis*, 17(2):223–252.

Donovan, D. M. & McIntyre, M. D. (1985). Therapeutic issues in sexual abuse (Letter). *Journal of the American Academy of Child Psychiatry*, 24(5):663–664.

Donovan, D. M. & McIntyre, D. (in press). Child Psychotherapy. In: *Treatment Strategies in Child and Adolescent Psychiatry*, ed., J. Simeon & H. B. Ferguson. New York: Human Sciences Press.

Duke P. & Turan, K. (1987). *Call Me Anna*. New York: Bantam Books.

Ellenberger, HF (1973). La notion de Kairos in psychothérapie. *Annales de Psychothérapie*, 4:4–14.

Emde, R. N., Gaensbauer, T J., Harmon, R. J. (1976). *Emotional Expression in Infancy: A Biobehavioral Study (Psychological Issues*, Monograph 37, Vol. 10). New York: International Universities Press.

Emslie, G. J. & Rosenfeld, A. (1983). Incest reported by children and adolescents hospitalized for severe psychiatric problems. *American Journal Of Psychiatry*, 140:708–711.

Eth, S. & Pynoos, R. S. [Eds.] (1985). *Post-Traumatic Stress Disorder in Children*. Washington, D.C.: American Psychiatric Press.

Everson, M. D. & Boat, B. W. (1989). False allegations of sexual abuse by children and adolescents. *Journal of the American Academy of Child and Adolescent Psychiatry*, 28(2):230–235.

Faller, K. C. (1988). *Child Sexual Abuse: An Interdisciplinary Manual for Diagnosis, Case Management and Treatment*. New York: Columbia University Press.

Fein, G. & Rivkin, M. (Eds.) (1986). *The Young Child at Play*. Washington, D.C.: National Association for the Education of Young Children.

Fifer, W. P. (1980). Early attachment: Maternal voice preferences in one- and three-day old infants. Unpublished doctoral dissertation, University of North Carolina at Greensboro.

Figley C. R. [ed.] (1985). *Trauma and Its Wake: The Study and Treatment of Post-Traumatic Stress Disorder*. New York: Brunner/Mazel.

Figley, C. R. [Ed.] (1986). *Trauma and Its Wake: Traumatic Stress Theory, Research, and Intervention*. New York: Brunner/Mazel.

Fish-Murray CC, Koby EV & van der Kolk BA (1987). Evolving ideas: The effect of abuse on children's thought. In: BA van der Kolk, (Ed.), *Psychological Trauma*. Washington, D.C.: American Psychiatric Press.

Frankenthal, K. (1969). Autohypnosis and other aids for survival in situations of extreme stress. *International Journal of Clinical and Experimental Hypnosis*, 17:153–159.

Frankl, V. (1962). *Man's Search for Meaning: An Introduction to Logotherapy*. Boston: Beacon Press.

Freud, S. (1900). *The Interpretation of Dreams. Standard Edition*, 4:261. London: Hogarth Press, 1975.

Freud, S. (1923). *The Ego and The Id, The Standard Edition of The Complete Psychological Works, Vol. 14*. W. W. Norton & Co.

Froning, M. L. (1988). Allegations of sexual abuse then and now (Letter). *Journal of the American Academy of Child and Adolescent Psychiatry*, 27(5):665–666.

Gardner, H (1982). *Developmental Psychology*, 2nd Edition. Boston: Little, Brown.

Gardner, H. (1983). *Frames of Mind: The Theory of Multiple Intelligences*. New York: Basic Books, Inc.

Gilligan, C. (1982). *In a Different Voice*. Cambridge (Mass.): Harvard University Press.

Goodman, J, Silberstein, R. & Mandell, W. (1963). Adopted children brought to child psychiatric clinics. *Arch. Gen. Psychiatry*, 9:451–456.

Grabe, P. V. [Ed.] (1986). *Adoption Resources for Mental Health Professionals*. Mercer (PA): Children's Aid Society in Mercer County.

Green, A. (1980). *Child Maltreatment*. New York: Jason Aronson.

Green, A. (1986). True and false allegations of sexual abuse in child custody disputes. *Journal of the American Academy of Child and Adolescent Psychiatry*, 25(4):449–456.

Greenberg, M. S. & van der Kolk, B. (1987). Retrieval and integration of traumatic memories with the "painting cure." In: van der Kolk, B. A. (1987), *Psychological Trauma*. Washington, D.C.: American Psychiatric Press.

Greenfield, P. M. (1980). Towards an operational and logical analysis of intentionality. In: Olson, D. (Ed.), *The Social Foundations of Cognition and Language: Essays in Honor of Jerome S. Bruner*. New York: W. W. Norton & Co., 254–279.

Grice, H. P. (1967). Logic and conversation. Unpublished manuscript of William James Lectures, Harvard University (cited in Bruner, 1974).

Grinker, R. R. & Spiegel, J. J. (1945). *Men Under Stress*. New York: McGraw-Hill.

Haley, J. (1973). *Uncommon Therapy*. New York: W. W. Norton.

Harper, M. (1969). Déjà vu and depersonalization in normal subjects. *Australian and New Zealand Journal of Psychiatry*, 3:67–74.

Henderson, S. (1974). Care-eliciting behavior in man. *Journal of Nervous and Mental Diseases*, 159(3):172–181.

Hinsie, L. E. & Campbell, R. J. (1970). *Psychiatric Dictionary, Fourth Edition*. New York: Oxford.

Horowitz, M. J. (1986). *Stress Response Syndromes*. New York: Jason Aronson.

Horowitz et al (1984). Unpublished manuscript cited in Everson, M. D. & Boat, B. W. (1989). False allegations of sexual abuse by children and adolescents. *Journal of the American Academy of Child and Adolescent Psychiatry*, 28(2):230–235.

Humphrey, M. E. & Ounsted, C. (1963). Adoptive families referred for psychiatric advice I: the children. *Br. J. Psychiat.*, 109:599–608.

Hussain, A. & Chapel, J. L. (1983). History of incest in girls admitted to a psychiatric hospital for severe psychiatric problems. *American Journal of Psychiatry*, 140-591-593.

Inhelder, B. (1976). Operatory thought processes in psychotic children. In: *Piaget and His School: A Reader In Developmental Psychology*. Edited by B. Inhelder & H. H. Chipman. New York: Springer-Verlag.

Jacobson, A., Koehler, J. E., & Jones-Brown, C. (1987). The failure of routine assessment to detect histories of assault experienced by psychiatric patients. *Hosp. Comm. Psychiat.*, 38,4:386–389.

Jerome, L. (1986). Overrepresentation of adopted children attending a children's mental health centre. *Can. J. Psychiat.*, 31:526–531.

Jones, D. P. H. & McGraw, J. M. (1987). Reliable and fictitious accounts of sexual abuse of children. *Journal of Interpersonal Violence*, 2:27–45.

Kappelman, M. (1982). When to tell adopted child. *Human Sexuality.*, 16,11:43–44.

Kaplan, H. I. & Saddock, B. (1985). *Comprehensive Textbook of Psychiatry/IV*. Baltimore: Williams & Wilkins.

Kelman, H. (1960). Kairos and the therapeutic process. *J. Existential Psychol.*, 1:233–269.

Kellman-Pringle, M. L. (1961). The incidents of some supposedly adverse family conditions and of lefthandedness in schools for maladjusted children. *Br. J. Educ. Psychol.*, 31:183–193.

Kielholz, A (1956). Vom Kairos. *Schweizerische medizinische Wochenschrift*, 86(35):982–984.

Klein, C. (1988). Teaching disabilities [review of *The Learning Mystique: A Critical Look at "Learning Disabilities"* by Gerald Coles]. *Readings*, 3(4):4–7.

Kluft, R. P. (1984). Treatment of multiple personality disorder: A study of 33 cases. *Psychiatric Clinics of North America*, 7:9–29.

Kluft, R. P. (1987). Longterm effects of child abuse. Paper presented at the Annual Meeting of the American Academy of Child and Adolescent Psychiatry, Washington, D.C., 10/21/87.

Kohl, H. (1988). The mislabled. [Review of *The Learning Mystique: A Critical Look at "Learning Disabilities"*, by Gerald Coles]. *The Nation*. April 16:542–543.

Kohlberg, L. (1981). *The Philosophy of Moral Development*. San Francisco: Harper and Row.

Kolata, G. (1987). Associations or rules in language learning? *Science*, 237:133–134.

Krener, P. (1985). After incest: secondary prevention? *Journal of the American Academy of Child & Adolescent Psychiatry*. 24:231–234.

Krystal, H. (1968). *Massive Psychic Trauma*. New York: International Universities Press.

Laplanche, J. & Pontalis, J.-B. (1973). *The Language of Psycho-Analysis*. New York: W. W. Norton.

Linsky, L. (1967). Referring. In *The Encyclopedia of Philosophy*. New York: MacMillan Publishing Co, Onc. & The Free Press, 95–99.

Looney, J. G. (1980). Treatment planning in child psychiatry. *J. Am. Acad. Child Psychiat*, 23,5:529–536.

Ludwig, A. M. (1983). The psychobiological functions of dissociation. *American Journal of Clinical Hypnosis*, 26:93–99.

Luke, J. L. (1978). Sleeping arrangements of sudden infant death syndrome victims in the District of Columbia—A preliminary report. *J. Forensic Sciences*, 23(2): 379–383.

Lytle, J. (1988). Is special education serving minority students? *Harvard Educational Review*, 58:116–120.

Masson, J. M. (1984). *The Assault on the Truth: Freud's Suppression of the Seduction Theory*. New York: Farrar, Straus and Giroux.

McDermott, J. F., Jr. & Char, W. F. (1984). Stage-related models of psychotherapy with children. *J. Am. Acad. Child Psychiat.*, 23, 5:537–543.

McGoldrick, M. & Gerson, R. (1985). *Genograms in Family Assessment*. New York: W. W. Norton.

Meltzoff, A. N. (1988). Infant imitation after a 1-week delay: long term memory for novel acts and multiple stimuli. *Developmental Psychology*, 24(4):470–476.

Meltzoff, A N. & Moore, M. K. (1977). Imitation of facial and manual gestures by human neonates. *Science*, 198:75–78.

Menlove, F. L. (1965). Aggressive symptoms in emotionally disturbed adopted children. *Child Dev.*, 36:519–532.

Miller, G. A. & Gildea, P. M. (1987). How children learn words. *Scientific American*, 257:95–99.

Moskowitz, B. A. (1978). The Acquisition of Language, *Scientific American*, November.

Mounin, G. (1970). *Introduction à la Sémiologie*. Paris: Les Editions de Minuit.

Myers, D. & Grant, G. (1970). A study of depersonalization in students. *British Journal of Psychiatry*, 121:59–65.

National Committee for Adoption (1985). *Adoption Factbook: United States Data, Issues, Regulations and Resources*. Washington, D.C.: National Committee for Adoption.

Nemiah, J. C. (1981). Dissociative disorders. In Freeman, A. M. & Kaplan, H. I. (Eds.), *Comprehensive Textbook of Psychiatry, Third Edition*. Baltimore: Williams & Wilkins.

Niederland WG (1961). The survivor syndrome: further observations and dimensions. *Journal of the American Psychoanalytic Association*, 29(2):413–425.

Novick, J., Benson, R. & Rembar, J. (1981). Patterns of termination in an outpatient clinic for children and adolescents. *J. Amer. Acad. Child Psychiatry*, 20:834–844.

Oram, K. (1978). Developmental aspects of "childhood schizophrenia": A structural analysis using a Piagetian and psychoanalytic approach. Unpublished doctoral dissertation, City University, New York.

Panneton, R. K. & DeCasper, A. J. (1984). Newborns prefer intrauterine heartbeat sounds to male voices. Paper presented at the International Conference on Infant Studies, New York.

Peters, J. J. (1979). Children who are victims of sexual assault and the psychology of offenders. *American Journal of Psychotherapy*, 30:399–421.

Piaget, J. (1968). Autobiography. In Boring, E. G., Langfield, H. S., Werner, H. & Yerkes, R. M. (eds.), *History of Psychology in Autobiography*, Vol 4: 237–256. New York: Russell & Russell (1952).

Piaget, J. (1972). *The Principles of Genetic Epistemology*. London: Routledge & Kegan Paul. (1970).

Pilowsky, I. (1969). Abnormal illness behavior. *British Journal of Medical Psychology*, 42:347–351.

Pines, M. (1988). Review of Gerald Coles' *The Learning Mystique: A Critical Look At "Learning Disabilities." Washington Post Book World*, 2/7/88.

Prechtl, H. F. R. (1974). The behavioral states of the newborn infant (a review). *Brain Research*, 76:184–212.

Prechtl, H. F. R. & O'Brien, M. J. (1982). Behavioral states of the full term newborn. Emergence of a concept. In P. Stratton (Ed.), *Psychobiology of the Human Newborn*. New York: Wiley.

Prechtl, H. F. R., Theorell, K. & Blair, A. W. (1973). Behavioral state cycles in abnormal infants. *Developmental Medicine and Child Neurology*, 15:606–615.

Putnam, F. W. (1987). Dissociative disorders: A developmental perspective. Paper read at the Symposium "Long-Term Effects of Childhood Sexual Abuse." Annual Meeting, American Academy of Child and Adolescent Psychiatry, Washington, D.C., 10/22/87.

Putnam, F. W. (1989). *Multiple Personality Disorder*. New York: Guildford Press.

Pynoos, R. S. & Eth, S. (1986). Witness to violence: The child interview. *J. Am. Acad. Child Psychiat.*, 25(3):306–319.

Reid, W. H. (1989). *DSM-III Training Guide*. New York: Brunner/Mazel.

Roberts, W. (1960). Normal and abnormal depersonalization. *Journal of Mental Science*, 106:478–493.

Robie, G. F., Payne, G. G., & Morgan, M. A. (1989). Selective delivery of an acardiac, acephalic twin. *New England Journal of Medicine*, 20(8):512–513.

Rogers, C. R. (1955). Persons or science: A philosophical question. *American Psychologst*, 10:267–278.

Rogers, C. S. & Sawyers, J. K. (1988). *Play in the Lives of Children*. Washington, D.C.: National Association for the Education of Young Children.

Rothenberg, M. B. (1980). Is there an unconscious national conspiracy against children in the United States? *Clinical Pediatrics*, 19(5):10–24.

Rutter, M. & Hersov, L. (Eds.) (1985). *Child and Adolescent Psychiatry: Modern Approaches*. Oxford: Blackwell.

Saussure, F. de (1959). *Course in General Linguistics*. New York: Philosophical Library.

Schecter, M. (1960). Observations on adopted children. *Arch. Gen. Psychiat.*, 3:21–32.

Schetky, D. H. & Green, A. H. (1988). *Child Sexual Abuse*. New York: Brunner/Mazel.

Schmid-Kitsikis, E. (1976). The cognitive mechanisms underlying problem-solving in psychotic and mentally retarded children. In: *Piaget and His School: A Reader in Developmental Psychology*. Edited by B. Inhelder & H. H. Chipman. New York: Springer-Verlag.

Schwam, J. S. & Tuskan, M. K. (1979). The adopted Child. In: *Basic Handbook of Child Psychiatry*, ed. I. N. Berlin & L. A. Stone. New York: Basic Books, 4: 342–348.

Searle, J. R. (1969). *Speech acts: an essay in the philosophy of language*. London: Cambridge University Press.

Sedman, G. (1966). Depersonalization in a group of normal subjects. *British Journal of Psychiatry*, 112:907–912.

Seligman, M. E. P., Maier, S. F. & Geer, J. (1968). The alleviation of learned helplessness in the dog. *J. Abnorm. Psychol.*, 73:256–262.

Senior, N. & Hamadi, E. (1985). Emotionally disturbed, adopted, inpatient adolescents. *Child Psychiat. Hum. Develop.*, 15,3:189–197.

Shackelford, M. D. (1977). The structure of thought in schizophrenic children: A Piagetian analysis. Unpublished doctoral dissertation, City University, New York.

Sholevar, G. P., Burland, J. Al., Frank, J. L., et al (1989). Psychoanalytic treatment of children and adolescents. *Am. J. Acad. Child Adolesc. Psychiatry*, 28(5): 685–690.

Siegel, L. S. & Brainerd, C. J. (eds.), *Alternatives to Piaget*. London: Academic Press.

Sirles, E. A., Smith, J. A., & Kusama, H. (1989). Psychiatric status of intrafamilial child sexual abuse victims. *Journal of the American Academy of Child and Adolescent Psychiatry*, 28(2):225–229.

Sloate, P. L., Voyat, G. (1983). Cognitive and asffective features in childhood psychosis. *Am. J. Psychotherapy*, 37(3):376–386.

Sophocles (no date). *Oedipus Tryrannus*. In: *Greek Dramas*, trans. T. Francklin, p. 183. New York: D. Appleton & Co, 1904.

Spence, M. J. & DeCasper, A. J. (in press). Prenatal experience with low-frequency maternal voice sounds influences neonatal perception of maternal voice samples. *Infant Behavior and Development*.

Spiegel, D. (1984). Multiple personality as a post-traumatic stress disorder. *Psychiatric Clinics of North America*, 7:101–110.

Spitzer, R. (1989). *DSM-III-R Casebook — A Learning Companion to the Diagnostic and Statistical Manual of Mental Disorders, Third Edition, Revised.* Washington, D.C.: American Psychiatric Press.

Starr, R. J., Jr. (1987). Clinical judgment of abuse-proneness based on parent-child interactions. *Child Abuse and Neglect*, 11:87–92.

Strawson, P. F. (1950). On referring. *Mind*. (Reprinted in Flew, A. G. N. [Ed.], *Essays in Conceptual Analysis*. London: Macmillan, 1956.

Sugarman, M. & Kuehnle, K. (1987, Nov.). Sexual abuse of very young children in the context of divorce visitation. Paper presented at the boston Institute for the Development of Infants and Parents, Twelfth Annual Conference.

Tanguay, P. (1985). Piaget: new and improved. *Newsletter of the Am. Acad. Child Psychiat.* (Fall, 1985):10–12.

Tennant, C., Bebbington, P. & Hurry, J. (1980). Parental death in childhood and risk of adult depressive disorders: a review. *Psychological Medicine*, 10:289.

Terr, L. C. (1979). Children of Chowchilla: A study of psychic trauma. In: The *Psychoanalytic Study of the Child*, Vol 34., Edited by A. J. Solnit, R. S. Eissler, A. Freud et al. New Haven: Yale University Press, 547–623.

Terr, L. C. (1981). "Forbidden Games" Post-traumatic child's play. *J. Am. Acad. Child Psychiat.*, 20(4):741–760.

Terr, L. C. (1983a). Chowchilla revisited: The effects of psychic trauma four years after a school bus kidnapping. *Am. J. Psychiat.*, 140:1543–1550.

Terr, L. C. (1983b). Life attitudes, dreams, and psychic trauma in a group of "normal" children. *J. Am. Acad. Child Adolesc. Psychiat.*, 22:221–230.

Terr, L. C. (1985a). Remembered images in psychic trauma: one explanation for the supernatural. *Psychoanalytic Study of the Child*, 40:493–533.

Terr, L. C. (1985b). Children traumatized in small groups. In: *Post-traumatic Stress Disorder in Children*, edited by S. Eth & R. S. Pynoos. Washington, D.C.: American Psychiatric Press, 47–70.

Terr, L. C. (1986). The child psychiatrist and the child witness: Traveling companions by necessity, if not by design. *Journal of the American Academy of Child and Adolescent Psychiatry*, 25(4):462–472.

Terr, L. C. (1987). Childhood trauma and the creative product: a look at the early lives and later works of Poe, Wharton, Magritte, Hitchcock, and Bergman. *Psychoanalytic Study of the Child*, 42:545–572.

Terr, L. C. (1988). What happens to early memories of trauma? A study of twenty children under age five at the time of documented traumatic events. *J. Am. Acad. Child Adol. Psychiatry*, 27(1):96–104.

Thoennes, N. & Pearson, J. (1987). Summary of findings from the sexual abuse allegations project. Project of the Research Unit of The Association of Family and Conciliation Courts. (To be published in the American Bar Association publication "Sexual Abuse Allegations in Custody-Visitation Cases.")

van der Kolk, B. A. (1987). *Psychological Trauma*. Washington, D.C.: American Psychiatric Press.

van der Kolk, B. A. & Greenberg, The psychobiology of the trauma response: hyperarousal, constriction, and addiction to traumatic reexposure. In: van der Kolk, B. A. (1987), *Psychological Trauma*. Washington, D.C.: American Psychiatric Press.

van der Kolk, B. A., Greenberg, M. S., Boyd, H., et al. (1985). Inescapable shock, neurotransmitters and addiction to trauma: towards a psychobiology of post traumatic stress. *Biol. Psychiatry*, 20:314–325.

van der Kolk, B. A. & Kadish, W. (1987). Amnesia, dissociation, and the return of the repressed. In: van der Kolk, B. A. (1987), *Psychological Trauma*. Washington, D.C.: American Psychiatric Press.

von Knorring, A-L, Bohman, M. & Sigvardsson, S. (1982). Early life experiences and psychiatric disorders: an adoptee study. *Acta psychiat. scand.*, 65:283-291.

Voyat, G. (1979). Psychosis: a cognitive and psychodynamic perspective. In: M. Poulson (ed.), *Piagetian Theory and Implications for Helping Professions*. Los Angeles: Southern California Press.

Webster's New Collegiate Dictionary (1961). Springfiled (Mass.): G. & C. Merriam Co.

Wender, P. H., Ketty, S. S., Rosenthal, D., Schulsinger, F., Ortmann, J. & Lunde, I. (1986). Psychiatric disorders in the biological and adoptive families of adopted individuals with affective disorders. *Arch. Gen. Psychiat.*, 43:923-929.

Wheelis, A. (1973). *How People Change*. New York: Harper & Row.

Williams. G. J. & Money. J. (1980). *Traumatic Abuse and Neglect of Children at Home*. Baltimore: Johns Hopkins.

Wilson, P. & Hersov, L. (1985). Individual and group psychotherapy. In Rutter, M. & Hersov, L. (Eds.), *Textbook of Child and Adolescent Psychiatry: Modern Approaches*. Oxford: Blackwell Scientific, 826-838.

Wolff, L. (1988). *Postcards From The End Of The World. Child Abuse in Freud's Vienna*. New York: Antheneum.

Wolf, P. H. (1963). Observations on the early development of smiling. In: Foss, B. (Ed.), *Determinants of Infant Behavior*, Vol. 2. London: Methuen.

Wolff, P. H. (1987). *The Development of Behavioral States And The Expression Of Emotions In Early Infancy*. Chicago: University of Chicago Press.

Work, H. H. & Anderson, H. (1971). Studies in adoption requests for psychiatric treatment. *Am. J. Psychiat.*, 127:948-950.

Index